DISCOVERING IDEAS
An Anthology for Writers

Fourth Edition

DISCOVERING IDEAS
An Anthology for Writers

Fourth Edition

JEAN WYRICK
Colorado State University

HARCOURT BRACE COLLEGE PUBLISHERS

*Fort Worth   Philadelphia   San Diego   New York   Orlando   Austin   San Antonio
Toronto   Montreal   London   Sydney   Tokyo*

Publisher:	Ted Buchholz
Acquisitions Editor:	Michael Rosenberg
Developmental Editor:	Camille Adkins
Project Editoral:	Publications Development Company and Katherine Lincoln
Production Manager:	Kathleen Ferguson
Art Director:	Nick Welch
Permissions Editor:	Julia Stewart

Cover Image: Dato Shushanja. *Composition XV.* 1985. Oil on Canvas. 116 × 70 cm. Courtesy of International Images, Ltd., Sewickley, PA.

Address editorial correspondence to:
301 Commerce Street, Suite 3700,
Fort Worth, Texas 76102

Address orders to:
6277 Sea Harbor Drive,
Orlando, Florida 32887
1-800-782-4479 (outside Florida)
1-800-433-0001 (inside Florida)

Library of Congress Cataloging-in-Publication Data

Discovering ideas : an anthology for writers / [edited by] Jean
  Wyrick. — 4th ed.
        p.   cm.
    Includes index.
    ISBN 0-15-501134-0
    1. College readers.   2. English language—Rhetoric.   I. Wyrick,
Jean.
PE1417.D57   1994
808'.0427—dc20   93-38338
                                                         CIP

Acknowledgments begin on page 414

Printed in the United States of America

4 5 6 7 8 9 0 1 2 3   067   9 8 7 6 5 4 3 2 1

THIS BOOK IS FOR DAVID, SARAH, KATE, AND AUSTIN

TO THE TEACHER

Composed of twenty-six new readings and thirty-seven selections recommended by users of the third edition, this fourth edition of *Discovering Ideas* is again dedicated to those composition teachers (myself included) who have been listening to their students complain, "I have nothing to write about." Over the years, many of us have turned to essay anthologies to show our students good prose styles and to help them find interesting essay topics. Unfortunately, we have been disappointed too often by textbook authors who have chosen essays that illustrate particular rhetorical strategies—but at the expense of engaging subject matter that would encourage class discussion and lead naturally to writing assignments. Some of the other textbooks have also insisted upon anthologizing selections that are well known but too long or complex, essays whose prose styles far exceed both the grasp of our students and the scope of our courses.

This textbook is called *Discovering Ideas* for two reasons. First, like most anthologies, it is designed to help students find new techniques and strategies they can analyze and then incorporate into their own writing. But the book is also so titled because it is a collection of essays, stories, and poems carefully selected *to help writers discover new ideas and create opinions that they want to talk and write about.* Each selection in this new edition has demonstrated that it can evoke varied responses, generate discussion, and encourage fresh, imaginative thinking on issues students can react to. And in turn, each one can help motivate students to discover thoughtful essay topics that avoid those mechanical or unfocused compositions that frustrate writing teachers. In other words, these selections try to inspire rather than intimidate, to stimulate rather than subdue.

The sixty-three selections are divided into nine categories that interest students: Growing Up; Exploring Our Diversity; People at Leisure; Education: Teaching and Learning; Life Confronts Death; Observing Our World; Social Issues: Freedoms and Choices; Scenes of Our Past; and Language: Reading, Writing, Creating. Teachers who have used this book in another edition may note two changes in the sections. The section called "Exploring Our Diversity" was previously called "Men and Women" and is now expanded to include selections discussing issues of culture, race, economic class, and physical ability, as well as gender. The section once called "Perceiving Our Environment" has also been changed slightly, to include various views of urban and country life.

Each of the nine sections contains five essays and concludes with a poem and a short story that complement the theme. Each section presents selections by authors who are old favorites (such as Mark Twain, E. B. White, Kate Chopin, Sherwood Anderson, and James Thurber) and contemporary authors (such as Maya Angelou, Ellen Goodman, Richard Rodriguez, Louise Erdrich, and Barbara Ehrenreich). This edition also introduces readers to several new writers, including Brenda Bell, Diane Sylvain, and Laurie Ouellette.

The selections present a variety of styles, tones, and organizational patterns and offer students opportunities to read and study not only traditional essays but also speeches, editorials, newspaper articles, satire, autobiographical narratives, short stories, and poems. In addition, many of the selections have what Sheridan Baker calls "an argumentative edge": controversial positions that students may challenge in essays of their own. Finally, this edition contains nine humorous pieces that make their points in clear but lighthearted ways.

This book also contains two tables of contents to help teachers organize their courses. An annotated thematic table of contents makes the choice of essays, poems, or stories easy for teachers who wish to assign individual selections rather than entire sections; a second table of contents is also included to aid those instructors who wish to emphasize rhetorical modes and strategies as well as thematic concerns. Essays are listed in the rhetorical table of contents under their primary strategy of development, with the major secondary strategies noted in parentheses for quick reference.

Next in importance to the selections themselves in any college anthology is the apparatus that enables both the teachers and students to use the book more efficiently. This book offers a number of features not always available in other textbooks. "Why Read Essays?" explains to the students the purposes of studying other people's writing, and "How to Read an Essay" then shows them how to become critical readers. The step-by-step process for marking and analyzing the essays in this text should prepare the students for class discussions and help train them to recognize and remember important techniques and ideas. A sample essay, marked according to the steps in the how-to-read process, is included as a model.

New to this edition is a student response to the professional essay, with brief marginal notes outlining organization. Readers are invited to critique this essay and compare their own ideas to it. Discussing the sample response may help some students understand more clearly how the readings can lead to discovery of a good essay topic. Of course, the student essay reprinted here is not intended to illustrate the only kind of appropriate student response, but rather is presented to show one of the many essays a reading might generate.

Another new feature in this edition is the explanation of a half-dozen prewriting or "pump-primer" techniques, designed to help student writers focus topics and actually begin writing. Sample student responses are provided to clarify these techniques so that teachers may assign them in or out of class. The section of the text called "Modes and Strategies: An Introduction to Essays" has been retained in this edition to provide a brief overview of the traditional strategies of organization and development that students may wish to use in their essays.

Each selection in this book is accompanied by a brief biographical note about its author, as well as a vocabulary list, questions on content, structure, and style, and suggestions for writing. The questions are not divided into separate sections on "content" and "form" because to do so not only leads to repetition but also implies that *what* one says can be easily distinguished from *how* one says it. Instead, the questions generally follow the order of the selection itself so that as a student rereads he or she can quickly answer the questions. Many of the suggestions for writing ask the students to write essays based on personal experiences; others ask for essays that might profit from local interviews or library research. Topics call for developing papers by a variety of strategies so that the students may practice organizing their writing in a number of ways.

Discovering Ideas is a textbook that can be used in any college composition course. By simultaneously providing models of good writing and provocative, challenging ideas, this book should help teachers guide their students from analytical reading to thoughtful discussions, and, ultimately, to the writing of their own insightful essays.

Instructor's Manual

A new Instructor's Manual, prepared by Kimberly Miller, containing teaching suggestions for each selection, answers to each set of questions, and definitions for all vocabulary words, is available. To request an Instructor's Manual, contact your Harcourt Brace sales representative.

ACKNOWLEDGMENTS

I would like to thank English Acquisitions Editor Michael Rosenberg for his continuing support of this project and its author. Special thanks go to Camille Adkins, Developmental Editor; without her valuable assistance, wise counsel, and good humor, this edition would not have seen publication. I am continually grateful to Kimberly Miller, who skillfully and graciously assisted me on so many tasks in this edition and who also wrote the excellent Instructor's Manual.

In addition, I appreciate the expertise of Katherine Vardy Lincoln, Project Editor, for overseeing production of this edition, and I thank Julia Stewart for devoting much time and energy to acquiring permissions for the selections in this book. Van Strength was also very helpful in the early stages of selection for this edition. Many thanks to Nick Welch, Design Supervisor; Kathy Ferguson, Senior Production Manager; and Ilse Wolfe-West, Marketing Manager, for all their good work. Nancy Land and her staff at Publications Development Company also did a fine job on production.

A number of colleagues across the country offered thoughtful advice for this edition. I would like to acknowledge Professors John M. Hansen, Catonsville Community College; Stephen C. Holder, Central Michigan University; Maryl Jo Peltzie, Glendale College; and Norman Tederous, Niagara County Community College.

And, as always, much love and appreciation to my husband, David Hall, and our children, Sarah, Kate, and Austin, for their patience and support during the preparation of this edition.

CONTENTS

Thematic Contents

*New to this edition.

4. EDUCATION: TEACHING AND LEARNING

promoted by today's popular culture, this educator
argues that schools should return to the study of role
models, men and women who led exemplary lives
of compassion, commitment, and ethical courage.

5.   LIFE CONFRONTS DEATH

6. OBSERVING OUR WORLD

8. SCENES OF OUR PAST

Rhetorical Contents

The essays in this text are listed here according to their primary mode or strategy of development. Other important modes and strategies found in each essay are noted in parentheses below the selection's title.

TO THE STUDENT

WHY READ ESSAYS?

Studying the essays in this text should help you become a better writer in several ways. First, a close reading of the opinions and arguments expressed by these authors may spark new thoughts and reactions that will lead you to devise interesting essay topics of your own; second, discovering the various ways others have organized, developed, and explained their material should give you some new ideas about selecting your own strategies and supporting details. Familiarizing yourself with the effective stylistic devices and diction of other writers may also stimulate you to use language in ways you've never tried before. And finally, evaluating the prose of others should make you more aware of the writing process itself. Each writer represented in this book faced a series of problems similar to those you face when you write; each had to make decisions regarding organization, development, coherence, sentence style, tone, and so forth, just as you do. By asking questions ("Why did the writer begin the essay this way?" "Why is this term defined here?" "Why compare this event to that one?" and so forth), you will begin to see how the writer put the essay together—and that knowledge will help you put your essay together.

Questioning the choices of other writers should also help you become a better editor as you rewrite and polish your prose because you will acquire the habit of asking yourself questions such as: Does this point need more supporting evidence? Is my reasoning clear and logical here? Does my conclusion fall flat? In other words, the skills you practice as a critical reader are those you'll need to become a skillful writer.

How to Read an Essay

How do you become a critical reader? One way you can better understand not only the content but also the composition of the essays in this text is by practicing a process of analysis involving the steps explained next. This analytical process demands at least two readings, some marking of the text, and some brief note taking. While this procedure may seem time-consuming at first, the benefits to you as both reader and writer are well worth the extra minutes.

First, read the essay through without marking anything. Then jot down a sentence or two summarizing your general impression. Consider what you think the author was trying to do and how well he or she succeeded (a typical response might be "argued for tuition hike—unconvincing, boring—too many confusing statistics"). Then return to the beginning of the essay and, as you reread, follow these steps and answer these questions:

1. Note any *publication information* and biographical data on the *author.* Knowing the source of the material you're reading may make a difference in your evaluation. Is the author qualified to discuss this subject? Is he or she obviously biased in any way? To whom was the essay written? Is the essay out of date?

2. Look at the *title* and *introduction.* Do they draw you into the essay? Do they help set the essay's tone?

3. Frequently writers will present their main point (*thesis*) early in the essay; the thesis may be stated plainly in one or more sentences or it may be implied. Once you've located the main point, underline the sentence or note the area in which it is implied with the word "thesis" or with a capital "T" in the margin so that you can refer to it easily.

4. As you reread the essay, you will discover important statements that support the thesis. These statements are sometimes found in *topic sentences,* which often occur near the beginning or at the end of body paragraphs. So that you can quickly find each of these supporting points later, number each one and place two or three key words in the margin by each number. (*Hint:* writers often use subheadings to announce a new point; watch for these and also for any italicized or underlined words.) Writing down these key words will also help you remember the *content* of the essay.

5. Each time you discover one of the essay's key statements, ask yourself how the author *develops* that idea. For instance, does he or she try to support or prove the point by providing examples, statistics, or testimony; by comparing or contrasting it to something else; or by describing, classifying, or defining the subject? A writer can use one method of development or any combination, but each major point in an essay should be explained clearly and logically. Underdeveloped ideas or ones supported only by generalizations, biased sources, or emotional outpourings are not ultimately convincing.

6. As you move through the essay, circle any words you don't know that you feel are essential to the author's meaning. Look these up in a dictionary if their context does not provide a definition. Next, underline or put a star by important or especially effective statements; put a question mark by those passages you think are weak, exaggerated, or untrue. Use the top and bottom margins to jot brief responses, raise questions, or make note of new ideas (or possible essay topics). Most of these markings and notes will help you assess the essay's effectiveness in your final evaluation.

7. To help you structure your own essay, you may find it useful to note how the writer moved from one point to the next. Bracketing the *transition devices* that link the paragraphs can make you aware of the ways a good writer subtly creates a smooth flow from idea to idea. (You might not have time to do this throughout the essay, but try marking a few paragraphs.)

8. Look closely at the essay's *conclusion.* Does it emphasize the author's thesis without being boring or repetitive?

9. Consider the essay's *tone,* the writer's *voice.* Is it ironic, sarcastic, serious, informal, humorous, or what? An inappropriate tone can undercut an author's intended effect on the reader. For instance, a flippant, overly informal tone may offend the reader who takes seriously the subject in question; a sarcastic tone may signal a writer who's too angry to be logical. On the other hand, a coolly rational tone can be convincing, and sometimes humor can be persuasive in a way that nothing else can. Creating the right tone is important.

10. The author's *style* is important, too. Does he or she use figurative language (for example, similes, metaphors, personification) in an arresting way? Literary allusions? Specialized diction? Does he or she use any sentence patterns that are especially effective? Repetition of words or phrases? Writers use a variety of stylistic devices to make their prose vivid and memorable; you may want to study some of the devices you find so that you can try using them in your own essays.

Once you have completed these ten steps, you are ready to make your final evaluation of the essay. Review your notes and markings; they should help you quickly locate the important parts of the essay and your impressions of those parts. Is the essay's thesis supported by enough logically developed, persuasive points? Is each point as clear, convincing, and well stated as it should be? Is the essay organized effectively? What strengths and weaknesses did you find after this critical reading? Has your original evaluation changed? If so, write a new assessment of the essay. Add any other comments you want to remember about this piece of writing.

Finally, after this critical reading of the essay, have you discovered any new ideas, strategies, or techniques you wish to incorporate into *your* writing?

Sample Annotated Essay

Here is an essay marked and annotated according to the criteria listed on pages 4–5.

Our Youth Should Serve

STEVEN MULLER

Steven Muller is a former president of Johns Hopkins University. This essay appeared in *Newsweek* in 1978.

> title forecasts thesis

> Educator writing about young people

> general audience, educated

1   Too many young men and women now leave school without a well-developed sense of purpose. If they go right to work after high school, many are not properly prepared for careers. But if they enter college instead, many do not really know what to study or what to do afterward. Our society does not seem to be doing much to encourage and use the best instincts and talents of our young.

> Introduction sets up the problem

2   [On the one hand,] I see the growing problems of each year's new generation of high-school graduates. After twelve years of schooling—and television—many of them want to participate actively in society; but they face either a job with a limited future or more years in educational institutions. Many are wonderfully idealistic: they have talent and energy to offer, and they seek the meaning in their lives that comes from giving of oneself to the

> the problem for young people

common good. But they feel almost rejected by a society that has too few jobs to offer them and that asks nothing of them except to avoid trouble. They want to be part of a new solution; instead society perceives them as a problem. They seek a cause; but their elders preach only self-advancement. They need experience on which to base choice; yet society seems to put a premium on the earliest possible choice, based inescapably on the least experience.

Style : note parallelism stressing the difficult situation

Necessary Tasks

the problem for society

3 [On the other hand,] I see an American society sadly in need of social services that we can afford less and less at prevailing costs of labor. Some tasks are necessary but constitute no career; they should be carried out, but not as anyone's lifetime occupation. Our democracy profoundly needs public spirit, but the economy of our labor system primarily encourages self-interest. The Federal government spends billions on opportunity grants for post-secondary education, but some of us wonder about money given on the basis only of need. We ask the young to volunteer for national defense, but not for the improvement of our society. As public spirit and public services decline, so does the quality of life. So I ask myself why cannot we put it all together and ask our young people to volunteer in peacetime to serve America?

? — suchas ?

? Not sure what he means

} Thesis

4 I recognize that at first mention, universal national youth service may sound too much like compulsory military service or the Hitler Youth or the Komsomol. I do not believe it has to be like that at all. It need not require uniforms or camps, nor a vast new Federal bureaucracy, nor vast new public expenditures. And it should certainly not be compulsory.

A clarifies his proposal—tells what it isn't (contrast, definition) Youth section of the Soviet Communist Party

5   A voluntary program of universal national youth service does of course require compelling incentives. Two could be provided. Guaranteed job training would be one. Substantial Federal assistance toward post-secondary education would be the other. This would mean that today's complex measures of Federal aid to students would be ended, and that there would also be no need for tuition tax credits for post-secondary education. Instead, prospective students would *earn* their assistance for post-secondary education by volunteering for national service, and only those who earned assistance would receive it. Present Federal expenditures for the assistance of students in post-secondary education would be converted into a simple grant program, modeled on the post–World War II GI Bill of Rights.

1. incentives
a. job training
b. Federal assistance for education

(contrast — unlike complex federal aid)

(comparison — more like GI Bill)

Volunteers

2. Duties

6   But what, you say, would huge numbers of high-school graduates do as volunteers in national service? They could be interns in public agencies, local, state and national. They could staff day-care programs, neighborhood health centers, centers to counsel and work with children; help to maintain public facilities, including highways, railbeds, waterways and airports; engage in neighborhood-renewal projects, both physical and social. Some would elect military service, others the Peace Corps. Except for the latter two alternatives and others like them, they could live anywhere they pleased. They would not wear uniforms. They would be employed and supervised by people already employed locally in public-agency careers.

(examples — jobs)

How would this differ from the present volunteer army?

7   Volunteers would be paid only a subsistence wage, because they would receive the benefits of job training (not necessarily confined to one

3. Low Pay (cites reasons)

task) as well as assistance toward post-secondary education if they were so motivated and qualified. If cheap mass <u>housing</u> for some groups of volunteers were needed, supervised participants in the program could rebuild decayed dwellings in metropolitan areas.

But how could the volunteers afford essentials like food?

8   [All that] might work. But perhaps an even more attractive version of universal national youth service might include private industrial and commercial enterprise as well. A private employer would volunteer to select a stated number of volunteers. He would have their labor at the universally applied subsistence wage; in return he would offer guaranteed job training as well as the exact equivalent of what the Federal government would have to pay for assistance toward post-secondary education. The inclusion of volunteer private employers would greatly amplify job-training opportunities for the youth volunteers, and would greatly lessen the costs of the program in public funds.

4. Role of private employees

(description — benefits to both employers & employees)

Direct Benefits

5.

9   The direct benefits of [such a universal national-youth-service program] would be significant. Every young man and woman would face a meaningful role in society after high school. Everyone would receive job training, and the right to earn assistance toward post-secondary education. Those going on to post-secondary education would have their education interrupted by a constructive work experience. <u>There is evidence that</u> they would thereby become <u>more highly motivated and successful students, particularly if their work experience related closely to subsequent vocational interests.</u> Many participants <u>might locate careers</u> by means of their national-service assignments.

projects results

from where?

10   No union jobs need be lost, because skilled
workers would be needed to give job training.
Many public services would be performed by cheap
labor, but there would be no youth army. And the
intangible, <u>indirect benefits</u> would be the greatest
of all. Young people could regard themselves as
more useful and needed. They could serve this
country for a two-year period as volunteers, and
<u>earn</u> job training and/or assistance toward post-
secondary education. <u>There is more self-esteem
and motivation in earned than in unearned benefits.</u> Universal national youth service may be no
panacea. But in my opinion the idea merits serious
and imaginative consideration.

Margin notes:

Counters a possible problem

6. Indirect Benefits

Conclusion: stresses benefits & calls for consideration of proposal

a remedy for all ills

<u>First Impression</u>: Muller wants a volunteer youth corps to provide certain public services — many benefits — clearly organized arguments.

<u>Final Evaluation</u>: Muller is persuasive, although the low pay would be a problem for many. I especially like the idea of getting work experience before college — working might have helped me decide on the major and career I wanted. (<u>Possible essay topic</u>: Some people — or just me? — should work a year before starting college.)

<u>Other Notes</u>: Organization and development: Muller's essay is an argument — good use of examples, reasons, comparison, contrast, description, cause-effect relationships. Many specific details. He might have given essay more of a personal tone by adding some testimony from students or by citing some real experiences. Style and tone: Muller is serious, straightforward, forceful, sincere. No jargon or pompous language. Note parallelism for emphasis (¶ 2).

Student Response to Sample Essay

After reading one of the selections in this text, your instructor may ask you to write an essay that responds to the ideas in the essay, story, or poem. Your instructor may ask for an essay developed by personal experience, or for an argumentative "agree or disagree" essay, or for a paper that researches some idea, or for another kind of essay altogether. Perhaps the topic or type of essay will be your choice.

The following essay, written by Jennifer H., was a response to a journal assignment that asked students to agree or disagree with Muller, using personal experience to support their position. If you were Jennifer's partner in a revision workshop, what suggestions would you offer to help make her next draft more effective and polished?

Youth Service: An Idea Whose Time Has Come

Title: topic and writer's stance

1   In "Our Youth Should Serve," former university president Steven Muller argues that a volunteer youth service would help both our country's social needs and those high school graduates who have had to choose between taking a low-paying job or starting college with no clear sense of direction. Because of the year I spent working before I began college last Fall, I agree with Muller completely. The Youth Service is an organization that should be started as soon as possible.

Introduction briefly summarizes Muller's main point; states writer's thesis

2   After I graduated from high school, I didn't start college because I didn't have enough money saved and I really didn't know what I wanted to study and I was tired of school, so I figured I'd work for a while. But of course I wasn't really trained for anything, so my first job was as a sales clerk in a department store at the mall where my friends and I used to hang out. The job paid minimum wage and I had to dress nicely everyday, which actually cost me money since my wardrobe

Paragraphs 2–4 offer personal experiences showing why the writer's job was not rewarding

basically consisted of jeans and oversized t-shirts. Financially, I was barely breaking even.

3   I worked 38 hours a week, but my work schedule changed from week to week so it was hard to plan ahead. Sometimes I worked evening shifts, Sunday afternoons, and Saturdays, and sometimes I didn't. But ALWAYS on holidays, which meant goodbye to any fun stuff with my friends on the Fourth of July and any other special days because the store always had big sales and needed extra floor people.

4   But the worst part was the job itself. Since I started right after graduation, it was swim suit time. Because I had the least seniority on the floor, it seems like all I did all day long was clean out dressing rooms with dozens of two-piece swim suits thrown all over the floor. It took forever to match up the tops and bottoms, right patterns and right sizes, and then came the struggle of trying to neatly hang them back up on these crazy little double hangers so that everything would be facing the right way and all the straps would be untwisted. It was frustrating!

5   It took me less than one year's worth of work at that store to know that I wanted more out of life than a low-paying, boring job. So last Spring I spent a lot of time talking to the counselor here at Logan [Community College]. She helped me explore my interests, and now I am enrolled in the medical technology program. While I'm not exactly sure yet which specialization I will choose, I am happy knowing the area I want to work in. I think that if I could have done a year of national service I might have been assigned as a volunteer in a hospital or nursing home and might have discovered my interest in that field earlier. I also would have had money to apply to my tuition, instead of having to go into major debt like I am now with school loans. And I'm positive that some

Paragraph 5 contrasts job to experience youth service might have provided

kind of national service would have made me feel
more useful to society like Muller says than hanging up swim suits for eight hours a day did!

6   Right now our government seems very interested in the idea of volunteer national service for
high school graduates. My sister will graduate
next year and she's in more or less the same place
I was two years ago. I hope she has the opportunity that Muller suggests in his essay. I know I
would encourage her in that direction.

Conclusion: hope for
sister as future
graduate.

If you had been asked to respond to Muller's essay, would you agree
or disagree with his ideas? What evidence would *your* essay include to
clarify or support your position?

Modes and Strategies: An Introduction to Essays

For ease of understanding, communication may be divided into four
types (or "modes" as they are often called): exposition, narration, description, and argumentation. The four modes may be defined briefly
as follows:

- Exposition: the writer intends to explain or inform

- Narration: the writer intends to tell a story or recount an event

- Description: the writer intends to create in words a picture of a
  person, place, object, or feeling

- Argumentation: the writer intends to convince or persuade.

While we commonly refer to exposition, argumentation, description, and narration as the basic types of prose, in reality it is difficult
to find any one mode in a pure form. In fact, almost all essays are

combinations of two or more modes; it would be virtually impossible, for instance, to write a story—narration—without including description or to argue without also giving some information. Nevertheless, by determining a writer's *main* purpose, we can usually identify an essay or prose piece as primarily exposition, argumentation, description, or narration. In other words, an article may include a brief description of a new mousetrap, but if the writer's main intention is to explain how the trap works, then we may designate the essay as exposition. In most cases, the primary mode of any essay will be readily apparent to the reader.

Here, then, is a brief introduction to the modes and the most frequently used patterns of organization. Learning to recognize and analyze prose patterns as they appear in the essays in this text will ultimately help you select the most effective plan for organizing and developing your own writing.

I.   Exposition

There are a variety of ways to organize an expository essay, depending upon the writer's purpose. The most common *strategies,* or patterns, of organization include development by example, comparison and contrast, definition, analysis and classification, process analysis, and causal analysis. An essay may be identified as having a primary strategy of development (for instance, an essay telling how to operate a computer is a piece of process analysis), or an essay may use a variety of strategies to explain its points.

STRATEGY ONE: *Development by Example*

Using examples to illustrate, clarify, or support an idea is probably the most common method of development. If a writer wants to make a point about the dangers of nuclear wastes, he or she may cite specific examples—actual harm done to people or studies of potential hazards—to support his or her claims rather than relying on vague generalizations. In addition to making general statements specific and thus more convincing, good examples can explain and clarify unfamiliar, abstract, or difficult concepts. Examples also make prose more vivid and interesting by giving readers something concrete to think about as they note each point in the essay. A general statement decrying animal abuse, for instance, is probably more effective accompanied by several reports of unnecessary experiments.

Sometimes writers use a number of brief examples to support or explain their ideas; at other times one long, detailed example (called an *extended example*) or a combination of the two types is more useful. Regardless of the number, the writer should always select examples that are clear, persuasive, and relevant to the subject under discussion.

STRATEGY TWO: *Development by Comparison and Contrast*

Comparison (pointing out similarities) and contrast (pointing out differences) is another common expository method. Writers frequently use comparison and contrast to make a point ("the many similarities in style clearly suggest that Ernest Hemingway was influenced by Stephen Crane"), assert superiority or advantages ("Mom's is a better place to eat than McHenry's"), or clarify the unfamiliar ("the new aid-to-education plan will be set up like the GI Bill").

Essays of comparison and contrast are often organized one of two ways. The writer may present all the information on subject A and then turn to all the information on subject B, being careful to make the basis for comparison/contrast clear through use of connecting phrases, such as "unlike those responsible for the friendly service at restaurant A, the employees of restaurant B are cold, distant, and uncooperative." Or the writer may choose to compare/contrast the two subjects on one point, then another, and then another, and so forth. Whichever plan the writer adopts, he or she probably will use numerous examples to clarify his or her points; the writer will also employ transition devices wisely to avoid a choppy "seesaw" effect.

STRATEGY THREE: *Development by Definition*

When readers do not understand a particular term central to a writer's point, the entire meaning of the essay may be lost or clouded. For instance, a writer arguing for the repeal of a law he or she considers too liberal must first make clear his or her use of "liberal" before the readers know whether they agree. Other essays may define new or unusual words found in slang, dialects, or jargon, or they may provide interpretations of vague, abstract, or controversial terms (such as "pornography," "success," or "mercy killing"). Depending upon the subject, a writer might define a word or expression by giving synonyms, stating some examples, comparing or contrasting to similar terms, explaining a process, presenting the history, describing the parts, or using any combination of these and other methods.

STRATEGY FOUR: *Development by Classification*

Writers who use analysis or classification try to make a subject easier to understand by breaking it down into its parts or by separating it into groups, types, or categories for a particular purpose or audience. For example, if the classified ads in the newspaper were not listed under categories such as "Houses to Rent" and "Help Wanted," we would have to search through countless ads to find the service or item we wanted. Some essays of analysis or classification are serious and informative (the parts of a new labor-management agreement or the kinds of birds native to a specific area); others are just for fun (kinds of blind dates to avoid or reasons to overspend one's bank account). Notice that this section of this text uses classification to make clear both the four basic categories of communication (exposition, narration, description, and argumentation) and the six strategies of exposition.

STRATEGY FIVE: *Development by Process Analysis*

Process analysis identifies and explains what steps must be taken to complete an operation or procedure. A *directional* process tells the reader how to do or make something; a directional process essay might explain how to buy a used car or how to knit a sweater. An *informative* process tells how something is or was made or done that could not be duplicated by the reader. For example, an informative process essay might describe how the French Revolution started or how scientists created DNA in the laboratory or how a particular airplane operates. Both kinds of essays should state the steps of the process clearly and accurately in logical, chronological order.

STRATEGY SIX: *Development by Causal Analysis*

Causal analysis explains the cause-and-effect relationship between two elements. Essays that discuss the conditions producing X analyze *causes* (political events leading to Pearl Harbor); essays that discuss the results produced by X analyze *effects* (jogging's benefits to potential heart-attack victims). Some essays, of course, discuss both causes and effects of an event or condition. In any case, the writer must make the analysis clear enough so that the reader is convinced the cause-effect relationship does, in fact, exist.

II. Narration

Not all narratives are fictional, nor are they all synonymous with short stories or novels. Essay writers often use stories to illustrate, explain, or support some larger point; for instance, an essay narrating a childhood event might stress the importance of an understanding teacher. Shorter narratives may also illustrate ideas in expository and argumentative essays. A successful narrative, regardless of length, frequently depends upon the writer's ability to create believable characters, events, and dialogue through the use of vivid details. The narrative should also maintain a clear point of view, an appropriate time sequence, and a smooth pace.

III. Description

The writer of description creates a word-picture of persons, places, objects, abstract qualities, and emotions, using a careful selection of details to make an impression on the reader. An essay can be almost entirely description, but more often than not description is used in expository, narrative, and argumentative essays to make them more vivid, understandable, and convincing. Sometimes the writer of description tries to be *objective* (the factual detailing of a business transaction or cancer operation), but frequently the writer wants to convey a particular attitude toward the subject; this approach is called *subjective* or *impressionistic* (the joyful description of a baby at play). In both kinds of description, the writer selects only those details that will communicate the appropriate mood to the readers, and those details should be arranged in an order that will most effectively present the picture. Good description uses specific, sensory details to help the reader understand and imagine the subject the writer wants to reproduce. Frequently, a writer will use figurative language, such as metaphors or similes, to clarify the unfamiliar or abstract subject or simply to make the description more distinct and memorable.

IV.   *Argumentation*

An argumentative essay presents the writer's stand on some subject and then offers reasons, facts, and examples to support that position. The writer may want the reader to agree, to support a cause, to change behavior, or to take action—but whatever the goal, the essay must be convincing and persuasive. Consequently, the writer must provide more than mere opinion; he or she must offer enough logical evidence to back up the essay's position. Writers may use any of a number of expository methods to develop their arguments, such as definition, comparison, cause and effect, and illustration. They may argue *inductively* (move from specific evidence to a generalization) or *deductively* (move from an accepted generality to a specific claim), and they may also employ testimony from authorities, statistics, factual information, or personal experience. Many writers of argument find it useful to state and refute the opposition's major points, a practice that not only helps convince the readers but also shows them that the writer has thoroughly investigated and thought out his or her position. No matter what sort of evidence or organization of that evidence a writer selects, he or she should maintain a sincere, rational tone and should avoid making any logical fallacies, such as hasty generalizations (conclusions based on insufficient or unrepresentative evidence), *non sequiturs* (conclusions that do not follow from the facts), or arguments *ad hominem* (attacks on the opponent's character rather than on the argument).

D ISCOVERING *Y OUR* I DEAS

Getting Started (Or Soup-Can Labels Can Be Fascinating)

For many writers, getting started is the hardest part. You may have no-ticed that when it is time to begin a writing assignment, you suddenly develop an enormous desire to defrost your refrigerator, water your plants, or sharpen your pencils for the fifth time. If this situation sounds familiar, you may find it reassuring to know that many profes-sionals undergo these same strange compulsions before they begin writ-ing. Jean Kerr, author of *Please Don't Eat the Daisies,* admits that she often finds herself in the kitchen reading soup-can labels—or any-thing—in order to prolong the moments before taking pen in hand. John C. Calhoun, vice-president under Andrew Jackson, insisted he had to plow his fields before he could write, and Joseph Conrad, author of *Lord Jim* and other novels, is said to have cried on occasion from the sheer dread of sitting down to compose his stories.

To spare you as much hand-wringing as possible, this section will present some practical suggestions for discovering some ideas for your essay. Let's suppose that you have been assigned an essay topic or that you've found an idea in one of the essays in this text that interests you. But now you're stuck. Deciding on something to write about this sub-ject suddenly looks as easy as nailing Jell-O to your kitchen wall. What should you say? What would be the purpose of your essay? What would be interesting for you to write about and for readers to hear about?

At this point you may profit from trying several prewriting exer-cises, designed to help you generate some ideas about your topic. The exercises described next are, in a sense, "pump primers" that will get your creative juices flowing again. Because all writers compose differ-ently, not all of these exercises will work for you—in fact, some of them may lead you nowhere. Nevertheless, try all of them at least once or twice; you may be surprised to discover that some pump-primer techniques work better with some subjects than with others.

Pump-Primer Techniques

1. Listing

Try jotting down all the ideas that pop into your head about your topic. Free-associate; don't hold back anything. Try to brainstorm for at least ten minutes.

A quick list on jogging might look like this:

fun	races
healthy	both sexes
relieves tension	any age group
no expensive equipment	running with friend or spouse
shoes	too much competition
poor shoes won't last	great expectations
shin splints	good for lungs
fresh air	improves circulation
good for heart	firming
jogging paths vs. streets	no weight loss
hard surfaces	warm-ups before run
muscle cramps	cool-downs after
going too far	getting discouraged
going too fast	hitting the wall
sense of accomplishment	marathons

As you read over the list, look for connections among ideas or one large idea that encompasses several small ones. In this list you might first notice that many of the ideas focus on improving health (heart, lungs, circulation), but you discard that subject because a "jogging improves health" essay is too obvious; it's a topic that's been done too many times to say anything new. A closer look at your list, however, turns up a number of ideas that concern how *not* to jog or reasons why someone might become discouraged and quit a jogging program. You begin to think of friends who might have stuck with jogging as you have if only they'd warmed up properly beforehand, chosen the right places to run, paced themselves more realistically, and so on. You decide, therefore, to write an essay telling first-time joggers how to start a successful program, how to avoid a number of problems, from shoes to track surfaces, that might otherwise defeat their efforts before they've given the sport a chance.

2. Freewriting

Some people simply need to start writing to find a focus. Take out several sheets of blank paper, give yourself at least ten to fifteen minutes, and begin writing whatever comes to mind on your subject. Don't worry about spelling, punctuation, or even complete sentences. Don't change, correct, or delete anything. If you run out of things to say, write "I can't think of anything to say" until you can find a new thought. At the end of the time period you may discover that by continuously writing you will have written yourself into an interesting topic.

Here are examples of freewriting from students who were given ten minutes to write on the general topic of "nature."

Student 1:

I'm really not the outdoorsy type. I'd rather be inside somewhere than out in Nature tromping through the bushes. I don't like bugs and snakes and stuff like that. Lots of my friends like to go hiking around or camping but I don't. Secretly, I think maybe one of the big reasons I really don't like being out in Nature is because I'm deathly afraid of bees. When I was a kid I was out in the woods and ran into a swarm of bees and got stung about a million times, well, it felt like a million times. I had to go to the hospital for a few days. Now every time I'm outside somewhere and something, anything, flies by me I'm terrified. Totally paranoid. Everyone kids me because I immediately cover my head. I keep hearing about killer bees heading this way, my worst nightmare come true. . . .

Student 2:

We're not going to have any Nature left if people don't do something about the environment. Despite all the media attention to recycling, we're

> still trashing the planet left and right. People talk
> big about "saving the environment" but then do
> such stupid things all the time. Like smokers who
> flip their cigarette butts out their car windows.
> Do they think those filters are just going to disap-
> pear overnight? The parking lot by this building
> is full of butts this morning where someone
> dumped their car ashtray. This campus is full of
> pop cans, I can see at least three empties under
> desks in this classroom right now. . . .

These two students reacted quite differently to the same general subject. The first student responded personally, thinking about her own relationship to "nature" (defined as being out in the woods), whereas the
second student associated nature with environmental concerns. More
freewriting might lead student 1 to a humorous essay on her bee phobia
or even to an inquiry about those dreaded killer bees; student 2 might
write an interesting paper suggesting ways college students could clean
up their campus or easily recycle their aluminum cans.

Often freewriting will not be as coherent as these two samples;
sometimes freewriting goes nowhere or in circles. But it's a technique
worth trying. By allowing our minds to roam freely over a subject,
without worrying about "correctness" or organization, we may remember or discover topics we want to write about or investigate, topics we
feel strongly about and wish to introduce to others.

3. Looping *

Looping is a variation on freewriting that works amazingly well for
many people, including those who are frustrated rather than helped by
freewriting.

Let's assume you've been assigned that old standby "My Summer Vacation." First, you must find a focus, something specific and important
to say. Take out several sheets of blank paper and begin to freewrite, as
described previously. Write for at least ten minutes. At the end of this

---

* This technique is suggested by Peter Elbow in *Writing Without Teachers* (New York: Ox-
ford University Press, 1975).

period, read over what you've written and try to identify a central idea that has emerged. This idea may be an important thought that occurred to you in the middle or at the end of your writing, or perhaps it was the idea you liked best for whatever reason. It may be the idea that was pulling you onward when time ran out. In other words, look for the thought that stands out, that seems to indicate the direction of your thinking. Put this thought or idea into one sentence called the "center-of-gravity sentence." You have now completed loop 1.

To begin loop 2, use your center-of-gravity sentence as a jumping-off point for another ten minutes of freewriting. Stop, read what you've written, and complete loop 2 by composing another center-of-gravity sentence. Use this second sentence to start loop 3. You should write at least three loops and three center-of-gravity sentences. At the end of three loops, you may find that you have focused on a specific topic that might lead to a good essay. If you're not satisfied with your topic at this point, by all means try two or three more loops until your subject is sufficiently narrowed and focused.

Here's an example of one student's looping exercise:

Summer Vacation

Loop 1

I think summer vacations are very important aspects of living. They symbolize getting away from daily routines, discovering places and people that are different. When I think of vacations I think mostly of traveling somewhere too far to go, say, for a weekend. It is a chance to get away and relax and not think about most responsibilities. Just have a good time and enjoy yourself. Vacations can also be a time of gathering with family and friends.

Center-of-gravity sentence

Vacations are meant to be used for traveling.

Loop 2

Vacations are meant for traveling. Last summer my family and I drove to Yellowstone National Park. I didn't want to go at first. I thought looking at geysers would be dumb and boring. I was really obnoxious all the way up there and made lots of

smart remarks about getting eaten by bears. Luckily, my parents ignored me and I'm glad they did,
because Yellowstone turned out to be wonderful.
It's not just Old Faithful—there's lots more to
see like these colorful boiling pools and boiling
patches of mud. I got interested in the thermody-
namics of the pools and how new ones are surfac-
ing all the time, and how algae make the pools
different colors.

Center-of-gravity sentence

Once I got interested in Yellowstone's amazing
pools, my vacation turned out great.

Loop 3

Once I got interested in the pools, I had a good
time, mainly because I felt I was seeing something
really unusual. I knew I'd never see anything like
this again unless I went to Iceland or New Zealand
(highly unlikely!). I felt like I was learning a lot,
too. I liked the idea of learning a lot about the inside of the earth without having to go to class and
study books. I really hated to leave—Mom and
Dad kidded me on the way back about how much
I'd griped about going on the trip in the first
place. I felt pretty dumb. But I was really glad I'd
given the Park a closer look instead of holding on
to my view of it as a boring bunch of water foun-
tains. I would have had a terrible time, but now
I hope to go back someday. I think the experience
made me more open-minded about trying new
places.

Center-of-gravity sentence

My vacation this summer was special because I
was willing to put aside my expectations of boredom and learn some new ideas about the strange
environment at Yellowstone.

At the end of three loops, this student has moved from the general
subject of "summer vacation" to the more focused idea that her willingness to learn about a new place played an important part in the enjoyment of her vacation. Although her last center-of-gravity sentence

still contains some vague words ("special," "new ideas," "strange environment"), the thought stated here may eventually lead to an essay that will not only say something about this student's vacation but may also persuade the readers to reconsider their attitude toward taking trips to new places.

4. The Boomerang

Still another variation on freewriting is the technique called the boomerang, named appropriately because, like the Australian stick, it invites your mind to travel over a subject from opposite directions to produce new ideas.

Suppose, for example, members of your class have been asked to write about their major field of study, which in your case is Liberal Arts. Begin by writing a statement that comes into your mind about majoring in the Liberal Arts and then freewrite on that statement for five minutes. Then write a second statement that approaches the subject from an opposing point of view, and freewrite again for five minutes. Continue this pattern several times. Boomeranging, like looping, can help writers see their subject in a new way and consequently help them find an idea to write about.

Here's an abbreviated sample of boomeranging:

1. Majoring in the Liberal Arts is impractical in today's world.
   [Freewrite for five minutes.]

2. Majoring in the Liberal Arts is practical in today's world.
   [Freewrite for five minutes.]

3. Liberal Arts is a particularly enjoyable major for me.
   [Freewrite for five minutes.]

4. Liberal Arts is not always an enjoyable major for me.
   [Freewrite for five minutes.]

And so on.

By continuing to "throw the boomerang" across your subject, you may not only find your focus but also gain insight into other people's views of your topic, which can be especially valuable if your paper will address a controversial issue or one that you feel is often misunderstood.

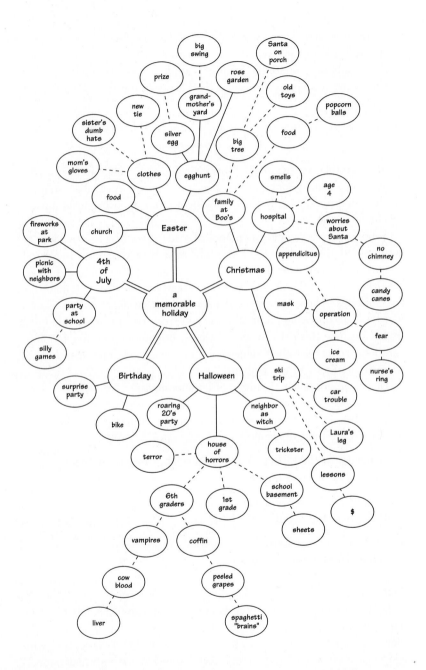

5. *Clustering*

Another excellent technique is clustering (sometimes called "mapping"). Place your general subject in a circle in the middle of a blank sheet of paper and begin to draw other lines and circles that radiate from the original subject. Cluster those ideas that seem to fall together. At the end of ten minutes see if a topic emerges from any of your groups of ideas.

Ten minutes of clustering on the subject of "A Memorable Holiday" might look like the drawing on page 26. This student may wish to brainstorm further on the Christmas he spent in the hospital with a case of appendicitis or perhaps the Halloween he first experienced a house of horrors. By using clustering, he has recollected some important details about a number of holidays that may help him focus on an occasion he wants to describe in his paper.

6. *Cubing*

Still another way to generate ideas is cubing. Imagine a six-sided cube that looks something like this:

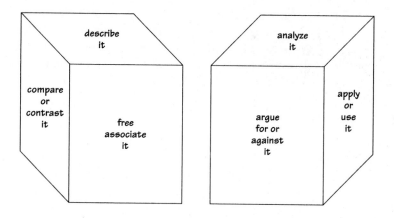

Mentally, roll your subject around the cube and freewrite the answers to the questions that follow. Write whatever comes to mind for ten or fifteen minutes; don't concern yourself with the "correctness" of what you write.

a. *Describe it:*   What does your subject look like? What size, colors, textures does it have? Any special features worth noting?

b. *Compare or contrast it:*   What is your subject similar to? What is your subject different from? In what ways?

c. *Free-associate it:*   What does this subject remind you of? What does it call to mind? What memories does it conjure up?

d. *Analyze it:*   How does it work? How are the parts connected? What is its significance?

e. *Argue for or against it:*   What arguments can you make for or against your subject? What advantages or disadvantages does it have? What changes or improvements should be made?

f. *Apply it:*   What are the uses of your subject? What can you do with it?

A student who had recently volunteered at a homeless shelter wrote the following responses about her experience:

a. *Describe it:*   I and five other members of my campus organization volunteered three Saturdays to work at the shelter here in town. We mainly helped in the kitchen, preparing, serving, and cleaning up after meals. At the dinners we served about 70 homeless people, mostly men but also some families with small children and babies.

b. *Compare or contrast it:*   I had never done anything like this before so it's hard to compare or contrast it to anything. It was different though from what I expected. I hadn't really thought much about the people who would be there—or to be honest I think I thought they would be pretty weird or sad and I was kind of dreading going there after I volunteered. But the people were just regular normal people. And they were very, very polite to us.

c. *Free-associate it:*   Some of the people there reminded me of some of my relatives! John, the kitchen manager, said most of the people were just temporarily "down on their luck" and that reminded me of my aunt and uncle who came to stay with us for a while when I was in high school after my uncle lost his job.

d. *Analyze it:*   I feel like I got a lot out of my experience. I think I had some wrong ideas about "the homeless" and working there made me think more about them as real people not just a faceless group.

e. *Argue for or against it:*   I would encourage others to volunteer there. The work isn't hard and it isn't scary. It makes you appreciate what you've got and also makes you think about what you or your family might do if things went wrong for a while. It also makes you feel good to do something for people you don't even know.

f. *Apply it:*   I feel like I am more knowledgeable when I hear people talk about the poor or the homeless in this town, especially those people who criticize those who use the shelter.

After you've written your responses, see if any one or more of them give you an idea for a paper. The student who wrote the preceding responses decided she wanted to write an article for her campus newspaper encouraging people to volunteer at the shelter not only to provide much-needed help but also to challenge their own preconceived notions about the homeless in her college town. Cubing helped her realize she had something valuable to say about her experience and gave her a purpose for writing.

Once you think you've found a purpose and a focus for your essay, you're probably ready to start drafting. But if you're still stuck—or if you experience Writer's Block along the way—by all means, turn to Donald Murray's excellent essay "Twenty-Six Ways to Start Writing" in Section 9 of this text. In addition to the good advice there, here's one more recommendation: try to relax. No one—not even the very best professional writer—produces perfect prose every time pen hits paper. If you're blocked, you may be trying too hard; if your expectations of your first draft are too high, you may not be able to write at all for fear of failure. You just might be holding yourself back by being a perfectionist at this point. You can always revise and polish your prose in other drafts—the first important step is jotting down your ideas. Remember that once the first word or phrase appears on your blank page, a major battle has been won.

GROWING UP

Discovery of a Father

Sherwood Anderson was an American novelist and short-story writer, who was best known for *Winesburg, Ohio* (1919), a collection of interrelated stories set in a small Midwestern town. Some of his other works include *Horses and Men* (1923), *Dark Laughter* (1925), *Sherwood Anderson's Notebook* (1926), and *Death in the Woods and Other Stories* (1933). This autobiographical sketch about his father is from *Sherwood Anderson's Memoirs* (1942).

1   YOU HEAR it said that fathers want their sons to be what they feel they cannot themselves be, but I tell you it also works the other way. A boy wants something very special from his father. I know that as a small boy I wanted my father to be a certain thing he was not. I wanted him to be a proud, silent, dignified father. When I was with other boys and he passed along the street, I wanted to feel a flow of pride. "There he is. That is my father."

2   But he wasn't such a one. He couldn't be. It seemed to me then that he was always showing off. Let's say someone in our town had got up a show. They were always doing it. The druggist would be in it, the shoe-store clerk, the horse doctor, and a lot of women and girls. My father would manage to get the chief comedy part. It was, let's say, a Civil War play and he was a comic Irish soldier. He had to do the most absurd things. They thought he was funny, but I didn't.

3   I thought he was terrible. I didn't see how mother could stand it. She even laughed with the others. Maybe I would have laughed if it hadn't been my father.

4   Or there was a parade, the Fourth of July or Decoration Day. He'd be in that, too, right at the front of it, as Grand Marshal or something, on a white horse hired from a livery stable.

5   He couldn't ride for shucks. He fell off the horse and everyone hooted with laughter, but he didn't care. He even seemed to like it. I remember once when he had done something ridiculous, and right out on Main Street, too. I was with some other boys and they were laughing and shouting at him and he was shouting back and having as good a time as they were. I ran down an alley back of some stores and there in the Presbyterian Church sheds I had a good long cry.

6   Or I would be in bed at night and father would come home a little lit up and bring some men with him. He was a man who was never alone. Before he went broke, running a harness shop, there were always a lot of men loafing in the shop. He went broke, of course, because he gave too much credit. He couldn't refuse it and I thought he was a fool. I had got to hating him.

7   There'd be men I didn't think would want to be fooling around with him. There might even be the superintendent of our schools and a quiet man who ran the hardware store. Once I remember there was a white-haired man who was a cashier of the bank. It was a wonder to me they'd want to be seen with such a windbag. That's what I thought he was. I know now what it was that attracted them. It was because life in our town, as in all small towns, was at times pretty dull and he livened it up. He made them laugh. He could tell stories. He'd even get them to singing.

8   If they didn't come to our house they'd go off, say at night, to where there was a grassy place by a creek. They'd cook food there and drink beer and sit about listening to his stories.

9   He was always telling stories about himself. He'd say this or that wonderful thing had happened to him. It might be something that made him look like a fool. He didn't care.

10   If an Irishman came to our house, right away father would say he was Irish. He'd tell what county in Ireland he was born in. He'd tell things that happened there when he was a boy. He'd make it seem so real that, if I hadn't known he was born in southern Ohio, I'd have believed him myself.

11   If it was a Scotchman the same thing happened. He'd get a burr into his speech. Or he was a German or a Swede. He'd be anything the other man was. I think they all knew he was lying, but they seemed to like him just the same. As a boy that was what I couldn't understand.

12   And there was mother. How could she stand it? I wanted to ask but never did. She was not the kind you asked such questions.

13   I'd be upstairs in my bed, in my room above the porch, and father would be telling some of his tales. A lot of father's stories were about the Civil War. To hear him tell it he'd been in about every battle. He'd known Grant, Sherman, Sheridan and I don't know how many others. He'd been particularly intimate with General Grant so that when Grant went East to take charge of all the armies, he took father along.

14   "I was an orderly at headquarters and Sim Grant said to me, 'Irve' he said, 'I'm going to take you along with me.'"

15   It seems he and Grant used to slip off sometimes and have a quiet drink together. That's what my father said. He'd tell about the day Lee surrendered and how, when the great moment came, they couldn't find Grant.

16   "You know," my father said, "about General Grant's book, his memoirs. You've read of how he said he had a headache and how, when he got word that Lee was ready to call it quits, he was suddenly and miraculously cured.

17   "Huh," said father. "He was in the woods with me.

18   "I was in there with my back against a tree. I was pretty well corned. I had got hold of a bottle of pretty good stuff.

19   "They were looking for Grant. He had got off his horse and come into the woods. He found me. He was covered with mud.

20   "I had the bottle in my hand. What'd I care? The war was over. I knew we had them licked."

21   My father said that he was the one who told Grant about Lee. An orderly riding by had told him, because the orderly knew how thick he was with Grant. Grant was embarrassed.

22   "But, Irve, look at me. I'm all covered with mud," he said to father.

23   And then, my father said, he and Grant decided to have a drink together. They took a couple of shots and then, because he didn't want Grant to show up potted before the immaculate Lee, he smashed the bottle against the tree.

24   "Sim Grant's dead now and I wouldn't want it to get out on him," my father said.

25   That's just one of the kind of things he'd tell. Of course the men knew he was lying, but they seemed to like it just the same.

26   When we got broke, down and out, do you think he ever brought anything home? Not he. If there wasn't anything to eat in the house, he'd go off visiting around at farmhouses. They all wanted him. Sometimes he'd stay away for weeks, mother working to keep us fed, and then home he'd come bringing, let's say, a ham. He'd got it from some farmer friend. He'd slap it on the table in the kitchen. "You bet I'm going to see that my kids have something to eat," he'd say, and mother would just stand smiling at him. She'd never say a word about all the weeks and months he'd been away, not leaving us a cent for food. Once

I heard her speaking to a woman in our street. Maybe the woman had dared to sympathize with her. "Oh," she said, "it's all right. He isn't ever dull like most of the men in this street. Life is never dull when my man is about."

27   But often I was filled with bitterness, and sometimes I wished he wasn't my father. I'd even invent another man as my father. To protect my mother I'd make up stores of a secret marriage that for some strange reason never got known. As though some man, say the president of a railroad company or maybe a Congressman, had married my mother, thinking his wife was dead and then it turned out she wasn't.

28   So they had to hush it up but I got born just the same. I wasn't really the son of my father. Somewhere in the world there was a very dignified, quite wonderful man who was really my father. I even made myself half believe these fancies.

29   And then there came a certain night. He'd been off somewhere for two or three weeks. He found me alone in the house, reading by the kitchen table.

30   It had been raining and he was very wet. He sat and looked at me for a long time, not saying a word. I was startled, for there was on his face the saddest look I had ever seen. He sat for a time, his clothes dripping. Then he got up.

31   "Come on with me," he said.

32   I got up and went with him out of the house. I was filled with wonder but I wasn't afraid. We went along a dirt road that led down into a valley, about a mile out of town, where there was a pond. We walked in silence. The man who was always talking had stopped his talking.

33   I didn't know what was up and had the queer feeling that I was with a stranger. I don't know whether my father intended it so. I don't think he did.

34   The pond was quite large. It was still raining hard and there were flashes of lightning followed by thunder. We were on a grassy bank at the pond's edge when my father spoke, and in the darkness and rain his voice sounded strange.

35   "Take off your clothes," he said. Still filled with wonder, I began to undress. There was a flash of lightning and I saw that he was already naked.

36   Naked, we went into the pond. Taking my hand he pulled me in. It may be that I was too frightened, too full of a feeling of strangeness, to speak. Before that night my father had never seemed to pay any attention to me.

37   "And what is he up to now?" I kept asking myself. I did not swim very well, but he put my hand on his shoulder and struck out into the darkness.

38   He was a man with big shoulders, a powerful swimmer. In the darkness I could feel the movement of his muscles. We swam to the far edge of the pond and then back to where we had left our clothes. The rain continued and the wind blew. Sometimes my father swam on his back and when he did he took my hand in his large powerful one and moved it over so that it rested always on his shoulder. Sometimes there would be a flash of lightning and I could see his face clearly.

39   It was as it was earlier, in the kitchen, a face filled with sadness. There would be the momentary glimpse of his face and then again the darkness, the wind, and the rain. In me there was a feeling I had never known before.

40   It was a feeling of closeness. It was something strange. It was as though there were only we two in the world. It was as though I had been jerked suddenly out of myself, out of my world of the schoolboy, out of a world in which I was ashamed of my father.

41   He had become blood of my blood; he the strong swimmer and I the boy clinging to him in the darkness. We swam in silence and in silence we dressed in our wet clothes, and went home.

42   There was a lamp lighted in the kitchen and when we came in, the water dripping from us, there was my mother. She smiled at us. I remember that she called us "boys."

43   "What have you boys been up to," she asked, but my father did not answer. As he had begun the evening's experience with me in silence, so he ended it. He turned and looked at me. Then he went, I thought, with a new and strange dignity out of the room.

44   I climbed the stairs to my own room, undressed in the darkness and got into bed. I couldn't sleep and did not want to sleep. For the first time I knew that I was the son of my father. He was a story teller as I was to be. It may be that I even laughed a little softly there in the darkness. If I did, I laughed knowing that I would never again be wanting another father.

QUESTIONS ON CONTENT, STRUCTURE, AND STYLE

1. From whose point of view is this narrative presented?

2. Before the swimming incident, Anderson saw his father as what kind of a person?

3. In the first part of the essay what technique does Anderson primarily use to characterize his father for the readers?

4. Does Anderson use enough descriptive details to convey his impression of his father? Point out some of the more effective examples.

5. Why does Anderson use dialogue in the story about General Grant?

6. Do all the people in town share Anderson's earlier view of his father? What other qualities did he have? How do you know?

7. In paragraph 30 and again in paragraph 39, Anderson refers to his father's face as full of sadness. Why do you think his father, ordinarily so cheerful, looked so sad?

8. After Anderson swims with his father, how do his feelings change?

9. Try to explain in your own words why you think Anderson saw his father differently after the swimming incident.

10. Describe the tone of this essay. What do the choice of words and sentence type contribute to this tone?

VOCABULARY

dignified (1)
absurd (2)
immaculate (23)

SUGGESTIONS FOR WRITING

1. Perhaps as a child you also had a relative you considered odd or even embarrassing. Write an essay describing your view of this person. Did your opinion of this person change? If so, explain why.

2. In the swimming scene, Anderson tries to show a moment in which a great change in important feelings occurred. Write an essay that captures such a moment in your own life.

3. Think of the people in your life who have strongly influenced your beliefs, goals, or personality. Select one person to write about and focus your essay on a specific event that shows clearly how this person affected your character.

Graduation

MAYA ANGELOU

Maya Angelou is an American author, actress, journalist, and civil-rights activist. She has written several volumes of poetry and four popular autobiographical works, including her most recent memoir *All God's Children Need Traveling Shoes* (1986). Angelou received national attention when she read her poem "On the Pulse of Morning" at the 1993 inauguration of President Bill Clinton. This essay is a chapter from her autobiography, *I Know Why the Caged Bird Sings* (1970).

1   THE CHILDREN in Stamps[1] trembled visibly with anticipation. Some adults were excited too, but to be certain the whole young population had come down with graduation epidemic. Large classes were graduating from both the grammar school and the high school. Even those who were years removed from their own day of glorious release were anxious to help with preparations as a kind of dry run. The junior students who were moving into the vacating classes' chairs were tradition-bound to show their talents for leadership and management. They strutted through the school and around the campus exerting pressure on the lower grades. Their authority was so new that occasionally if they pressed a little too hard it had to be overlooked. After all, next term was coming, and it never hurt a sixth grader to have a play sister in the eighth grade, or a tenth-year student to be able to call a twelfth grader Bubba. So all was endured in a spirit of shared understanding.

---

[1] A small town in Arkansas where Angelou and her brother Bailey were raised by their grandmother ("Momma").

But the graduating classes themselves were the nobility. Like travelers with exotic destinations on their minds, the graduates were remarkably forgetful. They came to school without their books, or tablets or even pencils. Volunteers fell over themselves to secure replacements for the missing equipment. When accepted, the willing workers might or might not be thanked, and it was of no importance to the pregraduation rites. Even teachers were respectful of the now quiet and aging seniors, and tended to speak to them, if not as equals, as beings only slightly lower than themselves. After tests were returned and grades given, the student body, which acted like an extended family, knew who did well, who excelled, and what piteous ones had failed.

2   Unlike the white high school, Lafayette County Training School distinguished itself by having neither lawn, nor hedges, nor tennis court, nor climbing ivy. Its two buildings (main classrooms, the grade school and home economics) were set on a dirt hill with no fence to limit either its boundaries or those of bordering farms. There was a large expanse to the left of the school which was used alternately as a baseball diamond or a basketball court. Rusty hoops on the swaying poles represented the permanent recreational equipment, although bats and balls could be borrowed from the P.E. teacher if the borrower was qualified and if the diamond wasn't occupied.

3   Over this rocky area relieved by a few shady tall persimmon trees the graduating class walked. The girls often held hands and no longer bothered to speak to the lower students. There was a sadness about them, as if this old world was not their home and they were bound for higher ground. The boys, on the other hand, had become more friendly, more outgoing. A decided change from the closed attitude they projected while studying for finals. Now they seemed not ready to give up the old school, the familiar paths and classrooms. Only a small percentage would be continuing on to college—one of the South's A & M (agricultural and mechanical) schools, which trained Negro youths to be carpenters, farmers, handymen, masons, maids, cooks and baby nurses. Their future rode heavily on their shoulders, and blinded them to the collective joy that had pervaded the lives of the boys and girls in the grammar school graduating class.

4   Parents who could afford it had ordered new shoes and ready-made clothes for themselves from Sears and Roebuck or Montgomery Ward. They also engaged the best seamstresses to make the floating graduating

dresses and to cut down secondhand pants which would be pressed to a military slickness for the important event.

5   Oh, it was important, all right. Whitefolks would attend the ceremony, and two or three would speak of God and home, and the Southern way of life, and Mrs. Parsons, the principal's wife, would play the graduation march while the lower-grade graduates paraded down the aisles and took their seats below the platform. The high school seniors would wait in empty classrooms to make their dramatic entrance.

6   In the Store I was the person of the moment. The birthday girl. The center. Bailey had graduated the year before, although to do so he had had to forfeit all pleasures to make up for his time lost in Baton Rouge.

7   My class was wearing butter-yellow pique dresses, and Momma launched out on mine. She smocked the yoke into tiny crisscrossing puckers, then shirred the rest of the bodice. Her dark fingers ducked in and out of the lemony cloth as she embroidered raised daisies around the hem. Before she considered herself finished she had added a crocheted cuff on the puff sleeves, and a pointy crocheted collar.

8   I was going to be lovely. A walking model of all the various styles of fine hand sewing and it didn't worry me that I was only twelve years old and merely graduating from the eighth grade. Besides, many teachers in Arkansas Negro schools had only that diploma and were licensed to impart wisdom.

9   The days had become longer and more noticeable. The faded beige of former times had been replaced with strong and sure colors. I began to see my classmates' clothes, their skin tones, and the dust that waved off pussy willows. Clouds that lazed across the sky were objects of great concern to me. Their shiftier shapes might have held a message that in my new happiness and with a little bit of time I'd soon decipher. During that period I looked at the arch of heaven so religiously my neck kept a steady ache. I had taken to smiling more often, and my jaws hurt from the unaccustomed activity. Between the two physical sore spots, I suppose I could have been uncomfortable, but that was not the case. As a member of the winning team (the graduating class of 1940) I had outdistanced unpleasant sensations by miles. I was headed for the freedom of open fields.

10   Youth and social approval allied themselves with me and we trammeled memories of slights and insults. The wind of our swift passage remodeled my features. Lost tears were pounded to mud and then to dust.

Years of withdrawal were brushed aside and left behind, as hanging ropes of parasitic moss.

11   My work alone had awarded me a top place and I was going to be one of the first called in the graduating ceremonies. On the classroom blackboard, as well as on the bulletin board in the auditorium, there were blue stars and white stars and red stars. No absences, no tardinesses, and my academic work was among the best of the year. I could say the preamble to the Constitution even faster than Bailey. We timed ourselves often: WethepeopleoftheUnitedStatesinordertoformamoreperfectunion. . . ." I had memorized the Presidents of the United States from Washington to Roosevelt in chronological as well as alphabetical order.

12   My hair pleased me too. Gradually the black mass had lengthened and thickened, so that it kept at last to its braided pattern, and I didn't have to yank my scalp off when I tried to comb it.

13   Louise and I had rehearsed the exercises until we tired out ourselves. Henry Reed was class valedictorian. He was a small, very black boy with hooded eyes, a long, broad nose and an oddly shaped head. I had admired him for years because each term he and I vied for the best grades in our class. Most often he bested me, but instead of being disappointed I was pleased that we shared top places between us. Like many Southern Black children, he lived with his grandmother, who was as strict as Momma and as kind as she knew how to be. He was courteous, respectful and soft-spoken to elders, but on the playground he chose to play the roughest games. I admired him. Anyone, I reckoned, sufficiently afraid or sufficiently dull could be polite. But to be able to operate at a top level with both adults and children was admirable.

14   His valedictory speech was entitled "To Be or Not to Be." The rigid tenth-grade teacher had helped him to write it. He'd been working on the dramatic stresses for months.

15   The weeks until graduation were filled with heady activities. A group of small children were to be presented in a play about buttercups and daisies and bunny rabbits. They could be heard throughout the building practicing their hops and their little songs that sounded like silver bells. The older girls (non-graduates, of course) were assigned the task of making refreshments for the night's festivities. A tangy scent of ginger, cinnamon, nutmeg and chocolate wafted around the

home economics building as the budding cooks made samples for themselves and their teachers.

16   In every corner of the workshop, axes and saws split fresh timber as
the woodshop boys made sets and stage scenery. Only the graduates
were left out of the general bustle. We were free to sit in the library at
the back of the building or look in quite detachedly, naturally, on the
measures being taken for our event.

17   Even the minister preached on graduation the Sunday before. His
subject was "Let your light so shine that men will see your good works
and praise your Father, Who is in Heaven." Although the sermon was
purported to be addressed to us, he used the occasion to speak to back-
sliders, gamblers and general ne'er-do-wells. But since he had called
our names at the beginning of the service we were mollified.

18   Among Negroes the tradition was to give presents to children going
only from one grade to another. How much more important this was
when the person was graduating at the top of the class. Uncle Willie
and Momma had sent away for a Mickey Mouse watch like Bailey's.
Louise gave me four embroidered handkerchiefs. (I gave her three crocheted doilies.) Mrs. Sneed, the minister's wife, made me an under-
skirt to wear for graduation, and nearly every customer gave me a
nickel or maybe even a dime with the instruction "Keep on moving to
higher ground," or some such encouragement.

19   Amazingly the great day finally dawned and I was out of bed before
I knew it. I threw open the back door to see it more clearly, but
Momma said, "Sister, come away from that door and put your robe on."

20   I hoped the memory of that morning would never leave me. Sunlight
was itself still young, and the day had none of the insistence maturity
would bring it in a few hours. In my robe and barefoot in the backyard,
under cover of going to see about my new beans, I gave myself up to the
gentle warmth and thanked God that no matter what evil I had done in
my life He had allowed me to live to see this day. Somewhere in my
fatalism I had expected to die, accidentally, and never have the chance
to walk up the stairs in the auditorium and gracefully receive my hard-
earned diploma. Out of God's merciful bosom I had won reprieve.

21   Bailey came out in his robe and gave me a box wrapped in Christmas
paper. He said he had saved his money for months to pay for it. It felt
like a box of chocolates, but I knew Bailey wouldn't save money to buy
candy when we had all we could want under our noses.

22   He was as proud of the gift as I. It was a soft-leather-bound copy of a collection of poems by Edgar Allan Poe, or, as Bailey and I called him, "Eap." I turned to "Annabel Lee" and we walked up and down the garden rows, the cool dirt between our toes, reciting the beautifully sad lines.

23   Momma made a Sunday breakfast although it was only Friday. After we finished the blessing, I opened my eyes to find the watch on my plate. It was a dream of a day. Everything went smoothly and to my credit. I didn't have to be reminded or scolded for anything. Near evening I was too jittery to attend to chores, so Bailey volunteered to do all before his bath.

24   Days before, we had made a sign for the Store and as we turned out the lights Momma hung the cardboard over the doorknob. It read clearly: CLOSED. GRADUATION.

25   My dress fitted perfectly and everyone said that I looked like a sunbeam in it. On the hill, going toward the school, Bailey walked behind with Uncle Willie, who muttered, "Go on, Ju." He wanted him to walk ahead with us because it embarrassed him to have to walk so slowly. Bailey said he'd let the ladies walk together, and the men would bring up the rear. We all laughed, nicely.

26   Little children dashed by out of the dark like fireflies. Their crepe-paper dresses and butterfly wings were not made for running and we heard more than one rip, dryly, and the regretful "uh uh" that followed.

27   The school blazed without gaiety. The windows seemed cold and unfriendly from the lower hill. A sense of ill-fated timing crept over me, and if Momma hadn't reached for my hand I would have drifted back to Bailey and Uncle Willie, and possibly beyond. She made a few slow jokes about my feet getting cold, and tugged me along to the now-strange building.

28   Around the front steps, assurance came back. There were my fellow "greats," the graduating class. Hair brushed back, legs oiled, new dresses and pressed pleats, fresh pocket handkerchiefs and little handbags, all homesewn. Oh, we were up to snuff, all right. I joined my comrades and didn't even see my family go in to find seats in the crowded auditorium.

29   The school band struck up a march and all classes filed in as had been rehearsed. We stood in front of our seats, as assigned, and on a signal from the choir director, we sat. No sooner had this been accomplished than the band started to play the national anthem. We rose again and sang the song, after which we recited the pledge of allegiance. We

remained standing for a brief minute before the choir director and the principal signaled to us, rather desperately I thought, to take our seats. The command was so unusual that our carefully rehearsed and smooth-running machine was thrown off. For a full minute we fumbled for our chairs and bumped into each other awkwardly. Habits change or solidify under pressure, so in our state of nervous tension we had been ready to follow our usual assembly pattern: the American National Anthem, then the pledge of allegiance, then the song every Black person I knew called the Negro National Anthem. All done in the same key, with the same passion and most often standing on the same foot.

30   Finding my seat at last, I was overcome with a presentiment of worse things to come. Something unrehearsed, unplanned, was going to happen, and we were going to be made to look bad. I distinctly remember being explicit in the choice of pronoun. It was "we," the graduating class, the unit, that concerned me then.

31   The principal welcomed "parents and friends" and asked the Baptist minister to lead us in prayer. His invocation was brief and punchy, and for a second I thought we were getting back on the high road to right action. When the principal came back to the dais, however, his voice had changed. Sounds always affected me profoundly and the principal's voice was one of my favorites. During assembly it melted and lowed weakly into the audience. It had not been in my plan to listen to him, but my curiosity was piqued and I straightened up to give him my attention.

32   He was talking about Booker T. Washington, our "late great leader," who said we can be as close as the fingers on the hand, etc. . . . Then he said a few vague things about friendship and the friendship of kindly people to those less fortunate than themselves. With that his voice nearly faded, thin, away. Like a river diminishing to a stream and then to a trickle. But he cleared his throat and said, "Our speaker tonight, who is also our friend, came from Texarkana to deliver the commencement address, but due to the irregularity of the train schedule, he's going to, as they say, 'speak and run.'" He said that we understood and wanted the man to know that we were most grateful for the time he was able to give us and then something about how we were willing always to adjust to another's program, and without more ado—"I give you Mr. Edward Donleavy."

33   Not one but two white men came through the door offstage. The shorter one walked to the speaker's platform, and the tall one moved over to the center seat and sat down. But that was our principal's seat,

and already occupied. The dislodged gentleman bounced around for a long breath or two before the Baptist minister gave him his chair, then with more dignity than the situation deserved, the minister walked off the stage.

34   Donleavy looked at the audience once (on reflection, I'm sure that he wanted only to reassure himself that we were really there), adjusted his glasses and began to read from a sheaf of papers.

35   He was glad "to be here and to see the work going on just as it was in the other schools."

36   At the first "Amen" from the audience I willed the offender to immediate death by choking on the word. But Amen's and Yes, sir's began to fall around the room like rain through a ragged umbrella.

37   He told us of the wonderful changes we children in Stamps had in store. The Central School (naturally, the white school was Central) had already been granted improvements that would be in use in the fall. A well-known artist was coming from Little Rock to teach art to them. They were going to have the newest microscopes and chemistry equipment for their laboratory. Mr. Donleavy didn't leave us long in the dark over who made these improvements available to Central High. Nor were we to be ignored in the general betterment scheme he had in mind.

38   He said that he had pointed out to people at a very high level that one of the first-line football tacklers at Arkansas Agricultural and Mechanical College had graduated from good old Lafayette County Training School. Here fewer Amen's were heard. Those few that did break through lay dully in the air with the heaviness of habit.

39   He went on to praise us. He went on to say how he had bragged that "one of the best basketball players at Fisk sank his first ball right here at Lafayette County Training School."

40   The white kids were going to have a chance to become Galileos and Madame Curies and Edisons and Gauguins, and our boys (the girls weren't even in on it) would try to be Jesse Owenses and Joe Louises.

41   Owens and the Brown Bomber were great heroes in our world, but what school official in the white-goddom of Little Rock had the right to decide that those two men must be our only heroes? Who decided that for Henry Reed to become a scientist he had to work like George Washington Carver, as a bootblack, to buy a lousy microscope? Bailey was obviously always going to be too small to be an athlete, so which concrete angel glued to what country seat had decided that if my

brother wanted to become a lawyer he had to first pay penance for his skin by picking cotton and hoeing corn and studying correspondence books at night for twenty years?

42   The man's dead words fell like bricks around the auditorium and too many settled in my belly. Constrained by hard-learned manners I couldn't look behind me, but to my left and right the proud graduating class of 1940 had dropped their heads. Every girl in my row had found something new to do with her handkerchief. Some folded the tiny squares into love knots, some into triangles, but most were wadding them, then pressing them flat on their yellow laps.

43   On the dais, the ancient tragedy was being replayed. Professor Parsons sat, a sculptor's reject, rigid. His large, heavy body seemed devoid of will or willingness, and his eyes said he was no longer with us. The other teachers examined the flag (which was draped stage right) or their notes, or the window which opened on our now-famous playing diamond.

44   Graduation, the hush-hush magic time of frills and gifts and congratulations and diplomas, was finished for me before my name was called. The accomplishment was nothing. The meticulous maps, drawn in three colors of ink, learning and spelling decasyllabic words, memorizing the whole of *The Rape of Lucrece*—it was nothing. Donleavy had exposed us.

45   We were maids and farmers, handymen and washerwomen, and anything higher that we aspired to was farcical and presumptuous. Then I wished that Gabriel Prosser and Nat Turner had killed all whitefolks in their beds and that Abraham Lincoln had been assassinated before the signing of the Emancipation Proclamation, and that Harriet Tubman had been killed by that blow on her head and Christopher Columbus had drowned in the *Santa Maria*.

46   It was awful to be Negro and have no control over my life. It was brutal to be young and already trained to sit quietly and listen to charges brought against my color with no chance of defense. We should all be dead. I thought I should like to see us all dead, one on top of the other. A pyramid of flesh with the whitefolks on the bottom, as the broad base, then the Indians with their silly tomahawks and teepees and wigwams and treaties, the Negroes with their mops and recipes and cotton sacks and spirituals sticking out of their mouths. The Dutch children should all stumble in their wooden shoes and break their necks. The French should choke to death on the Louisiana Purchase

(1803) while silkworms ate all the Chinese with their stupid pigtails. As a species, we were an abomination. All of us.

47   Donleavy was running for election, and assured our parents that if he won we could count on having the only colored paved playing field in that part of Arkansas. Also—he never looked up to acknowledge the grunts of acceptance—also, we were bound to get some new equipment for the home economics building and the workshop.

48   He finished, and since there was no need to give any more than the most perfunctory thank-you's, he nodded to the men on the stage, and the tall white man who was never introduced joined him at the door. They left with the attitude that now they were off to something really important. (The graduation ceremonies at Lafayette County Training School had been a mere preliminary.)

49   The ugliness they left was palpable. An uninvited guest who wouldn't leave. The choir was summoned and sang a modern arrangement of "Onward, Christian Soldiers," with new words pertaining to graduates seeking their place in the world. But it didn't work. Elouise, the daughter of the Baptist minister, recited "Invictus," and I could have cried at the impertinence of "I am the master of my fate: I am the captain of my soul."

50   My name had lost its ring of familiarity and I had to be nudged to go and receive my diploma. All my preparations had fled. I neither marched up to the stage like a conquering Amazon, nor did I look in the audience for Bailey's nod of approval. Marguerite Johnson, I heard the name again, my honors were read, there were noises in the audience of appreciation, and I took my place on the stage as rehearsed.

51   I thought about colors I hated: ecru, puce, lavender, beige and black.

52   There was shuffling and rustling around me, then Henry Reed was giving his valedictory address, "To Be or Not to Be." Hadn't he heard the whitefolks? We couldn't be, so the question was a waste of time. Henry's voice came out clear and strong. I feared to look at him. Hadn't he got the message? There was no "nobler in the mind" for Negroes because the world didn't think we had minds, and they let us know it. "Outrageous fortune"? Now, that was a joke. When the ceremony was over I had to tell Henry Reed some things. That is, if I still cared. Not "rub," Henry, "erase." "Ah, there's the erase." Us.

53   Henry had been a good student in elocution. His voice rose on tides of promise and fell on waves of warnings. The English teacher had helped him to create a sermon winging through Hamlet's soliloquy. To

be a man, a doer, a builder, a leader, or to be a tool, an unfunny joke, a crusher of funky toadstools. I marveled that Henry could go through with the speech as if we had a choice.

54   I had been listening and silently rebutting each sentence with my eyes closed; then there was a hush, which in an audience warns that something unplanned is happening. I looked up and saw Henry Reed, the conservative, the proper, the A student, turn his back to the audience and turn to us (the proud graduating class of 1940) and sing, nearly speaking,

> Lift ev'ry voice and sing
> Till earth and heaven ring
> Ring with the harmonies of Liberty . . .²

It was the poem written by James Weldon Johnson. It was the music composed by J. Rosamond Johnson. It was the Negro National Anthem. Out of habit we were singing it.

55   Our mothers and fathers stood in the dark hall and joined the hymn of encouragement. A kindergarten teacher led the small children onto the stage and the buttercups and daisies and bunny rabbits marked time and tried to follow:

> Stony the road we trod
> Bitter the chastening rod
> Felt in the days when hope, unborn, had died.
> Yet with a steady beat
> Have not our weary feet
> Come to the place for which our fathers sighed?

56   Every child I knew had learned that song with his ABC's and along with "Jesus Loves Me This I Know." But I personally had never heard it before. Never heard the words, despite the thousands of times I had sung them. Never thought they had anything to do with me.

57   On the other hand, the words of Patrick Henry had made such an impression on me that I had been able to stretch myself tall and

² "Lift Ev'ry Voice and Sing"—words by James Weldon Johnson and music by J. Rosamond Johnson. © Copyrighted: Edward B. Marks Music Corporation. Used by permission.

trembling and say, "I know not what course others may take, but as for me, give me liberty or give me death."

58   And now I heard, really for the first time:

> We have come over a way that with tears has been watered,
> We have come, treading our path through the blood of the
>   slaughtered.

59   While echoes of the song shivered in the air, Henry Reed bowed his head, said "Thank you," and returned to his place in the line. The tears that slipped down many faces were not wiped away in shame.

60   We were on top again. As always, again. We survived. The depths had been icy and dark, but now a bright sun spoke to our souls. I was no longer simply a member of the proud graduating class of 1940; I was a proud member of the wonderful, beautiful Negro race.

61   Oh, Black known and unknown poets, how often have your auctioned pains sustained us? Who will compute the lonely nights made less lonely by your songs, or the empty pots made less tragic by your tales?

62   If we were a people much given to revealing secrets, we might raise monuments and sacrifice to the memories of our poets, but slavery cured us of that weakness. It may be enough, however, to have it said that we survive in exact relationship to the dedication of our poets (include preachers, musicians and blues singers).

QUESTIONS ON CONTENT, STRUCTURE, AND STYLE

1. In paragraph 1, how does Angelou characterize the members of the graduating classes?

2. Study paragraph 10; what level of diction is used there? Why?

3. Why are the students confused when they are signaled to sit down after reciting the pledge of allegiance? Why is Angelou upset?

4. What is Angelou's reaction to Donleavy's speech?

5. Why does she make the wishes she does in paragraphs 45 and 46? How has her mood changed from the earlier part of the day?

6. Why is the reading of the poem "Invictus" particularly ironic to her?

7. Why does Angelou "hear" the words of the Negro National Anthem for the first time? What effect do they have on her?

8. Why does Angelou end this selection by addressing "Black known and unknown poets"? How does the tone in the last two paragraphs differ from the rest of the essay?

9. Does Angelou use enough detail in her story to make it vivid and believable? Support your answer with some examples.

10. What was Angelou's purpose in telling about this incident?

VOCABULARY

trammeled (10)	*farcical (45)*	*palpable (49)*
explicit (30)	*presumptuous (45)*	*impertinence (49)*
penance (41)	*perfunctory (48)*	*rebutting (54)*
meticulous (44)		

SUGGESTIONS FOR WRITING

1. Write an essay explaining what Angelou learned from this experience and how, through her use of characterization and description, she communicates this lesson to her reader.

2. Recent times have seen a rise in the number of racist incidents on campuses and in our neighborhoods. Analyze an incident you have witnessed or experienced, and write an essay that explains your feelings or perhaps suggests solutions.

3. Write an essay describing an incident that you feel taught you something important about your view of yourself.

They Stole Our Childhood

LEE GOLDBERG

Lee Goldberg was a junior majoring in mass communications at the University of California, Los Angeles, when he wrote this essay for "My Turn" column appearing in the March 1983 "On Campus" edition of *Newsweek* magazine.

1   WE'RE THE wonderful generation.

2   We are the kids who were "so adult" when our divorced parents readjusted to the rigors of being suddenly single. We are the kids who discovered sex so early in our lives and were such overachievers in school.

3   We are looked on by our elders with admiration and awe. And yet, if you wipe away the surface gloss, you will find that we are actually victims, casualties of our parents' need for us to grow up fast. That which we are praised for is our biggest problem.

4   Day-to-day family life for us was a contradiction between what we saw on "The Brady Bunch" and "Courtship of Eddie's Father" and what we were actually living. We were supposed to be thinking about the big dance, playing baseball, getting new handlebars on our bikes, gossiping about our favorite TV stars and, when our parents weren't around, dressing up in their clothes and looking at ourselves in the mirror.

5   Instead we found ourselves not only dressing up in their clothes, but adopting their state of mind as well. We worried about whether mom would receive her child-support check, whether our parent's date for tonight would become a breakfast guest tomorrow, whether our little sister would ever remember what it was like to have two parents under one roof.

6   Our parents were always so proud of our capacity to make it on our own, to "be adult." Parents were thinking of us less like children and more like peers. Suddenly we kids weren't being treated like kids anymore.

7   Part of being adult was not indulging the child in us that hungered for affection. Our generation, it seems, turned to sex for the affection we lacked at home. As we saw it, needing a hug wasn't very adult.

Sleeping with someone was. It was an acceptable way to ask for the physical affirmation of self-worth that we weren't getting from our parents, who we saw doing little hugging and a lot of sleeping around.

8   We found that spending more time at school or work was a welcome alternative to going home in the afternoons. The media had taught us that coming home from school meant milk and cookies, TV and playing with friends, mom or a babysitter in the kitchen, and dad back from work at 6. Suddenly, going home meant confronting dad's new girl-friend, mom's unpaid bills or playing parent to our younger siblings and our parents, too.

9   It's no wonder so many of us, barely into our 20s, feel as though we've already been married and raised children. In divorce, parents seem to become teen-agers, and the kids become the adults. Many of our younger brothers and sisters see us more as their parents than their real parents. As our parents pursued careers and re-entered the dating scene, we children coped by forming our own little mini-families, with the older kids parenting for the younger siblings. It was common for single mothers to joke about how their eldest son played doting father, checking out her dates and offering sage advice. Or for parents to find their younger kids wouldn't accept candy from them unless an older sister OK'd it first.

10   Our parents expected us to understand their problems and frustra-tions, to grasp the complex machinations of divorce proceedings and the emotional hazards they faced by dating again. More than under-standing, they even solicited our advice and guidance in these delicate matters. Our parents sometimes pressured us into becoming partici-pants in their divorce proceedings, encouraging us to take sides. We found ourselves having to withdraw from them just to protect ourselves from the potential pain that could be caused by mixed parental loy-alties in the midst of courtroom warfare.

11   We were rewarded with approval: "my kids are so grown-up," "my kids can handle things," "my kids coped so well," "my kids can make it on their own," "my kids are so together." What we missed was a chance to be childish, immature and unafraid to admit we didn't have it all together.

12   We pay the price when we need parents to turn to and don't have them—as we toil with our first serious relationships and when our long-suppressed childish side rears its playful head.

13   Divorce didn't just split up our parents. It stole our childhood.

14   Our parents are paying, too. They ache for the closeness with us they never had and may never get. They try to grasp memories of our childhood and come up nearly empty. They find themselves separated from their children and wonder how the gap appeared. Some wake up to realize that they know their gas-station attendant better than their children.

15   The cure is not to curb divorce. We can start by realizing that this generation, which may have it together intellectually, paid with its adolescence. What needs rethinking are the attitudes and expectations of parents. Kids who are mature are fine. Kids who are "so adult" need help.

QUESTIONS ON CONTENT, STRUCTURE, AND STYLE

1. Why does Goldberg begin his essay with a series of parallel statements about "the wonderful generation"?

2. In addition to the loss of a traditional family, what, according to Goldberg, have divorces taken from children? Why?

3. Goldberg offers numerous examples of adult worries that children of divorce have been forced to assume. Identify two or three examples you find persuasive.

4. In what ways have the "adult" children tried to cope with their situations?

5. What expository technique does Goldberg use in paragraphs 4 and 5 and within paragraph 8 to emphasize his point about television and real-life families?

6. Goldberg notes that parents often praise children who appear "so grown-up" and "so together." Why does he see such approval as a problem for both children and parents?

7. Near the end of the essay, why does Goldberg restate the thesis of his essay?

8. How does Goldberg conclude his essay? Do you find his conclusion effective? Why?

9. Describe the tone of this essay. Give some examples of Goldberg's clearly presented "voice."

10. Do you think Goldberg has accurately and persuasively illustrated the problems of today's children of divorce? Why or why not?

VOCABULARY

rigors (2)   *machinations (10)*
casualties (3)   *solicited (10)*
siblings (8)

SUGGESTIONS FOR WRITING

1. Think about the couples you know, and then write an essay analyzing the major effect(s) on your life of one divorce or of one happy marriage.

2. Interview as many children of divorce as you can find. Do they agree with Goldberg's thesis? Use the results of your survey as evidence in an essay that either argues for or against Goldberg's point of view.

3. The traditional family today is fast being replaced by families with joint custody or with children "blended" from different marriages. Such families have their advantages and disadvantages, their successes and failures. Write about a nontraditional family arrangement you know well, making clear your attitude toward the family life it represents.

Road Warrior

DIANE SYLVAIN

Diane Sylvain is an artist who lives in Paonia, Colorado, where she also writes for the *High Country News*. She has published articles in both major newspapers in Denver, Colorado—the *Post* and the *Rocky Mountain News*. This article originally appeared on February 18, 1993, in the *Rocky Mountain News* "Colorado People" magazine.

1   I GREW up in a series of cluttered, crowded cars, elbowing my two brothers for back seat space as we stared out the windows at America flying by.

2   We were Air Force brats—not a name we chose; it was a careless sort of packing label that was slapped on to us by strangers, as if we were merely an extra set of baggage following Dad down the highway. We were always the new family on the block, the new kids in the classroom, waiting uncomfortably for the moment when the teacher would ask us to stand up in front of everyone and explain where we came from. I went to 10 schools in 12 years, so I was asked that question a lot.

3   Where was I from? A good question. Nowhere, I sometimes think. Sometimes, everywhere.

4   When I was a child we always had cardboard boxes to play with and in and build things out of, boats and robots and forts and mazes. We had the excitement of the long vacations we took, curiously open-ended, as we left one home behind us and headed toward another never seen. We never went to Europe, and we envied those who did, but we saw Chugwater, Wyoming, and Wewahitchka, Florida; Dinwiddie, Virginia, and the tiny town of George, Washington. We tramped across Civil War battlefields and western ghost towns and prehistoric Indian ruins—and we admired the Big Well in Greensburg, Kansas, and got our Official Dinosaur Hunting Licenses in Vernal, Utah.

5   I loved the tacky roadside museums full of mangy two-headed goats, the postcards of giant fish and jackalopes, the gift shops crammed with strangely inscribed souvenir ashtrays and fragrant little cedar boxes

that showed the Last Supper. There were times when it was as exciting and wonderful as a carnival road show, an epic, gypsy-free, in which the Sylvain family starred and triumphed.

6   But life on the road was not always a song. Two of us spent much of the time fighting motion sickness in hot cars. Bladders were always too small and never synchronized. There were strained budgets and strained tempers and bad weather and bouts of car trouble. There were losses— irreplaceable things that vanished in transit—such as the box of old and precious Christmas ornaments Auntie Hazel gave us—the closest thing we had to an heirloom. And somewhere there is a shoebox full of the tape-recorded letters my father sent us during his year in Vietnam— things whose value could never be named, lost as completely as if swallowed by a monstrous black hole.

7   For a child, there were other losses: like the rocks I gathered from the streams of the Cascade Mountains—not because I cared about geology, but because the stones were smooth and bright and smelled enchantingly of the green darkness under huge, wet trees. We lost our swingsets and sandpits and favorite climbing trees. We left our schools, and occasionally our pets. Hardest of all, we left our friends.

8   Arrival in a new place was a schizophrenic blend of delight and anxiety—finding a new house, learning a new neighborhood, meeting people, unpacking and assembling our new lives. But this was eclipsed—if we moved during the school year—by the indescribable terror of the first day in a new school, finding out that the rest of the class had gotten halfway through the multiplication table while we were still waltzing across Texas—or entering a hot classroom in Leisure City, Florida, to find that everyone else was taking a test in Spanish and that no exception was to be made for me, just because I was a newcomer whose only previous acquaintance with the language was watching "Speedy Gonzales" on the Bugs Bunny show back in Moses Lake, Washington.

9   I worried that no one would talk to me, that I would forget my teacher's name or my locker combination—or that I would leave school at the end of the day and not remember what town I was in, unable to guess where my new house lay, and without a road map to lead me home.

10   I don't regret my wandering childhood. It knitted my family tightly together, opened my mind to different ways of thinking and gave me a sense of self.

11   After enough practice, you can get used to saying good-bye. It is an American kind of life, this riding off into the sunset without looking

back. It can seem like a kind of freedom: to toss your past carelessly over your shoulder and never have to look back to see where it comes down.

12   But I always remember how it felt to be a child, passing through nameless small towns at twilight, when night flowed around the old car like deep, black water. I fell achingly in love with everything I left behind, and knew that pieces of my heart were being scattered in the wake of our passage.

13   It was then that I first glimpsed how much we have to lose in this life by never getting to know what we have while it is ours.

QUESTIONS ON CONTENT, STRUCTURE, AND STYLE

1. How does the title of this essay, "Road Warrior," reflect its content?

2. What is the dominant idea in Sylvain's essay? Is the thesis clearly stated or is it implied?

3. This essay was originally published in a newspaper for a general audience. Would the essay be most effective for those, like Sylvain, who "grew up in a series of . . . cars"? Explain.

4. Sylvain describes her childhood journeys in terms of emotion—the excitement of the road, the fear of a new school, the sense of loss when they must pack up and leave again. Which of these experiences is so vividly described that it evoked memories of similar emotions in you as the reader? Explain your choice.

5. Describe Sylvain's tone. Is it wistful? Bitter? Nostalgic? Something else? Choose a few lines from the essay to support your answer.

6. In paragraph 12 Sylvain writes, "It is an American kind of life, this riding off into the sunset without looking back." What popular cultural image is she alluding to here? How does this affect her essay's message?

7. Sylvain uses figurative language, particularly simile and metaphor, throughout the essay. List some examples you found effective.

8. How does Sylvain use small details to emphasize the effect of frequent moves on her family. For example, what does the line "When

I was a child we always had cardboard boxes to play with" reveal? Cite other examples of such "showing" details in the essay.

9. Consider Sylvain's use of travel imagery (for example, "packing label" in paragraph 2, "carnival road show" in paragraph 5). What other images does she use to sustain the travel motif throughout the essay?

10. How does the final paragraph change the overall impact of the essay? Are readers prepared for this conclusion? Explain.

VOCABULARY

mangy (5)   *transit (6)*
inscribed (5)   *eclipsed (8)*
synchronized (6)   *twilight (12)*

SUGGESTIONS FOR WRITING

1. Re-read the last paragraph of the essay and consider your own experiences. Write a well-detailed essay describing something you never knew you had until it was lost.

2. Like Sylvain, did you move often while you were growing up? Or did you remain in the same area for most of your life? How important is a "sense of place" to your own identity? In an informal essay, describe how your neighborhood or your many moves influenced you.

3. Some sociologists argue that our society's increasing mobility in the past few decades, as families move from city to city and state to state, is destroying, or at least altering, our sense of community. Do you agree? Explain your views in an essay supported by specific examples from your own experience.

Halloween

ANNA QUINDLEN

Anna Quindlen is a contemporary journalist, columnist, and novelist. She is well-known for her column on modern life, "Life in the 30s," which appears in *The New York Times*. Her novel, *Object Lessons,* was published in 1991. This essay is from her collection of columns called *Living Out Loud,* published in 1988.

1   WHEN I was a little girl, I loved Halloween because it was the only day of the year when I was beautiful. I had friends who went out dressed as hobos and clowns and witches, but I never would. I was always a princess or a ballet dancer, Sleeping Beauty or Cinderella. (One year I wanted to go as Barbie. "Out of the question," said my mother flatly, and it occurs to me now that her reply worked on several levels.)

2   It was the only day of the year when I wore satin or net or hoops, the only day of the year when my thin lips were carmine and full and the mole on my upper lip, blackened with eyebrow pencil, became a beauty mark. I remember one Halloween, when I wore my cousin Mary Jane's flower-girl dress, blue net over blue chiffon over blue satin, with a skirt as big around at the bottom as a hula hoop, as one of the happiest nights of my life. I had a wand with a silver star on the end made of tinfoil, and a tiara that was borrowed from a girl down the street who was last year's prom princess. My hair had been set in pin curls, and waves rose all over my head like a cross between Shirley Temple and Elsa Lanchester in *Bride of Frankenstein*. I looked in the mirror on the back of my closet door and saw someone I was not, and loved her. The night was sharp, as perfect Halloween nights always are, but I would not wear a coat. I caught cold, and didn't care.

3   I suppose one of the things that makes me saddest about modern life, right up there with the fact that most of the furniture is so cheesy, is that Halloween has fallen into some disrepute. The candy is not good for you. The store-bought costumes stink. And behind every door a mother is supposed to imagine that there's a man with candied apples

whose recipe for caramelization includes rat poison. My children don't go far on Halloween, at least in part because they are city kids. They visit a few neighbors, get just enough stuff to make a kind of promising rustle in the bottom of their bags. They are amazed at even this much license; the rest of the year they live with a woman whose idea of a good time is a bag of yogurt raisins. They must think I've lost it when I stand before the jack-o'-lantern at the kitchen table, grinning maniacally at one of those miniature Mr. Goodbars. I have never in my life eaten a Mr. Goodbar, except in the aftermath of Halloween.

4   In the way they do—must, I suppose—my children are galvanized by Halloween because I am, just as they make a big fuss about throwing autumn leaves up in the air and letting them tumble over their heads. They take their cue from me. The little one is still a bit confused, but the elder caught fire last year. "I want to be a clown," he said. And even though, throughout the month, he ricocheted between wanting to be a bumblebee and a bunny, he always inevitably came back to wanting to be a clown. His cheeks were painted with red circles, the tip of his nose was blue, and although he was sick for four days beforehand he insisted on dragging himself around to a half-dozen houses in his satin clown costume with the pompoms and the big ruffle around his reedy neck. A sensitive, thoughtful little boy, who loves to laugh but never likes to feel laughed at, he looked in the mirror and saw someone he was not. "I look really great," he said.

5   (By contrast, the little one was a bunny, quite himself in artificial white pile. "Hop, hop, hop," he said for three hours. "Hop, hop, hop," he said for two weeks afterward. Of course, I chose the costume, and when he chooses for himself perhaps he will choose something more contrary to his essential nature. Like a clerical collar. This year he is a black cat, which is just right.)

6   This year the elder boy is a witch, which is just right, too. He says he loves witches because they are mean and nasty, although he is not mean and nasty at all. He will wear a black robe, a pointed hat, and wrinkles made of eyeliner. A broom but no wig. "I am a boy witch," he says with dignity.

7   I, of course, go along for the ride, at least for the next few years, until the day when they say "Mo-om!" in that unpleasant, whiny voice and march off by themselves with their pillowcases, their voices muffled behind their masks. Last year I thought seriously about dressing up

as something for the sake of verisimilitude—I'm short, I could pass!—
but abandoned the idea in a rare moment of complete and total common
sense. This year I will not be so foolish.

8   The other day on the telephone a friend recalled one of the saddest
moments of her youth: the night when her sister came home in tears
and announced that she had become too old to go out on Halloween. I
remember it, too—that night looking into the mirror at a Gypsy, with
hoop earrings and a rakish headscarf and an off-the-shoulder peasant
blouse, and knowing in a kind of clear, horrible grown-up way that it
was something I was not. And getting door duty from then on in, giving out M & M's to kids who were rowdy, jubilant, somehow freed
from themselves, and happy not to find behind the door one of those
moms who gave out apples. I've been on door duty every Halloween
since. Last year I suppose I wanted to make one last stab at the magic.
But the wand's been passed.

QUESTIONS ON CONTENT, STRUCTURE, AND STYLE

1. Why is Quindlen saddened by the current view of Halloween?
   What does she feel has been lost?

2. Why does Quindlen begin her essay with a long description of herself as a child at Halloween? Why was this holiday especially important to her?

3. What does the allusion to Shirley Temple and Elsa Lanchester add
   to Quindlen's description of herself? Why do you think her
   mother refused to allow her to go as Barbie?

4. As a mother at Halloween, Quindlen's personality transforms in
   what ways? How does she use humor to communicate this change?

5. Evaluate Quindlen's use of details as she describes her sons' costumes. Cite some details that help the reader understand the boys'
   distinct personalities through their choice of disguise.

6. Quindlen occasionally uses dialogue in this essay. What do these
   direct quotations add to her descriptions?

7. Why does Quindlen remember so vividly the Halloween she
   dressed as a Gypsy? What change had occurred and why is this an
   important change in children's lives?

8. Why does Quindlen mention her friend's sister who came home in tears? Why doesn't she just talk about her own experience?

9. What does Quindlen mean when she says "the wand's been passed"? Why is that image appropriate for the conclusion of this essay?

10. Do you agree with Quindlen that Halloween has fallen into "disrepute"? If so, do you share her attitude of regret for what has been lost? Why or why not?

Vocabulary

carmine (2)	maniacally (3)	verisimilitude (7)
chiffon (2)	galvanized (4)	rakish (8)
tiara (2)	clerical (5)	jubilant (8)

Suggestions for Writing

1. Can you identify a moment in your life when, as Quindlen did, you realized that you had outgrown some activity that had been important to you as a child? Write an essay that describes your realization that you were becoming more adult, that "the wand had passed." Were you sad like Quindlen or pleased?

2. Halloween is clearly an important holiday to Quindlen. Select a holiday (or ritual) that is important to you, your family, or your community. Write an essay that explains the significance of this holiday in a way that all readers can understand. Or, if you prefer, focus on the one holiday you remember best. What made this time so special?

3. Many elementary schools have outlawed Halloween celebrations under pressure from various groups/parents. While some parents argue for the magic of the holiday, others complain of the danger, the candy consumption, the pro-violence costuming, or the increase of juvenile crime associated with the "tricks" of Halloween. Investigate these and other objections and write an essay arguing your position: Is Halloween a holiday we should abandon?

We Real Cool

GWENDOLYN BROOKS

Gwendolyn Brooks is an American poet and teacher who won a Pulitzer Prize for *Annie Allen* in 1949. She is the author of many books of poetry, including *A Street in Bronzeville* (1945), *The Bean Eaters* (1960), *Riot* (1969), and *Beckonings* (1975). She has also written an autobiography, *Report from Part I* (1972), and several books for children. This poem is from *Selected Poems* (1959).

> *The Pool Players.*
> *Seven at the Golden Shovel.* [1]
>
> We real cool. We
> Left school. We
>
> Lurk late. We
> Strike straight. We
>
> 5 Sing sin. We
> Thin gin. We
>
> Jazz June. We
> Die soon.

QUESTIONS ON CONTENT, STRUCTURE, AND STYLE

1. Who are the "we" of this poem? What is the setting of the poem?

2. Characterize the people described in the poem. How does Brooks, in only eight short lines, create a clear picture of these people?

3. Why does Brooks use a series of short, parallel sentences? What do the sound and rhythm contribute to the creation of the scene and characters?

4. What sort of rhyme scheme appears in the poem? What does it contribute to the poem's rhythm?

[1] The Golden Shovel is a Chicago pool hall.

5. Throughout the poem Brooks uses alliteration, the repetition of consonant sounds. Identify some examples of alliteration and explain what the repetition of sound adds to the poem.

6. Does a shift in tone occur in the poem? What effect do the last three words have on the reader?

7. Why do you think Brooks chose to write from a first person plural ("we") point of view? Why not write about "them"?

8. What was Brooks' purpose in writing this poem? What was she trying to say about such young people?

9. The first two lines following the title of the poem are presented much like the cast and scene are announced for a play. In what way is this poem a modern drama?

10. One literary critic has noted that this poem, written decades ago, has much in common with today's "rap" music. Do you see any similarities in sound or theme?

VOCABULARY

lurk (line 3)

SUGGESTIONS FOR WRITING

1. Investigate the status of gangs in your community or in a nearby urban area. Write an essay on this growing problem in our cities; you might focus on the major causes of recent conflicts or suggest some solutions.

2. Write an essay on some aspect of the dropout problem in your community or former high school. What, for example, is your opinion of the law, now current in several states, that bars high school dropouts from holding driver's licenses?

3. What is the price of being "cool" today? Have you or someone you know ever felt pressured to conform to a standard or commit an action that you felt was silly, unreasonable, or morally wrong? Write an essay aimed at younger students and, based on your experience, give them some advice about being "cool."

A & P

JOHN UPDIKE

*John Updike began his writing career as a staff member of The New
Yorker from 1955 to 1957. Since that time he has written numerous
short stories and over a dozen novels, including Trust Me (1987), Rabbit
Run (1960), Couples (1968), and The Centaur, which won the 1964 Na-
tional Book Award for Fiction. "A & P" was originally published in The
New Yorker and then appeared in Pigeon Feathers and Other Stories (1962).*

1   In walks these three girls in nothing but bathing suits. I'm in the third
checkout slot, with my back to the door, so I don't see them until
they're over by the bread. The one that caught my eye first was the
one in the plaid green two-piece. She was a chunky kid, with a good
tan and a sweet broad soft-looking can with those two crescents of
white just under it, where the sun never seems to hit, at the top of the
backs of her legs. I stood there with my hand on a box of HiHo crack-
ers trying to remember if I rang it up or not. I ring it up again and the
customer starts giving me hell. She's one of these cash-register-
watchers, a witch about fifty and rouge on her cheekbones and no eye-
brows, and I know it made her day to trip me up. She'd been watching
cash registers for fifty years and probably never seen a mistake before.

2   By the time I got her feathers smoothed and her goodies into a
bag—she gives me a little snort in passing, if she'd been born at the
right time they would have burned her over in Salem—by the time I
get her on her way the girls had circled around the bread and were
coming back, without a pushcart, back my way along the counters, in
the aisle between the checkouts and the Special bins. They didn't even
have shoes on. There was the chunky one, with the two-piece—it was
bright green and the seams on the bra were still sharp and her belly
was still pretty pale so I guessed she just got it (the suit)—there was
this one, with one of those chubby berryfaces, the lips all bunched
together under her nose, this one, and a tall one, with black hair that
hadn't quite frizzed right, and one of these sunburns right across
under the eyes, and a chin that was too long—you know, the kind of

girl other girls think is very "striking" and "attractive" but never quite makes it, as they very well know, which is why they like her so much—and then the third one, that wasn't quite so tall. She was the queen. She kind of led them, the other two peeking around and making their shoulders round. She didn't look around, not this queen, she just walked straight on slowly, on these long white primadonna legs. She came down a little hard on her heels, as if she didn't walk in bare feet that much, putting down her heels and then letting the weight move along to her toes as if she was testing the floor with every step, putting a little deliberate extra action into it. You never know for sure how girls' minds work (do you really think it's a mind in there or just a little buzz like a bee in a glass jar?) but you got the idea she had talked the other two into coming in here with her, and now she was showing them how to do it, walk slow and hold yourself straight.

3   She had on a kind of dirty-pink—beige maybe, I don't know—bathing suit with a little nubble all over it and, what got me, the straps were down. They were off her shoulders looped loose around the cool tops of her arms, and I guess as a result the suit had slipped a little on her, so all around the top of the cloth there was this shining rim. If it hadn't been there you wouldn't have known there could have been anything whiter than those shoulders. With the straps pushed off, there was nothing between the top of the suit and the top of her head except just *her,* this clean bare plane of the top of her chest down from the shoulder bones like a dented sheet of metal tilted in the light. I mean, it was more than pretty.

4   She had a sort of oaky hair that the sun and salt had bleached, done up in a bun that was unravelling, and a kind of prim face. Walking into the A & P with your straps down, I suppose it's the only kind of face you *can* have. She held her head so high her neck, coming up out of those white shoulders, looked kind of stretched, but I didn't mind. The longer her neck was, the more of her there was.

5   She must have felt in the corner of her eye me and over my shoulder Stokesie in the second slot watching, but she didn't tip. Not this queen. She kept her eyes moving across the racks, and stopped, and turned so slow it made my stomach rub the inside of my apron, and buzzed to the other two, who kind of huddled against her for relief, and then they all three of them went up the cat-and-dog-food—breakfast-cereal—macaroni—rice—raisins—seasonings—spreads—

spaghetti—soft-drinks—crackers-and-cookies aisle. From the third slot I look straight up this aisle to the meat counter, and I watched them all the way. The fat one with the tan sort of fumbled with the cookies, but on second thought she put the package back. The sheep pushing their carts down the aisle—the girls were walking against the usual traffic (not that we have one-way signs or anything)—were pretty hilarious. You could see them, when Queenie's white shoulders dawned on them, kind of jerk, or hop, or hiccup, but their eyes snapped back to their own baskets and on they pushed. I bet you could set off dynamite in an A & P and the people would by and large keep reaching and checking oatmeal off their lists and muttering "Let me see, there was a third thing, began with A, asparagus, no, ah, yes, applesauce!" or whatever it is they do mutter. But there was no doubt, this jiggled them. A few houseslaves in pin curls even looked around after pushing their carts past to make sure what they had seen was correct.

6   You know, it's one thing to have a girl in a bathing suit down on the beach, where what with the glare nobody can look at each other much anyway, and another thing in the cool of the A & P, under the fluorescent lights, against all those stacked packages, with her feet padding along naked over our checkerboard green-and-cream rubber-tile floor.

7   "Oh Daddy," Stokesie said beside me. "I feel so faint."

8   "Darling," I said. "Hold me tight." Stokesie's married, with two babies chalked up on his fuselage already, but as far as I can tell that's the only difference. He's twenty-two, and I was nineteen this April.

9   "Is it done?" he asks, the responsible married man finding his voice. I forgot to say he thinks he's going to be manager some sunny day, maybe in 1990 when it's called the Great Alexandrov and Petrooshki Tea Company or something.

10   What he meant was, our town is five miles from a beach, with a big summer colony out on the Point, but we're right in the middle of town, and the women generally put on a shirt or shorts or something before they get out of the car into the street. And anyway these are usually women with six children and varicose veins mapping their legs and nobody, including them, could care less. As I say, we're right in the middle of town, and if you stand at our front doors you can see two banks and the Congregational church and the newspaper store and three real-estate offices and about twenty-seven old freeloaders tearing up Central Street because the sewer broke again. It's not as if we're on the

Cape; we're north of Boston and there's people in this town haven't seen the ocean for twenty years.

11   The girls had reached the meat counter and were asking McMahon something. He pointed, they pointed, and they shuffled out of sight behind a pyramid of Diet Delight peaches. All that was left for us to see was old McMahon patting his mouth and looking after them sizing up their joints. Poor kids, I began to feel sorry for them, they couldn't help it.

12   Now here comes the sad part of the story, at least my family says it's sad, but I don't think it's so sad myself. The store's pretty empty, it being Thursday afternoon, so there was nothing much to do except lean on the register and wait for the girls to show up again. The whole store was like a pinball machine and I didn't know which tunnel they'd come out of. After a while they come around out of the far aisle, around the light bulbs, records at discount of the Caribbean Six or Tony Martin Sings or some such gunk you wonder they waste the wax on, six-packs of candy bars, and plastic toys done up in cellophane that fall apart when a kid looks at them anyway. Around they come, Queenie still leading the way, and holding a little gray jar in her hand. Slots Three through Seven are unmanned and I could see her wondering between Stokes and me, but Stokesie with his usual luck draws an old party in baggy gray pants who stumbles up with four giant cans of pineapple juice (what do these bums *do* with all that pineapple juice? I've often asked myself) so the girls come to me. Queenie puts down the jar and I take it into my fingers icy cold. Kingfish Fancy Herring Snacks in Pure Sour Cream: 49. Now her hands are empty, not a ring or a bracelet, bare as God made them, and I wonder where the money's coming from. Still with that prim look she lifts a folded dollar bill out of the hollow at the center of her nubbled pink top. The jar went heavy in my hand. Really, I thought that was so cute.

13   Then everybody's luck begins to run out. Lengel comes in from haggling with a truck full of cabbages on the lot and is about to scuttle into that door marked manager behind which he hides all day when the girls touch his eye. Lengel's pretty dreary, teaches Sunday school and the rest, but he doesn't miss that much. He comes over and says, "Girls, this isn't the beach."

14   Queenie blushes, though maybe it's just a brush of sunburn I was noticing for the first time, now that she was so close."My mother asked me to pick up a jar of herring snacks." Her voice kind of startled me, the

way voices do when you see the people first, coming out so flat and
dumb yet kind of tony, too, the way it ticked over "pick up" and "snacks."
All of a sudden I slid right down her voice into her living room. Her
father and the other men were standing around in ice-cream coats and
bow ties and the women were in sandals picking up herring snacks on
toothpicks off a big glass plate and they were all holding drinks the color
of water with olives and sprigs of mint in them. When my parents have
somebody over they get lemonade and if it's a real racy affair Schlitz in
tall glasses with "They'll Do It Every Time" cartoons stencilled on.

15   "That's all right," Lengel said. "But this isn't the beach." His repeating this struck me as funny, as if it had just occurred to him, and he had
been thinking all these years the A & P was a great big dune and he was
the head lifeguard. He didn't like my smiling—as I say he doesn't miss
much—but he concentrates on giving the girls that sad Sunday-school-
superintendent stare.

16   Queenie's blush is no sunburn now, and the plump one in plaid, that
I like better from the back—a really sweet can—pipes up, "We weren't
doing any shopping. We just came in for the one thing."

17   "That makes no difference," Lengel tells her, and I could see from
the way his eyes went that he hadn't noticed she was wearing a two-
piece before. "We want you decently dressed when you come in here."

18   "We are decent," Queenie says suddenly, her lower lip pushing, getting sore now that she remembers her place, a place from which the
crowd that runs the A & P must look pretty crummy. Fancy Herring
Snacks flashed in her very blue eyes.

19   "Girls, I don't want to argue with you. After this come in here with
your shoulders covered. It's our policy." He turns his back. That's policy for you. Policy is what the kingpins want. What the others want is
juvenile delinquency.

20   All this while, the customers had been showing up with their carts
but, you know, sheep, seeing a scene, they had all bunched up on
Stokesie, who shook open a paper bag as gently as peeling a peach, not
wanting to miss a word. I could feel in the silence everybody getting
nervous, most of all Lengel, who asks me, "Sammy, have you rung up
their purchase?"

21   I thought and said "No" but it wasn't about that I was thinking. I go
through the punches, 4, 9, groc, tot—it's more complicated than you
think, and after you do it often enough, it begins to make a little song,
that you hear words to, in my case "Hello (bing) there, you (gung)

happy *pee*-pul *(splat)!*" the *splat* being the drawer flying out. I uncrease the bill, tenderly as you may imagine, it just having come from between the two smoothest scoops of vanilla I had ever known there were, and pass a half and a penny into her narrow pink palm, and nestle the herrings in a bag and twist its neck and hand it over, all the time thinking.

22   The girls, and who'd blame them, are in a hurry to get out, so I say "I quit" to Lengel quick enough for them to hear, hoping they'll stop and watch me, their unsuspecting hero. They keep right on going, into the electric eye; the door flies open and they flicker across the lot to their car, Queenie and Plaid and Big Tall Goony-Goony (not that as raw material she was so bad), leaving me with Lengel and a kink in his eyebrow.

23   "Did you say something, Sammy?"

24   "I said I quit."

25   "I thought you did."

26   "You didn't have to embarrass them."

27   "It was they who were embarrassing us."

28   I started to say something that came out "Fiddle-de-do." It's a saying of my grandmother's, and I know she would have been pleased.

29   "I don't think you know what you're saying," Lengel said.

30   "I know you don't," I said. "But I do." I pull the bow at the back of my apron and start shrugging it off my shoulders. A couple of customers that had been heading for my slot begin to knock against each other, like scared pigs in a chute.

31   Lengel sighs and begins to look very patient and old and gray. He's been a friend of my parents' for years. "Sammy, you don't want to do this to your Mom and Dad," he tells me. It's true, I don't. But it seems to me that once you begin a gesture it's fatal not to go through with it. I fold the apron, "Sammy" stitched in red on the pocket, and put it on the counter, and drop the bow tie on top of it. The bow tie is theirs, if you've ever wondered. "You'll feel this for the rest of your life," Lengel says, and I know that's true, too, but remembering how he made that pretty girl blush makes me so scrunchy inside I punch the No Sale tab and the machine whirs "pee-pul" and the drawer splats out. One advantage to this scene taking place in summer, I can follow this up with a clean exit, there's no fumbling around getting your coat and galoshes, I just saunter into the electric eye in my white shirt that my mother ironed the night before, and the door heaves itself open, and outside the sunshine is skating around on the asphalt.

32   I look around for my girls, but they're gone, of course. There wasn't anybody but some young married screaming with her children about some candy they didn't get by the door of a powder-blue Falcon station wagon. Looking back in the big windows, over the bags of peat moss and aluminum lawn furniture stacked on the pavement, I could see Lengel in my place in the slot, checking the sheep through. His face was dark gray and his back stiff, as if he's just had an injection of iron, and my stomach kind of fell as I felt how hard the world was going to be to me hereafter.

QUESTIONS ON CONTENT, STRUCTURE, AND STYLE

1. Who narrates this story? Why did Updike pick this narrator instead of another character?

2. Characterize Sammy's view of women by pointing out some of his opinions and descriptions of them.

3. Who are "sheep"? What is Sammy's attitude toward them? Toward his boss?

4. How does he see Queenie and her friends?

5. What do Sammy's opinions about other people reveal about *him*?

6. Why does Sammy quit his job? Are his motives entirely what he says they are?

7. Is his action admirable or misguided? Why?

8. What does Sammy mean in the last line of the story when he says he knows "how hard the world was going to be to me hereafter"? To what, if any, extent is Sammy exaggerating?

9. Is this a humorous or serious story? Defend your answer.

10. An "initiation story" is a tale in which a young person learns something important—and often disillusioning—about becoming an adult. Such stories often deal with a loss of innocence or youthful naiveté. Would you call "A & P" an initiation story? Why/why not?

VOCABULARY

crescents (1)   *nubble (3)*
prima donna (2)   *fuselage (8)*
deliberate (2)

SUGGESTIONS FOR WRITING

1. Write an essay describing an experience from your adolescence that convinced you that the world was going to be harder on you than you had imagined.

2. Write an essay comparing Sammy's attitude toward his job to your attitude toward any job you have held. Did you learn any lessons from working at your job that Sammy might need to know someday?

3. Novelist Joseph Heller once wrote, "How did I get here? Somebody pushed me. Somebody must have set me off in this direction and clusters of other hands must have touched themselves to the controls at various times, for I would not have picked this way for the world." Have you ever wondered how you ended up somewhere, in some surprising situation? Did someone really push you or did you allow yourself to be swept along? Write an essay that analyzes your participation in a particular incident, making clear your role in determining your own fate.

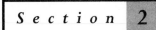

Section **2**

EXPLORING OUR DIVERSITY

"Just Walk on By: A Black Man Ponders His Power to Alter Public Space"

BY BRENT STAPLES

"Building the Third Wave: Reflections of a Young Feminist"

BY LAURIE OUELLETTE

"Aria"

BY RICHARD RODRIGUEZ

"The Men We Carry in Our Minds"

BY SCOTT RUSSELL SANDERS

"A Day on Wheels"

BY CHERYL A. DAVIS

"Dear John Wayne"

BY LOUISE ERDRICH

"The Story of an Hour"

BY KATE CHOPIN

Just Walk on By: A Black Man Ponders His Power to Alter Public Space

BRENT STAPLES

Brent Staples has written articles for a number of newspapers and journals, including the *Chicago Sun-Times, The New York Times Magazine,* and
Harper's. He is currently the assistant editor of the Metropolitan section
of *The New York Times.* This selection originally appeared in *Ms.* magazine
in September, 1986.

1 MY FIRST victim was a woman—white, well dressed, probably in her
early twenties. I came upon her late one evening on a deserted street in
Hyde Park, a relatively affluent neighborhood in an otherwise mean,
impoverished section of Chicago. As I swung onto the avenue behind
her, there seemed to be a discreet, uninflammatory distance between
us. Not so. She cast back a worried glance. To her, the youngish black
man—a broad six feet two inches with a beard and billowing hair, both
hands shoved into the pockets of a bulky military jacket—seemed menacingly close. After a few more quick glimpses, she picked up her pace
and was soon running in earnest. Within seconds she disappeared into
a cross street.

2   That was more than a decade ago. I was twenty-two years old, a
graduate student newly arrived at the University of Chicago. It was in
the echo of that terrified woman's footfalls that I first began to know
the unwieldy inheritance I'd come into—the ability to alter public space
in ugly ways. It was clear that she thought herself the quarry of a mugger, a rapist, or worse. Suffering a bout of insomnia, however, I was
stalking sleep, not defenseless wayfarers. As a softy who is scarcely able
to take a knife to a raw chicken—let alone hold it to a person's throat—
I was surprised, embarrassed, and dismayed all at once. Her flight made
me feel like an accomplice in tyranny. It also made it clear that I was
indistinguishable from the muggers who occasionally seeped into the
area from the surrounding ghetto. That first encounter, and those that
followed, signified that a vast, unnerving gulf lay between nighttime
pedestrians—particularly women—and me. And I soon gathered that
being perceived as dangerous is a hazard in itself. I only needed to turn

a corner into a dicey situation, or crowd some frightened, armed person in a foyer somewhere, or make an errant move after being pulled over by a policeman. Where fear and weapons meet—and they often do in urban America—there is always the possibility of death.

3   In that first year, my first away from my hometown, I was to become thoroughly familiar with the language of fear. At dark, shadowy intersections in Chicago, I could cross in front of a car stopped at a traffic light and elicit the *thunk, thunk, thunk, thunk* of the driver—black, white, male, or female—hammering down the door locks. On less traveled streets after dark, I grew accustomed to but never comfortable with people who crossed to the other side of the street rather than pass me. Then there were the standard unpleasantries with police, doormen, bouncers, cab drivers, and others whose business it is to screen out troublesome individuals *before* there is any nastiness.

4   I moved to New York nearly two years ago and I have remained an avid night walker. In central Manhattan, the near-constant crowd cover minimizes tense one-on-one street encounters. Elsewhere—visiting friends in SoHo, where sidewalks are narrow and tightly spaced buildings shut out the sky—things can get very taut indeed.

5   Black men have a firm place in New York mugging literature. Norman Podhoretz[1] in his famed (or infamous) 1963 essay, "My Negro Problem—And Ours," recalls growing up in terror of black males; they "were tougher than we were, more ruthless," he writes— and as an adult on the Upper West Side of Manhattan, he continues, he cannot constrain his nervousness when he meets black men on certain streets. Similarly, a decade later, the essayist and novelist Edward Hoagland extols a New York where once "Negro bitterness bore down mainly on other Negroes." Where some see mere panhandlers, Hoagland sees "a mugger who is clearly screwing up his nerve to do more than just *ask* for money." But Hoagland has "the New Yorker's quick-hunch posture for broken-field maneuvering," and the bad guy swerves away.

6   I often witness that "hunch posture," from women after dark on the warrenlike streets of Brooklyn where I live. They seem to set their faces on neutral and, with their purse straps strung across their chests bandolier style, they forge ahead as though bracing themselves against

---

[1] A literary critic and editor.

being tackled. I understand, of course, that the danger they perceive is not a hallucination. Women are particularly vulnerable to street violence, and young black males are drastically overrepresented among the perpetrators of that violence. Yet these truths are no solace against the kind of alienation that comes of being ever the suspect, against being set apart, a fearsome entity with whom pedestrians avoid making eye contact.

7   It is not altogether clear to me how I reached the ripe old age of twenty-two without being conscious of the lethality nighttime pedestrians attributed to me. Perhaps it was because in Chester, Pennsylvania, the small, angry industrial town where I came of age in the 1960s, I was scarcely noticeable against a backdrop of gang warfare, street knifings, and murders. I grew up one of the good boys, had perhaps a half-dozen fist fights. In retrospect, my shyness of combat has clear sources.

8   Many things go into the making of a young thug. One of those things is the consummation of the male romance with the power to intimidate. An infant discovers that random flailings send the baby bottle flying out of the crib and crashing to the floor. Delighted, the joyful babe repeats those motions again and again, seeking to duplicate the feat. Just so, I recall the points at which some of my boyhood friends were finally seduced by the perception of themselves as tough guys. When a mark cowered and surrendered his money without resistance, myth and reality merged—and paid off. It is, after all, only manly to embrace the power to frighten and intimidate. We, as men, are not supposed to give an inch of our lane on the highway; we are to seize the fighter's edge in work and in play and even in love; we are to be valiant in the face of hostile forces.

9   Unfortunately, poor and powerless young men seem to take all this nonsense literally. As a boy, I saw countless tough guys locked away; I have since buried several, too. They were babies, really—a teenage cousin, a brother of twenty-two, a childhood friend in his mid-twenties—all gone down in episodes of bravado played out in the streets. I came to doubt the virtues of intimidation early on. I chose, perhaps even unconsciously, to remain a shadow—timid, but a survivor.

10   The fearsomeness mistakenly attributed to me in public places often has a perilous flavor. The most frightening of these confusions occurred

in the late 1970s and early 1980s when I worked as a journalist in Chicago. One day, rushing into the office of a magazine I was writing for with a deadline story in hand, I was mistaken for a burglar. The office manager called security and, with an ad hoc posse, pursued me through the labyrinthine halls, nearly to my editor's door. I had no way of proving who I was. I could only move briskly toward the company of someone who knew me.

11   Another time I was on assignment for a local paper and killing time before an interview. I entered a jewelry store on the city's affluent Near North Side. The proprietor excused herself and returned with an enormous red Doberman pinscher straining at the end of a leash. She stood, the dog extended toward me, silent to my questions, her eyes bulging nearly out of her head. I took a cursory look around, nodded, and bade her good night. Relatively speaking, however, I never fared as badly as another black male journalist. He went to nearby Waukegan, Illinois, a couple of summers ago to work on a story about a murderer who was born there. Mistaking the reporter for the killer, police hauled him from his car at gunpoint and but for his press credentials would probably have tried to book him. Such episodes are not uncommon. Black men trade tales like this all the time.

12   In "My Negro Problem—And Ours," Podhoretz writes that the hatred he feels for blacks makes itself known to him through a variety of avenues—one being his discomfort with that "special brand of paranoid touchiness" to which he says blacks are prone. No doubt he is speaking here of black men. In time, I learned to smother the rage I felt at so often being taken for a criminal. Not to do so would surely have led to madness—via that special "paranoid touchiness" that so annoyed Podhoretz at the time he wrote the essay.

13   I began to take precautions to make myself less threatening. I move about with care, particularly late in the evening. I give a wide berth to nervous people on subway platforms during the wee hours, particularly when I have exchanged business clothes for jeans. If I happen to be entering a building behind some people who appear skittish, I may walk by, letting them clear the lobby before I return, so as not to seem to be following them. I have been calm and extremely congenial on those rare occasions when I've been pulled over by the police.

14   And on late-evening constitutionals along streets less traveled by, I employ what has proved to be an excellent tension-reducing measure:

I whistle melodies from Beethoven and Vivaldi and the more popular classical composers. Even steely New Yorkers hunching toward night-time destinations seem to relax, and occasionally they even join in the tune. Virtually everybody seems to sense that a mugger wouldn't be warbling bright, sunny selections from Vivaldi's *Four Seasons*. It is my equivalent of the cowbell that hikers wear when they know they are in bear country.

QUESTIONS ON CONTENT, STRUCTURE, AND STYLE

1. Why does Staples refer to his "first victim" in his opening paragraph? What effect does such language have on the reader?

2. Why does Staples begin with a story that occurred over ten years ago? What did that event—and others like it—make clear for him?

3. What other personal experiences does Staples tell the reader? What details add to the realism of the scenes he describes?

4. How does Staples feel about his "victims" and their fear of him?

5. Why does Staples include comments from writers Norman Podhoretz and Edward Hoagland in paragraphs 5 and 12?

6. What stereotype does Staples criticize when he refers to "the consummation of the male romance with the power to intimidate" (paragraph 8)? What results does this stereotype ultimately produce?

7. Why is the discussion of this stereotype important to Staples' essay on his ability to alter public space?

8. Why does Staples tell about his experience in his magazine's office and the episode in the jewelry store? About his colleague's experience in Waukegan, Illinois?

9. How has Staples altered his own behavior in public places? Are the other people in Staples' stories the only "victims"?

10. What were Staples' primary purposes in writing this essay? What effect do you think he was trying to have on the reader? Did he succeed?

VOCABULARY

affluent (1)	quarry (2)	intimidate (8)
impoverished (1)	dicey (2)	bravado (9)
discreet (1)	foyer (2)	ad hoc (10)
uninflammatory (1)	errant (2)	labyrinthine (10)
menacingly (1)	solace (6)	cursory (11)
unwieldy (2)	lethality (7)	constitutionals (14)

SUGGESTIONS FOR WRITING

1. Staples' essay is, in part, about perception—how we are seen by others—and the dangers of stereotyping. Have you ever been a victim of someone's faulty perception, of someone's discrimination? Did you react with anger or fear or did you, like Staples, change your behavior in some way? Write an essay explaining your experience, your reaction to it, and your advice to others who may find themselves in similar situations.

2. Think of a time when your irrational response or prejudice toward someone may have caused him or her to feel alienated, excluded, suspected, or loathed. Write an essay that examines the causes and effects of your behavior and how you might respond differently if you could repeat the episode.

3. Staples criticizes the notion that "manly" men must "embrace the power to frighten and intimidate" and then cites some examples of aggressive behavior dictated by such a notion. What elements in our society promote this harmful view of "manliness"? Write an essay focused on a primary cause of this stereotype, citing enough examples to make your case convincing. How might this stereotype be changed?

Building the Third Wave:
Reflections of a Young Feminist

LAURIE OUELLETTE

Born in 1966, Laurie Ouellette is an associate editor for the New York magazine *On the Issues,* where this essay originally appeared in 1992. Holding a B.A. in journalism and an M.A. in media studies, she is also a contributor to a number of publications, including *The Utne Reader* and *The Independent Film and Video Monthly,* frequently writing about media and culture.

1 I AM a member of the first generation of women to benefit from the gains of the 1970s women's movement without having participated in its struggles. I grew up on the sidelines of feminism—too young to take part in the moments, debates, and events that would define the women's movement while at the same time experiencing firsthand the societal changes that feminism had demanded.

2 Ironically, it is due to the modest success of feminism that many young women like myself were raised with an illusion of equality. I never really thought much about feminism as I was growing up, but looking back, I believe I've always had feminist inclinations. Having divorced parents and a father who was ambivalent about his parental responsibilities probably has much to do with this. I was only five when my parents separated in 1971, and I couldn't possibly have imagined or understood the ERA marches, consciousness-raising groups, or triumphal passing of *Roe* v. *Wade* that shortly would make history. Certainly I couldn't have defined the word *feminism.* Still, watching my young mother struggle emotionally and financially as a single parent made the concept of gender injustice painfully clear, teaching me a lesson that would follow me always.

3 My first real introduction to feminism came secondhand. During the height of the seventies' women's movement, I watched my mother become "liberated" after the breakup of yet another marriage. It was she, not I, who sought some answers from the counterculture of the

time. It was confusing, if not terrifying, to watch her dramatically change her life—and, by association, mine—during those years, transforming herself into a woman I barely recognized. She quit her job and returned to college and then graduate school, working odd jobs and devoting her time to books and meetings and new-age therapy and talking it all out with her never-ending supply of free-spirited divorced comrades. I was thirteen the year I found her copy of *The Women's Room,* a book which so intrigued me that I read it cover to cover in the course of only a few nights. Like the heroine of the book, my mother was becoming "independent" and "hip," but I had never been so miserable.

4   Like most women my age, though, I never really considered feminism in terms of my own life until I reached college. It was during those years that I first took an interest in feminist classics such as *The Feminine Mystique, Sisterhood Is Powerful,* and *Sexual Politics.* As powerful as these texts were, they seemed to express the anger of an earlier generation, simultaneously captivating and excluding me. Reading them so long after the excitement of their publication made my own consciousness-raising seem anticlimactic. These books and countless others that I encountered seemed to speak more to my mother's generation than mine. They explained a great deal about the limited choices awaiting such women and attempted to guide them in ways to overcome patriarchal oppression. But I, like many of my white, middle-class friends, saw women's liberation from quite a different perspective. Many of us really believed that we wouldn't have to worry about issues like discrimination, oppression, and getting stuck in the housewife role. Indeed, many of my friends considered my interest in feminism "radical" and irrelevant to the times.

5   Although I participated in feminist activities sporadically in college, including prochoice demonstrations, it was really in my experiences outside of that environment where my feminist politics took root. Several events stand out as catalysts. First was an internship I held at a public television station while in college. Armed with an eager attitude and practical experience, I felt my enthusiasm wane when I was given mainly menial and secretarial tasks to perform while my male co-interns, who had less experience than I, were frequently asked to do editing assignments and were invited along on shoots. I had never before experienced sexual discrimination, and in fact honestly believed it was something I would never have to face. In retrospect, this experience marked my first realization that there was much work to be done in creating a world

where women and men were treated with equal respect, on the job and off.

6   Living in an inner-city neighborhood and my involvement in community issues there were also important. I saw the dire need for drastic political change in the lives of the poor women, elderly women, and women of color who were my neighbors. Watching these women, many of them single parents, struggling daily to find shelter, child care, and food made me realize that they, unlike me, had not been touched at all by the gains of the seventies' women's movement. How could women's liberation possibly be perceived as won when these women had been so forgotten? I began to reconsider feminism in an attempt to find the answers.

7   Today I am among the minority of young women who have committed themselves to feminism in the hopes of achieving social and political goals for all women. While we are attempting to carve out a place for ourselves in a movement still heavily dominated by another generation, the majority of young women have been reluctant to do the same. Confused about their roles in relation to the media stereotypes about feminists or intimidated by the legacy of the women's movement past, many have become "no, but" feminists. That is, they approve of—indeed, demand—equal pay, economic independence, sexual freedom, and reproductive choice but are still reluctant to define themselves with the label "feminist." The results of a recent poll by *In View,* a magazine for college women, is typical of many surveys that report this contradiction. Of the 514 female undergraduates surveyed by *In View,* 90 percent agreed that men and women should earn equal pay for equal work; 93 percent said that women want equality with men; 84 percent agreed that women should have access to birth control, regardless of age or marital status; 90 percent believed that sexism still exists. Still, only 16 percent of the women said they were definitely feminists.

8   Yet the evidence clearly shows that young women's situations are dismal: *Roe* v. *Wade* is under fire, and if overturned, my generation and those to come will be affected most profoundly; parental consent laws, which require parental notification or permission for abortion, have been mandated in many states; date rape and violence against women have become epidemics on college campuses and everywhere; eating disorders, linked to the unreasonable societal standards for women's body sizes, have claimed the lives of thousands of us; and we still can expect to earn 70 cents for every dollar earned by men. Sure, our chances of

having professional careers are greater. However, more of us than in any previous generation have grown up in single-parent families—we have seen the myth of the "supermom" professional "bringing home that bacon and frying it up in a pan" and can call it for what it is. In these hard economic times, young women can look forward to mandatory full-time jobs and second shifts of house care and child care in their homes. Where are the parental-leave policies, the flexible schedules, the adequate health care, the subsidized day care, and the male cooperation that will ease these situations? As yet, nowhere to be found, and considering the present political climate, there doesn't seem to be much hope for the near future.

9   Given all this, what can explain why so many young women have shunned feminism? In her survey of young women, *Feminist Fatale: Voices from the Twentysomething Generation Explore the Future of the Women's Movement,* Paul Kamen found that media-fueled stereotypes of feminists as "man-bashers" and "radical extremists" were behind the fact that many young women don't identify with the women's movement.

10   But these are not the only reasons. Kamen also points to the lack of young feminist role models as an important factor. The failure of a major feminist organization such as NOW to reach out to a wider spectrum of women, including young women, must be acknowledged as a part of this problem. While individual chapters do have young feminist committees and sometimes officers, they and the national office are led and staffed primarily by older women, and consequently often fail to reflect the interests and needs of a complex generation of young women.

11   Yet another reason young women have turned away from feminism may lie within its history. If the young women who have gained the most from feminism—that is, white, middle-class women who took advantage of increased accessibility to higher education and professional employment—have been reluctant to associate themselves with feminism, it is hardly surprising that most economically disadvantaged women and women of color, who have seen fewer of those gains, have not been eager to embrace feminism either. The women's movement of the seventies has been called an upper-middle-class white women's movement, and to a large degree I believe that is true. More than a few young feminists— many influenced by feminists of color such as Flo Kennedy, Audre Lorde, and bell hooks—have realized that feminism must also acknowledge issues of race and class to reach out to those women whose concerns have been overlooked by the women's movement of the past.

Indeed, numerous statistics, including a poll by the *New York Times,* have noted that young African-American women are more likely than white women to acknowledge many of the concerns conducive to a feminist agenda, including a need for job training and equal earning power outside the professional sector. But for them, feminism has not provided the only answer. Only by making issues of class and race a priority can feminism hope to influence the lives of the millions of women for whom the daily struggle to survive, not feminist activism, is a priority. Will ours be the first generation of feminists to give priority to fighting cuts in Aid to Families with Dependent Children, establishing the right to national health care, day care, and parental leave, and bringing to the forefront other issues pertinent to the daily struggle of many women's lives? If there is to be a third wave of feminism, they must.

12   While the women's movement of the seventies focused primarily on the ERA, getting women into high-paying, powerful occupations, and combating sexual discrimination in the workplace, these issues— though still critical—must not be the only goals of feminism. My sister is an example. We have taken very different paths indeed. I have focused on attending graduate school and writing about women's issues; she has chosen to forfeit similar plans, for now, in favor of marrying young and raising a family. Does she signify a regression into the homemaker role of the 1950s? On the contrary. In fact, she is among the feminists I most respect, even though she herself believes that the feminist movement may not have a place for her because of the choices she has made. For her, issues such as getting midwifery legalized and covered by insurance plans, providing information about the importance of breastfeeding to rural mothers, countering the male-dominated medical establishment by using and recommending natural and alternative healing methods, protecting the environment, and raising her own daughter with positive gender esteem are central to what she defines as a feminist agenda. Who am I to say that she—and other young women like her who are attempting to reclaim the power and importance of motherhood— aren't correct? If there is to be a third wave of feminism, it must acknowledge and support a wide range of choices for all women.

13   Surely the greatest challenge facing all young women is the frightening assault on reproductive rights, and if any issue can unite women from all backgrounds, it is this. While we have never known the horrors of coat-hanger abortions, we have seen our reproductive rights drastically shrink. If the legacy of the women's movement has left

young women confused about their roles in a structure still heavily dominated by older white women, this is one issue on which the torch must be shared. If feminism is to succeed in challenging this patriarchal assault on women's bodies, a coalition of women from all backgrounds will have to join forces to address the underlying assumptions of this attack. Young women have been among the first to organize on this fight, witnessed by the proliferation of prochoice activity on college campuses around the United States. Still, if this movement is to progress beyond a single-issue campaign, uniting women inside and outside the academy in the name of feminism, it will mean expanding the agenda: insisting upon birth control options for all women and giving equal energy to addressing the lack of educational opportunities, child care, day care, and health care options that are fundamental to the campaign for reproductive choice.

14   Only by recognizing and helping provide choices for all women, and supporting all women in their struggles to obtain those choices, will the women of my generation, the first raised in the shadow of the second wave and witness to its triumphs and failures, be able to build a successful third wave of the feminist movement. The initial step must be to reclaim the word *feminism* as an appealing, empowering term in women's lives by building a movement that commits to all women while recognizing their multiple concerns.

QUESTIONS ON CONTENT, STRUCTURE, AND STYLE

1. In what ways, according to Ouellette, are feminists of her generation different from those of earlier generations?

2. What inaccurate assumptions does she believe many young women make about women's rights today?

3. What inconsistencies does Ouellette see between the views of young women as revealed in surveys and their rejection of the term "feminism"?

4. According to Ouellette, what is a "no, but" feminist?

5. What must the feminist movement do if it is to gain new ground, according to this essay?

6. Why does Ouellette open the essay with a discussion of her own experience? How does this affect her argument?

7. Why, according to Ouellette, have young women "shunned feminism"?

8. What is Ouellette's purpose in writing this essay? Describe reading audiences that would react strongly—perhaps in a variety of ways—to this essay.

9. Describe Ouellette's tone, citing specific examples from the essay.

10. Ouellette mentions her sister as an example of one type of feminist among many. Would her essay be strengthened by the inclusion of more such examples? Explain.

VOCABULARY

feminism (1)	*catalysts (5)*	*subsidized (8)*
inclinations (2)	*wane (5)*	*shunned (9)*
triumphal (2)	*dire (6)*	*coalition (13)*
anticlimactic (4)	*mandated (8)*	*empowering (14)*
sporadically (5)		

SUGGESTIONS FOR WRITING

1. Ouellette notes that she has had "feminist inclinations" from early childhood because of her family experience. In an essay developed by example, show how your views of gender roles have been shaped by your family.

2. As a man or woman, do you define yourself as a feminist? If so, what are the key reasons? If not, why not? Present your case in a well-developed essay.

3. In what ways are your views of gender different from those of your parents? In what ways do you hope your children's views will be different from those of your own generation? Compare these three generational perspectives in an essay supported by personal experience, the experience of others, and current or past events.

Aria

RICHARD RODRIGUEZ

Richard Rodriguez, the son of Mexican immigrants, was born in California, where he received a B.A. from Stanford. He earned an M.A. from Columbia University and studied Renaissance literature in London on a Fulbright Fellowship. He wrote his autobiography, *Hunger of Memory: The Education of Richard Rodriguez,* from which this selection is taken, in 1982. His most recent books include *Mexico's Children* (1992) and *Days of Obligation: An Argument with My Mexican Father* (1992).

1   SUPPORTERS OF bilingual education today imply that students like me miss a great deal by not being taught in their family's language. What they seem not to recognize is that, as a socially disadvantaged child, I considered Spanish to be a private language. What I needed to learn in school was that I had the right—and the obligation—to speak the public language of *los gringos.* The odd truth is that my first-grade classmates could have become bilingual, in the conventional sense of that word, more easily than I. Had they been taught (as upper-middle-class children are often taught early) a second language like Spanish or French, they could have regarded it simply as that: another public language. In my case such bilingualism could not have been so quickly achieved. What I did not believe was that I could speak a single public language.

2   Without question, it would have pleased me to hear my teachers address me in Spanish when I entered the classroom. I would have felt much less afraid. I would have trusted them and responded with ease. But I would have delayed—for how long postponed?—having to learn the language of public society. I would have evaded—and for how long could I have afforded to delay?—learning the great lesson of school, that I had a public identity.

3   Fortunately, my teachers were unsentimental about their responsibility. What they understood was that I needed to speak a public language. So their voices would search me out, asking me questions. Each time I'd hear them, I'd look up in surprise to see a nun's face frowning at me.

I'd mumble, not really meaning to answer. The nun would persist, 'Richard, stand up. Don't look at the floor. Speak up. Speak to the entire class, not just to me!' But I couldn't believe that the English language was mine to use. (In part, I did not want to believe it.) I continued to mumble. I resisted the teacher's demands. (Did I somehow suspect that once I learned public language my pleasing family life would be changed?) Silent, waiting for the bell to sound, I remained dazed, diffident, afraid.

4   Because I wrongly imagined that English was intrinsically a public language and Spanish an intrinsically private one, I easily noted the difference between classroom language and the language of home. At school, words were directed to a general audience of listeners. ('Boys and girls.') Words were meaningfully ordered. And the point was not self-expression alone but to make oneself understood by many others. The teacher quizzed: 'Boys and girls, why do we use that word in this sentence? Could we think of a better word to use there? Would the sentence change its meaning if the words were differently arranged? And wasn't there a better way of saying much the same thing?' (I couldn't say. I wouldn't try to say.)

5   Three months. Five. Half a year passed. Unsmiling, ever watchful, my teachers noted my silence. They began to connect my behavior with the difficult progress my older sister and brother were making. Until one Saturday morning three nuns arrived at the house to talk to our parents. Stiffly, they sat on the blue living room sofa. From the doorway of another room, spying the visitors, I noted the incongruity—the clash of two worlds, the faces and voices of school intruding upon the familiar setting of home. I overheard one voice gently wondering, 'Do your children speak only Spanish at home, Mrs. Rodriguez?' While another voice added, 'That Richard especially seems so timid and shy.'

6   *That Rich-heard!*

7   With great tact the visitors continued, 'Is it possible for you and your husband to encourage your children to practice their English when they are home?' Of course, my parents complied. What would they not do for their children's well-being? And how could they have questioned the Church's authority which those women represented? In an instant, they agreed to give up the language (the sounds) that had revealed and accentuated our family's closeness. The moment after the visitors left, the change was observed. *'Ahora,* speak to us *en inglés,'* my father and mother united to tell us.

8   At first, it seemed a kind of game. After dinner each night, the family gathered to practice 'our' English. (It was still then *inglés,* a language foreign to us, so we felt drawn as strangers to it.) Laughing, we would try to define words we could not pronounce. We played with strange English sounds, often overanglicizing our pronunciations. And we filled the smiling gaps of our sentences with familiar Spanish sounds. But that was cheating, somebody shouted. Everyone laughed. In school, meanwhile, like my brother and sister, I was required to attend a daily tutoring session. I needed a full year of special attention. I also needed my teachers to keep my attention from straying in class by calling out, *Rich-heard*—their English voices slowly prying loose my ties to my other name, its three notes, *Ri-car-do.* Most of all I needed to hear my mother and father speak to me in a moment of seriousness in broken—suddenly heartbreaking—English. The scene was inevitable: One Saturday morning I entered the kitchen where my parents were talking in Spanish. I did not realize that they were talking in Spanish however until, at the moment they saw me, I heard their voices change to speak English. Those *gringo* sounds they uttered startled me. Pushed me away. In that moment of trivial misunderstanding and profound insight, I felt my throat twisted by unsounded grief. I turned quickly and left the room. But I had no place to escape to with Spanish. (The spell was broken.) My brother and sisters were speaking English in another part of the house.

9   Again and again in the days following, increasingly angry, I was obliged to hear my mother and father: 'Speak to us *en inglés.' (Speak.)* Only then did I determine to learn classroom English. Weeks after, it happened: One day in school I raised my hand to volunteer an answer. I spoke out in a loud voice. And I did not think it remarkable when the entire class understood. That day, I moved very far from the disadvantaged child I had been only days earlier. The belief, the calming assurance that I belonged in public, had at last taken hold.

10   Shortly after, I stopped hearing the high and loud sounds of *los gringos.* A more and more confident speaker of English, I didn't trouble to listen to *how* strangers sounded, speaking to me. And there simply were too many English-speaking people in my day for me to hear American accents anymore. Conversations quickened. Listening to persons who sounded eccentrically pitched voices, I usually noted their sounds for an initial few seconds before I concentrated on *what* they were saying. Conversations became content-full. Transparent. Hearing someone's *tone* of voice—angry or questioning or sarcastic or happy or

sad—I didn't distinguish it from the words it expressed. Sound and word were thus tightly wedded. At the end of a day, I was often be-mused, always relieved, to realize how 'silent,' though crowded with words, my day in public had been. (This public silence measured and quickened the change in my life.)

11   At last, seven years old, I came to believe what had been technically true since my birth: I was an American citizen.

12   But the special feeling of closeness at home was diminished by then. Gone was the desperate, urgent, intense feeling of being at home; rare was the experience of feeling myself individualized by family intimates. We remained a loving family, but one greatly changed. No longer so close; no longer bound tight by the pleasing and troubling knowledge of our public separateness. Neither my older brother nor sister rushed home after school anymore. Nor did I. When I arrived home there would often be neighborhood kids in the house. Or the house would be empty of sounds.

13   Following the dramatic Americanization of their children, even my parents grew more publicly confident. Especially my mother. She learned the names of all the people on our block. And she decided we needed to have a telephone installed in the house. My father continued to use the word *gringo*. But it was no longer charged with the old bit-terness or distrust. (Stripped of any emotional content, the word sim-ply became a name for those Americans not of Hispanic descent.) Hearing him, sometimes, I wasn't sure if he was pronouncing the Spanish word *gringo* or saying gringo in English.

14   Matching the silence I started hearing in public was a new quiet at home. The family's quiet was partly due to the fact that, as we children learned more and more English, we shared fewer and fewer words with our parents. Sentences needed to be spoken slowly when a child ad-dressed his mother or father. (Often the parent wouldn't understand.) The child would need to repeat himself. (Still the parent misunder-stood.) The young voice, frustrated, would end up saying, 'Never mind'—the subject was closed. Dinners would be noisy with the clink-ing of knives and forks against dishes. My mother would smile softly between her remarks; my father at the other end of the table would chew and chew his food, while he stared over the heads of his children.

15   My *mother!* My *father!* After English became my primary language, I no longer knew what words to use in addressing my parents. The old Spanish words (those tender accents of sound) I had used earlier—

mamá and *papá*—I couldn't use anymore. They would have been too painful reminders of how much had changed in my life. On the other hand, the words I heard neighborhood kids call *their* parents seemed equally unsatisfactory. *Mother* and *Father; Ma, Papa, Pa, Dad, Pop* (how I hated the all-American sound of that last word especially)—all these terms I felt were unsuitable, not really terms of address for *my* parents. As a result, I never used them at home. Whenever I'd speak to my parents, I would try to get their attention with eye contact alone. In public conversations, I'd refer to 'my parents' or 'my mother and father.'

16   My mother and father, for their part, responded differently, as their children spoke to them less. She grew restless, seemed troubled and anxious at the scarcity of words exchanged in the house. It was she who would question me about my day when I came home from school. She smiled at small talk. She pried at the edges of my sentences to get me to say something more. (What?) She'd join conversations she overheard, but her intrusions often stopped her children's talking. By contrast, my father seemed reconciled to the new quiet. Though his English improved somewhat, he retired into silence. At dinner he spoke very little. One night his children and even his wife helplessly giggled at his garbled English pronunciation of the Catholic Grace before Meals. Thereafter he made his wife recite the prayer at the start of each meal, even on formal occasions, when there were guests in the house. Hers became the public voice of the family. On official business, it was she, not my father, one would usually hear on the phone or in stores, talking to strangers. His children grew so accustomed to his silence that, years later, they would speak routinely of his shyness. (My mother would often try to explain: Both his parents died when he was eight. He was raised by an uncle who treated him like little more than a menial servant. He was never encouraged to speak. He grew up alone. A man of few words.) But my father was not shy, I realized, when I'd watch him speaking Spanish with relatives. Using Spanish, he was quickly effusive. Especially when talking with other men, his voice would spark, flicker, flare alive with sounds. In Spanish, he expressed ideas and feelings he rarely revealed in English. With firm Spanish sounds, he conveyed confidence and authority English would never allow him.

17   The silence at home, however, was finally more than a literal silence. Fewer words passed between parent and child, but more profound was the silence that resulted from my inattention to sounds. At about the time I no longer bothered to listen with care to the sounds of

English in public, I grew careless about listening to the sounds family members made when they spoke. Most of the time I heard someone speaking at home and didn't distinguish his sounds from the words people uttered in public. I didn't even pay much attention to my parents' accented and ungrammatical speech. At least not at home. Only when I was with them in public would I grow alert to their accents. Though, even then, their sounds caused me less and less concern. For I was increasingly confident of my own public identity.

18   I would have been happier about my public success had I not sometimes recalled what it had been like earlier, when my family had conveyed its intimacy through a set of conveniently private sounds. Sometimes in public, hearing a stranger, I'd hark back to my past. A Mexican farmworker approached me downtown to ask directions to somewhere. '¿Hijito . . . ?' he said. And his voice summoned deep longing. Another time, standing beside my mother in the visiting room of a Carmelite convent, before the dense screen which rendered the nuns shadowy figures, I heard several Spanish-speaking nuns—their busy, singsong overlapping voices—assure us that yes, yes, we were remembered, all our family was remembered in their prayers. (Their voices echoed faraway family sounds.) Another day, a dark-faced old woman—her hand light on my shoulder—steadied herself against me as she boarded a bus. Her Spanish voice came near, like the face of a never-before-seen relative in the instant before I was kissed. Her voice, like so many of the Spanish voices I'd hear in public, recalled the golden age of my youth. Hearing Spanish then, I continued to be a careful, if sad, listener to sounds. Hearing a Spanish-speaking family walking behind me, I turned to look. I smiled for an instant, before my glance found the Hispanic-looking faces of strangers in the crowd going by.

QUESTIONS ON CONTENT, STRUCTURE, AND STYLE

1. What is Rodriguez's attitude toward his "unsentimental" teachers and their demands?

2. What, overall, is Rodriguez's opinion of bilingual education in our schools?

3. What was Rodriguez's main point in telling about his childhood and his family? Is there a conflict between his view of bilingual education and his feelings toward his family?

4. What distinctions does Rodriguez make between a private language and a public language? Why was this distinction important in his case?

5. Why does Rodriguez include the story about his parents speaking Spanish in the kitchen? What does he mean when he says, "The spell was broken"?

6. What were the consequences of Rodriguez's learning English? How did he change?

7. How does Rodriguez show the effects of learning English on his relationship to his family? Does he include enough details to make the effects clear to the reader?

8. How does Rodriguez convince the reader that his parents' personalities and family roles changed as well? Were these changes good or bad?

9. Why does Rodriguez end his essay with the stories of the Mexican farmworker, the nuns in the convent, and the woman on the bus? What do they represent for him?

10. Summarize what you think Rodriguez has gained and lost in achieving what he refers to as his "public success." How do you think proponents of the bilingual education movement would react to this essay? Supporters of laws that declare English our official language?

VOCABULARY

bilingual (1)
diffident (3)
intrinsically (4)
incongruity (5)

complied (7)
overanglicizing (8)
inevitable (8)
eccentrically (10)

intrusions (16)
garbled (16)
effusive (16)

SUGGESTIONS FOR WRITING

1. Interview someone who grew up in this country whose family came from or was strongly influenced by another culture or country. Write an essay that explains the most difficult problem this person (or you?) faced becoming "a public success." What was gained or lost in the process?

2. Rodriguez's essay reveals some of the problems posed by the questions of bilingual education in our schools. Drawing on your own experiences or those of others, write an essay that presents your views on this controversial issue.

3. Investigate the laws, passed in over a dozen states, that proclaim English as our official language. Are these laws a racist backlash against the increasing ethnic and cultural diversity in our country? According to Arturo Vargas of the Mexican-American Legal Defense and Educational Fund, "That's what English-only has been all about—a reaction to the growing population and influence of Hispanics." Research this controversy and write an essay arguing your position.

The Men We Carry in Our Minds

Scott Russell Sanders

Scott Russell Sanders is a professor of English at Indiana University who has written many books, including fiction, biography, folktales, children's stories, and literary criticism. His essays appear in two collections, *The Paradise of Bombs* (1987), from which "The Men We Carry in Our Minds" is taken, and *Secrets of the Universe: Scenes from the Journey Home* (1991).

1   "THIS MUST be a hard time for women," I say to my friend Anneke. "They have so many paths to choose from, and so many voices calling them."

2   "I think it's a lot harder for men," she replies.

3   "How do you figure that?"

4   "The women I know feel excited, innocent, like crusaders in a just cause. The men I know are eaten up with guilt."

5   We are sitting at the kitchen table drinking sassafras tea, our hands wrapped around the mugs because this April morning is cool and drizzly. "Like a Dutch morning," Anneke told me earlier. She is Dutch herself, a writer and midwife and peacemaker, with the round face and sad eyes of a woman in a Vermeer painting who might be waiting for the

rain to stop, for a door to open. She leans over to sniff a sprig of lilac, pale lavender, that rises from a vase of cobalt blue.

6   "Women feel such pressure to be everything, do everything," I say. "Career, kids, art, politics. Have their babies and get back to the office a week later. It's as if they're trying to overcome a million years' worth of evolution in one lifetime."

7   "But we help one another. We don't try to lumber on alone, like so many wounded grizzly bears, the way men do." Anneke sips her tea. I gave her a mug with owls on it, for wisdom. "And we have this deep-down sense that we're in the *right*—we've been held back, passed over, used—while men feel they're in the wrong. Men are the ones who've been discredited, who have to search their souls."

8   I search my soul. I discover guilty feelings aplenty—toward the poor, the Vietnamese, Native Americans, the whales, an endless list of debts—a guilt in each case that is as bright and unambiguous as a neon sign. But toward women I feel something more confused, a snarl of shame, envy, wary tenderness, and amazement. This muddle troubles me. To hide my unease I say, "You're right, it's tough being a man these days."

9   "Don't laugh." Anneke frowns at me, mournful-eyed, through the sassafras steam. "I wouldn't be a man for anything. It's much easier being the victim. All the victim has to do is break free. The persecutor has to live with his past."

10   How deep is that past? I find myself wondering after Anneke has left. How much of an inheritance do I have to throw off? Is it just the beliefs I breathed in as a child? Do I have to scour memory back through father and grandfather? Through St. Paul? Beyond Stonehenge and into the twilit caves? I'm convinced the past we must contend with is deeper even than speech. When I think back on my childhood, on how I learned to see men and women, I have a sense of ancient, dizzying depths. The back roads of Tennessee and Ohio where I grew up were probably closer, in their sexual patterns, to the campsites of Stone Age hunters than to the genderless cities of the future into which we are rushing.

11   The first men, besides my father, I remember seeing were black convicts and white guards, in the cottonfield across the road from our farm on the outskirts of Memphis. I must have been three or four. The prisoners wore dingy gray-and-black zebra suits, heavy as canvas, sodden with sweat. Hatless, stooped, they chopped weeds in the fierce

heat, row after row, breathing the acrid dust of boll-weevil poison. The overseers wore dazzling white shirts and broad shadowy hats. The oiled barrels of their shotguns flashed in the sunlight. Their faces in memory are utterly blank. Of course those men, white and black, have become for me an emblem of racial hatred. But they have also come to stand for the twin poles of my early vision of manhood—the brute toiling animal and the boss.

12   When I was a boy, the men I knew labored with their bodies. They were marginal farmers, just scraping by, or welders, steelworkers, carpenters; they swept floors, dug ditches, mined coal, or drove trucks, their forearms ropy with muscle; they trained horses, stoked furnaces, built tires, stood on assembly lines wrestling parts onto cars and refrigerators. They got up before light, worked all day long whatever the weather, and when they came home at night they looked as though somebody had been whipping them. In the evenings and on weekends they worked on their own places, tilling gardens that were lumpy with clay, fixing broken-down cars, hammering on houses that were always too drafty, too leaky, too small.

13   The bodies of the men I knew were twisted and maimed in ways visible and invisible. The nails of their hands were black and split, the hands tattooed with scars. Some had lost fingers. Heavy lifting had given many of them finicky backs and guts weak from hernias. Racing against conveyor belts had given them ulcers. Their ankles and knees ached from years of standing on concrete. Anyone who had worked for long around machines was hard of hearing. They squinted, and the skin of their faces was creased like the leather of old work gloves. There were times, studying them, when I dreaded growing up. Most of them coughed, from dust or cigarettes, and most of them drank cheap wine or whiskey, so their eyes looked bloodshot and bruised. The fathers of my friends always seemed older than the mothers. Men wore out sooner. Only women lived into old age.

14   As a boy I also knew another sort of men, who did not sweat and break down like mules. They were soldiers, and so far as I could tell they scarcely worked at all. During my early school years we lived on a military base, an arsenal in Ohio, and every day I saw GIs in the guardshacks, on the stoops of barracks, at the wheels of olive drab Chevrolets. The chief fact of their lives was boredom. Long after I left the Arsenal I came to recognize the sour smell the soldiers gave off as that of souls in limbo. They were all waiting—for wars, for transfers,

for leaves, for promotions, for the end of their hitch—like so many braves waiting for the hunt to begin. Unlike the warriors of older tribes, however, they would have no say about when the battle would start or how it would be waged. Their waiting was broken only when they practiced for war. They fired guns at targets, drove tanks across the churned-up fields of the military reservation, set off bombs in the wrecks of old fighter planes. I knew this was all play. But I also felt certain that when the hour for killing arrived, they would kill. When the real shooting started, many of them would die. This was what soldiers were *for,* just as a hammer was for driving nails.

15   Warriors and toilers: those seemed, in my boyhood vision, to be the chief destinies for men. They weren't the only destinies, as I learned from having a few male teachers, from reading books, and from watching television. But the men on television—the politicians, the astronauts, the generals, the savvy lawyers, the philosophical doctors, the bosses who gave orders to both soldiers and laborers—seemed as remote and unreal to me as the figures in tapestries. I could no more imagine growing up to become one of these cool, potent creatures than I could imagine becoming a prince.

16   A nearer and more hopeful example was that of my father, who had escaped from a red-dirt farm to a tire factory, and from the assembly line to the front office. Eventually he dressed in a white shirt and tie. He carried himself as if he had been born to work with his mind. But his body, remembering the earlier years of slogging work, began to give out on him in his fifties, and it quit on him entirely before he turned sixty-five. Even such a partial escape from man's fate as he had accomplished did not seem possible for most of the boys I knew. They joined the Army, stood in line for jobs in the smoky plants, helped build highways. They were bound to work as their fathers had worked, killing themselves or preparing to kill others.

17   A scholarship enabled me not only to attend college, a rare enough feat in my circle, but even to study in a university meant for the children of the rich. Here I met for the first time young men who had assumed from birth that they would lead lives of comfort and power. And for the first time I met women who told me that men were guilty of having kept all the joys and privileges of the earth for themselves. I was baffled. What privileges? What joys? I thought about the maimed, dismal lives of most of the men back home. What had they stolen from their wives and daughters? The right to go five days a week, twelve months a year, for thirty or forty years to a steel mill or a coal mine?

The right to drop bombs and die in war? The right to feel every leak in the roof, every gap in the fence, every cough in the engine, as a wound they must mend? The right to feel, when the lay-off comes or the plant shuts down, not only afraid but ashamed?

18   I was slow to understand the deep grievances of women. This was because, as a boy, I had envied them. Before college, the only people I had ever known who were interested in art or music or literature, the only ones who read books, the only ones who ever seemed to enjoy a sense of ease and grace were the mothers and daughters. Like the menfolk, they fretted about money, they scrimped and made-do. But, when the pay stopped coming in, they were not the ones who had failed. Nor did they have to go to war, and that seemed to me a blessed fact. By comparison with the narrow, ironclad days of fathers, there was an expansiveness, I thought, in the days of mothers. They went to see neighbors, to shop in town, to run errands at school, at the library, at church. No doubt, had I looked harder at their lives, I would have envied them less. It was not my fate to become a woman, so it was easier for me to see the graces. Few of them held jobs outside the home, and those who did filled thankless roles as clerks and waitresses. I didn't see, then, what a prison a house could be, since houses seemed to me brighter, handsomer places than any factory. I did not realize—because such things were never spoken of—how often women suffered from men's bullying. I did learn about the wretchedness of abandoned wives, single mothers, widows; but I also learned about the wretchedness of lone men. Even then I could see how exhausting it was for a mother to cater all day to the needs of young children. But if I had been asked, as a boy, to choose between tending a baby and tending a machine, I think I would have chosen the baby. (Having now tended both, I know I would choose the baby.)

19   So I was baffled when the women at college accused me and my sex of having cornered the world's pleasures. I think something like my bafflement has been felt by other boys (and by girls as well) who grew up in dirt-poor farm country, in mining country, in black ghettos, in Hispanic barrios, in the shadows of factories, in Third World nations—any place where the fate of men is as grim and bleak as the fate of women. Toilers and warriors. I realize now how ancient these identities are, how deep the tug they exert on men, the undertow of a thousand generations. The miseries I saw, as a boy, in the lives of nearly all men I continue to see in the lives of many—the body-breaking toil, the tedium, the call to be tough, the humiliating powerlessness, the battle for a living and for territory.

20   When the women I met at college thought about the joys and privileges of men, they did not carry in their minds the sort of men I had
known in my childhood. They thought of their fathers, who were
bankers, physicians, architects, stockbrokers, the big wheels of the big
cities. These fathers rode the train to work or drove cars that cost
more than any of my childhood houses. They were attended from
morning to night by female helpers, wives and nurses and secretaries.
They were never laid off, never short of cash at month's end, never
lined up for welfare. These fathers made decisions that mattered. They
ran the world.

21   The daughters of such men wanted to share in this power, this glory.
So did I. They yearned for a say over their future, for jobs worthy of
their abilities, for the right to live at peace, unmolested, whole. Yes, I
thought, yes yes. The difference between me and these daughters was
that they saw me, because of my sex, as destined from birth to become
like their fathers, and therefore as an enemy to their desires. But I
knew better. I wasn't an enemy, in fact or in feeling. I was an ally. If I
had known, then, how to tell them so, would they have believed me?
Would they now?

QUESTIONS ON CONTENT, STRUCTURE, AND STYLE

1. Why does Sanders open his essay with a conversation? How does
    this dialogue affect his readers?

2. In what way does this opening dialogue prepare the reader for the
    main idea of Sanders's essay?

3. How does Sanders feel about Anneke's views?

4. Sanders uses first person point-of-view to present his experiences
    and show how they shaped him. Does this use of first person pre-
    vent the reader from fully identifying with his essay? Explain.

5. Describe Sanders's tone, choosing a few lines or phrases that best
    illustrate it.

6. Is this essay more effectively directed at male readers, female read-
    ers, or both sexes? Why?

7. What does Sanders mean when he writes, "Warriors and toilers:
    those seemed, in my boyhood vision, to be the chief destinies
    for men"?

8. Sanders addresses both gender and economic class barriers. Explain how he faces both these forces at college.

9. Sanders often asks questions in his writing (paragraphs 10, 17, and 21, for example). How does this affect the impact of the essay on the reader?

10. Writers often open or close their essays with rhetorical questions—that is, a question where a particular answer is assumed. Consider Sanders's concluding line. Is this question hypothetical? Do you sense that Sanders knows the answers? Explain your view.

VOCABULARY

Vermeer (5)	*acrid (11)*	*tapestries (15)*
lumber (7)	*toilers (15)*	*expansiveness (18)*
unambiguous (8)	*savvy (15)*	*tedium (19)*

SUGGESTIONS FOR WRITING

1. Sanders' essay is titled "The Men We Carry in Our Minds." Who are the men or women you carry in your mind? In an essay developed by description and specific example, show how these men or women have helped shape you and your views.

2. Compare Laurie Ouellette's essay on feminism (pp. 83–88) to "The Men We Carry in Our Minds." At first glance they may appear to be about very different issues. Are they, however? (Consider, for example, their discussions of economic class.) Write an essay assessing the common ground between these two points of view.

3. Sanders writes that he was slow to understand "the deep grievances of women. . . . because, as a boy, I had envied them" and continues, "It was not my fate to become a woman, so it was easier for me to see the graces." Consider your own view of the opposite sex. What elements of the lives of the opposite sex do you envy? In an essay, present two or three qualities and then thoroughly examine each one. Are each of your perceptions accurate when put under scrutiny or is some of your envy misplaced?

A Day on Wheels

Cheryl A. Davis

Cheryl A. Davis was an associate at the Center for Investigative Reporting in San Francisco when this essay was published in 1987. As a consultant and a journalist, she has written many articles, often focusing on disability-related issues. This essay first appeared in the magazine *The Progressive*.

1   "MAN, IF I was you, I'd shoot myself," said the man on the subway platform. No one else was standing near him. I realized he was talking to me.

2   "Luckily, you're not," I said, gliding gracefully away.

3   For me, this was not an unusual encounter; indeed, it was a typical episode in my continuing true-life sitcom, "Day on Wheels."

4   A train ride can be an occasion for silent meditation in the midst of mechanical commotion. Unfortunately, I rarely get to meditate.

5   I attract attention. I pretend to ignore them, the eyes that scrutinize me and then quickly glance away. I try to avoid the gratuitous chats with loosely wrapped passengers. Usually, I fail. They may be loosely wrapped, but they're a persistent lot.

6   I use a wheelchair; I am not "confined" to one. Actually, I get around well. I drive a van equipped with a wheelchair-lift to the train station. I use a powered wheelchair with high-amperage batteries to get to work. A manual chair, light enough to carry, enables me to visit the "walkies" who live upstairs and to ride in their Volkswagens.

7   My life has been rich and varied, but my fellow passengers assume that, as a disabled person, I must be horribly deprived and so lonely that I will appreciate any unsolicited overture.

8   "Do you work?" a woman on the train asked me recently.

9   I said I did.

10   "It's nice that you have something to keep you busy, isn't it?"

11   Since we are thought of as poor invalids in need of chatting up, people are not apt to think too hard about what they are saying to us. It seems odd, since they also worry about the "right" way to talk to disabled people.

12   "How do you take a bath?" another woman asked me, apropos of nothing.

13   One day, an elderly man was staring at me as I read the newspaper.

14   "Would you like to read the sports section?" I asked him.

15   "How many miles can that thing go before you need new batteries?" he responded.

16   When I was a little girl, I once saw a woman whose teeth looked strange. "Mommy, that lady has funny teeth," I said. My mother explained that it was not *comme il faut* to offer up personal observations about other people's appearances. I thought everyone's mommy taught that, but I was wrong.

17   For many years, I was in what some of us call "the phyz-diz-biz"— developing housing and educational programs for disabled people. I was active in the disability-rights movement. I went to "special" schools offering the dubious blessing of a segregated education. As a result, I have known several thousand disabled people, at one time or another, across the United States.

18   For those whose disablement is still recent, the gratuitous remarks and unsolicited contributions can be exceptionally hurtful. It takes time to learn how to protect yourself. To learn how to do it gracefully can take a lifetime.

19   Many of us take the position that the people who bother us are to be pitied for their ignorance. We take it upon ourselves to "educate" them. We forgive them their trespasses and answer their questions patiently and try to straighten them out.

20   Others prefer to ignore the rude remarks and questions altogether. I tried that, but it didn't work. There was one woman on the train who tipped the scales for me.

21   "You're much too pretty to be in a wheelchair," she said.

22   I stared straight ahead, utterly frozen in unanticipated rage.

23   Undaunted, she grabbed my left arm below the elbow to get my attention.

24   "I said, 'You're much too pretty to be in a wheelchair.'"

25   In my fury, I lost control. Between my brain and my mouth, the mediating force of acquired tact had vanished.

26   "What do you think?" I snapped. "That God holds a beauty contest and if you come in first, you don't have to be in one?"

27   She turned away and, a moment later, was chatting with an old woman beside her as if nothing had been said at all. But I was mortified, and I moved to the other end of the train car.

28   For that one lapse, I flagellated myself all afternoon. When I got home, I telephoned one of my more socially adroit disabled friends for advice.

29   Nick is a therapist, a Ph.D. from Stanford, and paraplegic. "How do you deal with the other bozos on the bus?" I asked him.

30   "I just say, 'Grow up,'" Nick answered.

31   That was a bit haughtier than I could pull off, I told him.

32   "Well, look," he said, "if those words don't do it, find something else. The main thing is to get them to stop bothering you, right?"

33   "Yes, but—"

34   "But what?"

35   "Nick, if I'm *too* rude, they won't learn a thing. They'll just tell themselves I'm maladjusted."

36   "Then tell them their behavior is inappropriate."

37   "Inappropriate. That's marvelous!" I decided to try it next time.

38   "Next time" arrived last week. I didn't see the man coming. I was on the train platform, and he approached me from behind and tapped me on the shoulder.

39   "What's your disability?" he asked, discarding civilities.

40   I turned and looked at him. "That is not an appropriate question to ask a stranger," I said quietly.

41   "Well, *I* have schizophrenia," he said proudly.

42   "I didn't ask you."

43   "I feel rejected," he said.

44   "Well, then don't say things like that to people you don't know."

45   The train came and we got on together. I offered him a conciliatory remark, and he quieted down. Clearly he was not the best person for my new approach, but I think I'm headed in the right direction.

QUESTIONS ON CONTENT, STRUCTURE, AND STYLE

1. What is the significance of the essay's title? What does this indicate about Davis's tone?

2. Why does Davis open the essay with the scene on the subway platform? What response does this provoke in the reader?

3. What is the distinction Davis emphasizes when she writes, "I use a wheelchair; I am not 'confined' to one"? How does this statement reflect her purpose in writing this essay?

4. According to Davis, how do most people view the disabled?

5. Why does Davis seek a new response to use in her encounters with intrusive people?

6. "A Day on Wheels" is developed by multiple example, a strategy that places a premium on specific detail. Which example is most vivid and effective in reaching the reader? Least effective? Explain your choices.

7. Davis frequently uses dialogue to show her interaction with others. Why is this more effective than a past-tense description of these encounters would be?

8. How does Davis's tone affect the reader? How did you react to the essay at the end of paragraph 3? 16? 26? 45?

9. What is Davis's thesis? At what point is it clear to the reader?

10. Consider the essay's concluding scene. How does the fact that the intrusive stranger also has a disabling condition impact Davis's message and tone?

VOCABULARY

gratuitous (5)
amperage (6)
overture (7)
apropos (12)
comme il faut (16)

dubious (17)
trespasses (19)
undaunted (23)
mediating (25)
tact (25)

flagellated (28)
adroit (28)
maladjusted (35)
conciliatory (45)

SUGGESTIONS FOR WRITING

1. As an answer to Davis, write an essay describing how you feel when you meet a disabled person. Are her perceptions about you correct? Are you unsure how to act or what to say? Did you recognize yourself in Davis's essay? Offer an honest assessment of why we behave as we do in these encounters, offering specific examples, when possible, to support your answer.

2. Review Davis's use of dialogue and then recreate a scene from your own experience when a stranger asked you unwanted questions.

Use the dialogue to let your reader "hear" what you heard and said that day.

3. In an essay developed by multiple example, show either how you have been prejudged based on some outwardly visible trait (some examples include race, beauty, weight, wealth, disabilities) or how you have prejudged others.

Dear John Wayne

LOUISE ERDRICH

Louise Erdrich is the descendant of a German immigrant and a Chippewa Indian. Her poetry, stories, and novels, including *Love Medicine* (1984), which won the National Book Critics' Circle Award, and *Tracks* (1988), often focus on the lives of contemporary Native Americans. Her most recent works are *Baptism of Desire* (1991), a volume of poetry, and *The Crown of Columbus* (1991), a novel co-authored with her husband, Michael Dorris. This poem is from a collection called *Jacklight,* published in 1984.

August and the drive-in picture is packed.
We lounge on the hood of the Pontiac
surrounded by the slow-burning spirals they sell
at the window, to vanquish the hordes of mosquitoes.
5   Nothing works. They break through the smoke-screen for blood.

Always the look-out spots the Indians first,
spread north to south, barring progress.
The Sioux, or Cheyenne, or some bunch
in spectacular columns, arranged like SAC missiles,
10   their feathers bristling in the meaningful sunset.

The drum breaks. There will be no parlance.
Only the arrows whining, a death-cloud of nerves
swarming down on the settlers
who die beautifully, tumbling like dust weeds

15 into the history that brought us all here
together: this wide screen beneath the sign of the bear.

The sky fills, acres of blue squint and eye
that the crowd cheers. His face moves over us,
a thick cloud of vengeance, pitted
20 like the land that was once flesh. Each rut,
each scar makes a promise: *It is*
not over, this fight, not as long as you resist.

Everything we see belongs to us.
A few laughing Indians fall over the hood
25 slipping in the hot spilled butter.
The eye sees a lot, John, but the heart is so blind.
How will you know what you own?
He smiles, a horizon of teeth
the credits reel over, and then the white fields
30 again blowing in the true-to-life dark.
The dark films over everything.
We get into the car
scratching our mosquito bites, speechless and small
as people are when the movie is done.
35 We are back in ourselves.

How can we help but keep hearing his voice,
the flip side of the sound-track, still playing:
Come on, boys, we've got them
where we want them, drunk, running.
40 *They will give us what we want, what we need:*
The heart is a strange wood inside of everything
we see, burning, doubling, splitting out of its skin.

QUESTIONS ON CONTENT, STRUCTURE, AND STYLE

1. What is the setting of this poem? What is the effect of the image "this wide screen beneath the sign of the bear"?

2. Who are the "we" of the first stanza? From whose point of view is this poem presented?

3. What sort of movie is on the screen? What lines reveal the movie's plot? How are the Indians presented? the settlers?

4. Whose face is referred to in stanza 4? What characteristics does this person represent to many Americans who grew up in the 1950s?

5. What contrasts are presented between the action on the screen and the reality of the present? For example, what parallel does Erdrich draw between the mosquitoes and the "swarming" arrows? Indians on guard and SAC missiles?

6. What do the Indians find humorous about the movie? How does their state of mind change after the movie is over, when "the dark films over everything"?

7. Why do the Indians keep hearing a voice that says, "we've got them where we want them"? To what does "drunk" and "running" refer?

8. Why is the name of the Indians' car particularly ironic?

9. What is your interpretation of the last two lines of the poem?

10. Summarize into a few sentences the main idea of this poem. What was Erdrich's purpose? For whom do you think she was writing this poem?

VOCABULARY

vanquish (line 4)   parlance (line 11)
hordes (line 4)   vengeance (line 19)

SUGGESTIONS FOR WRITING

1. Erdrich's poem presents stereotypes that were popular in films and popular literature until the 1960s. Today's movies about Native Americans frequently stress their sense of honor, courage, and kinship with nature. Write an essay in which you argue that today's films have or have not replaced old stereotypes with new ones. Use as many films as possible to support your view.

2. Should schools whose athletic teams sport names such as "Redskins," "Chiefs," or "Braves" change their names? Are war-painted team mascots ("Willie Wampum"), war-cry yells, or tomahawk chops offensive? Assume that your school has had an Indian symbol for over 50 years, but now some community leaders are calling for an image

that they feel will be less denigrating. Write an editorial for your local newspaper arguing for or against the change.

3. Many Native American groups have protested against the excavation of their burial grounds and the consequent display of their ancestors' artifacts and bones in many American museums, including the Smithsonian. Investigate the arguments on both sides of this controversy, and write an essay that presents your view of the issue.

The Story of an Hour

KATE CHOPIN

Kate Chopin was a nineteenth-century writer whose stories appeared in such magazines as *The Atlantic Monthly, Century,* and *Saturday Evening Post.* She published two collections of short stories and two novels; one of her novels, *The Awakening* (1899), was considered so shocking in its story of a married woman who desired a life of her own that it was removed from some library shelves. "The Story of an Hour" was first published in *Vogue* in 1894.

1   KNOWING THAT Mrs. Mallard was afflicted with a heart trouble, great care was taken to break to her as gently as possible the news of her husband's death.

2   It was her sister Josephine who told her, in broken sentences, veiled hints that revealed in half concealing. Her husband's friend Richards was there, too, near her. It was he who had been in the newspaper office when intelligence of the railroad disaster was received, with Brently Mallard's name leading the list of "killed." He had only taken the time to assure himself of its truth by a second telegram, and had hastened to forestall any less careful, less tender friend in bearing the sad message.

3   She did not hear the story as many women have heard the same, with a paralyzed inability to accept its significance. She wept at once, with sudden, wild abandonment, in her sister's arms. When the storm

of grief had spent itself she went away to her room alone. She would have no one follow her.

4   There stood, facing the open window, a comfortable, roomy arm-chair. Into this she sank, pressed down by a physical exhaustion that haunted her body and seemed to reach into her soul.

5   She could see in the open square before her house the tops of trees that were all aquiver with the new spring life. The delicious breath of rain was in the air. In the street below a peddler was crying his wares. The notes of a distant song which some one was singing reached her faintly, and countless sparrows were twittering in the eaves.

6   There were patches of blue sky showing here and there through the clouds that had met and piled each above the other in the west facing her window.

7   She sat with her head thrown back upon the cushion of the chair quite motionless, except when a sob came up into her throat and shook her, as a child who has cried itself to sleep continues to sob in its dreams.

8   She was young, with a fair, calm face, whose lines bespoke repression and even a certain strength. But now there was a dull stare in her eyes, whose gaze was fixed away off yonder on one of those patches of blue sky. It was not a glance of reflection, but rather indicated a sus-pension of intelligent thought.

9   There was something coming to her and she was waiting for it, fear-fully. What was it? She did not know; it was too subtle and elusive to name. But she felt it, creeping out of the sky, reaching toward her through the sounds, the scents, the color that filled the air.

10   Now her bosom rose and fell tumultuously. She was beginning to recognize this thing that was approaching to possess her, and she was striving to beat it back with her will—as powerless as her two white slender hands would have been.

11   When she abandoned herself a little whispered word escaped her slightly parted lips. She said it over and over under her breath: "Free, free, free!" The vacant stare and the look of terror that had followed it went from her eyes. They stayed keen and bright. Her pulses beat fast, and the coursing blood warmed and relaxed every inch of her body.

12   She did not stop to ask if it were not a monstrous joy that held her. A clear and exalted perception enabled her to dismiss the suggestion as trivial.

13   She knew that she would weep again when she saw the kind, tender hands folded in death; the face that had never looked save with love

upon her, fixed and gray and dead. But she saw beyond that bitter moment a long procession of years to come that would belong to her absolutely. And she opened and spread her arms out to them in welcome.

14   There would be no one to live for during those coming years; she would live for herself. There would be no powerful will bending her in that blind persistence with which men and women believe they have a right to impose a private will upon a fellow creature. A kind intention or a cruel intention made the act seem no less a crime as she looked upon it in that brief moment of illumination.

15   And yet she had loved him—sometimes. Often she had not. What did it matter! What could love, the unsolved mystery, count for in face of this possession of self-assertion which she suddenly recognized as the strongest impulse of her being.

16   "Free! Body and soul free!" she kept whispering.

17   Josephine was kneeling before the closed door with her lips to the keyhole, imploring for admission. "Louise, open the door! I beg; open the door—you will make yourself ill. What are you doing, Louise? For heaven's sake open the door."

18   "Go away. I am not making myself ill." No; she was drinking in a very elixir of life through that open window.

19   Her fancy was running riot along those days ahead of her. Spring days, and summer days, and all sorts of days that would be her own. She breathed a quick prayer that life might be long. It was only yesterday she had thought with a shudder that life might be long.

20   She arose at length and opened the door to her sister's importunities. There was a feverish triumph in her eyes, and she carried herself unwittingly like a goddess of Victory. She clasped her sister's waist, and together they descended the stairs. Richards stood waiting for them at the bottom.

21   Some one was opening the front door with a latchkey. It was Brently Mallard who entered, a little travel-stained, composedly carrying his gripsack and umbrella. He had been far from the scene of accident, and did not even know there had been one. He stood amazed at Josephine's piercing cry; at Richards' quick motion to screen him from the view of his wife.

22   But Richards was too late.

23   When the doctors came they said she had died of heart disease—of joy that kills.

QUESTIONS ON CONTENT, STRUCTURE, AND STYLE

1. According to her doctors, what kills Mrs. Mallard? Do you agree with their diagnosis?

2. Why is the ending of the story ironic?

3. What is Mrs. Mallard's immediate reaction to the news of her husband's death?

4. During what season is the story set? Why did Chopin select this season?

5. What is the feeling Mrs. Mallard senses "creeping out of the sky"?

6. What does Mrs. Mallard recognize as the "strongest impulse of her being"?

7. Chopin uses what kind of imagery to describe Mrs. Mallard after her revelation?

8. Is Mr. Mallard a villain in this story?

9. Is this story critical of men only? Support your views with reference to the story.

10. If you did not know that this story was published in 1894, what year or era would you have guessed? Why?

VOCABULARY

forestall (2)   imploring (17)
aquiver (5)   elixir (18)
elusive (9)   importunities (20)
tumultuously (10)

SUGGESTIONS FOR WRITING

1. Chopin's story notes the "blind persistence with which men and women believe they have a right to impose a private will upon a fellow creature." Write an essay about a period in your life during which you felt someone was unfairly trying to influence or control your thinking or actions. How did you resolve this situation? What lessons did you learn?

2. Think of a time when an important relationship changed because you changed in some way. Consider, for example, changes associated with graduations, leaving home, marriages, divorces, new schools or careers. Write an essay contrasting your feelings before and after this significant change. What might readers learn about themselves after reading about your experience?

3. Write an essay analyzing Chopin's use of imagery and setting in this story. What do they add to the readers' understanding of Mrs. Mallard's character and dreams?

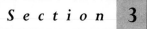

Section 3

PEOPLE AT LEISURE

"The Plug-In Drug: TV and the American Family"
BY MARIE WINN

"Attitude"
BY GARRISON KEILLOR

"My Car: Finally, A Room of One's Own"
BY ELLEN GOODMAN

"Horrors!"
BY DAVE BARRY

"Not Being There"
BY ROGER EBERT

"Eating Poetry"
BY MARK STRAND

"The Secret Life of Walter Mitty"
BY JAMES THURBER

The Plug-In Drug:
TV and the American Family

MARIE WINN

Marie Winn is the author of *Children Without Childhood* (1983), numerous children's books, and many articles for such publications as *The New York Times Magazine* and *The Village Voice*. This essay is an excerpt from her book *The Plug-In Drug: Television, Children and Family,* published in 1977.

1   A QUARTER of a century after the introduction of television into American society, a period that has seen the medium become so deeply ingrained in American life that in at least one state the television set has attained the rank of a legal necessity, safe from repossession in case of debt along with clothes, cooking utensils, and the like, television viewing has become an inevitable and ordinary part of daily life. Only in the early years of television did writers and commentators have sufficient perspective to separate the activity of watching television from the actual content it offers the viewer. In those early days writers frequently discussed the effects of television on family life. However, a curious myopia afflicted those early observers: almost without exception they regarded television as a favorable, beneficial, indeed, wondrous influence upon the family.

2   "Television is going to be a real asset in every home where there are children," predicts a writer in 1949.

3   "Television will take over your way of living and change your children's habits, but this change can be a wonderful improvement," claims another commentator.

4   "No survey's needed, of course, to establish that television has brought the family together in one room," writes *The New York Times* television critic in 1949.

5   Each of the early articles about television is invariably accompanied by a photograph or illustration showing a family cozily sitting together before the television set, Sis on Mom's lap, Buddy perched on the arm of Dad's chair, Dad with his arm around Mom's shoulder. Who could have guessed that twenty or so years later Mom would be watching a drama in the kitchen, the kids would be looking at

119

cartoons in their rooms, while Dad would be taking in the ball game in the living room?

6   Of course television sets were enormously expensive in those early days. The idea that by 1975 more than 60 percent of American families would own two or more sets was preposterous. The splintering of the multiple-set family was something the early writers could not foresee. Nor did anyone imagine the number of hours children would eventually devote to television, the common use of television by parents as a child pacifier, the changes television would effect upon child-rearing methods, the increasing domination of family schedules by children's viewing requirements—in short, the *power* of the new medium to dominate family life.

7   After the first years, as children's consumption of the new medium increased, together with parental concern about the possible effects of so much television viewing, a steady refrain helped to soothe and reassure anxious parents. "Television always enters a pattern of influences that already exist: the home, the peer group, the school, the church, and culture generally," write the authors of an early and influential study of television's effects on children. In other words, if the child's home life is all right, parents need not worry about the effects of all that television watching.

8   But television does not merely influence the child; it deeply influences that "pattern of influences" that is meant to ameliorate its effects. Home and family life has changed in important ways since the advent of television. The peer group has become television-oriented, and much of the time children spend together is occupied by television viewing. Culture generally has been transformed by television. Therefore it is improper to assign to television the subsidiary role its many apologists (too often members of the television industry) insist it plays. Television is not merely one of a number of important influences upon today's child. Through the changes it has made in family life, television emerges as *the* important influence in children's lives today.

9   Television's contribution to family life has been an equivocal one. For while it has, indeed, kept the members of the family from dispersing, it has not served to bring them *together*. By its domination of the time families spend together, it destroys the special quality that distinguished one family from another, a quality that depends to a great extent on what a family *does*, what special rituals, games, recurrent jokes, familiar songs, and shared activities it accumulates.

10   "Like the sorcerer of old," writes Urie Bronfenbrenner,[1] "the television set casts its magic spell, freezing speech and action, turning the living into silent statues so long as the enchantment lasts. The primary danger of the television screen lies not so much in the behavior it produces—although there is danger there—as in the behavior it prevents: the talks, the games, the family festivities and arguments through which much of the child's learning takes place and through which his character is formed. Turning on the television set can turn off the process that transforms children into people."

11   Yet parents have accepted a television-dominated family life so completely that they cannot see how the medium is involved in whatever problems they might be having. A first-grade teacher reports:

12   "I have one child in the group who's an only child. I wanted to find out more about her family life because this little girl was quite isolated from the group, didn't make friends, so I talked to her mother. Well, they don't have time to do anything in the evening, the mother said. The parents come home after picking up the child at the baby-sitter's. Then the mother fixes dinner while the child watches TV. Then they have dinner and the child goes to bed. I said to this mother, 'Well, couldn't she help you fix dinner? That would be a nice time for the two of you to talk,' and the mother said, 'Oh, but I'd hate to have her miss "Zoom." It's such a good program!'"

13   Even when families make efforts to control television, too often its very presence counterbalances the positive features of family life. A writer and mother of two boys aged three and seven described her family's television schedule in an article in *The New York Times*:

> We were in the midst of a full-scale War. Every day was a new battle and every program was a major skirmish. We agreed it was a bad scene all around and were ready to enter diplomatic negotiations. . . . In principle we have agreed on two and a half hours of TV a day, "Sesame Street," "Electric Company" (with dinner gobbled up in between) and two half-hour shows between 7 and 8:30 which enables the grown-ups to eat in peace and prevents the two boys from destroying one another. Their pre-bedtime choice is

---

[1] Urie Bronfenbrenner was a professor in the Department of Human Development at Cornell University.

dreadful, because, as Josh recently admitted, "There's nothing much on I really like." So . . . it's "What's My Line" or "To Tell the Truth." . . . Clearly there is a need for first-rate children's shows at this time. . . .

14   Consider the "family life" described here: Presumably the father comes home from work during the "Sesame Street"—"Electric Company" stint. The children are either watching television, gobbling their dinner, or both. While the parents eat their dinner in peaceful privacy, the children watch another hour of television. Then there is only a half-hour left before bedtime, just enough time for baths, getting pajamas on, brushing teeth, and so on. The children's evening is regimented with an almost military precision. They watch their favorite programs, and when there is "nothing much on I really like," they watch whatever else is on—because *watching* is the important thing. Their mother does not see anything amiss with watching programs just for the sake of watching; she only wishes there were some first-rate children's shows on at those times.

15   Without conjuring up memories of the Victorian era with family games and long, leisurely meals, and large families, the question arises: isn't there a better family life available than this dismal, mechanized arrangement of children watching television for however long is allowed them, evening after evening?

16   Of course, families today still do *special* things together at times: go camping in the summer, go to the zoo on a nice Sunday, take various trips and expeditions. But their *ordinary* daily life together is diminished—that sitting around at the dinner table, that spontaneous taking up of an activity, those little games invented by children on the spur of the moment when there is nothing else to do, the scribbling, the chatting, and even the quarreling, all the things that form the fabric of a family, that define a childhood. Instead, the children have their regular schedule of television programs and bedtime, and the parents have their peaceful dinner together.

17   The author of the article in *The Times* notes that "keeping a family sane means mediating between the needs of both children and adults." But surely the needs of adults are being better met than the needs of the children, who are effectively shunted away and rendered untroublesome, while their parents enjoy a life as undemanding as that of any

childless couple. In reality, it is those very demands that young children make on a family that lead to growth, and it is the way parents accede to those demands that builds the relationships on which the future of the family depends. If the family does not accumulate its backlog of shared experiences, shared *everyday* experiences that occur and recur and change and develop, then it is not likely to survive as anything other than a caretaking institution.

Family Rituals

18   Ritual is defined by sociologists as "that part of family life that the family likes about itself, is proud of and wants formally to continue." Another text notes that "the development of a ritual by a family is an index of the common interest of its members in the family as a group."

19   What has happened to family rituals, those regular, dependable, recurrent happenings that gave members of a family a feeling of *belonging* to a home rather than living in it merely for the sake of convenience, those experiences that act as the adhesive of family unity far more than any material advantages?

20   Mealtime rituals, going-to-bed rituals, illness rituals, holiday rituals, how many of these have survived the inroads of the television set?

21   A young woman who grew up near Chicago reminisces about her childhood and gives an idea of the effects of television upon family rituals:

22   "As a child I had millions of relatives around—my parents both come from relatively large families. My father had nine brothers and sisters. And so every holiday there was this great swoop-down of aunts, uncles, and millions of cousins. I just remember how wonderful it used to be. These thousands of cousins would come and everyone would play and ultimately, after dinner, all the women would be in the front of the house, drinking coffee and talking, all the men would be in the back of the house, drinking and smoking, and all the kids would be all over the place, playing hide and seek. Christmas time was particularly nice because everyone always brought all their toys and games. Our house had a couple of rooms with go-through closets, so there were always kids running in a great circle route. I remember it was just wonderful.

23   "And then all of a sudden one year I remember becoming suddenly aware of how different everything had become. The kids were no longer playing Monopoly or Clue or the other games we used to play together. It was because we had a television set which had been turned on for a football game. All of that socializing that had gone on previously had ended. Now everyone was sitting in front of the television set, on a holiday, at a family party! I remember being stunned by how awful that was. Somehow the television had become more attractive."

24   As families have come to spend more and more of their time together engaged in the single activity of television watching, those rituals and pastimes that once gave family life its special quality have become more and more uncommon. Not since prehistoric times when cave families hunted, gathered, ate, and slept, with little time remaining to accumulate a culture of any significance, have families been reduced to such a sameness.

Real People

25   It is not only the activities that a family might engage in together that are diminished by the powerful presence of television in the home. The relationships of the family members to each other are also affected, in both obvious and subtle ways. The hours that the young child spends in a one-way relationship with television people, an involvement that allows for no communication or interaction, surely affect his relationships with real-life people.

26   Studies show the importance of eye-to-eye contact, for instance, in real-life relationships, and indicate that the nature of a person's eye-contact patterns, whether he looks another squarely in the eye or looks to the side or shifts his gaze from side to side, may play a significant role in his success or failure in human relationships. But no eye contact is possible in the child-television relationship, although in certain children's programs people purport to speak directly to the child and the camera fosters this illusion by focusing directly upon the person being filmed. (Mr. Rogers is an example, telling the child "I like you, you're special," etc.) How might such a distortion of real-life relationships affect a child's development of trust, of openness, of an ability to relate well to other *real* people?

27   Bruno Bettelheim[2] writes:

> Children who have been taught, or conditioned, to listen passively most of the day to the warm verbal communications coming from the TV screen, to the deep emotional appeal of the so-called TV personality, are often unable to respond to real persons because they arouse so much less feeling than the skilled actor. Worse, they lose the ability to learn from reality because life experiences are much more complicated than the ones they see on the screen. . . .

28   A teacher makes a similar observation about her personal viewing experiences:

29   "I have trouble mobilizing myself and dealing with real people after watching a few hours of television. It's just hard to make that transition from watching television to a real relationship. I suppose it's because there was no effort necessary while I was watching, and dealing with real people always requires a bit of effort. Imagine, then, how much harder it might be to do the same thing for a small child, particularly one who watches a lot of television every day."

30   But more obviously damaging to family relationships is the elimination of opportunities to talk, and perhaps more important, to argue, to air grievances, between parents and children and brothers and sisters. Families frequently use television to avoid confronting their problems, problems that will not go away if they are ignored but will only fester and become less easily resolvable as time goes on.

31   A mother reports:

32   "I find myself, with three children, wanting to turn on the TV set when they're fighting. I really have to struggle not to do it because I feel that's telling them this is the solution to the quarrel—but it's so tempting that I often do it."

33   A family therapist discusses the use of television as an avoidance mechanism:

34   "In a family I know the father comes home from work and turns on the television set. The children come and watch with him and the wife

[2] Bruno Bettelheim was a well-known psychologist and author who frequently wrote about children.

serves them their meal in front of the set. He then goes and takes a shower, or works on the car or something. She then goes and has her own dinner in front of the television set. It's a symptom of a deeper-rooted problem, sure. But it would help them all to get rid of the set. It would be far easier to work on what the symptom really means without the television. The television simply encourages a double avoidance of each other. They'd find out more quickly what was going on if they weren't able to hide behind the TV. Things wouldn't necessarily be better, of course, but they wouldn't be anesthetized."

35   The decreased opportunities for simple conversation between parents and children in the television-centered home may help explain an observation made by an emergency room nurse at a Boston hospital. She reports that parents just seem to sit there these days when they come in with a sick or seriously injured child, although talking to the child would distract and comfort him. "They don't seem to know *how* to talk to their own children at any length," the nurse observes. Similarly, a television critic writes in *The New York Times*: "I had just a day ago taken my son to the emergency ward of a hospital for stitches above his left eye, and the occasion seemed no more real to me than Maalot or 54th Street, south-central Los Angeles. There was distance and numbness and an inability to turn off the total institution. I didn't behave at all; I just watched. . . ."

36   A number of research studies substantiate the assumption that television interferes with family activities and the formation of family relationships. One survey shows that 78 percent of the respondents indicated no conversation taking place during viewing except at specified times such as commercials. The study notes: "The television atmosphere in most households is one of quiet absorption on the part of family members who are present. The nature of the family social life during a program could be described as 'parallel' rather than interactive, and the set does seem to dominate family life when it is on." Thirty-six percent of the respondents in another study indicated that television viewing was the only family activity participated in during the week.

37   In a summary of research findings on television's effect on family interactions James Gabardino states: "The early findings suggest that television had a disruptive effect upon interaction and thus presumably human development. . . . It is not unreasonable to ask: 'Is

the fact that the average American family during the 1950s came to include two parents, two children, and a television set somehow related to the psycho-social characteristics of the young adults of the 1970s?'"

Undermining the Family

38   In its effect on family relationships, in its facilitation of parental withdrawal from an active role in the socialization of their children, and in its replacement of family rituals and special events, television has played an important role in the disintegration of the American family. But of course it has not been the only contributing factor, perhaps not even the most important one. The steadily rising divorce rate, the increase in the number of working mothers, the decline of the extended family, the breakdown of neighborhoods and communities, the growing isolation of the nuclear family—all have seriously affected the family.

39   As Urie Bronfenbrenner suggests, the sources of family breakdown do not come from the family itself, but from the circumstances in which the family finds itself and the way of life imposed on it by those circumstances. "When those circumstances and the way of life they generate undermine relationships of trust and emotional security between family members, when they make it difficult for parents to care for, educate and enjoy their children, when there is no support or recognition from the outside world for one's role as a parent and when time spent with one's family means frustration of career, personal fulfillment, and peace of mind, then the development of the child is adversely affected," he writes.

40   But while the roots of alienation go deep into the fabric of American social history, television's presence in the home fertilizes them, encourages their wild and unchecked growth. Perhaps it is true that America's commitment to the television experience masks a spiritual vacuum, an empty and barren way of life, a desert of materialism. But it is television's dominant role in the family that anesthetizes the family into accepting its unhappy state and prevents it from struggling to better its condition, to improve its relationships, and to regain some of the richness it once possessed.

41   Others have noted the role of mass media in perpetuating an unsatisfactory *status quo*. Leisure-time activity, writes Irving Howe,[3] "must provide relief from work monotony without making the return to work too unbearable; it must provide amusement without insight and pleasure without disturbance—as distinct from art which gives pleasure through disturbance. Mass culture is thus oriented toward a central aspect of industrial society: the depersonalization of the individual." Similarly, Jacques Ellul[4] rejects the idea that television is a legitimate means of educating the citizen: "Education . . . takes place only incidentally. The clouding of his consciousness is paramount. . . ."

42   And so the American family muddles on, dimly aware that something is amiss but distracted from an understanding of its plight by an endless stream of television images. As family ties grow weaker and vaguer, as children's lives become more separate from their parents', as parents' educational role in their children's lives is taken over by television and schools, family life becomes increasingly more unsatisfying for both parents and children. All that seems to be left is Love, an abstraction that family members *know* is necessary but find great difficulty giving each other because the traditional opportunities for expressing love within the family have been reduced or destroyed.

43   For contemporary parents, love toward each other has increasingly come to mean successful sexual relations, as witnessed by the proliferation of sex manuals and sex therapists. The opportunities for manifesting other forms of love through mutual support, understanding, nurturing, even, to use an unpopular word, *serving* each other, are less and less available as mothers and fathers seek their independent destinies outside the family.

44   As for love of children, this love is increasingly expressed through supplying material comforts, amusements, and educational opportunities. Parents show their love for their children by sending them to good schools and camps, by providing them with good food and good doctors, by buying them toys, books, games, and a television set of their very own. Parents will even go further and express their love by attending PTA meetings to improve their children's schools, or by

[3] Irving Howe was an author, historian, critic, and professor of English at Hunter College in New York.
[4] Jacques Ellul is the author of books on religion and on our technological society.

joining groups that are acting to improve the quality of their children's television programs.

45   But this is love at a remove, and is rarely understood by children.
The more direct forms of parental love require time and patience,
steady, dependable, ungrudgingly given time actually spent *with* a
child, reading to him, comforting him, playing, joking, and working
with him. But even if a parent were eager and willing to demonstrate
that sort of direct love to his children today, the opportunities are diminished. What with school and Little League and piano lessons and, of
course, the inevitable television programs, a day seems to offer just
enough time for a good-night kiss.

QUESTIONS ON CONTENT, STRUCTURE, AND STYLE

1. How does Winn use the comments from early television critics to
   introduce her subject?

2. According to Winn, television does more than influence the child
   viewer. What larger effect does it have on the family?

3. How does Winn try to show that too often parents have accepted
   a "television-dominated family life"? Does she succeed?

4. What kinds of family rituals have been undermined by television?

5. How might television affect a child's relationships with people in
   general?

6. What other factors have contributed to the disintegration of the
   American family?

7. According to Winn, television anesthetizes the family into accepting what?

8. In Winn's opinion, how do some parents mistakenly demonstrate
   their love for their children? What should they do instead?

9. Evaluate Winn's use of evidence throughout the essay. What
   methods are most effective?

10. Winn argues the detrimental effects of watching too much televi-
    sion in general, in contrast to many critics who are opposed only
    to certain kinds of programs. Does this distinction hurt or help
    her argument?

VOCABULARY

inevitable (1)	*advent (8)*	*facilitation (38)*
myopia (1)	*equivocal (9)*	*perpetuating (41)*
ameliorate (8)	*shunted (17)*	*ungrudgingly (45)*

SUGGESTIONS FOR WRITING

1. Write an essay in which you discuss the effects of television on rituals or shared activities in your family. Do you agree with Winn's thesis?

2. Write an essay describing a family ritual or tradition and its effect on you. This tradition or ritual might be connected to a holiday or season; on the other hand, you might select something your family did on a daily basis that might appear insignificant to outsiders but that you feel greatly enriched the texture of your home life. What tradition might you wish to pass on to *your* children?

3. The Greeks had their Olympic games. The Romans are well-known for their orgies, gladiator contests, and Christian-eating lions. The Elizabethans watched both fighting bears and Shakespearean plays. How do you think people in the generations to come will judge our civilization if they base their view on our popular entertainment? Write an essay explaining what you think their judgment of our character would be, supporting your opinion with evidence from currently popular television, music, or movies.

Attitude

GARRISON KEILLOR

Garrison Keillor is a writer, storyteller, and humorist. He is the former host of National Public Radio's *A Prairie Home Companion* and currently hosts the *American Radio Company*. His works include *Lake Wobegon Days* (1985), *We Are Still Married* (1989), *WLT: A Radio Romance* (1991), and *Happy To Be Here* (1982), from which this selection is taken.

1   LONG AGO I passed the point in life when major-league ballplayers begin to be younger than yourself. Now all of them are, except for a few aging trigenarians and a couple of quadros who don't get around on the fastball as well as they used to and who sit out the second games of doubleheaders. However, despite my age (thirty-nine), I am still active and have a lot of interests. One of them is slow-pitch softball, a game that lets me go through the motions of baseball without getting beaned or having to run too hard. I play on a pretty casual team, one that drinks beer on the bench and substitutes freely. If a player's wife or girlfriend wants to play, we give her a glove and send her out to right field, no questions asked, and if she lets a pop fly drop six feet in front of her, nobody agonizes over it.

2   Except me. This year. For the first time in my life, just as I am entering the dark twilight of my slow-pitch career, I find myself taking the game seriously. It isn't the bonehead play that bothers me especially—the pop fly that drops untouched, the slow roller juggled and the ball then heaved ten feet over the first baseman's head and into the next diamond, the routine singles that go through outfielders' legs for doubles and triples with gloves flung after them. No, it isn't our stone-glove fielding or pussyfoot base-running or limp-wristed hitting that gives me fits, though these have put us on the short end of some mighty ridiculous scores this summer. It's our attitude.

3   Bottom of the ninth, down 18–3, two outs, a man on first and a woman on third, and our third baseman strikes out. *Strikes out!* In slow-pitch, not even your grandmother strikes out, but this guy does,

and after his third strike—a wild swing at a ball that bounces on the plate—he topples over in the dirt and lies flat on his back, laughing. *Laughing!*

4   Same game, earlier. They have the bases loaded. A weak grounder is hit toward our second baseperson. The runners are running. She picks up the ball, and she looks at them. She looks at first, at second, at home. We yell, "Throw it! Throw it!" and she throws it, underhand, at the pitcher, who has turned and run to back up the catcher. The ball rolls across the third-base line and under the bench. Three runs score. The batter, a fatso, chugs into second. The other team hoots and hollers, and what does she do? She shrugs and smiles ("Oh, silly me"); after all, it's only a game. Like the aforementioned strikeout artist, she treats her error as a joke. They have forgiven themselves instantly, which is unforgivable. It is *we* who should forgive them, who can say, "It's all right, it's only a game." They are supposed to throw up their hands and kick the dirt and hang their heads, as if this boner, even if it is their sixteenth of the afternoon—*this* is the one that really and truly breaks their hearts.

5   That attitude sweetens the game for everyone. The sinner feels sweet remorse. The fatso feels some sense of accomplishment; this is no bunch of rumdums he forced into an error but a team with some class. We, the sinner's teammates, feel momentary anger at her—dumb! dumb play!—but then, seeing her grief, we sympathize with her in our hearts (any one of us might have made that mistake or one worse), and we yell encouragement, including the shortstop, who, moments before, dropped an easy throw for a force at second. "That's all right! Come on! We got 'em!" we yell. "Shake it off! These turkeys can't hit!" This makes us all feel good, even though the turkeys now lead us by ten runs. We're getting clobbered, but we have a winning attitude.

6   Let me say this about attitude: Each player is responsible for his or her own attitude, and to a considerable degree you can *create* a good attitude by doing certain little things on the field. These are certain little things that ballplayers do in the Bigs, and we ought to be doing them in the Slows.

7   1. When going up to bat, don't step right into the batter's box as if it were an elevator. The box is your turf, your stage. Take possession of it slowly and deliberately, starting with a lot of back-bending, knee-stretching, and torso-revolving in the on-deck circle. Then,

approaching the box, stop outside it and tap the dirt off your spikes with your bat. You don't have spikes, you have sneakers, of course, but the significance of the tapping is the same. Then, upon entering the box, spit on the ground. It's a way of saying, "This here is mine. This is where I get my hits."

8   2. Spit frequently. Spit at all crucial moments. Spit correctly. Spit should be *blown,* not ptuied weakly with the lips, which often results in dribble. Spitting should convey forcefulness of purpose, concentration, pride. Spit down, not in the direction of others. Spit in the glove and on the fingers, especially after making a real knucklehead play; it's a way of saying, "I dropped the ball because my glove was dry."

9   3. At bat and in the field, pick up dirt. Rub dirt in the fingers (especially after spitting on them). Toss dirt, as if testing the wind for velocity and direction. Smooth the dirt. Be involved with dirt. If no dirt is available (e.g., in the outfield), pluck tufts of grass. Fielders should be grooming their areas constantly between plays, flicking away tiny sticks and bits of gravel.

10   4. Take your time. Tie your laces. Confer with your teammates about possible situations that may arise and conceivable options in dealing with them. Extend the game. Three errors on three consecutive plays can be humiliating if the plays occur within the space of a couple of minutes, but if each error is separated from the next by extensive conferences on the mound, lace-tying, glove adjustments, and arguing close calls (if any), the effect on morale is minimized.

11   5. Talk. Not just an occasional "Let's get a hit now" but continuous rhythmic chatter, a flow of syllables: "Hey babe hey babe c'mon babe good stick now hey babe long tater take him downtown babe . . . hey good eye good eye."

12   Infield chatter is harder to maintain. Since the slow-pitch pitch is required to be a soft underhand lob, infielders hesitate to say, "Smoke him babe hey low heat hey throw it on the black babe chuck it in there back him up babe no hit no hit." Say it anyway.

13   6. One final rule, perhaps the most important of all: When your team is up and has made the third out, the batter and the players who were left on base do not come back to the bench for their gloves. *They remain on the field, and their teammates bring their gloves out to them.* This requires some organization and discipline, but it pays off big in morale. It says, "Although we're getting our pants knocked off, still we must conserve our energy."

14   Imagine that you have bobbled two fly balls in this rout and now you have just tried to stretch a single into a double and have been easily thrown out sliding into second base, where the base runner ahead of you had stopped. It was the third out and a dumb play, and your opponents smirk at you as they run off the field. You are the goat, a lonely and tragic figure sitting in the dirt. You curse yourself, jerking your head sharply forward. You stand up and kick the base. How miserable! How degrading! Your utter shame, though brief, bears silent testimony to the worthiness of your teammates, whom you have let down, and they appreciate it. They call out to you now as they take the field, and as the second baseman runs to his position he says, "Let's get 'em now," and tosses you your glove. Lowering your head, you trot slowly out to right. There you do some deep knee bends. You pick grass. You find a pebble and fling it into foul territory. As the first batter comes to the plate, you check the sun. You get set in your stance, poised to fly. Feet spread, hands on hips, you bend slightly at the waist and spit the expert spit of a veteran ballplayer—a player who has known the agony of defeat but who always bounces back, a player who has lost a stride on the base paths but can still make the big play.

15   This is *ball,* ladies and gentlemen. This is what it's all about.

QUESTIONS ON CONTENT, STRUCTURE, AND STYLE

1. What problem does Keillor confront in this essay?

2. What is Keillor's solution to this problem?

3. What is the purpose of the six steps listed in the middle of this essay?

4. What is the tone of this essay? How seriously do you think Keillor intends his advice?

5. Why does Keillor present five paragraphs before he offers his list of advice? Is this introduction too long? Why or why not?

6. What is the effect of Keillor's personal experiences? Of his many specific details?

7. Why in paragraph 14 does Keillor create an imaginary scene with the reader as the ball player?

8. What is the effect of the last two sentences in the essay? Do they provide an appropriate conclusion to this essay?
9. Characterize Keillor's style. For example, what does dialogue add to his descriptions? Use of short or fragment sentences? Slang?
10. How might Keillor's thesis be applied to activities other than softball? Can you think of other examples in which attitude and performance have been linked in important ways for you?

VOCABULARY

trigenarians (1)	*rumdrums (5)*
quadros (1)	*velocity (9)*
remorse (5)	*degrading (14)*

SUGGESTIONS FOR WRITING

1. Write an essay in which you describe an "attitude problem" in another field or activity. Then offer steps, as Keillor did, that show how one may achieve the appropriate behavior and outlook.
2. Describe a time in your life when attitude made all the difference in your performance. Did your attitude help you succeed at something or did it contribute to your defeat?
3. Baseball fan and writer Joseph Epstein once noted that "Sport may be the toy department of life, but . . . at least on the field, it is the real thing." Write an essay in which you analyze the benefits you've received from playing a particular sport. Or, if you prefer, write an essay analyzing the enjoyment of a particular sport or team from your point of view as a loyal fan.

My Car: Finally, a Room of One's Own

ELLEN GOODMAN

Ellen Goodman has written for *Newsweek,* the *Detroit Free Press,* and the *Boston Globe.* Her popular newspaper column, "At Large," has been syndicated since 1976. She has won praise as a radio and television commentator, and in 1980 she won the Pulitzer Prize for distinguished commentary. Her essays have been collected in *Close to Home* (1979), *At Large* (1980), *Keeping in Touch* (1985), and *Making Sense* (1989). The following essay was published in 1990.

1   I HAVE just moved into a new car. I use the word "moved" advisedly. There were no massive crates to pack and unpack. Indeed, I was determined to travel lightly into this four-wheeler. All anyone actually needs to move into a new car, I said to myself primly, is the keys.

2   I have a history as a car slob. But as I unloaded my old car of its burdensome past—five years worth of sweatpants, sneakers, T-shirts, umbrellas, coffee cups, hats, tapes, pens, parking tickets, receipts, magazines, notebooks, pennies, plastic forks and window scrapers in various stages of disrepair—I believed that I could unload myself of old habits.

3   This motor vehicle would be pristine. A clean slate. Passengers would be able to eat off my floormats. People who peered into my windows would assume that my last name was Hertz.

4   For the first month, I did deal with the car as if I were renting it. I felt like a guest in a hotel who wasn't quite sure how the shower handles worked. I did everything but sign the register when I entered the car. And (this is crucial) when I checked out, I left nothing behind.

5   But, as I began to feel at home, I did in fact move in. With all my belongings. The sneakers, the sweatpants, the hat . . . .

6   Now, I have come to the rationalization that my car functions in life as my mobile home. And I am one of those people who like things homey.

7   I say this defensively because my husband has a different attitude and, fortunately, a different car. I have, however, consulted with any number of friends on this subject. For a surprisingly large number of us, the car is the modern equivalent of what Virginia Woolf once described as a room of her own. To mess up.

8   My car goes to work and comes home with me, and waits in the parking lot like Mary's little lamb. It tags along for errands and other assorted pit stops. Sooner or later anything that can't fit into a pocket or pocketbook takes semi-permanent residence inside its doors and trunk. Because you never know when you'll need it, you take it with you.

9   Inevitably it begins to serve the function of a knapsack, a locker room, a laundry, workspace and a closet.

10   In my defense, I am not without restraint. I did not put bumper stickers on my mobile home anymore than I would add psychedelic posters to my living room. I have pledged to remove litter on a semiannual basis and empty the pennies out of the ashtray on Arbor Day.

11   But quite frankly I have given up on keeping the new car a showroom. The people who have immaculate cars are people who buy aerosol cans with new-car-smell spray. They are people who prefer to live in showrooms.

12   I am a nester, and I have the twigs in the trunk to prove it. So, I have moved in. I feel more comfortable with my mobile home each day. It's got a real look to it, you know. The lived-in look.

Questions on Content, Structure, and Style

1. What is Goodman's purpose in writing this essay? Why might readers enjoy reading about her relationship to her new car?

2. How does the list of items in paragraph 2 clarify Goodman's relationship to past cars?

3. How did Goodman intend to treat her new car? To what does Hertz (paragraph 3) refer?

4. How does the comparison to a hotel room clarify Goodman's early relationship to her car?

5. After a month or so in her new car, how does Goodman's attitude change? What has the car become for her?

6. In 1929, writer Virginia Woolf urged women to find their own identities, for each to create a "a room of one's own." How does Goodman incorporate this metaphor into her essay?

7. In addition to providing transportation, what functions does Goodman's car perform?

8. From what two kinds of car-owners does Goodman distinguish herself? Why does she call herself a "nester"?

9. How is Goodman's conclusion linked to her introductory comments about her car?

10. How does Goodman's relationship to her car compare to yours or to others you know? If you own or frequently drive a particular car, would you characterize yourself as a "car slob" or a "hotel guest" or somewhere in between? Select a descriptive term or phrase that best describes your attitude.

VOCABULARY

advisedly *(1)*   homey *(6)*
pristine *(3)*   immaculate *(11)*
rationalization *(6)*   nester *(12)*

SUGGESTIONS FOR WRITING

1. Americans are well known for their love affairs with cars. Has there ever been a special car in your life? Write an essay describing this relationship, using ample specific details and images as Goodman did to characterize you and your car.

2. Many families take vacations involving long car trips; these trips often provide the basis for humorous family storytelling in later years. Think of your best or worst family car trip. Write an essay that retells and then analyzes your funniest or most memorable story. What did your car trip ultimately reveal about you and the members of your family?

3. Write a humorous essay describing the messiest person you know (you? a roommate? a friend or family member?). Analyze this person's messy habits—are there patterns in the mess-making? Is this

person's messiness an attempt to define a space or an identity? Or, if you prefer, write an essay contrasting the sloppy vs. neat habits of two people you know. (Remember that humorous essays present a thesis as well as amusing description. What claim might you argue by using these people as evidence?)

Horrors!

DAVE BARRY

Dave Barry is a contemporary humorist who writes a nationally syndicated column distributed by Knight-Ridder newspapers. He is the author of many books, including *Claw Your Way to the Top: How to Become the Head of a Major Corporation in Roughly a Week* (1986); *Dave Barry Slept Here: A Sort of History of the United States* (1989); *Dave Barry Turns 40* (1991); and *Dave Barry Does Japan* (1992). This essay first appeared in newspapers in May 1990.

1   RECENTLY I'VE been reading horror novels at bedtime. I'm talking about those paperbacks with names like "The Brainsucker," full of scenes like this:

2   "As Marge stepped through the doorway into the darkening mansion, she felt a sense of foreboding, caused, perhaps, by the moaning of the wind, or the creaking of the door, or possibly the Kentucky Fried Chicken bucket full of eyeballs."

3   Of course, if Marge had the intelligence of paint, she'd stop right there. "Wait a minute," she'd say. "I'm getting the hell out of this novel." Then she'd leap off the page, sprint across my bedspread, and run into my son's bedroom to become a character in a safe book like "Horton Hears a Who."

4   But Marge, in the hallowed horror-novel-character tradition, barges straight ahead, down gloomy corridors where she has to cut through the foreboding with a machete, despite the obvious fact that something hideous is about to happen, probably involving the forced evacuation of her skull cavity by a demonic being with the underworld Roto-Rooter

franchise. So I'm flinching as I turn each page, thinking, "What a mo-ron this woman is!" And Marge is thinking: "Well, I may be a moron, but at least I'm not stupid enough to be READING this."

5   And of course Marge is right. I should know better than to read hor-ror books, or watch horror movies, because—this is not easy for a 42-year-old male to admit—I BELIEVE THEM. I have always believed them. When I was a child, I was routinely terrified by horror movies, even the comically inept ones where, when Lon Chaney turned into a werewolf, you could actually see the makeup person's hand darting into the picture to attach more fake fur to his face.

6   For years, after I saw "The Exorcist," I felt this need to be around priests. Friends would say, "What do you want to do tonight?" And I'd say, "Let's take in a Mass!"

7   I'm still this way, even though I'm a grown-up parent, constantly reassuring my son about his irrational fears, telling him don't be silly, there aren't any vampires in the guest bathroom. Part of my brain—the rational part, the part that took the SAT tests—actually believes this; but a much more powerful part, the Fear Lobe, takes the possibility of bathroom vampires far more seriously than it takes, for example, the U.S. trade deficit.

8   And so late at night, when I finish my horror novel and take the dogs out into the yard, which is very dark, I am highly alert. My brain's SAT Sector, trying to be cool, is saying, "Ha ha! This is merely your yard!" But the Fear Lobe is saying: "Oh, yes, this is exactly the kind of place that would attract The Brainsucker."

9   And so I start sauntering back toward the house, trying to look as casual as possible considering that every few feet I suddenly whirl around to see if anything's behind me. Soon I am sauntering at upwards of 35 miles per hour, and the Fear Lobe is screaming "IT'S COMING!" and even the SAT Sector has soaked its mental armpits and now I'm openly sprinting through the darkness, almost to the house, and WHAT'S THAT NOISE BEHIND ME OH NO PLEASE AAAIIIEEEE WHUMP I am struck violently in the back by Earnest, our Toyota-sized main dog, who has located a cache of valuable dog poo and shrewdly elected to roll in it, and is now generously attempting to share the experience with me.

10   Thus the spell of horror is broken, and my SAT Sector reasserts control and has a good laugh at what a silly goose I was, and I walk calmly back inside and close the door, just seconds before the tentacle reaches it.

QUESTIONS ON CONTENT, STRUCTURE, AND STYLE

1. What is Barry's purpose in writing this essay?

2. What is the general tone of this article? At what point did this tone become apparent to you?

3. How does Barry use exaggeration to create the article's tone? Cite some examples to illustrate your answer.

4. Consider Barry's discussion of "Marge." Why do you suppose he includes this specific scene? Why is this more humorous than a simple description of horror novels in general?

5. Does this essay have a stated thesis? If so, where? If not, does it need one?

6. Why does Barry include the detailed description of his excursion into the backyard?

7. Consider the "fear lobe" and the "SAT sector." Why does Barry use these terms instead of simply describing certain behaviors?

8. The article ends with Barry closing the door "just seconds before the tentacle reaches it." What does this tell the reader?

9. Barry's columns appear in a number of newspapers across the country. What specific audience might he have envisioned for this particular piece? Why?

10. Writers often poke fun at a subject to make a point. Do you agree with Barry's view of horror novels and films? Did you enjoy his humor or find it too absurd?

VOCABULARY

foreboding (2)	*sector (7)*	*cache (9)*
hallowed (4)	*lobe (7)*	*shrewdly (9)*
inept (5)	*sauntering (9)*	*elected (9)*

SUGGESTIONS FOR WRITING

1. Like Dave Barry, many people are drawn to horror novels and movies. If you, too, are a fan of horror, consider why. In a

well-developed essay, using your own experience as support, explain why so many people are fascinated by entertainment that
terrifies them.

2. Using Barry's essay as a model, write a humorous essay that tells of
   a time that you fell victim to your own horror-fed, over-active
   imagination and imagined lurking danger where there was none.

3. Some critics have argued that the public's insatiable appetite for horror novels and films is producing an increasingly hardened and violent society. In a persuasive essay, argue in opposition to or in
   support of this statement using your own experience, the experience of others, or past and present events as evidence for your claim.

Not Being There

ROGER EBERT

Nationally known film critic Roger Ebert started his career at the *Chicago
Sun-Times.* His syndicated movie reviews are now featured in over one
hundred newspapers. With his co-host Gene Siskel, Ebert has also presented film reviews on the television programs *Sneak Previews* (1977–
1982) and *At the Movies* (1982–present). He was awarded the Pulitzer
Prize for distinguished criticism in 1975 for his reviews and essays. This
essay appeared in the *Atlantic Monthly* in 1980.

1   LIKE MOST other people whose tastes began to form before television
became the dominant entertainment medium, I have a simple idea of
what it means to go to the movies. You buy your ticket and take a seat
in a large dark room with hundreds of strangers. You slide down in
your seat and make yourself comfortable. On the screen in front of
you, the movie image appears—enormous and overwhelming. If the
movie is a good one, you allow yourself to be absorbed in its fantasy,
and its dreams become part of your memories.

2   Television is not a substitute for that experience, and I have never
had a TV-watching experience of emotional intensity comparable to

my great movie-going experiences. Television is just not first class. The screen is too small. The image is technically inferior. The sound is disgracefully bad. As the viewer I can contain television—but the movies are so large they can contain me. I can't lose myself in a television image, and neither, I suspect, can most other people. That is why people are forever recreating movie memories in great detail, but hardly ever reminisce about old TV programs.

3   I believe, then, that to experience a movie fully you have to go to the movies. I enjoy television for other purposes, and my favorite TV programs are the live ones (sports, news, elections, talk shows), where immediacy helps compensate for the loss in intensity. Unlike a lot of movie buffs, I am not a fan of *The Late Show.* If a movie is good enough to stay up late for, it's too good to be watched through the dilution of television. I'll catch it later at a revival theater or a film society, or, if I never catch it again at least I'll think of it as a *movie* and not as late-night programming.

4   Maybe it's no wonder, then, that, with these personal biases, I was disturbed by some of the things I heard last March during a conference I went to in Colorado. The American Film Institute had taken over the Aspen Institute for three days, and invited forty-five people to gather for a discussion of the future of the feature film. By "feature film," they meant both theatrical and made-for-TV features, the latter including docudramas and TV miniseries.

5   The conference was weighted toward the TV people, among them executives of various pay-cable companies, and although several of us professed an interest in a discussion of content (that is, what movies are *about* these days), most of the talk was about "delivery" (how to sell television programming at a profit). What actually went out on the airwaves or cable systems would presumably take care of itself.

6   Many panelists' remarks were couched in a technological Newspeak that I had trouble understanding at first. *Software,* for example, was the word for TV programming—software to feed the hardware of our new home video entertainment centers. ("Software?" they said. "You know. That's a word for product." "Product?" I asked. "Yeah. Like a movie.") *Television consuming units* was another expression that gave me trouble until I realized it was a reference to human beings. *Windows* was a very interesting word. It referred to the various markets that a new movie could be sold to (or "shown through") once it was made. First there would be the theatrical window, a traditional booking in a

movie theater. Then came the network window—sale to commercial television. After that the windows came thick and fast: the pay-cable window, video cassette window, video disc window, airline in-flight window, and so on. In the hierarchy of these windows, the traditional practice of showing the movie in a theater seemed furthest from everybody's mind; the theatrical run was sort of a preliminary before the other markets could be carved up.

7   One of the enticing things about all the windows, I learned, was that a new movie could now be in the position of turning a profit before it was made. The pre-sales of subsidiary viewing rights would take the risk out of the initial investment.

8   The chilling thought occurred to me that, if a movie was already in profit, actually showing it in theaters could be risky because promotion, advertising, and overhead would be seen as liabilities instead of (in the traditional view) as an investment risk with a hope of profitable return. But no, I was assured, that was wrong. Movies would still have to play in theaters because the theatrical run "legitimized" them: they thus became "real" movies in the eyes of people buying them on cassettes or over pay cable.

9   Wonderful, I thought. The theatrical feature film, the most all-encompassing art form of the twentieth century, has been reduced to a necessary marketing preliminary for software.

10   If this was a pessimistic view, it was mild compared to some of the visions of the future held by the conference participants. An important TV writer-producer, one of the most likable people at the conference, calmly predicted that in ten years people would be sitting at home in front of their wall-size TV screens while (and I am indeed quoting) "marauding bands roam the streets." I thought he was joking, until he repeated the same phrase the next day.

11   What about going out to the movies? Another television executive said he used to go, but he had stopped. "You have to stand in line and be crowded in with all those people. And it's too expensive."

12   Well, apart from the fact that he could no doubt afford to buy a ticket for everyone in line, and that higher ticket prices only reflect general inflation, his view overlooked the fact that video cassettes and pay cable are at least as expensive as going out to the movies, especially when you consider the initial "hardware" investment. And for your money, you get to watch a TV image made up of dots arranged in 625 lines—an image that, even assuming your set has perfect adjustment

and color control, does not and cannot approach the quality of an image projected by light through celluloid.

13   But those technical considerations aside, why did this man and some of his colleagues have such a distaste for going out to the movies? I do it all the time. I feel it adds something to a movie-going experience to share it with other people. It's communal. A lot of the fun of seeing a movie such as *Jaws* or *Star Wars* comes, for me, from the massed emotion of the theater audience. When the shark attacks, we all levitate three inches above our seats, and come down screaming and laughing.

14   Watching *Jaws* on network TV isn't a remotely comparable experience. And watching a *comedy* in isolation can actually be a depressing experience. Our laughter during a movie comedy is an act of communication; an audience roaring with laughter is expressing its shared opinion about what's funny. I've watched comedies while I was alone in a room, and I've noticed that I don't laugh at all. Why should I? Who's to hear? And, perhaps because I don't laugh, those comedies don't seem as funny. Maybe it's essential to comedy that we're conscious of sharing it with other people; maybe, in human development, the first communication was a scream and the second was a laugh, and then they got around to words.

15   I made a modest proposal at Aspen. I suggested that some time and attention be given to perfecting cheaper and better home 16-mm movie projection systems, and that 16-mm rental and lending libraries be set up, like the Fotomat video cassette centers. I've gotten a lot of enjoyment out of 16-mm movie prints. The picture is larger, sharper, and brighter than television, so you can get a good idea of what the director had in mind. My suggestion was received with polite indifference, although, later, there was a lot of enthusiasm about reports that they're improving those giant-size TV screens you see in bars.

16   As anyone who has seen one knows, giant TV screens aren't the answer because they further dilute the already washed-out TV image. The TV signal has only 625 lines to contain its information no matter *how* large the screen is, and so a larger screen means a faded picture. TV retail outlets report that consumers seem to understand this, and that 17- and 19-inch sets are preferred to 21- and 24-inch screens because of the sharper image.

17   One evening over dinner, I finally got an interesting response to my suggestion about home 16-mm movie projectors. The problem with those, I was told, is that they can't be programmed by the pay-TV

systems. You sit in your own house operating your own projector, and the cable operators don't have access to it. They can't pipe their software into it and charge you for it. Why, you decide for yourself what and when to watch!

18   What is clearly happening is very alarming.

19   A superior system of technology—motion pictures—is being sold out in favor of an inferior but more profitable system—pay video hardware/software combinations. The theatrical motion picture, which remains such a desirable item that it's used to sell home cassette systems, is in danger of being held hostage. Truly daring and offbeat film subjects will become increasingly risky because they can't be easily presold for showing through other "windows."

20   The two edges that movies have enjoyed over television are greater quality and impact of image, and greater freedom of subject matter. Now television is poised to absorb and emasculate the movies, all in the name of home entertainment. It will serve us right, as we sit in front of our fuzzy giant-screen home video systems ten or twenty years from now, if there's nothing new or interesting to watch on them. Count me in with the marauding bands.

QUESTIONS ON CONTENT, STRUCTURE, AND STYLE

1. What is Ebert's thesis? Where is this most clearly stated?

2. What are the advantages of going to see a movie in a theater, according to Ebert?

3. What does Ebert believe is threatening the movie-going experience?

4. Ebert defines several terms he learned at the American Film Institute conference. Is his tone here the same as in the rest of the article? Why is Ebert disturbed by the conference proceedings?

5. Why, as Ebert discovers, do some people feel distaste for going to the movies? Do you agree with this view?

6. Ebert concludes his essay by noting that he will be part of "the marauding bands" ten to twenty years in the future. What is the significance of this reference and what point is he making?

7. Who is Ebert's intended audience? What response does he hope to evoke from his readers?

8. Do you agree with Ebert's view regarding the movie experience of the theater versus movies watched on television? Explain, using a specific example to illustrate your point.

9. The title of this essay is an allusion to a satirical novel by Jerzy Koszinski, *Being There;* this novel was made into a highly successful 1979 movie, starring Peter Sellers. It tells the story of a simple-minded gardener who only knows what he sees on television—and yet he rises to great political power and fame, adored by people who think he is brilliant. Why do you think Ebert chose his essay title? Does this title support Ebert's thesis?

10. What technological changes in the film-television entertainment field have occurred since Ebert wrote this essay? Do you think such changes are beneficial? Why/why not?

VOCABULARY

medium (1)	*enticing (7)*	*celluloid (12)*
immediacy (3)	*subsidiary (7)*	*communal (13)*
professed (5)	*legitimized (8)*	*dilute (16)*
hierarchy (6)	*marauding (10)*	*emasculate (20)*

SUGGESTIONS FOR WRITING

1. Write an essay that describes a time when you were "absorbed" by a theatrical experience (a movie or a live production of some kind). Does your experience support Ebert's views on the theater versus the home experience?

2. Write an essay that defines "a movie classic." Use a number of movies to illustrate your definition for your readers. Be sure that your essay avoids generalizations through use of many specific details.

3. It's been said that everyone is his or her own movie critic . . . and that same person is someone else's movie censor. If you could advise the movie industry, what would you tell them about today's films? Do they glorify or promote violence? Are they too simple-minded? Should the ratings system be revised? (Movie critic Michael Medved, for example, now argues that the PG-13 rating

should really be R-13 to give parents a clearer idea of certain films'
content.) Choose a topic and write an editorial addressing some
controversy in the film industry today.

Eating Poetry

MARK STRAND

From 1990 to 1993, Mark Strand served as America's Poet Laureate,
the youngest poet to hold this national honor. He now teaches at the
University of Utah as a professor of English. He has published eight collections of poetry, three children's books, and is a translator of Spanish
literature. A recent book of poetry is *The Continuous Life* (1990). This
poem originally appeared in the *New York Review of Books*.

Ink runs from the corners of my mouth.
There is no happiness like mine.
I have been eating poetry.

The librarian does not believe what she sees.
5 Her eyes are sad
and she walks with her hands in her dress.

The poems are gone.
The light is dim.
The dogs are on the basement stairs and coming up.

10 Their eyeballs roll,
their blond legs burn like brush.
The poor librarian begins to stamp her feet and weep.

She does not understand.
15 When I get on my knees and lick her hand,
she screams.

I am a new man.
I snarl at her and bark.
I romp with joy in the bookish dark.

QUESTIONS ON CONTENT, STRUCTURE, AND STYLE

1. Describe the person speaking in this poem. Is the person happy? Sad? Pensive? Depressed? What has he been doing?

2. Where does the action described in this poem take place?

3. What does the speaker mean when he says, "I have been eating poetry"? Why does the poet use "eating" imagery?

4. Contrast the speaker to the other person mentioned in the poem. How is she presented? Why are we told about her hands?

5. Contrast the speaker and the woman's reactions to the animals introduced in the poem. What do their responses tell you about these people?

6. What does the woman "not understand"?

7. The speaker declares he is a "new man." What has made him so?

8. What images characterize the speaker as an animal? Why does he undergo such a transformation?

9. What image does the phrase "bookish dark" conjure up for you? Why didn't the poet simply say "in the dark rows of books" or in the "dark room full of books"?

10. Is this poem about a man becoming a werewolf—or something else? Summarize what feeling you think the poet was trying to communicate in this poem and why he chose certain images to describe this feeling.

VOCABULARY

romp (line 18)

SUGGESTIONS FOR WRITING

1. Strand's poem expresses the great joy of reading poetry. Have you ever read something—a poem, novel, story, play, or work of nonfiction—that gave you great pleasure, changed your opinion, or affected your life in an important way? Write an essay explaining how the reading selection affected you as it did.

2. Think of a character from a poem or piece of fiction with whom you identify closely. Select two or three words that describe that person's character, and write an essay explaining why you share, admire, or identify with those values or traits.

3. Imagine that a close friend has asked you for a short reading list to take on a long ocean voyage. Select three to five of your favorite books, and explain in some detail why you would choose them. Do these books share a common theme? A type of hero or heroine that you admire? In addition to producing a list for your friend, use this essay to learn something valuable about yourself.

The Secret Life of Walter Mitty

JAMES THURBER

James Thurber was a famous American humorist who created numerous stories, sketches, cartoons, fables, and essays, often satirizing the relationship between men and women. His books include *My Life and Hard Times* (1933), *Fables for Our Time* (1943), *The Thurber Carnival* (1945), and *Thurber Country* (1953). This story appeared in *My World—and Welcome to It* (1942).

1   "WE'RE GOING through!" The Commander's voice was like thin ice breaking. He wore his full-dress uniform, with the heavily braided white cap pulled down rakishly over one cold gray eye. "We can't make it, sir. It's spoiling for a hurricane, if you ask me." "I'm not asking you, Lieutenant Berg," said the Commander. "Throw on the power lights! Rev her up to 8,500! We're going through!" The pounding of the cylinders increased; ta-pocketa-pocketa-pocketa-*pocketa-pocketa*. The Commander stared at the ice forming on the pilot window. He walked over and twisted a row of complicated dials. "Switch on No. 8 auxiliary!" he shouted. "Switch on No. 8 auxiliary!" repeated Lieutenant Berg. "Full strength in No. 3 turret!" shouted the Commander. "Full strength in No. 3 turret!" The crew, bending to their various tasks in the huge, hurtling eight-engined Navy hydroplane, looked at each other and

grinned. "The Old Man'll get us through," they said to one another. "The Old Man ain't afraid of Hell!" . . .

2   "Not so fast! You're driving too fast!" said Mrs. Mitty. "What are you driving so fast for?"

3   "Hmm?" said Walter Mitty. He looked at his wife, in the seat beside him, with shocked astonishment. She seemed grossly unfamiliar, like a strange woman who had yelled at him in a crowd. "You were up to fifty-five," she said. "You know I don't like to go more than forty. You were up to fifty-five." Walter Mitty drove on toward Waterbury in silence, the roaring of the SN202 through the worst storm in twenty years of Navy flying fading in the remote, intimate airways of his mind. "You're tensed up again," said Mrs. Mitty. "It's one of your days. I wish you'd let Dr. Renshaw look you over."

4   Walter Mitty stopped the car in front of the building where his wife went to have her hair done. "Remember to get those overshoes while I'm having my hair done," she said. "I don't need overshoes," said Mitty. She put her mirror back into her bag. "We've been all through that," she said, getting out of the car. "You're not a young man any longer." He raced the engine a little. "Why don't you wear your gloves? Have you lost your gloves?" Walter Mitty reached in a pocket and brought out the gloves. He put them on, but after she had turned and gone into the building and he had driven on to a red light, he took them off again. "Pick it up, brother," snapped a cop as the light changed, and Mitty hastily pulled on his gloves and lurched ahead. He drove around the streets aimlessly for a time, and then he drove past the hospital on his way to the parking lot.

5   . . ."It's the millionaire banker, Wellington McMillan," said the pretty nurse. "Yes?" said Walter Mitty, removing his gloves slowly. "Who has the case?" "Dr. Renshaw and Dr. Benbow, but there are two specialists here, Dr. Remington from New York and Dr. Pritchard-Mitford from London. He flew over." A door opened down a long, cool corridor and Dr. Renshaw came out. He looked distraught and haggard. "Hello, Mitty," he said. "We're having the devil's own time with McMillan, the millionaire banker and close personal friend of Roosevelt. Obstreosis of the ductal tract.[1] Tertiary. Wish you'd take a look at him." "Glad to," said Mitty.

[1] Obstreosis is a disease found mainly in pigs and cattle.

6   In the operating room there were whispered introductions: "Dr. Remington, Dr. Mitty. Dr. Pritchard-Mitford, Dr. Mitty." "I've read your book on streptothricosis," said Pritchard-Mitford, shaking hands. "A brilliant performance, sir." "Thank you," said Walter Mitty. "Didn't know you were in the states, Mitty," grumbled Remington. "Coals to Newcastle, bringing Mitford and me up here for a tertiary." "You are very kind," said Mitty. A huge, complicated machine, connected to the operating table, with many tubes and wires, began at this moment to go pocketa-pocketa-pocketa. "The new anaesthetizer is giving away!" shouted an intern. "There is no one in the East who knows how to fix it!" "Quiet, man!" said Mitty, in a low, cool voice. He sprang to the machine, which was now going pocketa-pocketa-queep-pocketa-queep. He began fingering delicately a row of glistening dials. "Give me a fountain pen!" he snapped. Someone handed him a fountain pen. He pulled a faulty piston out of the machine and inserted the pen in its place. "That will hold for ten minutes," he said. "Get on with the operation." A nurse hurried over and whispered to Renshaw, and Mitty saw the man turn pale. "Coreopsis has set in,"[2] said Renshaw nervously. "If you would take over, Mitty?" Mitty looked at him and at the craven figure of Benbow, who drank, and at the grave, uncertain faces of the two great specialists. "If you wish," he said. They slipped a white gown on him; he adjusted a mask and drew on thin gloves; nurses handed him shining . . .

7   "Back it up, Mac! Look out for that Buick!" Walter Mitty jammed on the brakes. "Wrong lane, Mac," said the parking-lot attendant, looking at Mitty closely. "Gee. Yeh," muttered Mitty. He began cautiously to back out of the lane marked "Exit Only." "Leave her sit there," said the attendant. "I'll put her away." Mitty got out of the car. "Hey, better leave the key." "Oh," said Mitty, handing the man the ignition key. The attendant vaulted into the car, backed it up with insolent skill, and put it where it belonged.

8   They're so damn cocky, thought Walter Mitty, walking along Main Street; they think they know everything. Once he had tried to take his chains off, outside New Milford, and he had got them wound around the axles. A man had had to come out in a wrecking car and unwind them, a young, grinning garage man. Since then Mrs. Mitty always made him drive to a garage to have the chains taken off. The

[2] Coreopsis is a plant, not a disease.

next time, he thought, I'll wear my right arm in a sling; they won't grin at me then. I'll have my right arm in a sling and they'll see I couldn't possibly take the chains off myself. He kicked at the slush on the sidewalk. "Overshoes," he said to himself, and he began looking for a shoe store.

9   When he came out into the street again, with the overshoes in a box under his arm, Walter Mitty began to wonder what the other thing was his wife had told him to get. She had told him, twice before they set out from their house for Waterbury. In a way he hated these weekly trips to town—he was always getting something wrong. Kleenex, he thought, Squibb's, razor blades? No. Toothpaste, toothbrush, bicarbonate, carborundum, initiative and referendum? He gave it up. But she would remember it. "Where's the what's-its-name?" she would ask. "Don't tell me you forgot the what's-its-name." A newsboy went by shouting something about the Waterbury trial.

10   . . ."Perhaps this will refresh your memory." The District Attorney suddenly thrust a heavy automatic at the quiet figure on the witness stand. "Have you ever seen this before?" Walter Mitty took the gun and examined it expertly. "This is my Webley-Vickers 50.80," he said calmly. An excited buzz ran around the courtroom. The judge rapped for order. "You are a crack shot with any sort of firearms, I believe?" said the District Attorney, insinuatingly. "Objection!" shouted Mitty's attorney. "We have shown that the defendant could not have fired the shot. We have shown that he wore his right arm in a sling on the night of the fourteenth of July." Walter Mitty raised his hand briefly and the bickering attorneys were stilled. "With any known make of gun," he said evenly, "I could have killed Gregory Fitzhurst at three hundred feet *with my left hand.*" Pandemonium broke loose in the courtroom. A woman's scream rose above the bedlam and suddenly a lovely, dark-haired girl was in Walter Mitty's arms. The District Attorney struck at her savagely. Without rising from his chair, Mitty let the man have it on the point of the chin. "You miserable cur!" . . .

11   "Puppy biscuit," said Walter Mitty. He stopped walking and the buildings of Waterbury rose up out of the misty courtroom and surrounded him again. A woman who was passing laughed. "He said 'Puppy biscuit,'" she said to her companion. "That man said 'Puppy biscuit' to himself." Walter Mitty hurried on. He went into an A & P, not the first one he came to but a smaller one farther up the street. "I want some biscuit for small, young dogs," he said to the clerk. "Any special brand, sir?" The

greatest pistol shot in the world thought a moment. "It says 'Puppies Bark for It' on the box," said Walter Mitty.

12   His wife would be through at the hairdresser's in fifteen minutes, Mitty saw in looking at his watch, unless they had trouble drying it; sometimes they had trouble drying it. She didn't like to get to the hotel first; she would want him to be there waiting for her as usual. He found a big leather chair in the lobby, facing a window, and he put the overshoes and the puppy biscuit on the floor beside it. He picked up an old copy of *Liberty* and sank down into the chair. "Can Germany Conquer the World through the Air?" Walter Mitty looked at the pictures of bombing planes and of ruined streets.

13   . . ."The cannonading has got the wind up in young Raleigh, sir," said the sergeant. Captain Mitty looked up at him through tousled hair. "Get him to bed," he said wearily, "with the others. I'll fly alone." "But you can't, sir," said the sergeant anxiously. "It takes two men to handle that bomber and the Archies are pounding hell out of the air. Von Richtman's circus is between here and Saulier." "Somebody's got to get that ammunition dump," said Mitty. "I'm going over. Spot of brandy?" He poured a drink for the sergeant and one for himself. War thundered and whined around the dugout and battered at the door. There was a rending of wood and splinters flew through the room. "A bit of a near thing," said Captain Mitty carelessly. "The box barrage is closing in," said the sergeant. "We only live once, sergeant," said Mitty, with his faint, fleeting smile. "Or do we?" He poured another brandy and tossed it off. "I never see a man could hold his brandy like you, sir," said the sergeant. "Begging your pardon, sir." Captain Mitty stood up and strapped on his huge Webley-Vickers automatic. "It's forty kilometers through hell, sir," said the sergeant. Mitty finished one last brandy. "After all," he said softly, "what isn't?" The pounding of the cannon increased; there was the rat-tat-tatting of machine guns, and from somewhere came the menacing pocketa-pocketa-pocketa of the new flame-throwers. Walter Mitty walked to the door of the dugout humming "Auprès de Ma Blonde." He turned and waved to the sergeant. "Cheerio!" he said. . . .

14   Something struck his shoulder. "I've been looking all over this hotel for you," said Mrs. Mitty. "Why do you have to hide in this old chair? How did you expect me to find you?" "Things close in," said Walter Mitty vaguely. "What?" Mrs. Mitty said. "Did you get the what's-its-name? The puppy biscuit? What's in that box?" "Overshoes," said Mitty.

"Couldn't you have put them on in the store?" "I was thinking," said Walter Mitty. "Does it ever occur to you that I am sometimes thinking?" She looked at him. "I'm going to take your temperature when I get you home," she said.

15   They went out through the revolving doors that made a faintly derisive whistling sound when you pushed them. It was two blocks to the parking lot. At the drugstore on the corner she said, "Wait here for me. I forgot something. I won't be a minute." She was more than a minute. Walter Mitty lighted a cigarette. It began to rain, rain with sleet in it. He stood up against the wall of the drugstore, smoking. . . . He put his shoulders back and his heels together. "To hell with the handkerchief," said Walter Mitty scornfully. He took one last drag on his cigarette and snapped it away. Then, with that faint, fleeting smile playing about his lips, he faced the firing squad, erect and motionless, proud and disdainful, Walter Mitty the Undefeated, inscrutable to the last.

Questions on Content, Structure, and Style

1. What kind of daydreams does Mitty have? Why?

2. Is there a "hero" in this story? A villain? Neither? Both?

3. What evidence is there that Mitty is dominated by people other than his wife?

4. Is this story meant to be funny or tragic? A comedy or a satire? Defend your answer.

5. What are the probable sources of Mitty's fantasies? What kinds of clichés do you see?

6. How does each fantasy arise?

7. What pieces of misinformation does Mitty incorporate into his fantasies?

8. How does Thurber use repetition for comic effect throughout Mitty's fantasies?

9. In what way is Mitty "Undefeated, inscrutable to the last"?

10. This story was published in 1942. Do you think Mitty's fantasies still flourish? Do any Walter Mittys exist today?

VOCABULARY

turret (1)	*tertiary (5)*	*derisive (15)*
distraught (5)	*carborundum (9)*	*disdainful (15)*
haggard (5)	*insinuatingly (10)*	*inscrutable (15)*

SUGGESTIONS FOR WRITING

1. In your leisure time how do you daydream yourself? As a rock star? As President? As a millionaire on your yacht? What does your favorite fantasy reveal about you and your goals in life? Is your favorite fantasy merely comic relief or is it a future you hope to attain? Write an essay describing and analyzing your favorite daydream.

2. Write a humorous essay or story describing the fantasies of a struggling college student, an aspiring politician, a second-rate actor, a crass yuppie, or some other figure worthy of satire. Try using some of Thurber's comical techniques. Be sure that your essay makes a satirical point about the personality or values of the character you select.

3. Thurber is well known for his essays and cartoons that comment on the "battle of the sexes." What aspects of male-female relationships does Thurber satirize in this story? Do you agree that his portrayal of Mitty and his wife contains some elements of truth about men and women? In your essay compare or contrast your views to those of Thurber's.

EDUCATION:
TEACHING AND LEARNING

The Teacher Who Changed My Life

NICHOLAS GAGE

Born in Greece in 1939, journalist and author Nicholas Gage is best-known for *Eleni* (1983), the story of his mother's life and execution in 1948 during the Greek civil war. The story of this murder and Gage's subsequent search for her killers was made into a well-received movie in 1985. The story of Gage's father, *A Place for Us* (1989), contains a version of the following essay, which also appeared in *Parade Magazine*.

1   THE PERSON who set the course of my life in the new land I entered as a young war refugee—who, in fact, nearly dragged me onto the path that would bring all the blessings I've received in America—was a salty-tongued, no-nonsense schoolteacher named Marjorie Hurd. When I entered her classroom in 1953, I had been to six schools in five years, starting in the Greek village where I was born in 1939.

2   When I stepped off a ship in New York Harbor on a gray March day in 1949, I was an undersized nine-year-old in short pants who had lost his mother and was coming to live with the father he didn't know. My mother, Eleni Gatzoyiannis, had been imprisoned, tortured, and shot by Communist guerrillas for sending me and three of my four sisters to freedom. She died so that her children could go to their father in the United States.

3   The portly, bald, well-dressed man who met me and my sisters seemed a foreign, authoritarian figure. I secretly resented him for not getting the whole family out of Greece early enough to save my mother. Ultimately, I would grow to love him and appreciate how he dealt with becoming a single parent at the age of fifty-six, but at first our relationship was prickly, full of hostility.

4   As Father drove us to our new home—a tenement in Worcester, Mass.—and pointed out the huge brick building that would be our first school in America, I clutched my Greek notebooks from the refugee camp, hoping that my few years of schooling would impress my teachers in this cold, crowded country. They didn't. When my father led me and my eleven-year-old sister to Greendale Elementary School, the grim-faced Yankee principal put the two of us in a class for the mentally retarded. There was no facility in those days for non-English-speaking children.

159

5   By the time I met Marjorie Hurd four years later, I had learned English, been placed in a normal, graded class and had even been chosen for
the college preparatory track in the Worcester public school system.
I was thirteen years old when our father moved us yet again, and I entered Chandler Junior High shortly after the beginning of seventh
grade. I found myself surrounded by richer, smarter, and better-dressed
classmates who looked askance at my strange clothes and heavy accent.
Shortly after I arrived, we were told to select a hobby to pursue during
"club hour" on Fridays. The idea of hobbies and clubs made no sense to
my immigrant ears, but I decided to follow the prettiest girl in my
class—the blue-eyed daughter of the local Lutheran minister. She led
me through the door marked "Newspaper Club" and into the presence of
Miss Hurd, the newspaper adviser and English teacher who would become my mentor and my muse.

6   A formidable, solidly built woman with salt-and-pepper hair, a steely
eye, and a flat Boston accent, Miss Hurd had no patience with layabouts.
"What are all you goof-offs doing here?" she bellowed at the would-be
journalists. "This is the Newspaper Club! We're going to put out a *newspaper*. So if there's anybody in this room who doesn't like work, I suggest
you go across to the Glee Club now, because you're going to work your
tails off here!"

7   I was soon under Miss Hurd's spell. She did indeed teach us to put
out a newspaper, skills I honed during my next twenty-five years as a
journalist. Soon I asked the principal to transfer me to her English class
as well. There, she drilled us on grammar until I finally began to understand the logic and structure of the English language. She assigned stories for us to read and discuss; not tales of heroes, like the Greek myths
I knew, but stories of underdogs—poor people, even immigrants, who
seemed ordinary until a crisis drove them to do something extraordinary. She also introduced us to the literary wealth of Greece—giving
me a new perspective on my war-ravaged, impoverished homeland. I began to be proud of my origins.

8   One day, after discussing how writers should write about what
they know, she assigned us to compose an essay from our own experience. Fixing me with a stern look, she added, "Nick, I want you to
write about what happened to your family in Greece." I had been trying to put those painful memories behind me and left the assignment
until the last moment. Then, on a warm spring afternoon, I sat in my

room with a yellow pad and pencil and stared out the window at the buds on the trees. I wrote that the coming of spring always reminded me of the last time I said goodbye to my mother on a green and gold day in 1948.

9   I kept writing, one line after another, telling how the Communist guerrillas occupied our village, took our home and food, how my mother started planning our escape when she learned that children were to be sent to re-education camps behind the Iron Curtain, and how, at the last moment, she couldn't escape with us because the guerrillas sent her with a group of women to thresh wheat in a distant village. She promised she would try to get away on her own, she told me to be brave and hung a silver cross around my neck, and then she kissed me. I watched the line of women being led down into the ravine and up the other side, until they disappeared around the bend—my mother a tiny brown figure at the end who stopped for an instant to raise her hand in one last farewell.

10   I wrote about our nighttime escape down the mountain, across the minefields, and into the lines of the Nationalist soldiers, who sent us to a refugee camp. It was there that we learned of our mother's execution. I felt very lucky to have come to America, I concluded, but every year, the coming of spring made me feel sad because it reminded me of the last time I saw my mother.

11   I handed in the essay, hoping never to see it again, but Miss Hurd had it published in the school paper. This mortified me at first, until I saw that my classmates reacted with sympathy and tact to my family's story. Without telling me, Miss Hurd also submitted the essay to a contest sponsored by the Freedoms Foundation at Valley Forge, and it won a medal. The Worcester paper wrote about the award and quoted my essay at length. My father, by then a "five-and-dime-store chef," as the paper described him, was ecstatic with pride, and the Worcester Greek community celebrated the honor to one of its own.

12   For the first time, I began to understand the power of the written word. A secret ambition took root in me. One day, I vowed, I would go back to Greece, find out the details of my mother's death, and write about her life, so her grandchildren would know of her courage. Perhaps I would even track down the men who killed her and write of their crimes. Fulfilling that ambition would take me thirty years.

13   Meanwhile, I followed the literary path that Miss Hurd had so forcefully set me on. After junior high, I became the editor of my school

paper at Classical High School and got a part-time job at the Worcester *Telegram and Gazette*. Although my father could only give me $50 and encouragement toward a college education, I managed to finance four years at Boston University with scholarships and part-time jobs in journalism. During my last year of college, an article I wrote about a friend who had died in the Philippines—the first person to lose his life working for the Peace Corps—led to my winning the Hearst Award for College Journalism. And the plaque was given to me in the White House by President John F. Kennedy.

14   For a refugee who had never seen a motorized vehicle or indoor plumbing until he was nine, this was an unimaginable honor. When the Worcester paper ran a picture of me standing next to President Kennedy, my father rushed out to buy a new suit in order to be properly dressed to receive the congratulations of the Worcester Greeks. He clipped out the photograph, had it laminated in plastic, and carried it in his breast pocket for the rest of his life to show everyone he met. I found the much-worn photo in his pocket on the day he died twenty years later.

15   In our isolated Greek village, my mother had bribed a cousin to teach her to read, for girls were not supposed to attend school beyond a certain age. She had always dreamed of her children receiving an education. She couldn't be there when I graduated from Boston University, but the person who came with my father and shared our joy was my former teacher, Marjorie Hurd. We celebrated not only my bachelor's degree but also the scholarships that paid my way to Columbia's Graduate School of Journalism. There, I met the woman who would eventually become my wife. At our wedding and at the baptisms of our three children, Marjorie Hurd was always there, dancing alongside the Greeks.

16   By then, she was Mrs. Rabidou, for she had married a widower when she was in her early forties. That didn't distract her from her vocation of introducing young minds to English literature, however. She taught for a total of forty-one years and continually would make a "project" of some balky student in whom she spied a spark of potential. Often these were students from the most troubled homes, yet she would alternately bully and charm each one with her own special brand of tough love until the spark caught fire. She retired in 1981 at the age of sixty-two but still avidly follows the lives and careers of former students while

overseeing her adult stepchildren and driving her husband on camping trips to New Hampshire.

17   Miss Hurd was one of the first to call me on December 10, 1987, when President Reagan, in his television address after the summit meeting with Gorbachev, told the nation that Eleni Gatzoyiannis's dying cry, "My children!" had helped inspire him to seek an arms agreement "for all the children of the world."

18   "I can't imagine a better monument for your mother," Miss Hurd said with an uncharacteristic catch in her voice.

19   Although a bad hip makes it impossible for her to join in the Greek dancing, Marjorie Hurd Rabidou is still an honored and enthusiastic guest at all our family celebrations, including my fiftieth birthday picnic last summer, where the shish kebab was cooked on spits, clarinets and *bouzoukis* wailed, and costumed dancers led the guests in a serpentine line around our Colonial farmhouse, only twenty minutes from my first home in Worcester.

20   My sisters and I felt an aching void because my father was not there to lead the line, balancing a glass of wine on his head while he danced, the way he did at every celebration during his ninety-two years. But Miss Hurd was there, surveying the scene with quiet satisfaction. Although my parents are gone, her presence was a consolation, because I owe her so much.

21   This is truly the land of opportunity, and I would have enjoyed its bounty even if I hadn't walked into Miss Hurd's classroom in 1953. But she was the one who directed my grief and pain into writing, and if it weren't for her I wouldn't have become an investigative reporter and foreign correspondent, recorded the story of my mother's life and death in *Eleni* and now my father's story in *A Place for Us,* which is also a testament to the country that took us in. She was the catalyst that sent me into journalism and indirectly caused all the good things that came after. But Miss Hurd would probably deny this emphatically.

22   A few years ago, I answered the telephone and heard my former teacher's voice telling me, in that won't-take-no-for-an-answer tone of hers, that she had decided I was to write and deliver the eulogy at her funeral. I agreed (she didn't leave me any choice), but that's one assignment I never want to do. I hope, Miss Hurd, that you'll accept this remembrance instead.

QUESTIONS ON CONTENT, STRUCTURE, AND STYLE

1. What is Gage's stated purpose in writing this essay? Are there other purposes as well?

2. According to Gage, what was Miss Hurd's greatest gift to him?

3. Gage's narrative covers many years—nearly his lifetime, in fact. Why is this broad span of time important to his message?

4. What key scene best captures the essence of Gage's regard for Miss Hurd and her impact on his life? Explain your choice.

5. Are there any details given that are not vital to the central idea of the essay? Explain your selections.

6. Often, a component of effective writing is vivid description. Choose two examples of effective description and indicate two sections of the essay where the reader might want more descriptive detail.

7. There are two important uses of dialogue in this essay. Find these sections and explain why Gage may have chosen to emphasize these particular moments, rather than others, with dialogue.

8. Consider Gage's use of transitions between paragraphs, listing examples of smooth transitions and noting those that are more abrupt.

9. The success of an essay can be judged by its impact on its readers. What specific audience would most benefit from Gage's piece? Why?

10. Gage uses several examples of Miss Hurd's behavior to illustrate her character. What traits emerge in the following paragraphs: 6, 8, 11, 15, 16, 17 and 18, 22? Why is this a more effective way of revealing her character to the reader than simply telling the audience what she was like?

VOCABULARY

refugee (1)

portly (3)

layabouts (6)

honed (7)

Iron Curtain (9)

mortified (11)

balky (16)

serpentine (19)

void (20)

bounty (21)

testament (21)

catalyst (21)

emphatically (21)

eulogy (22)

SUGGESTIONS FOR WRITING

1. Consider your own teachers. Like Gage, have you had a teacher that changed your life? Changed your goals? Changed your view of yourself? Write an essay showing your readers the impact that one teacher has had on you. Use specific examples to reveal how this person affected you.

2. Gage writes of two awards received as a young man that helped solidify his career choice. Have you ever received—or not received—an award that changed your goals as a result? Describe this incident in a well-detailed essay.

3. In paragraphs 4 and 5 Gage presents a vivid portrait of himself as an outsider in a new system—a system that he does not understand and that does not understand him. Choose a time in your life when you felt isolated in this way and describe the incident in an essay that might help others in a similar situation.

Shame

DICK GREGORY

Dick Gregory is a civil-rights activist who also directs health and nutrition programs. He is the author of a number of books, including *The Shadow That Scares Me* (1971), *Dick Gregory's Political Primer* (1971), and *Dick Gregory's Bible Tales* (1978). This narrative is taken from *nigger: An Autobiography* (1964).

1   I NEVER learned hate at home, or shame. I had to go to school for that. I was about seven years old when I got my first big lesson. I was in love with a little girl named Helene Tucker, a light-complected little girl with pigtails and nice manners. She was always clean and she was smart in school. I think I went to school mostly to look at her. I brushed my hair and even got me a little old handkerchief. It was a lady's handkerchief, but I didn't want Helene to see me wipe my nose on my hand. The pipes were frozen again, there was no water in the house, but I

washed my socks and shirt every night. I'd get a pot, and go over to Mr. Ben's grocery store, and stick my pot down into his soda machine. Scoop out some chopped ice. By evening the ice melted to water for washing. I got sick a lot that winter because the fire would go out at night before the clothes were dry. In the morning I'd put them on, wet or dry, because they were the only clothes I had.

2   Everybody's got a Helene Tucker, a symbol of everything you want. I loved her for her goodness, her cleanliness, her popularity. She'd walk down my street and my brothers and sisters would yell, "Here comes Helene," and I'd rub my tennis sneakers on the back of my pants and wish my hair wasn't so nappy and the white folks' shirt fit me better. I'd run out on the street. If I knew my place and didn't come too close, she'd wink at me and say hello. That was a good feeling. Sometimes I'd follow her all the way home, and shovel the snow off her walk and try to make friends with her Momma and her aunts. I'd drop money on her stoop late at night on my way back from shining shoes in the taverns. And she had a Daddy, and he had a good job. He was a paper hanger.

3   I guess I would have gotten over Helene by summertime, but something happened in that classroom that made her face hang in front of me for the next twenty-two years. When I played the drums in high school it was for Helene and when I broke track records in college it was for Helene and when I started standing behind microphones and heard applause I wished Helene could hear it, too. It wasn't until I was twenty-nine years old and married and making money that I really got her out of my system. Helene was sitting in that classroom when I learned to be ashamed of myself.

4   It was on a Thursday. I was sitting in the back of the room, in a seat with a chalk circle drawn around it. The idiot's seat, the trouble-maker's seat.

5   The teacher thought I was stupid. Couldn't spell, couldn't read, couldn't do arithmetic. Just stupid. Teachers were never interested in finding out that you couldn't concentrate because you were so hungry, because you hadn't had any breakfast. All you could think about was noontime, would it ever come? Maybe you could sneak into the cloak-room and steal a bite of some kid's lunch out of a coat pocket. A bite of something. Paste. You can't really make a meal out of paste, or put it on bread for a sandwich, but sometimes I'd scoop a few spoonfuls out of the paste jar in the back of the room. Pregnant people get strange tastes. I was pregnant with poverty. Pregnant with dirt and pregnant

with smells that made people turn away, pregnant with cold and pregnant with shoes that were never bought for me, pregnant with five other people in my bed and no Daddy in the next room, and pregnant with hunger. Paste doesn't taste too bad when you're hungry.

6   The teacher thought I was a troublemaker. All she saw from the front of the room was a little black boy who squirmed in his idiot's seat and made noises and poked the kids around him. I guess she couldn't see a kid who made noises because he wanted someone to know he was there.

7   It was on a Thursday, the day before the Negro payday. The eagle always flew on Friday. The teacher was asking each student how much his father would give to the Community Chest. On Friday night, each kid would get the money from his father, and on Monday he would bring it to the school. I decided I was going to buy me a Daddy right then. I had money in my pocket from shining shoes and selling papers, and whatever Helene Tucker pledged for her Daddy I was going to top it. And I'd hand the money right in. I wasn't going to wait until Monday to buy me a Daddy.

8   I was shaking, scared to death. The teacher opened her book and started calling out names alphabetically.

9   "Helene Tucker?"

10   "My Daddy said he'd give two dollars and fifty cents."

11   "That's very nice, Helene. Very, very nice indeed."

12   That made me feel pretty good. It wouldn't take too much to top that. I had almost three dollars in dimes and quarters in my pocket. I stuck my hand in my pocket and held onto the money, waiting for her to call my name. But the teacher closed her book after she called everybody else in the class.

13   I stood up and raised my hand.

14   "What is it now?"

15   "You forgot me."

16   She turned toward the blackboard. "I don't have time to be playing with you, Richard."

17   "My Daddy said he'd . . ."

18   "Sit down, Richard, you're disturbing the class."

19   "My Daddy said he'd give . . . fifteen dollars."

20   She turned and looked mad. "We are collecting this money for you and your kind, Richard Gregory. If your Daddy can give fifteen dollars you have no business being on relief."

21   "I got it right now, I got it right now, my Daddy gave it to me to turn in today, my Daddy said . . ."

22   "And furthermore," she said, looking right at me, her nostrils getting big and her lips getting thin and her eyes opening wide, "we know you don't have a Daddy."

23   Helene Tucker turned around, her eyes full of tears. She felt sorry for me. Then I couldn't see her too well because I was crying, too.

24   "Sit down, Richard."

25   And I always thought the teacher kind of liked me. She always picked me to wash the blackboard on Friday, after school. That was a big thrill, it made me feel important. If I didn't wash it, come Monday the school might not function right.

26   "Where are you going, Richard?"

27   I walked out of school that day, and for a long time I didn't go back very often. There was shame there.

28   Now there was shame everywhere. It seemed like the whole world had been inside that classroom, everyone had heard what the teacher had said, everyone had turned around and felt sorry for me. There was shame in going to the Worthy Boys Annual Christmas Dinner for you and your kind, because everybody knew what a worthy boy was. Why couldn't they just call it the Boys Annual Dinner, why'd they have to give it a name? There was shame in wearing the brown and orange and white plaid mackinaw the welfare gave to 3,000 boys. Why'd it have to be the same for everybody so when you walked down the street the people could see you were on relief? It was a nice warm mackinaw and it had a hood, and my Momma beat me and called me a little rat when she found out I stuffed it in the bottom of a pail full of garbage way over on Cottage Street. There was shame in running over to Mister Ben's at the end of the day and asking for his rotten peaches, there was shame in asking Mrs. Simmons for a spoonful of sugar, there was shame in running out to meet the relief truck. I hated that truck, full of food for you and your kind. I ran into the house and hid when it came. And then I started to sneak through alleys, to take the long way home so the people going into White's Eat Shop wouldn't see me. Yeah, the whole world heard the teacher that day, we all know you don't have a Daddy.

QUESTIONS ON CONTENT, STRUCTURE, AND STYLE

1. What is Gregory's purpose in telling this story? Where does his purpose first become clear to you?

2. For Gregory, who was Helene Tucker and why did her face remain in his memory for so long?

3. Are the events of this story told in strict chronological order? If not, where are the deviations and why are they included?

4. Does Gregory use enough vivid details to help his readers visualize the people and events of his narrative? Support your answer by citing some specific examples.

5. Which characters are most developed in this story? How does Gregory help his readers understand his characters' motivations?

6. What does the use of dialogue add to this story?

7. What are the effects of the parallel constructions that appear in paragraphs 5 and 28?

8. Point out several examples of slang and colloquial language in this story; why did Gregory use such language?

9. Evaluate the effectiveness of Gregory's conclusion.

10. Describe Gregory's "voice" in this narrative. Did you find the author's tone sincere or too full of self-pity?

VOCABULARY

nappy (2)
pregnant (5)
mackinaw (28)

SUGGESTIONS FOR WRITING

1. Write an essay describing the worst (or best) experience you ever had in school. Make your narrative as vivid as Gregory's.

2. School teaches us many "lessons" not contained in texts or lectures. Select one lesson about life you learned in school and write an essay—humorous or serious—about the way you discovered the "truth" about something important.

3. Sometimes as we look back, the teachers or courses we may have once complained bitterly about now don't seem so bad; for instance, a tough high school instructor may have actually done you a

favor by preparing you for a difficult college requirement. Write a then-and-now essay, one that contrasts your earlier opinion of a teacher or a course with the more mature view you hold today.

Teach Diversity—with a Smile

BARBARA EHRENREICH

Barbara Ehrenreich is an editor, writer, and political activist. Her essays on contemporary culture, women's issues, and social history have appeared in numerous publications including *The Nation, Time, New York Times, Esquire,* and *Mother Jones.* She is the coauthor of five books and the author of *The Hearts of Men: American Dreams and the Flight from Commitment* (1983). This essay originally appeared in *Time* magazine in 1991.

1 SOMETHING HAD to replace the threat of communism, and at last a workable substitute is at hand. "Multiculturalism," as the new menace is known, has been denounced in the media recently as the new McCarthyism, the new fundamentalism, even the new totalitarianism—take your choice. According to its critics, who include a flock of tenured conservative scholars, multiculturalism aims to toss out what it sees as the Eurocentric bias in education and replace Plato with Ntozake Shange and traditional math with the Yoruba number system. And that's just the beginning. The Jacobins of the multiculturalist movement, who are described derisively as P.C., or politically correct, are said to have launched a campaign reign of terror against those who slip and innocently say "freshman" instead of "freshperson," "Indian" instead of "Native American" or, may the Goddess forgive them, "disabled" instead of "differently abled."

2 So you can see what is at stake here: freedom of speech, freedom of thought, Western civilization and a great many professional egos. But before we get carried away by the mounting backlash against multiculturalism, we ought to reflect for a moment on the system that the P.C. people aim to replace. I know all about it; in fact it's just about all I

do know, since I—along with so many educated white people of my generation—was a victim of monoculturalism.

3   American history, as it was taught to us, began with Columbus' "discovery" of an apparently unnamed, unpeopled America, and moved on to the Pilgrims serving pumpkin pie to a handful of grateful red-skinned folks. College expanded our horizons with courses called Humanities or sometimes Civ, which introduced us to a line of thought that started with Homer, worked its way through Rabelais and reached a poignant climax in the pensées of Matthew Arnold. Graduate students wrote dissertations on what long-dead men had thought of Chaucer's verse or Shakespeare's dramas; foreign languages meant French or German. If there had been high technology in ancient China, kingdoms in black Africa or women anywhere, at any time, doing anything worth noticing, we did not know it, nor did anyone think to tell us.

4   Our families and neighborhoods reinforced the dogma of monoculturalism. In our heads, most of us '50s teenagers carried around a social map that was about as useful as the chart that guided Columbus to the "Indies." There were "Negroes," "whites" and "Orientals," the latter meaning Chinese and "Japs." Of religions, only three were known—Protestant, Catholic and Jewish—and not much was known about the last two types. The only remaining human categories were husbands and wives, and that was all the diversity the monocultural world could handle. Gays, lesbians, Buddhists, Muslims, Malaysians, Mormons, etc. were simply off the map.

5   So I applaud—with one hand, anyway—the multiculturalist goal of preparing us all for a wider world. The other hand is tapping its fingers impatiently, because the critics are right about one thing: when advocates of multiculturalism adopt the haughty stance of political correctness, they quickly descend to silliness or worse. It's obnoxious, for example, to rely on university administrations to enforce P.C. standards of verbal inoffensiveness. Racist, sexist and homophobic thoughts cannot, alas, be abolished by fiat but only by the time-honored methods of persuasion, education and exposure to the other guy's—or, excuse me, woman's—point of view.

6   And it's silly to mistake verbal purification for genuine social reform. Even after all women are "Ms." and all people are "he or she," women will still earn only 65¢ for every dollar earned by men. Minorities by any other name, such as "people of color," will still bear a hugely disproportionate burden of poverty and discrimination. Disabilities are not

just "different abilities" when there are not enough ramps for wheelchairs, signers for the deaf or special classes for the "specially" endowed. With all due respect for the new politesse, actions still speak louder than fashionable phrases.

7   But the worst thing about the P.C. people is that they are such poor advocates for the multicultural cause. No one was ever won over to a broader, more inclusive view of life by being bullied or relentlessly "corrected." Tell a 19-year-old white male that he can't say "girl" when he means "teen-age woman," and he will most likely snicker. This may be the reason why, despite the conservative alarms, P.C.-ness remains a relatively tiny trend. Most campuses have more serious and ancient problems: faculties still top-heavy with white males of the monocultural persuasion; fraternities that harass minorities and women; date rape; alcohol abuse; and tuition that excludes all but the upper fringe of the middle class.

8   So both sides would be well advised to lighten up. The conservatives ought to realize that criticisms of the great books approach to learning do not amount to totalitarianism. And the advocates of multiculturalism need to regain the sense of humor that enabled their predecessors in the struggle to coin the term P.C. years ago—not in arrogance but in self-mockery.

9   Beyond that, both sides should realize that the beneficiaries of multiculturalism are not only the "oppressed peoples" on the standard P.C. list (minorities, gays, etc.). The "unenlightened"—the victims of monoculturalism—are oppressed too, or at least deprived. Our educations, whether at Yale or at State U, were narrow and parochial and left us ill-equipped to navigate a society that truly is multicultural and is becoming more so every day. The culture that we studied was, in fact, one culture and, from a world perspective, all too limited and ingrown. Diversity is challenging, but those of us who have seen the alternative know it is also richer, livelier and ultimately more fun.

QUESTIONS ON CONTENT, STRUCTURE, AND STYLE

1. Define monoculturalism and multiculturalism.

2. What do conservatives see as threatening about the "P.C." movement, according to Ehrenreich?

3. What aspects of multiculturalism does Ehrenreich embrace? What limitations or faults does she find in "political correctness"?

4. What advice does Ehrenreich offer to both sides of the multiculturalism debate?

5. Describe the tone of this essay. What is Ehrenreich's purpose in writing? Consider paragraph 3, for example.

6. Who, according to Ehrenreich, will benefit from multiculturalism?

7. Who are the "'unenlightened'—the victims of monoculturalism"?

8. Explain Ehrenreich's distinction between "verbal purification" and "genuine social reform."

9. In paragraph 7, Ehrenreich offers the theoretical example of a young white man's likely reaction to "P.C." admonitions. How does this example affect her readers? Would additional examples be effective in her essay?

10. How does Ehrenreich support her argument? Logic? Reasoning? Emotional appeal? Relevant experiences? Explain.

VOCABULARY

McCarthyism (1)
fundamentalism (1)
Eurocentric (1)
Jacobins (1)
poignant (3)

pensées (3)
dissertations (3)
dogma (4)
advocates (5)

fiat (5)
politesse (6)
totalitarianism (8)
parochial (9)

SUGGESTIONS FOR WRITING

1. Review Ehrenreich's claims, noting those you agree and disagree with. Argue for or against one claim in an essay, stating your position and supporting it with specific evidence from your own experience or from research.

2. In two short essays, role play your reaction to Ehrenreich's piece as a reader who disagrees with the need for multiculturalism and as a proponent of "P.C." who believes that "verbal purification" is a step toward needed reform.

3. An offshoot of multiculturalism has been a renewed interest in the groups each of us belong to—ethnic, racial, national, gender-based, regional, religious, political, and so forth. What groups do you belong to? In an essay, discuss which of those groups have been well-represented in your education and which of those groups have been under-represented. How does this view of yourself affect your view of multiculturalism in education?

In Search of Heroes

PETER H. GIBBON

Peter H. Gibbon is headmaster at Hackley School in Tarrytown, New York. He has written over 30 articles for a number of publications, including the *New York Times* and *Newsday*. "In Search of Heroes" first appeared in the "My Turn" column of *Newsweek* magazine on January 18, 1993.

1   To TEACH about exemplary lives has been a goal of American and European education for hundreds of years. Schools automatically offered young people heroes and role models. How else to combat the ambiguities and temptations of adult life? Where else to find the good to be imitated and the evil to be avoided? And so young people read Plutarch's "Lives," were saturated in the pious maxims of McGuffey's "Readers" and inculcated with the triumphs of Washington, Jefferson and Lincoln.

2   Did this force-feeding of idealism in youth make our grandparents and great-grandparents better people? I couldn't say whether this is the case. I can say only that the tradition of education by exemplary lives has ended.

3   The end may have come during the '60s, with the counterculture, the youth rebellion and the questioning of authority. Certainly Vietnam, the assassinations and Watergate gave many an excuse for cynicism.

4   It may be partly the new trend in biographies, which looks into all corners of a subject's life and pitilessly probes for ordinariness and weakness. The private lives of our leaders are fair game, and we expect

(some even hope) to find dirt. Thus we learn that John F. Kennedy was sexually compulsive, that Lyndon Johnson was more often than not devious and that Sir Thomas More, one of my heroes, was vindictive, disputatious and vain.

5   It may be a new approach to history, which stresses that violence and exploitation were endemic in our past. The discovery of America and the settlement of our West, for example, do not represent the opening of opportunity or the creation of wealth but genocide, environmental rape and the injection of lawlessness, greed and materialism into Eden. Columbus becomes a killer instead of a discoverer.

6   If new trends in biography and history make it difficult to have heroes, what about our popular culture and the media? My students are inundated with images and bombarded with information. Has this increase in information given them heroes?

7   My generation was raised on "The Adventures of Ozzie and Harriet." My students watch "Married with Children." We admired Rock Hudson and even thought that was his name; my students know he died of AIDS. We loved "Shane" and "Gunsmoke"; they watch "Blazing Saddles" and "Saturday Night Live." We subscribed to Boys' Life. Even junior-high-school students relish National Lampoon and "Doonesbury." We listened to preachers like Billy Graham. They were amused by Tammy and Jimmy. I liked Elvis Presley. They like him, too, but they know he died bloated and drug-infected.

8   Because we read Boys' Life, were we Boy Scouts? Hardly. But I do think we were more trusting, naive, sentimental and less cynical. We had greater faith in the adult world (perhaps knowing less about it) and were more deferential to authority. We had some heroes.

9   While irreverence among the young is inevitable and, in some ways, desirable, I would argue that today irreverence, skepticism and mockery permeate our scholarship and culture to such a degree that the tradition of exemplary lives is destroyed and that it is difficult for the young to have heroes. In schools we offer students lives that are seriously flawed, juvenile novels that emphasize "reality" and a history that is uncertain and blemished. At home they roam among dozens of channels and videos that do not intend to uplift and offer no role models.

10   Sir Richard Livingstone, a 20th-century educator, tells us, "True education is the habitual vision of greatness." I am afraid that we have lost the vision of greatness in our schools and culture. We have traded exemplary lives and heroes for information, irony and reality. I am terrified

that our children are not being raised by exemplary lives and confident schools; nor by high culture, vigilant communities, families, churches and temples, but rather by an all-enveloping enemy culture interested in amusement, titillation and consumerism.

11   I have no easy answers for disappearing heroes and increasing irreverence, only a few modest suggestions. Portray old heroes as human beings, but let them remain heroic. Yes, Lincoln liked bawdy stories, was politically calculating and suffered from depression. But he also exhibited astonishing political and moral courage and always appealed to "the better angels of our nature."

12   For a shabby age, find new heroes and heroines. I recently discovered the letters and diaries of the German sculptor Käthe Kollwitz, who died in 1945. She endures personal despair, a world war and fascism; still she paints and draws, has compassion and thinks lofty thoughts.

13   In schools, give moral and ethical education the same importance as the presentation of reality. Teachers need to be more cautious and selective about introducing messiness and complexity to our children. Presenting "reality" is a rather empty educational goal if our reading lists and assignments produce disillusioned, dispirited students.

14   Intellectuals and columnists could be less mocking and disdainful of those in authority. Too often they look for weakness, find fault and are confident of easy answers for complex problems; and American young people conclude that there is only corruption and shallowness in high places and no heroes.

15   Hollywood and popular culture must be fought. The movies, the media and the popular-music industry offer their own heroes—most of whom are disdainful of normal life, hard work and fidelity. Instead, they glorify violence, excitement and aberration. The cumulative effect of such indoctrination is incalculable but frightening.

16   Of course, parents need not be victims of Hollywood, of pundits, of negligent schools or a cynical age. They are the first and most important educators. If they try to make their lives exemplary, so will their children.

QUESTIONS ON CONTENT, STRUCTURE, AND STYLE

1. Summarize the differences Gibbon sees between the education of the current generation and that of their predecessors.

2. According to Gibbon, what has caused the "tradition of education by exemplary lives" to end?

3. In paragraph 7, Gibbon contrasts the popular cultures of two generations. Why does he offer these specific examples? What response does this evoke in the reader?

4. How does Gibbon accomplish smooth transitions between paragraphs? Choose two transitions and explain their effectiveness.

5. What solutions does Gibbon offer for the problems of "disappearing heroes and increasing irreverence"?

6. Given that this essay was first published in *Newsweek*, a news magazine, who might be the "typical" reader for this piece? Is this the best audience for the essay? Is there another, more specific, audience that would be even more affected? Explain.

7. Gibbon offers a number of causes for the loss of the exemplary tradition as well as a number of solutions to the problem. Which cause is most convincingly presented? Which solution?

8. Do you agree that children are now being raised without heroes? Or is it simply time to redefine "hero"? Explain your viewpoint.

9. Throughout the essay, Gibbon uses the word "we." How does this point-of-view affect the reader's response to the essay?

10. Gibbon concludes his essay with an appeal to parents. How effective is this ending? Why do you suppose parents are not mentioned earlier in the essay?

VOCABULARY

exemplary (1)
ambiguities (1)
pious (1)
maxims (1)
inculcated (1)
compulsive (4)

devious (4)
vindictive (4)
disputatious (4)
endemic (5)
genocide (5)

inundated (6)
relish (7)
deferential (8)
vigilant (10)
pundits (16)

SUGGESTIONS FOR WRITING

1. Gibbon writes that his generation was "more deferential to authority" and notes that "While irreverence among the young is inevitable and, in some ways, desirable," it has permeated society to a negative extent. Do you agree? In a persuasive essay, argue your viewpoint.

2. Gibbon proposes that schools "give moral and ethical education the same importance as the presentation of reality." Are there problems that might arise from teaching morality? For example, who will define "moral," "immoral," "hero," or "villain"? Defend your views in a persuasive essay.

3. Sir Richard Livingstone is quoted in the essay as saying, "True education is the habitual vision of greatness." Do you agree with this statement? Write an essay arguing your views, first defining what you mean by "greatness." If appropriate for your essay, consider noting individuals who meet these standards of "greatness."

How to Make People Smaller Than They Are

NORMAN COUSINS

Norman Cousins was the editor of *Saturday Review* for over thirty-five years (1940–1971 and 1973–1977). His many books include *The Celebration of Life* (1974), and *The Healing Heart: Antidotes to Panic and Helplessness* (1983), and *Anatomy of an Illness* (1979). This essay was published as an editorial in *Saturday Review* in 1978.

1   THREE MONTHS ago in this space we wrote about the costly retreat from the humanities on all the levels of American education. Since that time, we have had occasion to visit a number of campuses and have been troubled to find that the general situation is even more serious than we had thought. It has become apparent to us that one of the biggest problems confronting American education today is the increasing vocationalization of our colleges and universities. Throughout the country, schools are under pressure to become job-training centers and employment agencies.

2   The pressure comes mainly from two sources. One is the growing determination of many citizens to reduce taxes—understandable and even commendable in itself, but irrational and irresponsible when connected

to the reduction or dismantling of vital public services. The second source of pressure comes from parents and students who tend to scorn courses of study that do not teach people how to become attractive to employers in a rapidly tightening job market.

3   It is absurd to believe that the development of skills does not also require the systematic development of the human mind. Education is being measured more by the size of the benefits the individual can extract from society than by the extent to which the individual can come into possession of his or her full powers. The result is that the life-giving juices are in danger of being drained out of education.

4   Emphasis on "practicalities" is being characterized by the subordination of words to numbers. History is seen not as essential experience to be transmitted to new generations, but as abstractions that carry dank odors. Art is regarded as something that calls for indulgence or patronage and that has no place among the practical realities. Political science is viewed more as a specialized subject for people who want to go into politics than as an opportunity for citizens to develop a knowledgeable relationship with the systems by which human societies are governed. Finally, literature and philosophy are assigned the role of add-ons—intellectual adornments that have nothing to do with "genuine" education.

5   Instead of trying to shrink the liberal arts, the American people ought to be putting pressure on colleges and universities to increase the ratio of the humanities to the sciences. Most serious studies of medical-school curricula in recent years have called attention to the stark gaps in the liberal education of medical students. The experts agree that the schools shouldn't leave it up to students to close those gaps.

6   We must not make it appear, however, that nothing is being done. In the past decade, the National Endowment for the Humanities has been a prime mover in infusing the liberal arts into medical education and other specialized schools. During this past year alone, NEH has given 108 grants to medical schools and research organizations in the areas of ethics and human values. Some medical schools, like the one at Pennsylvania State University, have led the way in both the number and the depth of courses offered in the humanities. Penn State has been especially innovative in weaving literature and philosophy into the full medical course of study. It is ironical that the pressure against the humanities should be manifesting itself at precisely the time when so many medical schools are at long last moving in this direction.

7   The irony of the emphasis being placed on careers is that nothing is more valuable for anyone who has had a professional or vocational education than to be able to deal with abstractions or complexities, or to feel comfortable with subtleties of thought or language, or to think sequentially. The doctor who knows only disease is at a disadvantage alongside the doctor who knows at least as much about people as he does about pathological organisms. The lawyer who argues in court from a narrow legal base is no match for the lawyer who can connect legal precedents to historical experience and who employs wide-ranging intellectual resources. The business executive whose competence in general management is bolstered by an artistic ability to deal with people is of prime value to his company. For the technologist, the engineering of consent can be just as important as the engineering of moving parts. In all these respects, the liberal arts have much to offer. Just in terms of career preparation, therefore, a student is shortchanging himself by shortcutting the humanities.

8   But even if it could be demonstrated that the humanities contribute nothing directly to a job, they would still be an essential part of the educational equipment of any person who wants to come to terms with life. The humanities would be expendable only if human beings didn't have to make decisions that affect their lives and the lives of others; if the human past never existed or had nothing to tell us about the present; if thought processes were irrelevant to the achievement of purpose; if creativity was beyond the human mind and had nothing to do with the joy of living; if human relationships were random aspects of life; if human beings never had to cope with panic or pain, or if they never had to anticipate the connection between cause and effect; if all the mysteries of mind and nature were fully plumbed; and if no special demands arose from the accident of being born a human being instead of a hen or a hog.

9   Finally, there would be good reason to eliminate the humanities if a free society were not absolutely dependent on a functioning citizenry. If the main purpose of a university is job training, then the underlying philosophy of our government has little meaning. The debates that went into the making of American society concerned not just institutions or governing principles but the capacity of humans to sustain those institutions. Whatever the disagreements were over other issues at the American Constitutional Convention, the fundamental question sensed by everyone, a question that lay over the entire assembly, was whether the

people themselves would understand what it meant to hold the ultimate power of society, and whether they had enough of a sense of history and destiny to know where they had been and where they ought to be going.
10   Jefferson was prouder of having been the founder of the University of Virginia than of having been President of the United States. He knew that the educated and developed mind was the best assurance that a political system could be made to work—a system based on the informed consent of the governed. If this idea fails, then all the saved tax dollars in the world will not be enough to prevent the nation from turning on itself.

QUESTIONS ON CONTENT, STRUCTURE, AND STYLE

1. What problem does Cousins present in paragraph 1?

2. What is his attitude toward this problem? What danger does he see? What are the sources of this problem?

3. What action does Cousins advocate?

4. What irony does Cousins point out in paragraph 6? Why is this paragraph included in this essay?

5. What is the topic sentence in paragraph 7? How is the rest of the paragraph developed? Is the paragraph effective?

6. What is the purpose of the last sentence in paragraph 7?

7. Summarize Cousins' main arguments for studying the humanities.

8. Describe the construction of the second sentence in paragraph 8. Why does Cousins use one long sentence instead of a series of shorter ones?

9. How does Cousins conclude his essay? Is it an effective ending?

10. Overall, how persuasive is Cousins' argument?

VOCABULARY

vocationalization (1)	infusing (6)	pathological (7)
dismantling (2)	innovative (6)	bolstered (7)
dank (4)	subtleties (7)	plumbed (8)
indulgence (4)	sequentially (7)	

SUGGESTIONS FOR WRITING

1. Write an essay in which you defend the "increasing vocationalization of our colleges."

2. Write an essay in which you criticize or defend a particular requirement for the college degree in your major.

3. Interview premed, business, and liberal arts advisers on your campus. Compare/contrast their views on the role of humanities in their students' education. Use their comments and your own views to create and argue for "the perfect college curriculum."

When I Heard the Learn'd Astronomer

WALT WHITMAN

Walt Whitman was a nineteenth-century American poet whose free-verse poems broke with conventional style and subject matter. Some of his most famous poems, including "Song of Myself," "Crossing Brooklyn Ferry," and "Passage to India," extoll the virtues of the common people and stress their unity with a universal oversoul. This poem was published in 1865.

When I heard the learn'd astronomer;
When the proofs, the figures, were ranged in columns before
    me;
When I was shown the charts and the diagrams, to add, divide,
    and measure them;
When I, sitting, heard the astronomer, where he lectured with
    much applause in the lecture-room,
5 How soon, unaccountable, I became tired and sick;
Till rising and gliding out, I wander'd off by myself,
In the mystical moist night-air, and from time to time,
Look'd up in perfect silence at the stars.

QUESTIONS ON CONTENT, STRUCTURE, AND STYLE

1. Who is the speaker of this poem?

2. In lines 1–4, where is the speaker? What is he/she listening to?

3. How does the speaker react to the lecture?

4. How do lines 5–8 differ in content from lines 1–4?

5. Why does the speaker stare at the stars?

6. Why do lines 1–4 contain repetition?

7. Why did the poet make lines 3 and 4 longer than the lines that follow them?

8. Characterize the sounds in "rising and gliding," "mystical moist," "time to time," and "silence at the stars." Why are these sounds included in lines 6–8? Why are there no similar groupings in lines 1–4?

9. Does this poem have a set rhythm or rhyme scheme?

10. How is this poem an example of development by contrast?

VOCABULARY

ranged (line 2)
unaccountable (line 5)

SUGGESTIONS FOR WRITING

1. Write an essay contrasting your reactions to an experience you first heard or read about and the actual event as you participated in it. (For example, was your first job or first day at college what you thought it would be?)

2. Write an essay in which you describe an interest you developed after hearing about the subject in a class.

3. Write an essay or poem in which you compare/contrast two attitudes towards a particular class, teacher, lesson, or theory.

Expelled

JOHN CHEEVER

John Cheever was an American novelist and short story writer, who frequently published in *The New Yorker*. His most famous novels are *The Wapshot Chronicle* (1957) and *The Wapshot Scandal* (1964); some of his stories are collected in *The Enormous Radio* (1953), *The Housebreaker of Shady Hill* (1958), and *The Stories of John Cheever* (1978). This story was his first published work, written after he himself was expelled from a private school.

1   IT DIDN'T come all at once. It took a very long time. First I had a skirmish with the English Department and then all the other departments. Pretty soon something had to be done. The first signs were cordialities on the part of the headmaster. He was never nice to anybody unless he was a football star, or hadn't paid his tuition, or was going to be expelled. That's how I knew.

2   He called me down to his office with the carved chairs arranged in a semicircle and the brocade curtains resting against the vacant windows. All about him were pictures of people who had got scholarships at Harvard. He asked me to sit down.

3   "Well, Charles," he said, "some of the teachers say you aren't getting very good marks."

4   "Yes," I said, "that's true." I didn't care about the marks.

5   "But Charles," he said, "you know the scholastic standard of this school is very high and we have to drop people when their work becomes unsatisfactory." I told him I knew that also. Then he said a lot of things about the traditions, and the elms, and the magnificent military heritage from our West Point founder.

6   It was very nice outside of his room. He had his window pushed open halfway and one could see the lawns pulling down to the road behind the trees and the bushes. The gravy-colored curtains were too heavy to move about in the wind, but some papers shifted around on his desk. In a little while I got up and walked out. He turned and started to work again. I went back to my next class.

7   The next day was very brilliant and the peach branches were full against the dry sky. I could hear the people talking and a phonograph playing. The sounds came through the peach blossoms and crossed the room. I lay in bed and thought about a great many things. My dreams had been thick. I remembered two converging hills, some dry apple trees, and a broken blue egg cup. That is all I could remember.

8   I put on knickers and a soft sweater and headed toward school. My hands shook on the wheel. I was like that all over.

9   Through the cloudy trees I could see the protrusion of the new tower. It was going to be a beautiful new tower and it was going to cost a great deal of money. Some thought of buying new books for the library instead of putting up a tower, but no one would see the books. People would be able to see the tower five miles off when the leaves were off the trees. It would be done by fall.

10   When I went into the building the headmaster's secretary was standing in the corridor. She was a nice sort of person with brown funnels of hair furrowed about a round head. She smiled. I guess she must have known.

The Colonel

11   Every morning we went up into the black chapel. The brisk headmaster was there. Sometimes he had a member of the faculty with him. Sometimes it was a stranger.

12   He introduced the stranger, whose speech was always the same. In the spring life is like a baseball game. In the fall it is like football. That is what the speaker always said.

13   The hall is damp and ugly with skylights that rattle in the rain. The seats are hard and you have to hold a hymnbook in your lap. The hymnbook often slips off and that is embarrassing.

14   On Memorial Day they have the best speaker. They have a mayor or a Governor. Sometimes they have a Governor's second. There is very little preference.

15   The Governor will tell us what a magnificent country we have. He will tell us to beware of the Red menace. He will want to tell us that the goddam foreigners should have gone home a hell of a long time ago. That they should have stayed in their own goddam countries if they didn't like ours. He will not dare say this though.

16   If they have a mayor the speech will be longer. He will tell us that our country is beautiful and young and strong. That the War is over, but that if there is another we must fight. He will tell us that war is a masculine trait that has brought present civilization to its fine condition. Then he will leave us and help stout women place lilacs on graves. He will tell them the same thing.

17   One Memorial Day they could not get a Governor or a mayor. There was a colonel in the same village who had been to war and who had a chest thick with medals. They asked him to speak. Of course he said he would like to speak.

18   He was a thin colonel with a soft nose that rested quietly on his face. He was nervous and pushed his wedding ring about his thin finger. When he was introduced he looked at the audience sitting in the uncomfortable chairs. There was silence and the dropping of hymnbooks like the water spouts in the aftermath of a heavy rain.

19   He spoke softly and quickly. He spoke of war and what he had seen. Then he had to stop. He stopped and looked at the boys. They were staring at their boots. He thought of the empty rooms in the other buildings. He thought of the rectangles of empty desks. He thought of the curtains on the stage and the four Windsor chairs behind him. Then he started to speak again.

20   He spoke as quickly as he could. He said war was bad. He said that there would never be another war. That he himself should stop it if he could. He swore. He looked at the young faces. They were all very clean. The boys' knees were crossed and their soft pants hung loosely. He thought of the empty desks and began to whimper.

21   The people sat very still. Some of them felt tight as though they wanted to giggle. Everybody looked serious as the clock struck. It was time for another class.

22   People began to talk about the colonel after lunch. They looked behind them. They were afraid he might hear them.

23   It took the school several weeks to get over all this. Nobody said anything, but the colonel was never asked again. If they could not get a Governor or a mayor they could get someone besides a colonel. They made sure of that.

Margaret Courtwright

24   Margaret Courtwright was very nice. She was slightly bald and pulled her pressed hair down across her forehead. People said that she was the

best English teacher in this part of the country, and when boys came back from Harvard they thanked her for the preparation she had given them. She did not like Edgar Guest, but she did like Carl Sandburg. She couldn't seem to understand the similarity. When I told her people laughed at Galsworthy she said that people used to laugh at Wordsworth. She did not believe people were still laughing at Wordsworth. That was what made her so nice.

25   She came from the West a long time ago. She taught school for so long that people ceased to consider her age. After having seen twenty-seven performances of "Hamlet" and after having taught it for sixteen years, she became a sort of immortal. Her interpretation was the one accepted on college-board papers. That helped everyone a great deal. No one had to get a new interpretation.

26   When she asked me for tea I sat in a walnut armchair with grapes carved on the head and traced and retraced the arms on the tea caddy. One time I read her one of my plays. She thought it was wonderful. She thought it was wonderful because she did not understand it and because it took two hours to read. When I had finished, she said, "You know that thing just took right hold of me. Really it just swept me right along. I think it's fine that you like to write. I once had a Japanese pupil who liked to write. He was an awfully nice chap until one summer he went down to Provincetown. When he came back he was saying that he could express a complete abstraction. Fancy . . . a complete abstraction. Well, I wouldn't hear of it and told him how absurd it all was and tried to start him off with Galsworthy again, but I guess he had gone just too far. In a little while he left for New York and then Paris. It was really too bad. One summer in Provincetown just ruined him. His marks fell down . . . he cut classes to go to symphony. . . ." She went into the kitchen and got a tray of tarts.

27   The pastries were flaky and covered with a white coating that made them shine in the dead sunlight. I watched the red filling burst the thin shells and stain the triangles of bright damask. The tarts were good. I ate most of them.

28   She was afraid I would go the way of her Japanese pupil. She doubted anyone who disagreed with Heine on Shakespeare and Croce on expression.

29   One day she called me into her antiseptic office and spoke to me of reading Joyce. "You know, Charles," she said, "this sex reality can be quite as absurd as a hypercritical regard for such subjects. You know that, don't you? Of course, you do." Then she went out of the room.

She had straight ankles and wore a gold band peppered with diamond chips on her ring finger. She seemed incapable of carrying the weight of the folds in her clothing. Her skirt was askew, either too long in front or hitching up on the side. Always one thing or the other.

30   When I left school she did not like it. She was afraid I might go too near Provincetown. She wished me good luck and moved the blotter back and forth on her desk. Then she returned to teaching "Hamlet."

31   Late in February Laura Driscoll got fired for telling her history pupils that Sacco and Vanzetti were innocent. In her farewell appearance the headmaster told everyone how sorry he was that she was going and made it all quite convincing. Then Laura stood up, told the headmaster that he was a damned liar, and waving her fan-spread fingers called the school a hell of a dump where everyone got into a rut.

32   Miss Courtwright sat closely in her chair and knew it was true. She didn't mind much. Professor Rogers with his anti-feminization movement bothered her a little, too. But she knew that she had been teaching school for a long time now and no movement was going to put her out of a job overnight—what with all the boys she had smuggled into Harvard and sixteen years of "Hamlet."

Laura Driscoll

33   History classes are always dead. This follows quite logically, for history is a dead subject. It has not the death of dead fruit or dead textiles or dead light. It has a different death. There is not the timeless quality of death about it. It is dead like scenery in the opera. It is on cracked canvas and the paint has faded and peeled and the lights are too bright. It is dead like old water in a zinc bathtub.

34   "We are going to study ancient history this year," the teacher will tell the pupils. "Yes, ancient history will be our field.

35   "Now of course, this class is not a class of children any longer. I expect the discipline to be the discipline of well bred young people. We shall not have to waste any time on the scolding of younger children. No. We shall just be able to spend all our time on ancient history.

36   "Now about questions. I shall answer questions if they are important. If I do not think them important I shall not answer them, for the year is short, and we must cover a lot of ground in a short time. That

is, if we all cooperate and behave and not ask too many questions we shall cover the subject and have enough time at the end of the year for review.

37   "You may be interested in the fact that a large percentage of this class was certified last year. I should like to have a larger number this year. Just think boys: wouldn't it be fine if a very large number—a number larger than last year—was certified? Wouldn't that be fine? Well, there's no reason why we can't do it if we all cooperate and behave and don't ask too many questions.

38   "You must remember that I have twelve people to worry about and that you have only one. If each person will take care of his own work and pass in his notebook on time it will save me a lot of trouble. Time and trouble mean whether you get into college or not, and I want you all to get into college.

39   "If you will take care of your own little duties, doing what is assigned to you, and doing it well, we shall all get along fine. You are a brilliant-looking group of young people, and I want to have you all certified. I want to get you into college with as little trouble as possible.

40   "Now about the books. . . ."

41   I do not know how long history classes have been like this. One time or another I suppose history was alive. That was before it died its horrible fly-dappled unquivering death.

42   Everyone seems to know that history is dead. No one is alarmed. The pupils and the teachers love dead history. They do not like it when it is alive. When Laura Driscoll dragged history into the classroom, squirming and smelling of something bitter, they fired Laura and strangled the history. It was too tumultuous. Too turbulent.

43   In history one's intellect is used for mechanical speculation on a probable century or background. One's memory is applied to a list of dead dates and names. When one begins to apply one's intellect to the mental scope of the period, to the emotional development of its inhabitants, one becomes dangerous. Laura Driscoll was terribly dangerous. That's why Laura was never a good history teacher.

44   She was not the first history teacher I had ever had. She is not the last I will have. But she is the only teacher I have ever had who could feel history with an emotional vibrance—or, if the person was too oblique, with a poetic understanding. She was five feet four inches tall, brown-haired, and bent-legged from horseback riding. All the boys thought Laura Driscoll was a swell teacher.

45   She was the only history teacher I have ever seen who was often ecstatical. She would stand by the boards and shout out her discoveries on the Egyptian cultures. She made the gargoylic churnings of Chartres in a heavy rain present an applicable meaning. She taught history as an interminable flood of events viewed through the distortion of our own immediacy. She taught history in the broad-handed rhythms of Hauptmann's drama, in the static melancholy of Egypt moving before its own shadow down the long sand, in the fluted symmetry of the Doric culture. She taught history as a hypothesis from which we could extract the evaluation of our own lives.

46   She was the only teacher who realized that, coming from the West, she had little business to be teaching these children of New England.

47   "I do not know what your reaction to the sea is," she would say. "For I have come from a land where there is no sea. My elements are the fields, the sun, the plastic cadence of the clouds and the cloudlessness. You have been brought up by the sea. You have been coached in the cadence of the breakers and the strength of the mind.

48   "My emotional viewpoints will differ from yours. Do not let me impose my perceptions upon you."

49   However, the college-board people didn't care about Chartres as long as you knew the date. They didn't care whether history was looked at from the mountains or the sea. Laura spent too much time on such trivia and all of her pupils didn't get into Harvard. In fact, very few of her pupils got into Harvard, and this didn't speak well for her.

50   While the other members of the faculty chattered over Hepplewhite legs and Duncan Phyfe embellishments, Laura was before five-handed Siva or the sexless compassion glorious in its faded polychrome. Laura didn't think much of America. Laura made this obvious and the faculty heard about it. The faculty thought America was beautiful. They didn't like people to disagree.

51   However, the consummation did not occur until late in February. It was cold and clear and the snow was deep. Outside the windows there was the enormous roaring of broken ice. It was late in February that Laura Driscoll said Sacco and Vanzetti were undeserving of their treatment.

52   This got everyone all up in the air. Even the headmaster was disconcerted.

53   The faculty met.

54   The parents wrote letters.

55   Laura Driscoll was fired.

56   "Miss Driscoll," said the headmaster during her last chapel at the school, "has found it necessary to return to the West. In the few months that we have had her with us, she has been a staunch friend of the academy, a woman whom we all admire and love and who, we are sure, loves and admires the academy and its elms as we do. We are all sorry Miss Driscoll is leaving us. . . ."

57   Then Laura got up, called him a damned liar, swore down the length of the platform and walked out of the building.

58   No one ever saw Laura Driscoll again. By the way everyone talked, no one wanted to. That was all late in February. By March the school was quiet again. The new history teacher taught dates. Everyone carefully forgot about Laura Driscoll.

59   "She was a nice girl," said the headmaster, "but she really wasn't made for teaching history. . . . No, she really wasn't a born history teacher."

Five Months Later

60   The spring of five months ago was the most beautiful spring I have ever lived in. The year before I had not known all about the trees and the heavy peach blossoms and the tea-colored brooks that shook down over the brown rocks. Five months ago it was spring and I was in school.

61   In school the white limbs beyond the study hall shook out a greenness, and the tennis courts became white and scalding. The air was empty and hard, and the vacant wind dragged shadows over the road. I knew all this only from the classrooms.

62   I knew about the trees from the window frames. I knew the rain only from the sounds on the roof. I was tired of seeing spring with walls and awnings to intercept the sweet sun and the hard fruit. I wanted to go outdoors and see the spring. I wanted to feel and taste the air and be among the shadows. That is perhaps why I left school.

63   In the spring I was glad to leave school. Everything outside was elegant and savage and fleshy. Everything inside was slow and cool and vacant. It seemed a shame to stay inside.

64   But in a little while the spring went. I was left outside and there was no spring. I did not want to go in again. I would not have gone in again for anything. I was sorry, but I was not sorry over the fact that I had

gone out. I was sorry that the outside and the inside could not have been open to one another. I was sorry that there were roofs on the classrooms and trousers on the legs of the instructors to insulate their contacts. I was not sorry that I had left school. I was sorry that I left for the reasons that I did.

65   If I had left because I had to go to work or because I was sick it would not have been so bad. Leaving because you are angry and frustrated is different. It is not a good thing to do. It is bad for everyone.

66   Of course it was not the fault of the school. The headmaster and faculty were doing what they were supposed to do. It was just a preparatory school trying to please the colleges. A school that was doing everything the colleges asked it to do.

67   It was not the fault of the school at all. It was the fault of the system—the noneducational system, the college-preparatory system. That was what made the school so useless.

68   As a college-preparatory school it was a fine school. In five years they could make raw material look like college material. They could clothe it and breed it and make it say the right things when the colleges asked it to talk. That was its duty.

69   They weren't prepared to educate anybody. They were members of a college-preparatory system. No one around there wanted to be educated. No sir.

70   They presented the subjects the colleges required. They had math, English, history, languages, and music. They once had had an art department but it had been dropped. "We have enough to do," said the headmaster, "just to get all these people into college without trying to teach them art. Yes sir, we have quite enough to do as it is."

71   Of course there were literary appreciation and art appreciation and musical appreciation, but they didn't count for much. If you are young, there is very little in Thackeray that is parallel to your own world. Van Dyke's "Abbé Scaglia" and the fretwork of Mozart quartets are not for the focus of your ears and eyes. All the literature and art that holds a similarity to your life is forgotten. Some of it is even forbidden.

72   Our country is the best country in the world. We are swimming in prosperity and our President is the best president in the world. We have larger apples and better cotton and faster and more beautiful machines. This makes us the greatest country in the world. Unemployment is a myth. Dissatisfaction is a fable. In preparatory school America is beautiful. It is the gem of the ocean and it is too bad. It is bad because people

believe it all. Because they become indifferent. Because they marry and reproduce and vote and they know nothing. Because the tempered newspaper keeps its eyes ceilingwards and does not see the dirty floor. Because all they know is the tempered newspaper.

73   But I will not say any more. I do not stand in a place where I can talk.

74   And now it is August. The orchards are stinking ripe. The tea-colored brooks run beneath the rocks. There is sediment on the stone and no wind in the willows. Everyone is preparing to go back to school. I have no school to go back to.

75   I am not sorry. I am not at all glad.

76   It is strange to be so very young and to have no place to report to at nine o'clock. That is what education has always been. It has been laced curtseys and perfumed punctualities.

77   But now it is nothing. It is symmetric with my life. I am lost in it. That is why I am not standing in a place where I can talk.

78   The school windows are being washed. The floors are thick with fresh oil.

79   Soon it will be time for the snow and the symphonies. It will be time for Brahms and the great dry winds.

QUESTIONS ON CONTENT, STRUCTURE, AND STYLE

1. Charles doesn't name "it" in the opening paragraph. What is "it"? What is gained by having Charles tell his own story?

2. In paragraph 6 Charles doesn't say how he feels but describes the setting instead. What does this imply about his mood? Where else does Cheever use this technique to show rather than tell mood?

3. In paragraph 9 why does Charles say, "but no one would see the books." What does this paragraph suggest about the school?

4. What happened during the Colonel's speech? Why does he stand out in Charles' mind?

5. What was different about Laura Driscoll and her approach to history?

6. Who does Charles believe is the better teacher, Margaret Courtwright or Laura Driscoll? Which details suggest his opinion? Why does he mention college boards?

7. How does Charles describe spring? What is the difference between spring "outside" and spring "inside"? What role does nature play in this story?

8. Why does Charles quit school? Is he sorry? What does he see in his future?

9. Evaluate Charles' tone in paragraph 72. What is he criticizing?

10. Summarize what you think Cheever is saying about some college-preparatory schools. Do you agree with his view?

VOCABULARY

skirmish (1)	oblique (44)	interminable (45)
protrusion (9)	ecstatical (45)	consummation (51)
askew (29)	gargoylic (45)	tempered (72)
tumultuous (42)		

SUGGESTIONS FOR WRITING

1. John Cheever makes a strong statement about what education should or shouldn't be. What does he value or not value? Write an essay in which you agree or disagree with him, using your own experience to support your opinion.

2. Cheever writes about four memorable people: the headmaster, the colonel, and two teachers. Whom do you recall from your school experience? Write an essay contrasting the teaching styles of two of these memorable people. Focus on specific events that illustrate their methods.

3. Have you ever quit school or thought seriously about leaving a school? Write an essay about your decision. You might direct your comments to someone making a similar decision. Explain why you think your decision to stay or go was a good or bad choice at the time. (Or, if you prefer, write an essay explaining why you have chosen to return to school after a brief or extended period.)

LIFE CONFRONTS DEATH

38 Who Saw Murder Didn't Call the Police

MARTIN GANSBERG

Martin Gansberg has been a reporter and editor for *The New York Times* since 1942 and has also written for such magazines as *Diplomat, Catholic Digest,* and *Facts.* This news story was published in *The New York Times* in 1964, shortly after the murder of Kitty Genovese.

1 FOR MORE than half an hour 38 respectable, law-abiding citizens in Queens watched a killer stalk and stab a woman in three separate attacks in Kew Gardens.

2 Twice the sound of their voices and the sudden glow of their bedroom lights interrupted him and frightened him off. Each time he returned, sought her out and stabbed her again. Not one person telephoned the police during the assault; one witness called after the woman was dead.

3 That was two weeks ago today. But Assistant Chief Inspector Frederick M. Lussen, in charge of the borough's detectives and a veteran of 25 years of homicide investigations, is still shocked.

4 He can give a matter-of-fact recitation of many murders. But the Kew Gardens slaying baffles him—not because it is a murder, but because the "good people" failed to call the police.

5 "As we have reconstructed the crime," he said, "the assailant had three chances to kill this woman during a 35-minute period. He returned twice to complete the job. If we had been called when he first attacked, the woman might not be dead now."

6 This is what the police say happened beginning at 3:20 A.M. in the staid, middle-class, tree-lined Austin Street area:

7 Twenty-eight-year-old Catherine Genovese, who was called Kitty by almost everyone in the neighborhood, was returning home from her job as manager of a bar in Hollis. She parked her red Fiat in a lot adjacent to the Kew Gardens Long Island Railroad Station, facing Mowbray Place. Like many residents of the neighborhood, she had parked there day after day since her arrival from Connecticut a year ago, although the railroad frowns on the practice.

8 She turned off the lights of her car, locked the door and started to walk the 100 feet to the entrance of her apartment at 82–70 Austin

Street, which is in a Tudor building, with stores on the first floor and apartments on the second.

9   The entrance to the apartment is in the rear of the building because the front is rented to retail stores. At night the quiet neighborhood is shrouded in the slumbering darkness that marks most residential areas.

10   Miss Genovese noticed a man at the far end of the lot, near a seven-story apartment house at 82–40 Austin Street. She halted. Then, nervously, she headed up Austin Street toward Lefferts Boulevard, where there is a call box to the 102nd Police Precinct in nearby Richmond Hill.

"He Stabbed Me"

11   She got as far as a street light in front of a bookstore before the man grabbed her. She screamed. Lights went on in the 10-story apartment house at 82–67 Austin Street, which faces the bookstore. Windows slid open and voices punctuated the early-morning stillness.

12   Miss Genovese screamed: "Oh, my God, he stabbed me! Please help me! Please help me!"

13   From one of the upper windows in the apartment house, a man called down: "Let that girl alone!"

14   The assailant looked up at him, shrugged and walked down Austin Street toward a white sedan parked a short distance away. Miss Genovese struggled to her feet.

15   Lights went on. The killer returned to Miss Genovese, now trying to make her way around the side of the building by the parking lot to get to her apartment. The assailant stabbed her again.

16   "I'm dying!" she shrieked. "I'm dying!"

A City Bus Passed

17   Windows were opened again, and lights went on in many apartments. The assailant got into his car and drove away. Miss Genovese staggered to her feet. A city bus, Q-10, the Lefferts Boulevard line to Kennedy International Airport, passed. It was 3:35 A.M.

18   The assailant returned. By then, Miss Genovese had crawled to the back of the building, where the freshly painted brown doors to the

apartment house held out hope of safety. The killer tried the first door, she wasn't there. At the second door, 82–62 Austin Street, he saw her slumped on the floor at the foot of the stairs. He stabbed her a third time—fatally.

19   It was 3:50 by the time the police received their first call, from a man who was a neighbor of Miss Genovese. In two minutes they were at the scene. The neighbor, a 70-year-old woman and another woman were the only persons on the street. Nobody else came forward.

20   The man explained that he had called the police after much deliberation. He had phoned a friend in Nassau County for advice and then he had crossed the roof of the building to the apartment of the elderly woman to get her to make the call.

21   "I didn't want to get involved," he sheepishly told the police.

Suspect Is Arrested

22   Six days later, the police arrested Winston Moseley, a 29-year-old business-machine operator, and charged him with homicide. Moseley had no previous record. He is married, has two children and owns a home at 133–19 Sutter Avenue, South Ozone Park, Queens. On Wednesday, a court committed him to Kings County Hospital for psychiatric observation.

23   When questioned by the police, Moseley also said that he had slain Mrs. Annie May Johnson, 24, of 146–12 133d Avenue, Jamaica, on Feb. 29 and Barbara Kralik, 15, of 174–17 140th Avenue, Springfield Gardens, last July. In the Kralik case, the police are holding Alvin L. Mitchell, who is said to have confessed that slaying.

24   The police stressed how simple it would have been to have gotten in touch with them. "A phone call," said one of the detectives, "would have done it." The police may be reached by dialing "O" for operator or SPring 7-3100. . . .

25   Today witnesses from the neighborhood, which is made up of one-family homes in the $35,000 to $60,000 range with the exception of the two apartment houses near the railroad station, find it difficult to explain why they didn't call the police. . . .

26   A housewife, knowingly if quite casually, said, "We thought it was a lover's quarrel." A husband and wife both said, "Frankly, we were

afraid." They seemed aware of the fact that events might have been different. A distraught woman, wiping her hands in her apron, said, "I didn't want my husband to get involved."

27   One couple, now willing to talk about that night, said they heard the first screams. The husband looked thoughtfully at the bookstore where the killer first grabbed Miss Genovese.

28   "We went to the window to see what was happening," he said, "but the light from our bedroom made it difficult to see the street." The wife, still apprehensive, added: "I put out the light and we were able to see better."

29   Asked why they hadn't called the police, she shrugged and replied: "I don't know."

30   A man peeked out from a slight opening in the doorway to his apartment and rattled off an account of the killer's second attack. Why hadn't he called the police at the time? "I was tired," he said without emotion. "I went back to bed."

31   It was 4:25 A.M. when the ambulance arrived to take the body of Miss Genovese. It drove off. "Then," a solemn police detective said, "the people came out."

QUESTIONS ON CONTENT, STRUCTURE, AND STYLE

1. This article originally appeared in a newspaper, *The New York Times.* In what ways do paragraphs in newspaper stories differ from paragraphs in essays?

2. Describe the effect of the first paragraph; how does it attract the reader's attention?

3. What is the function of the first five paragraphs? Of paragraph 6? What happens between the first five paragraphs and the rest of the story?

4. Why does Gansberg put quotation marks around "good people" in paragraph 4?

5. Evaluate Gansberg's use of objective reporting. Is he always objective?

6. Analyze Gansberg's use of dialogue. How effective is it? Why?

7. How does Gansberg realistically recreate the scene of the murder?

8. In addition to reporting a news story about murder, what was Gansberg's purpose in writing this article?

9. Would Gansberg's point have been more persuasive had he written an argumentative essay rather than this narrative? Why/why not?

10. Evaluate the conclusion of the article. Why did Gansberg choose the words of the detective for his ending?

VOCABULARY

borough (3)	staid (6)	deliberation (20)
recitation (4)	adjacent (7)	distraught (26)
baffles (4)	shrouded (9)	apprehensive (28)

SUGGESTIONS FOR WRITING

1. Write a narrative, using an event from your experience, to illustrate people's involvement or lack of involvement with others.

2. Write a newspaper editorial based on the Kitty Genovese incident or on a more recent, similar crime or rescue. (Consider, for example, the 1992 case of Reginald Denny, a truck driver beaten in the riots following the first Rodney King trial; his rescuers saw the beating on live television and rushed to his aid.)

3. Write an essay detailing the precautions one might take to avoid becoming the victim of an attacker. You may wish to gather information from your campus police or from a local crime crisis center.

To Bid the World Farewell

JESSICA MITFORD

Jessica Mitford was born in England but is now an American citizen. She has written many articles and books, including *The Trial of Dr. Spock* (1969), *Kind and Usual Punishment* (1973), *A Fine Old Conflict* (1977), *Poison Penmanship* (1979), and, most recently, *The American Way of Birth* (1992). This essay is a part of her best-selling exposé *The American Way of Death* (1963).

1   EMBALMING IS indeed a most extraordinary procedure, and one must wonder at the docility of Americans who each year pay hundreds of millions of dollars for its perpetuation, blissfully ignorant of what it is all about, what is done, how it is done. Not one in ten thousand has any idea of what actually takes place. Books on the subject are extremely hard to come by. They are not to be found in most libraries or bookshops.

2   In an era when huge television audiences watch surgical operations in the comfort of their living rooms, when, thanks to the animated cartoon, the geography of the digestive system has become familiar territory even to the nursery school set, in a land where the satisfaction of curiosity about almost all matters is a national pastime, the secrecy surrounding embalming can, surely, hardly be attributed to the inherent gruesomeness of the subject. Custom in this regard has within this century suffered a complete reversal. In the early days of American embalming, when it was performed in the home of the deceased, it was almost mandatory for some relative to stay by the embalmer's side and witness the procedure. Today, family members who might wish to be in attendance would certainly be dissuaded by the funeral director. All others, except apprentices, are excluded by law from the preparation room.

3   A close look at what does actually take place may explain in large measure the undertaker's intractable reticence concerning a procedure that has become his major *raison d'être*. [1] Is it possible he fears that public

[1] Reason for being.

information about embalming might lead patrons to wonder if they really want this service? If the funeral men are loath to discuss the subject outside the trade, the reader may, understandably, be equally loath to go on reading at this point. For those who have the stomach for it, let us part the formaldehyde curtain. . . .

4   The body is first laid out in the undertaker's morgue—or rather, Mr. Jones is reposing in the preparation room—to be readied to bid the world farewell.

5   The preparation room in any of the better funeral establishments has the tiled and sterile look of a surgery, and indeed the embalmer-restorative artist who does his chores there is beginning to adopt the term "dermasurgeon" (appropriately corrupted by some mortician-writers as "demisurgeon") to describe his calling. His equipment, consisting of scalpels, scissors, augers, forceps, clamps, needles, pumps, tubes, bowls and basins, is crudely imitative of the surgeon's as is his technique, acquired in a nine- or twelve-month post-high-school course in an embalming school. He is supplied by an advanced chemical industry with a bewildering array of fluids, sprays, pastes, oils, powders, creams, to fix or soften tissue, shrink or distend it as needed, dry it here, restore the moisture there. There are cosmetics, waxes and paints to fill and cover features, even plaster of Paris to replace entire limbs. There are ingenious aids to prop and stabilize the cadaver: a Vari-Pose Head Rest, the Edwards Arm and Hand Positioner, the Repose Block (to support the shoulders during the embalming), and the Throop Foot Positioner, which resembles an old-fashioned stocks.

6   Mr. John H. Eckels, president of the Eckels College of Mortuary Science, thus describes the first part of the embalming procedure: "In the hands of a skilled practitioner, this work may be done in a comparatively short time and without mutilating the body other than by slight incision—so slight that it scarcely would cause serious inconvenience if made upon a living person. It is necessary to remove the blood, and doing this not only helps in the disinfecting, but removes the principal cause of disfigurements due to discoloration."

7   Another textbook discusses the all-important time element: "The earlier this is done, the better, for every hour that elapses between death and embalming will add to the problems and complications encountered. . . ." Just how soon should one get going on the embalming? The author tells us, "On the basis of such scanty information made

available to this profession through its rudimentary and haphazard system of technical research, we must conclude that the best results are to be obtained if the subject is embalmed before life is completely extinct—that is, before cellular death has occurred. In the average case, this would mean within an hour after somatic death." For those who feel that there is something a little rudimentary, not to say haphazard, about this advice, a comforting thought is offered by another writer. Speaking of fears entertained in early days of premature burial, he points out, "One of the effects of embalming by chemical injection, however, has been to dispel fears of live burial." How true; once the blood is removed, chances of live burial are indeed remote.

8   To return to Mr. Jones, the blood is drained out through the veins and replaced by embalming fluid pumped in through the arteries. As noted in *The Principles and Practices of Embalming,* "every operator has a favorite injection and drainage point—a fact which becomes a handicap only if he fails or refuses to forsake his favorites when conditions demand it." Typical favorites are the carotid artery, femoral artery, jugular vein, subclavian vein. There are various choices of embalming fluid. If Flextone is used, it will produce a "mild flexible rigidity. The skin retains a velvety softness, the tissues are rubbery and pliable. Ideal for women and children." It may be blended with B. and G. Products Company's Lyf-Lyk tint, which is guaranteed to reproduce "nature's own skin texture . . . the velvety appearance of living tissue." Suntone comes in three separate tints: Suntan; Special Cosmetic Tint, a pink shade "especially indicated for young female subjects"; and Regular Cosmetic Tint, moderately pink.

9   About three to six gallons of a dyed and perfumed solution of formaldehyde, glycerin, borax, phenol, alcohol and water is soon circulating through Mr. Jones, whose mouth has been sewn together with a "needle directed upward between the upper lip and gum and brought out through the left nostril," with the corners raised slightly "for a more pleasant expression." If he should be bucktoothed, his teeth are cleaned with Bon Ami and coated with colorless nail polish. His eyes, meanwhile, are closed with flesh-tinted eye caps and eye cement.

10   The next step is to have at Mr. Jones with a thing called a trocar. This is a long, hollow needle attached to a tube. It is jabbed into the abdomen, poked around the entrails and chest cavity, the contents of which are pumped out and replaced with "cavity fluid." This done, and the hole in the abdomen sewn up, Mr. Jones's face is heavily creamed

(to protect the skin from burns which may be caused by leakage of the chemicals), and he is covered with a sheet and left unmolested for a while. But not for long—there is more, much more, in store for him. He has been embalmed, but not yet restored, and the best time to start the restorative work is eight to ten hours after embalming, when the tissues have become firm and dry.

11   The object of all this attention to the corpse, it must be remembered, is to make it presentable for viewing in an attitude of healthy repose. "Our customs require the presentation of our dead in the semblance of normality . . . unmarred by the ravages of illness, disease or mutilation," says Mr. J. Sheridan Mayer in his *Restorative Art*. This is rather a large order since few people die in the full bloom of health, unravaged by illness and unmarked by some disfigurement. The funeral industry is equal to the challenge: "In some cases the gruesome appearance of a mutilated or disease-ridden subject may be quite discouraging. The task of restoration may seem impossible and shake the confidence of the embalmer. This is the time for intestinal fortitude and determination. Once the formative work is begun and affected tissues are cleaned or removed, all doubts of success vanish. It is surprising and gratifying to discover the results which may be obtained."

12   The embalmer, having allowed an appropriate interval to elapse, returns to the attack, but now he brings into play the skill and equipment of sculptor and cosmetician. Is a hand missing? Casting one in plaster of Paris is a simple matter. "For replacement purposes, only a cast of the back of the hand is necessary; this is within the ability of the average operator and is quite adequate." If a lip or two, a nose or an ear should be missing, the embalmer has at hand a variety of restorative waxes with which to model replacements. Pores and skin texture are simulated by stippling with a little brush, and over this cosmetics are laid on. Head off? Decapitation cases are rather routinely handled. Ragged edges are trimmed, and head joined to torso with a series of splints, wires and sutures. It is a good idea to have a little something at the neck—a scarf or high collar—when time for viewing comes. Swollen mouth? Cut out tissue as needed from inside the lips. If too much is removed, the surface contour can easily be restored by padding with cotton. Swollen necks and cheeks are reduced by removing tissue through vertical incisions made down each side of the neck. "When the deceased is casketed, the pillow will hide the suture incisions . . . as an extra precaution against leakage, the suture may be painted with liquid sealer."

13   The opposite condition is more likely to present itself—that of emaciation. His hypodermic syringe now loaded with massage cream, the embalmer seeks out and fills the hollowed and sunken areas by injection. In this procedure the backs of the hands and fingers and the under-chin area should not be neglected.

14   Positioning the lips is a problem that recurrently challenges the ingenuity of the embalmer. Closed too tightly, they tend to give a stern, even disapproving expression. Ideally, embalmers feel, the lips should give the impression of being ever so slightly parted, the upper lip protruding slightly for a more youthful appearance. This takes some engineering, however, as the lips tend to drift apart. Lip drift can sometimes be remedied by pushing one or two straight pins through the inner margin of the lower lip and then inserting them between the two front upper teeth. If Mr. Jones happens to have no teeth, the pins can just as easily be anchored in his Armstrong Face Former and Denture Replacer. Another method to maintain lip closure is to dislocate the lower jaw, which is then held in its new position by a wire run through holes which have been drilled through the upper and lower jaws at the midline. As the French are fond of saying, *il faut souffrir pour être belle.* [2]

15   If Mr. Jones has died of jaundice, the embalming fluid will very likely turn him green. Does this deter the embalmer? Not if he has intestinal fortitude. Masking pastes and cosmetics are heavily laid on, burial garments and casket interiors are color-correlated with particular care, and Jones is displayed beneath rose-colored lights. Friends will say, "How *well* he looks." Death by carbon monoxide, on the other hand, can be rather a good thing from the embalmer's viewpoint: "One advantage is the fact that this type of discoloration is an exaggerated form of a natural pink coloration." This is nice because the healthy glow is already present and needs but little attention.

16   The patching and filling completed, Mr. Jones is now shaved, washed and dressed. Cream-based cosmetic, available in pink, flesh, suntan, brunette and blond, is applied to his hands and face, his hair is shampooed and combed (and, in the case of Mrs. Jones, set), his hands manicured. For the horny-handed son of toil special care must be taken; cream should be applied to remove ingrained grime, and the nails cleaned. "If he were not in the habit of having them manicured in life,

---

[2] "One must suffer in order to be beautiful."

trimming and shaping is advised for better appearance—never questioned by kin."

17 Jones is now ready for casketing (this is the present participle of the verb "to casket"). In this operation his right shoulder should be depressed slightly "to turn the body a bit to the right and soften the appearance of lying flat on his back." Positioning the hands is a matter of importance, and special rubber positioning blocks may be used. The hands should be cupped slightly for a more lifelike, relaxed appearance. Proper placement of the body requires a delicate sense of balance. It should lie as high as possible in the casket, yet not so high that the lid, when lowered, will hit the nose. On the other hand, we are cautioned, placing the body too low "creates the impression that the body is in a box."

18 Jones is next wheeled into the appointed slumber room where a few last touches may be added—his favorite pipe placed in his hand or, if he was a great reader, a book propped into position. (In the case of little Master Jones a Teddy bear may be clutched.) Here he will hold open house for a few days, visiting hours 10 A.M. to 9 P.M.

QUESTIONS ON CONTENT, STRUCTURE, AND STYLE

1. By studying the first three paragraphs, summarize both Mitford's reason for explaining the embalming process and her attitude toward undertakers who wish to keep their patrons uninformed about this procedure.

2. Mitford's essay is developed by *process analysis;* that is, it explains what steps must be taken to complete an operation or procedure. Process essays may be identified as either *directional* or *informative.* A directional process tells the reader how to do or make something; an informative process describes the steps by which someone other than the reader does or makes something, or how something was done or made in the past. Is Mitford's essay a directional or informative process analysis?

3. Does this process flow smoothly from step to step? Identify the transition devices connecting the paragraphs.

4. Does Mitford use enough specific details to help you visualize each step as it occurs? Point out examples of details which create vivid descriptions by appealing to your sense of sight, smell, or touch.

5. How does the technique of using the hypothetical "Mr. Jones" make the explanation of the process more effective? Why didn't Mitford simply refer to "the corpse" or "a body" throughout her essay?

6. What is Mitford's general attitude toward this procedure? the overall tone of the essay? Study Mitford's choice of words and then identify the tone in each of the following passages:

"The next step is to have at Mr. Jones with a thing called a trocar." (10)

"The embalmer, having allowed an appropriate interval to elapse, returns to the attack. . . ." (12)

"Friends will say, 'How *well* he looks.'" (15)

"On the other hand, we are cautioned, placing the body too low 'creates the impression that the body is in a box.'" (17)

"Here he will hold open house for a few days, visiting hours 10 A.M. to 9 P.M." (18)

What other words and passages reveal Mitford's attitude and tone?

7. Why does Mitford repeatedly quote various undertakers and textbooks on the embalming and restorative process ("'needle directed upward between the upper lip and gum and brought out through the left nostril'")? Why is the quote in paragraph 7 that begins, "'On the basis of such scanty information made available to this profession through its rudimentary and haphazard system of technical research . . .'" particularly effective in emphasizing Mitford's attitude toward the funeral industry?

8. What does Mitford gain by quoting euphemisms (dandified terms replacing more offensive words) used by the funeral business, such as "dermasurgeon," "Repose Block," and "slumber room"?

9. What are the connotations of the words "jabbed," "poked," and "left unmolested" in paragraph 10? What effect is Mitford trying to produce with the series of questions (such as "Head off?") in paragraph 12?

10. Evaluate Mitford's last sentence. Does it successfully sum up the author's attitude and conclude the essay?

VOCABULARY

docility (1)	ingenious (5)	pliable (8)
inherent (2)	cadaver (5)	semblance (11)
intractable (3)	somatic (7)	stippling (12)
reticence (3)	dispel (7)	

SUGGESTIONS FOR WRITING

1. By supplying information about the embalming process, did Mitford change your attitude toward this procedure or toward the funeral industry? Should we subject our dead to this process? Are there advantages Mitford fails to mention? Write an essay defending your position.

2. Consider other American customs, such as those associated with the traditional wedding or the celebration of holidays. Are there any rituals you disapprove of? If so, write an essay explaining your criticisms, making your case as detailed and vivid as Mitford's.

3. Write a process essay in which you leave step-by-step instructions for carrying out your own funeral. Detail the location, music, speakers, and events so that the appropriate mood will be set. What is the dominant impression you are creating? Why?

The Right to Die

NORMAN COUSINS

Norman Cousins served as editor of *Saturday Review* for over thirty-five years (1940–1971 and 1973–1977). His many books include *The Celebration of Life* (1974), *Anatomy of an Illness* (1979), and *The Healing Heart: Antidotes to Panic and Helplessness* (1983). This essay was published as an editorial in *Saturday Review* in 1975.

1   THE WORLD of religion and philosophy was shocked recently when Henry P. Van Dusen and his wife ended their lives by their own hands. Dr. Van Dusen had been president of Union Theological Seminary; for

more than a quarter-century he had been one of the luminous names in Protestant theology. He enjoyed world status as a spiritual leader. News of the self-inflicted death of the Van Dusens, therefore, was profoundly disturbing to all those who attach a moral stigma to suicide and regard it as a violation of God's laws.

2   Dr. Van Dusen had anticipated this reaction. He and his wife left behind a letter that may have historic significance. It was very brief, but the essential point it made is now being widely discussed by theologians and could represent the beginning of a reconsideration of traditional religious attitudes toward self-inflicted death. The letter raised a moral issue: does an individual have the obligation to go on living even when the beauty and meaning and power of life are gone?

3   Henry and Elizabeth Van Dusen had lived full lives. In recent years, they had become increasingly ill, requiring almost continual medical care. Their infirmities were worsening, and they realized they would soon become completely dependent for even the most elementary needs and functions. Under these circumstances, little dignity would have been left in life. They didn't like the idea of taking up space in a world with too many mouths and too little food. They believed it was a misuse of medical science to keep them technically alive.

4   They therefore believed they had the right to decide when to die. In making that decision, they weren't turning against life as the highest value; what they were turning against was the notion that there were no circumstances under which life should be discontinued.

5   An important aspect of human uniqueness is the power of free will. In his books and lectures, Dr. Van Dusen frequently spoke about the exercise of this uniqueness. The fact that he used his free will to prevent life from becoming a caricature of itself was completely in character. In their letter, the Van Dusens sought to convince family and friends that they were not acting solely out of despair or pain.

6   The use of free will to put an end to one's life finds no sanction in the theology to which Pitney Van Dusen was committed. Suicide symbolizes discontinuity; religion symbolizes continuity, represented as its quintessence by the concept of the immortal soul. Human logic finds it almost impossible to come to terms with the concept of nonexistence. In religion, the human mind finds a larger dimension and is relieved of the ordeal of a confrontation with non-existence.

7   Even without respect to religion, the idea of suicide has been abhorrent throughout history. Some societies have imposed severe penalties on the families of suicides in the hope that the individual who sees no

reason to continue his existence may be deterred by the stigma his self-destruction would inflict on loved ones. Other societies have enacted laws prohibiting suicide on the grounds that it is murder. The enforcement of such laws, of course, has been an exercise in futility.

8 Customs and attitudes, like individuals themselves, are largely shaped by the surrounding environment. In today's world, life can be prolonged by science far beyond meaning or sensibility. Under these circumstances, individuals who feel they have nothing more to give to life, or to receive from it, need not be applauded, but they can be spared our condemnation.

9 The general reaction to suicide is bound to change as people come to understand that it may be a denial, not an assertion, of moral or religious ethics to allow life to be extended without regard to decency or pride. What moral or religious purpose is celebrated by the annihilation of the human spirit in the triumphant act of keeping the body alive? Why are so many people more readily appalled by an unnatural form of dying than by an unnatural form of living?

10 "Nowadays," the Van Dusens wrote in their last letter, "it is difficult to die. We feel that this way we are taking will become more usual and acceptable as the years pass.

11 "Of course, the thought of our children and our grandchildren makes us sad, but we still feel that this is the best way and the right way to go. We are both increasingly weak and unwell and who would want to die in a nursing home?

12 "We are not afraid to die. . . ."

13 Pitney Van Dusen was admired and respected in life. He can be admired and respected in death. "Suicide," said Goethe, "is an incident in human life which, however much disputed and discussed, demands the sympathy of every man, and in every age must be dealt with anew."

14 Death is not the greatest loss in life. The greatest loss is what dies inside us while we live. The unbearable tragedy is to live without dignity or sensitivity.

QUESTIONS ON CONTENT, STRUCTURE, AND STYLE

1. Why was it so shocking that the Van Dusens committed suicide?

2. What moral issue did the Van Dusens' letter raise?

3. What is Cousins' attitude toward suicide? Where does this attitude become clear?

4. How does Cousins use the Van Dusens to support his view on suicide?

5. How has suicide been regarded throughout history?

6. What change in attitude toward suicide does Cousins foresee? Why?

7. What does Cousins gain by quoting from the Van Dusens' letter?

8. Why does Cousins quote the philosopher Goethe?

9. According to Cousins, what is the "greatest loss in life"?

10. Evaluate Cousins' diction. Why, for example, does he use such phrases as "technically alive" (paragraph 3) and "prevent life from becoming a caricature of itself" (paragraph 5)?

VOCABULARY

luminous (1)	sanction (6)	sensibility (8)
stigma (1)	continuity (6)	annihilation (9)
infirmities (3)	quintessence (6)	appalled (9)
caricature (5)	abhorrent (7)	

SUGGESTIONS FOR WRITING

1. Do you agree that suicidal people should not be restrained? What about suicidal teenagers or children? Should doctors "assist" those who wish to end their lives? Most communities have a suicide prevention or mental health center of some kind. Contact your center and compare/contrast your attitude toward the "rights" of suicidal people to theirs. Then write an essay of your own on "The Right to Die."

2. Write an essay in support of or in opposition to Cousins' statement that "Death is not the greatest loss in life."

3. Should newborn infants who are severely handicapped be allowed to die? Should parents of such a baby be allowed to decide which medical treatment might be withheld? Write an essay that explains both sides of this complex controversy. Before you write, you might wish to read about some of the more famous cases in this area, such as the Baby Doe case (1982) in which the federal government tried to block the decision of the parents.

A Dying Art: The Classy Exit Line

LANCE MORROW

Shortly after graduating from Harvard, Lance Morrow began a career as a writer for *Time* that has spanned nearly thirty years. In addition to his award-winning essays and cover stories for the magazine, he has written several books, including *The Chief: A Memoir of Fathers and Sons* (1984), a chronicle of his relationship with his father, former *Saturday Evening Post* writer Hugh Morrow. This essay was first published in *Time* in 1984.

1   THERE WAS a time when the deathbed was a kind of proscenium, from which the personage could issue one last dramatic utterance, full of the compacted significance of his life. Last words were to sound as if all of the individual's earthly time had been sharpened to that point: he could now etch the grand summation. "More light!" the great Goethe of the Englightenment is said to have cried as he expired. There is some opinion, however, that what he actually said was "Little wife, give me your little paw."

2   In any case, the genre of great last words died quite a few years ago. There are those who think the last genuinely memorable last words were spoken in 1900, when, according to one version, the dying Oscar Wilde said, "Either that wallpaper goes, or I do."

3   Others set the date in 1904, when Chekhov on his deathbed declared, "It's a long time since I drank champagne." Appropriately, his coffin then rode to burial in a freight car marked FRESH OYSTERS.

4   Only now and then does one catch a handsome exit line today. Gary Gilmore, the murderer executed in Utah in 1977, managed a moment of brisk existentialist machismo when he told the warden, "Let's do it." There was a charm, a mist of the fey overlaying the terror, in the official last words that William Saroyan telephoned to the Associated Press before he died in 1981: "Everybody has got to die, but I have always believed an exception would be made in my case. Now what?" Last fall the British actor John Le Mesurier dictated to his wife his own death announcement, which ran in the *Times* of London. It said, "John Le

Mesurier wishes it to be known that he conked out on Nov. 15. He sadly misses family and friends."

5   Last words are a matter of taste, of course, and judgments about them tend to be subjective. A strong though eccentric case might be made for the final utterance of Britain's Lord Chief Justice Gordon Hewart, who died on a spring morning in 1944 with the words "Damn it! There's that cuckoo again!" Tallulah Bankhead used a splendid economy of language at her parting in New York City's St. Luke's Hospital in 1968. "Bourbon," she said. The Irish writer Brendan Behan rose to the occasion in 1964 when he turned to the nun who had just wiped his brow and said, "Ah, bless you, Sister, may all your sons be bishops." Some sort of award for sharp terminal repartee should be bestowed (posthumously) upon an uncle of Oliver Wendell Holmes, Jr., John Holmes, who lay dying in his Boston home in 1899. A nurse kept feeling his feet, and explained to someone in the room, "If his feet are warm, he is alive . . . Nobody ever died with his feet warm." Holmes rose out of his coma long enough to observe, "John Rogers[1] did!" Then he slipped away.

6   The great last words traditionally included in anthologies have usually been more serious than that, and often sound suspiciously perfect. *Le style, c'est l'homme.*[2] General Robert E. Lee is said to have gone in 1870 with just the right military-metaphysical command: "Strike the tent!" The great 18th century classicist and prig Nicolas Boileau managed a sentence of wonderfully plump self-congratulation: "It is a consolation to a poet on the point of death that he has never written a line injurious to good mortals."

7   While such goodbyes are usually retrospective, looking back on the life, they sometimes peer forward. Such lines derive considerable fascination from the fact that they have spoken at a vantage that is the closest that mortals can legitimately come to a glimpse of what lies on the other side. Thomas A. Edison said as he died in 1931, "It's very beautiful over there." (It is also possible, however, that he was referring to the view outside his window.) Voltaire had a mordant premonition. The lamp next to his deathbed flared momentarily, and his last words were "What? The flames already?"

---

[1] An English Protestant divine burned at the stake for heresy in 1555. [author's note]
[2] *Le style, c'est l'homme* is a French expression meaning "style makes the man."

8   Last words are supposed to be a drama of truth-telling, of nothing left to hide, nothing more to lose. Why, then, do they so often have that clunk of the bogus about them? Possibly because the majority of them may have been composed by others—keepers of the flame, hagiologists, busybodies. One hears the little sound of a pious fraud. The last breath is put into service to inflate the larger cause one last time, as with a regret that one has only one life to give for one's country. There is a long-running controversy, for example, over whether the younger Pitt, when departing this life, said, "My country! How I love my country!" or "I think I could eat one of Bellamy's pork pies."

9   As Hamlet says in *his* last words, "the rest is silence." Great terminal summations are a form of theater, really. They demand an audience—someone has to hear them, after all. More than that, they have been traditionally uttered with a high solemnity. Some last words have the irony of inadvertence—as when Civil War General John Sedgwick was heard to say during the battle of Spotsylvania Court House, "Why, they couldn't hit an elephant at this dist—" But premeditated last words—the deathbed equivalent of Neil Armstrong's "One small step for a man, one giant leap for mankind," the canned speech uttered when setting off for other worlds—have a Shakespearean grandiloquence about them.

10   Last words are not a congenial form of theater any more. Suitable stages no longer seem to be available for such death scenes, nor is there much inclination to witness them. People tend either to die suddenly, unexpectedly, without the necessary editorial preparation, or to expire in hospitals, under sedation and probably not during visiting hours. The sedative dusk descends hours or days before the last darkness.

11   Perhaps the demise of great last words has something to do with a decline in the 20th century of the augustness of death. The departure of a single soul was once an imposing occasion. An age of holocausts is less disposed to hear the individual goodbyes.

12   Perhaps some entrepreneur will try to revive the genre of last words by enlisting videotape, a newer form of theater. Customers could write their own final script—or choose appropriate last words from the company's handsome selection ("Pick the goodbye that is you"), and then, well before the actual end, videotape their own official death scenes. The trouble is that most people tend to be windy and predictable when asked to say a few words on an important occasion. Maybe the best way to be memorable at the end is to be enigmatic. When in doubt, simply mutter, "Rosebud."

QUESTIONS ON CONTENT, STRUCTURE, AND STYLE

1. How, according to this essay, did people once regard deathbed statements?

2. What is Morrow's thesis concerning great exit lines today?

3. What indications do you have that this essay is not intended to be an entirely serious treatment of its subject?

4. How does Morrow acquaint his audience with his notion of great last words?

5. Why is one suspicious of some of the more famous exit lines?

6. What characteristics do all great deathbed utterances have in common?

7. According to Morrow, why are there fewer outstanding exit lines in the modern ages?

8. What remedies does Morrow suggest in order to revive the genre of famous last words? Are his suggestions serious? Support your opinion.

9. Morrow's conclusion may be puzzling to some readers. To what does "Rosebud" refer? Is Morrow's ending a good choice for this essay?

10. Describe the overall effect of Morrow's use of quotations. Did he include too many or too few? Which were the most effective? Why?

VOCABULARY

proscenium (1)
genre (2)
existentialist (4)
fey (4)
repartee (5)
posthumously (5)
metaphysical (6)

prig (6)
retrospective (7)
mordant (7)
premonition (7)
bogus (8)
hagiologists (8)
inadvertence (9)

grandiloquence (9)
congenial (10)
demise (11)
augustness (11)
entrepreneur (12)
enigmatic (12)

Suggestions for Writing

1. Write your own memorable exit line; it might be humorous or serious. Then write an essay that explains why your exit line is a highly appropriate or symbolic comment on your life to this point. (To help you with this project, consider renting Orson Wells' great film *Citizen Kane*. Watch the way that Wells begins with the last word of a famous character and then uses a series of flashbacks to recreate the man's life and values.)

2. It's frequently lamented that too many people's tombstones should read "Died at 40. Buried at 70." Think of an older person you know who is living life to the fullest. Write an essay explaining this person's philosophy of life and show why such an approach to living is, in your opinion, admirable.

3. Write an essay that uses a number of quotations or anecdotes to illustrate its point. For instance, you might illustrate the lively art of the great insult, or the wit of a public figure, or the country wisdom of a friend or relative. Be sure that your essay has a clear thesis, a point you wish to make about your subject matter.

The Discus Thrower

Richard Selzer

Richard Selzer teaches surgery at Yale Medical School and has contributed both stories and essays to a number of magazines. He has published a collection of short stories, *Rituals of Surgery* (1974), and several collections of essays, including *Mortal Lessons* (1977) and *Taking the World in for Repairs* (1986). This essay was published in *Harper's* in 1977.

1   I spy on my patients. Ought not a doctor to observe his patients by any means and from any stance, that he might the more fully assemble evidence? So I stand in the doorways of hospital rooms and gaze. Oh, it is not all that furtive an act. Those in bed need only look up to discover me. But they never do.

2   From the doorway of Room 542 the man in the bed seems deeply tanned. Blue eyes and close-cropped white hair give him the appearance of vigor and good health. But I know that his skin is not brown from the sun. It is rusted, rather, in the last stage of containing the vile repose within. And the blue eyes are frosted, looking inward like the windows of a snowbound cottage. This man is blind. This man is also legless—the right leg missing from midthigh down, the left from just below the knee. It gives him the look of a bonsai, roots and branches pruned into the dwarfed facsimile of a great tree.

3   Propped on pillows, he cups his right thigh in both hands. Now and then he shakes his head as though acknowledging the intensity of his suffering. In all of this he makes no sound. Is he mute as well as blind?

4   The room in which he dwells is empty of all possessions—no get-well cards, small, private caches of food, day-old flowers, slippers, all the usual kickshaws of the sickroom. There is only the bed, a chair, a nightstand, and a tray on wheels that can be swung across his lap for meals.

5   "What time is it?" he asks.

6   "Three o'clock."

7   "Morning or afternoon?"

8   "Afternoon."

9   He is silent. There is nothing else he wants to know.

10   "How are you?" I say.

11   "Who is it?" he asks.

12   "It's the doctor. How do you feel?"

13   He does not answer right away.

14   "Feel?" he says.

15   "I hope you feel better," I say.

16   I press the button at the side of the bed.

17   "Down you go," I say.

18   "Yes, down," he says.

19   He falls back upon the bed awkwardly. His stumps, unweighted by legs and feet, rise in the air, presenting themselves. I unwrap the bandages from the stumps, and begin to cut away the black scabs and the dead, glazed fat with scissors and forceps. A shard of white bone comes loose. I pick it away. I wash the wounds with disinfectant and redress the stumps. All this while, he does not speak. What is he thinking behind those lids that do not blink? Is he remembering a time when he was whole? Does he dream of feet? Of when his body was not a rotting log?

20   He lies solid and inert. In spite of everything, he remains impressive, as though he were a sailor standing athwart a slanting deck.

21   "Anything more I can do for you?" I ask.

22   For a long moment he is silent.

23   "Yes," he says at last and without the least irony. "You can bring me a pair of shoes."

24   In the corridor, the head nurse is waiting for me.

25   "We have to do something about him," she says, "Every morning he orders scrambled eggs for breakfast, and, instead of eating them, he picks up the plate and throws it against the wall."

26   "Throws his plate?"

27   "Nasty. That's what he is. No wonder his family doesn't come to visit. They probably can't stand him any more than we can."

28   She is waiting for me to do something.

29   "Well?"

30   "We'll see," I say.

31   The next morning I am waiting in the corridor when the kitchen delivers his breakfast. I watch the aide place the tray on the stand and swing it across his lap. She presses the button to raise the head of the bed. Then she leaves.

32   In time the man reaches to find the rim of the tray, then on to find the dome of the covered dish. He lifts off the cover and places it on the stand. He fingers across the plate until he probes the eggs. He lifts the plate in both hands, sets it on the palm of his right hand, centers it, balances it. He hefts it up and down slightly, getting the feel of it. Abruptly, he draws back his right arm as far as he can.

33   There is the crack of the plate breaking against the wall at the foot of his bed and the small wet sound of the scrambled eggs dropping to the floor.

34   And then he laughs. It is a sound you have never heard. It is something new under the sun. It could cure cancer.

35   Out in the corridor, the eyes of the head nurse narrow.

36   "Laughed, did he?"

37   She writes something down on her clipboard.

38   A second aide arrives, brings a second breakfast tray, puts it on the nightstand, out of his reach. She looks over at me shaking her head and making her mouth go. I see that we are to be accomplices.

39   "I've got to feed you," she says to the man.

40   "Oh, no you don't," the man says.

41   "Oh, yes I do," the aide says, "after the way you just did. Nurse says so."

42   "Get me my shoes," the man says.

43   "Here's oatmeal," the aide says. "Open." And she touches the spoon to his lower lip.

44   "I ordered scrambled eggs," says the man.

45   "That's right," the aide says.

46   I step forward.

47   "Is there anything I can do?" I say.

48   "Who are you?" the man asks.

49   In the evening I go once more to that ward to make my rounds. The head nurse reports to me that Room 542 is deceased. She has discovered this quite by accident, she says. No, there had been no sound. Nothing. It's a blessing, she says.

50   I go into his room, a spy looking for secrets. He is still there in his bed. His face is relaxed, grave, dignified. After a while, I turn to leave. My gaze sweeps the wall at the foot of the bed, and I see the place where it has been repeatedly washed, where the wall looks very clean and very white.

QUESTIONS ON CONTENT, STRUCTURE, AND STYLE

1. How does Selzer establish the story's point of view?

2. Why does the patient throw his eggs on the wall each day? Why does he laugh?

3. Why does the patient repeatedly call for his shoes?

4. What is Selzer's attitude toward his patient? How do you know? What is the attitude of the head nurse?

5. What is Selzer's point in telling this story? Why doesn't he "do something" about the patient, as the nurse wants?

6. Why does Selzer use dialogue in some places rather than description?

7. What is the tone of this essay? Study the sentences in the essay. What effect does their length and construction have on the general tone?

8. Point out several examples of metaphor and simile. What does each of these add to the essay's effectiveness?

9. Why does Selzer end his essay by referring to the clean wall? Is it an effective conclusion? Why/why not?

10. Selzer's subtitle for this essay was "Do Not Go Gentle," a reference to a well-known poem by Dylan Thomas, reprinted on p. 222 of this text. Read through the poem; why is it an appropriate complement to this narrative?

VOCABULARY

furtive (1)   *caches (4)*   *inert (20)*
vile (2)   *kickshaws (4)*   *athwart (20)*
repose (2)   *shard (19)*   *irony (23)*
facsimile (2)

SUGGESTIONS FOR WRITING

1. Consider the death of a person you have known. Write an essay describing one way this death has affected you or your attitude toward dying.

2. Write an essay that explains your position toward keeping the dying or hopelessly ill alive through modern technology. It may help you focus your thoughts by pretending that the sick person is someone close to you, such as a member of your immediate family.

3. Should hospital care givers be legally required to withhold food or medicine if the patient demands such behavior? For instance, several years ago Elizabeth Bouvia, a victim of cerebral palsy that made her totally dependent upon the care of others, asked hospital personnel to allow her to starve to death. The hospital refused, and the case went to the courts. Write an essay in which you play the judge in this case or in a similar one. Write an essay that explains your decision. (See also question 3 on p. 212.)

Do Not Go Gentle into That Good Night

DYLAN THOMAS

Dylan Thomas, born in Wales, is one of the best-known poets of the twentieth century. Admired for his talent of reading as well as writing poetry, Thomas spent many months on tour in America between 1950 and 1953, where his outspoken and sometimes reckless behavior occasionally shocked the public. Some of his volumes of poetry include *The Map of Love* (1939), *Deaths and Entrances* (1946), and *Collected Poems* (1953).

Do not go gentle into that good night,
Old age should burn and rave at close of day;
Rage, rage against the dying of the light.

Though wise men at their end know dark is right,
5   Because their words had forked no lightning they
Do not go gentle into that good night.

Good men, the last wave by, crying how bright
Their frail deeds might have danced in a green bay,
Rage, rage against the dying of the light.

10   Wild men who caught and sang the sun in flight,
And learn, too late, they grieved it on its way,
Do not go gentle into that good night.

Grave men, near death, who see with blinding sight
Blind eyes could blaze like meteors and be gay,
15   Rage, rage against the dying of the light.

And you, my father, there on the sad height,
Curse, bless, me now with your fierce tears, I pray.
Do not go gentle into that good night.
Rage, rage against the dying of the light.

QUESTIONS ON CONTENT, STRUCTURE, AND STYLE

1. To whom is the poet speaking? Is this person old or young?

2. What does "that good night" refer to?

3. What, according to the poet, should old people do at the end of their lives?

4. What do wise men know about the "dark"? What do they do, nevertheless?

5. What other kinds of men rage against "the dying of the light"? Why does Thomas mention them?

6. List the metaphors Thomas uses for death. What do they all have in common?

7. What does Thomas ask his father to do to him? Why?

8. Characterize the speaker's tone of voice. Is it pleading? angry? insistent?

9. What effect does the repetition of lines (and sounds) have on the tone of the speaker's requests?

10. How might you paraphrase the poem's argument in one brief statement?

VOCABULARY

rave (line 2)
frail (line 8)
grieved (line 11)

SUGGESTIONS FOR WRITING

1. Read "The Discus Thrower," by Richard Selzer, p. 217. Why did Selzer subtitle his essay "Do Not Go Gentle"? Write an essay comparing and contrasting the attitude toward death held by Selzer's patient to that voiced by Dylan Thomas in his poem. Do their views toward death differ greatly from your own?

2. Adults are always, it seems, giving young people words of advice. But in this poem, Thomas is counseling his father. Write an essay

that explains either the best or worst piece of advice an older person ever gave you or an essay that explains advice that you would like to give to an older person, such as your father or mother, or to someone important in your life.

3. After looking up the literary term *villanelle,* write an essay analyzing Dylan's poem. How do the poem's structure, point of view, metaphors, and images communicate its theme? Or, if you prefer, compare/contrast this poem to another poem or literary work on a similar subject. How do the two writers' ideas and techniques differ?

The Cask of Amontillado

EDGAR ALLAN POE

Edgar Allan Poe, the adopted son of a wealthy Virginia merchant, attended West Point, but was expelled after a year because of his rowdy habits. Disowned by his father, Poe became a writer and an editor of the *Southern Literary Messenger,* from which he was eventually fired because of his instability. Depressed by the death of his cousin-wife, whom he married when she was but thirteen, and addicted to drugs and alcohol, Poe died, poor and ill, in mysterious circumstances. He is best known for his stories of mystery and terror ("Ligeia") and for his romantic poems ("To Helen") but is also recognized for his essays on literary criticism.

1   THE THOUSAND injuries of Fortunato I had borne as I best could, but when he ventured upon insult I vowed revenge. You, who so well know the nature of my soul, will not suppose, however, that I gave utterance to a threat. *At length* I would be avenged; this was a point definitely settled—but the very definitiveness with which it was resolved precluded the idea of risk. I must not only punish but punish with impunity. A wrong is unredressed when retribution overtakes its redresser. It is equally unredressed when the avenger fails to make himself felt as such to him who has done the wrong.

2   It must be understood that neither by word nor deed had I given Fortunato cause to doubt my good will. I continued, as was my wont, to smile in his face, and he did not perceive that my smile *now* was at the thought of his immolation.

3   He had a weak point—this Fortunato—although in other regards he was a man to be respected and even feared. He prided himself on his connoisseurship in wine. Few Italians have the true virtuoso spirit. For the most part their enthusiasm is adopted to suit the time and opportunity, to practise imposture upon the British and Austrian *millionaires.* In painting and gemmary, Fortunato, like his countrymen, was a quack, but in the matter of old wines he was sincere. In this respect I did not differ from him materially;—I was skillful in the Italian vintages myself, and bought largely whenever I could.

4   It was about dusk, one evening during the supreme madness of the carnival season, that I encountered my friend. He accosted me with excessive warmth, for he had been drinking much. The man wore motley. He had on a tight-fitting parti-striped dress, and his head was surmounted by the conical cap and bells. I was so pleased to see him that I thought I should never have done wringing his hand.

5   I said to him—"My dear Fortunato, you are luckily met. How remarkably well you are looking to-day. But I have received a pipe of what passes for Amontillado,[1] and I have my doubts."

6   "How?" said he. "Amontillado? A pipe? Impossible! And in the middle of the carnival!"

7   "I have my doubts," I replied; "and I was silly enough to pay the full Amontillado price without consulting you in the matter. You were not to be found, and I was fearful of losing a bargain."

8   "Amontillado!"

9   "I have my doubts."

10 "Amontillado!"

11 "And I must satisfy them."

12 "Amontillado!"

13 "As you are engaged, I am on my way to Luchresi. If any one has a critical turn it is he. He will tell me ———"

14 "Luchresi cannot tell Amontillado from Sherry."

15 "And yet some fools will have it that his taste is a match for your own."

[1] A Spanish sherry.

16   "Come, let us go."

17   "Whither?"

18   "To your vaults."

19   "My friend, no; I will not impose upon your good nature. I perceive you have an engagement. Luchresi ———"

20   "I have no engagement;—come."

21   "My friend, no. It is not the engagement, but the severe cold with which I perceive you are afflicted. The vaults are insufferably damp. They are encrusted with nitre."

22   "Let us go, nevertheless. The cold is merely nothing. Amontillado! You have been imposed upon. And as for Luchresi, he cannot distinguish Sherry from Amontillado."

23   Thus speaking, Fortunato possessed himself of my arm; and putting on a mask of black silk and drawing a *roquelaire*[2] closely about my person, I suffered him to hurry me to my palazzo.

24   There were no attendants at home; they had absconded to make merry in honor of the time. I had told them that I should not return until the morning, and had given them explicit orders not to stir from the house. These orders were sufficient, I well knew, to insure their immediate disappearance, one and all, as soon as my back was turned.

25   I took from their sconces two flambeaux, and giving one to Fortunato, bowed him through several suites of rooms to the archway that led into the vaults. I passed down a long and winding staircase, requesting him to be cautious as he followed. We came at length to the foot of the descent, and stood together upon the damp ground of the catacombs of the Montresors.

26   The gait of my friend was unsteady, and the bells upon his cap jingled as he strode.

27   "The pipe," he said.

28   "It is farther on," said I; "but observe the white web-work which gleams from these cavern walls."

29   He turned towards me, and looked into my eyes with two filmy orbs that distilled the rheum of intoxication.

30   "Nitre?" he asked at length.

31   "Nitre," I replied. "How long have you had that cough?"

32   "Ugh! ugh! ugh!—ugh! ugh! ugh!—ugh! ugh! ugh!—ugh! ugh! ugh!—ugh! ugh! ugh!"

---

[2] A cloak.

33   My poor friend found it impossible to reply for many minutes.

34   "It is nothing," he said at last.

35   "Come," I said, with decision, "we will go back; your health is precious. You are rich, respected, admired, beloved; you are happy, as once I was. You are a man to be missed. For me it is no matter. We will go back; you will be ill, and I cannot be responsible. Besides, there is Luchresi ———"

36   "Enough," he said; "the cough is a mere nothing; it will not kill me. I shall not die of a cough."

37   "True—true," I replied; "and, indeed, I had no intention of alarming you unnecessarily—but you should use all proper caution. A draught of this Medoc[3] will defend us from the damps."

38   Here I knocked off the neck of a bottle which I drew from a long row of its fellows that lay upon the mould.

39   "Drink," I said, presenting him the wine.

40   He raised it to his lips with a leer. He paused and nodded to me familiarly, while his bells jingled.

41   "I drink," he said, "to the buried that repose around us."

42   "And I to your long life."

43   He again took my arm, and we proceeded.

44   "These vaults," he said, "are extensive."

45   "The Montresors," I replied, "were a great and numerous family."

46   "I forget your arms."

47   "A huge human foot d'or, in a field azure; the foot crushes a serpent rampant whose fangs are imbedded in the heel."

48   "And the motto?"

49   "*Nemo me impune lacessit.*"[4]

50   "Good!" he said.

51   The wine sparkled in his eyes and the bells jingled. My own fancy grew warm with the Medoc. We had passed through long walls of piled skeletons, with casks and puncheons intermingling, into the inmost recesses of the catacombs. I paused again, and this time I made bold to seize Fortunato by an arm above the elbow.

52   "The nitre!" I said; "see, it increases. It hangs like moss upon the vaults. We are below the river's bed. The drops of moisture

---

[3] A French wine.
[4] No one attacks me without punishment.

trickle among the bones. Come, we will go back ere it is too late. Your cough ———"

53   "It is nothing," he said; "let us go on. But first, another draught of the Medoc."

54   I broke and reached him a flagon of De Grave. He emptied it at a breath. His eyes flashed with a fierce light. He laughed and threw the bottle upwards with a gesticulation I did not understand.

55   I looked at him in surprise. He repeated the movement—a grotesque one.

56   "You do not comprehend?" he said.

57   "Not I," I replied.

58   "Then you are not of the brotherhood."

59   "How?"

60   "You are not of the masons."

61   "Yes, yes," I said; "yes, yes."

62   "You? Impossible! A mason?"

63   "A mason," I replied.

64   "A sign," he said, "a sign."

65   "It is this," I answered, producing from beneath the folds of my *roquelaire* a trowel.

66   "You jest," he exclaimed, recoiling a few paces. "But let us proceed to the Amontillado."

67   "Be it so," I said, replacing the tool beneath the cloak and again offering him my arm. He leaned upon it heavily. We continued our route in search of the Amontillado. We passed through a range of low arches, descended, passed on, and descending again, arrived at a deep crypt, in which the foulness of the air caused our flambeaux rather to glow than flame.

68   At the most remote end of the crypt there appeared another less spacious. Its walls had been lined with human remains, piled to the vault overhead, in the fashion of the great catacombs of Paris. Three sides of this interior crypt were still ornamented in this manner. From the fourth side the bones had been thrown down, and lay promiscuously upon the earth, forming at one point a mound of some size. Within the wall thus exposed by the displacing of the bones, we perceived a still interior crypt or recess, in depth about four feet, in width three, in height six or seven. It seemed to have been constructed for no especial use within itself, but formed merely the interval between two of the

colossal supports of the roof of the catacombs, and was backed by one of their circumscribing walls of solid granite.

69   It was in vain that Fortunato, uplifting his dull torch, endeavored to pry into the depth of the recess. Its termination the feeble light did not enable us to see.

70   "Proceed," I said; "herein is the Amontillado. As for Luchresi ——"

71   "He is an ignoramus," interrupted my friend, as he stepped unsteadily forward, while I followed immediately at his heels. In an instant he had reached the extremity of the niche, and finding his progress arrested by the rock, stood stupidly bewildered. A moment more and I had fettered him to the granite. In its surface were two iron staples, distant from each other about two feet, horizontally. From one of these depended a short chain, from the other a padlock. Throwing the links about his waist, it was but the work of a few seconds to secure it. He was too much astounded to resist. Withdrawing the key I stepped back from the recess.

72   "Pass your hand," I said, "over the wall; you cannot help feeling the nitre. Indeed, it is *very* damp. Once more let me *implore* you to return. No? Then I must positively leave you. But I must first render you all the little attentions in my power."

73   "The Amontillado!" ejaculated my friend, not yet recovered from his astonishment.

74   "True," I replied; "the Amontillado."

75   As I said these words I busied myself among the pile of bones of which I have before spoken. Throwing them aside, I soon uncovered a quantity of building stone and mortar. With these materials and with the aid of my trowel, I began vigorously to wall up the entrance of the niche.

76   I had scarcely laid the first tier of the masonry when I discovered that the intoxication of Fortunato had in a great measure worn off. The earliest indication I had of this was a low moaning cry from the depth of the recess. It was *not* the cry of a drunken man. There was a long and obstinate silence. I laid the second tier, and the third, and the fourth; and then I heard the furious vibrations of the chain. The noise lasted for several minutes, during which, that I might hearken to it with the more satisfaction, I ceased my labors and sat down upon the bones. When at last the clanking subsided, I resumed the trowel, and finished without interruption the fifth, the sixth, and the seventh tier. The wall was now nearly upon a level with my breast. I again paused, and holding

the flambeaux over the mason-work, threw a few feeble rays upon the figure within.

77   A succession of loud and shrill screams, bursting suddenly from the throat of the chained form, seemed to thrust me violently back. For a brief moment I hesitated, I trembled. Unsheathing my rapier, I began to grope with it about the recess; but the thought of an instant reassured me. I placed my hand upon the solid fabric of the catacombs, and felt satisfied. I reapproached the wall; I replied to the yells of him who clamoured. I re-echoed, I aided, I surpassed them in volume and in strength. I did this, and the clamourer grew still.

78   It was now midnight, and my task was drawing to a close. I had completed the eighth, the ninth and the tenth tier. I had finished a portion of the last and the eleventh; there remained but a single stone to be fitted and plastered in. I struggled with its weight; I placed it partially in its destined position. But now there came from out the niche a low laugh that erected the hairs upon my head. It was succeeded by a sad voice, which I had difficulty in recognizing as that of the noble Fortunato. The voice said—

79   "Ha! ha! ha!—he! he! he!—a very good joke, indeed—an excellent jest. We will have many a rich laugh about it at the palazzo—he! he! he!—over our wine—he! he! he!"

80   "The Amontillado!" I said.

81   "He! he! he!—he! he! he!—yes, the Amontillado. But is it not getting late? Will not they be awaiting us at the palazzo, the Lady Fortunato and the rest? Let us be gone."

82   "Yes," I said, "let us be gone."

83   *"For the love of God, Montresor!"*

84   "Yes," I said, "for the love of God."

85   But to these words I hearkened in vain for a reply. I grew impatient. I called aloud—

86   "Fortunato!"

87   No answer. I called again—

86   "Fortunato!"

87   No answer. I called again—

88   "Fortunato!"

89   No answer still. I thrust a torch through the remaining aperture and let it fall within. There came forth in return only a jingling of the bells. My heart grew sick; it was the dampness of the catacombs that made it so. I hastened to make an end of my labour. I forced the last

stone into its position; I plastered it up. Against the new masonry I re-erected the old rampart of bones. For the half of a century no mortal has disturbed them. *In pace requiescat!*[5]

QUESTIONS ON CONTENT, STRUCTURE, AND STYLE

1. Who narrates this story? Why is first-person narration the best choice for this story?

2. What is Montresor's definition of revenge? Why does Poe present this definition at the beginning of the story?

3. Poe sets the story during what season? What does this setting add to the story? Why is Fortunato's costume ironic?

4. How does Montresor appeal to Fortunato's vanity to lure him into the catacombs?

5. Throughout the story Montresor ironically plays on words. Explain the irony you see, for instance, in the exchanges about Fortunato's cough (paragraphs 31–37) and the masons and the trowel (paragraphs 60–65).

6. Why are both Montresor's coat-of-arms and his family motto symbolic?

7. Poe creates a highly eerie underground scene. Cite some examples of sensory details that produce this setting. What role does repetition of sound play?

8. Is this story told in chronological order or as a flashback? When do you discover this answer? Why at that point? What would be lost if you knew earlier?

9. Who is "resting in peace"? Who is not? Has Montresor achieved the kind of revenge he described earlier in the story? Defend your answer.

10. Summarize what you think is Poe's attitude toward revenge, as presented in this story. Can one "punish with impunity"?

---

[5] May he rest in peace.

VOCABULARY

avenged (1)	redresser (1)	nitre (21)
precluded (1)	immolation (2)	trowel (65)
impunity (1)	connoisseurship (3)	clamored (77)
retribution (1)	motley (4)	aperture (89)

SUGGESTIONS FOR WRITING

1. Have you ever sought revenge but had your plan backfire on you for one reason or another? Write an essay about your experience, telling your readers what lesson you learned from the situation.

2. Literary critics often point to Poe's main character, Montresor, as an excellent example of the "unreliable narrator," someone whose point of view readers come to distrust. The unreliable narrator often reveals more about himself/herself than about the other characters in the story. Write an essay in which you analyze Poe's use of such a narrator. Or, if you prefer, write your own narrative essay or story from the point of view of a different kind of an unreliable narrator.

3. Poe's story offers at least two views of revenge. Write an essay in which you define some other abstract term (disloyalty, cowardice, friendship, courage, and so on) by using an extended narrative to explain and illustrate the concept. Consider using some of Poe's other techniques, such as setting, sensory details, or irony, to make your story vivid for your reader.

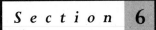

OBSERVING OUR WORLD

Two Ways of Viewing the River

SAMUEL CLEMENS (MARK TWAIN)

Samuel Clemens, whose pen name was Mark Twain, is regarded as one of America's most outstanding writers. Well known for his humorous stories and books, Twain was also a pioneer of fictional realism. His most famous novel, *The Adventures of Huckleberry Finn* (1884), is often hailed as a masterpiece. This selection is from the autobiographical book *Life on the Mississippi* (1883), which recounts Clemens' job as a riverboat pilot.

1   NOW WHEN I mastered the language of this water and had come to know every trifling feature that bordered the great river as familiarly as I knew the letters of the alphabet, I had made a valuable acquisition. But I had lost something, too. I had lost something which could never be restored to me while I lived. All the grace, the beauty, the poetry, had gone out of the majestic river! I still kept in mind a certain wonderful sunset which I witnessed when steamboating was new to me. A broad expanse of the river was turned to blood; in the middle distance the red hue brightened into gold, through which a solitary log came floating, black and conspicuous; in one place a long, slanting mark lay sparkling upon the water; in another the surface was broken by boiling, tumbling rings, that were as many-tinted as an opal; where the ruddy flush was faintest, was a smooth spot that was covered with graceful circles and radiating lines, ever so delicately traced; the shore on our left was densely wooded and the somber shadow that fell from this forest was broken in one place by a long, ruffled trail that shone like silver; and high above the forest wall a clean-stemmed dead tree waved a single leafy bough that glowed like a flame in the unobstructed splendor that was flowing from the sun. There were graceful curves, reflected images, woody heights, soft distances, and over the whole scene, far and near, the dissolving lights drifted steadily, enriching it every passing moment with new marvels of coloring.

2   I stood like one bewitched. I drank it in, in a speechless rapture. The world was new to me and I had never seen anything like this at home. But as I have said, a day came when I began to cease from noting the glories and the charms which the moon and the sun and the twilight wrought upon the river's face; another day came when I

ceased altogether to note them. Then, if that sunset scene had been repeated, I should have looked upon it without rapture, and should have commented upon it inwardly after this fashion: "This sun means that we are going to have wind to-morrow; that floating log means that the river is rising, small thanks to it; that slanting mark on the water refers to a bluff reef which is going to kill somebody's steamboat one of these nights, if it keeps on stretching out like that; those tumbling 'boils' show a dissolving bar and a changing channel there; the lines and circles in the slick water over yonder are a warning that that troublesome place is shoaling up dangerously; that silver streak in the shadow of the forest is the 'break' from a new snag and he has located himself in the very best place he could have found to fish for steamboats; that tall dead tree, with a single living branch, is not going to last long, and then how is a body ever going to get through this blind place at night without the friendly old landmark?"

3   No, the romance and beauty were all gone from the river. All the value any feature of it had for me now was the amount of usefulness it could furnish toward compassing the safe piloting of a steamboat. Since those days, I have pitied doctors from my heart. What does the lovely flush in a beauty's cheek mean to a doctor but a "break" that ripples above some deadly disease? Are not all her visible charms sown thick with what are to him the signs and symbols of hidden decay? Does he ever see her beauty at all, or doesn't he simply view her professionally and comment upon her unwholesome condition all to himself? And doesn't he sometimes wonder whether he has gained most or lost most by learning his trade?

QUESTIONS ON CONTENT, STRUCTURE, AND STYLE

1. What is Clemens contrasting in this essay? Identify his thesis.

2. What organizational pattern does he choose? Is his contrast clearly presented?

3. How does Clemens make a smooth transition to his second view of the river?

4. Why does Clemens refer to doctors in paragraph 3?

5. What is the purpose of the questions in paragraph 3? Why is the last question especially important?

6. Characterize the language Clemens uses in his description in paragraph 1. Is his diction appropriate?

7. Point out several examples of similes in paragraph 1; what do they add to the description of the sunset?

8. How does the language in the description in paragraph 2 differ from the diction in paragraph 1? What aspect of the river is emphasized there?

9. Identify an example of personification in paragraph 2. Why did Clemens add it to his description?

10. Describe the tone of this essay. Does it ever shift?

VOCABULARY

trifling (1)   *ruddy (1)*
acquisition (1)   *wrought (2)*
conspicuous (1)   *compassing (3)*

SUGGESTIONS FOR WRITING

1. Write an essay in which you contrast a first view of an object or scene to a later, less romantic view of the same object or scene. What conclusions can you draw from contrasting your perceptions?

2. Write an essay in which you, like Clemens, explain what you have gained or lost by mastering a trade or skill.

3. Describe a scene whose beauty also conceals its danger. Does the deception add to your enjoyment of the place?

Kids in the Mall

WILLIAM SEVERINI KOWINSKI

William Severini Kowinski is a writer of poetry, fiction, and nonfiction. He has published articles in a number of magazines, such as *Esquire, New Times,* and *The New York Times Magazine.* This selection is taken from his book-length study, *The Malling of America: An Inside Look at the Great Consumer Paradise* (1985), which investigates the effects of shopping malls on the lives of modern teenagers.

Butch heaved himself up and loomed over the group. "Like it was different for me," he piped. "My folks used to drop me off at the shopping mall every morning and leave me all day. It was like a big free baby-sitter, you know? One night they never came back for me. Maybe they moved away. Maybe there's some kind of a Bureau of Missing Parents I could check with."

–RICHARD PECK
Secrets of the Shopping Mall, a novel for teenagers

1   FROM HIS sister at Swarthmore, I'd heard about a kid in Florida whose mother picked him up after school every day, drove him straight to the mall, and left him there until it closed—all at his insistence. I'd heard about a boy in Washington who, when his family moved from one suburb to another, pedaled his bicycle five miles every day to get back to his old mall, where he once belonged.

2   These stories aren't unusual. The mall is a common experience for the majority of American youth; they have probably been going there all their lives. Some ran within their first large open space, saw their first fountain, bought their first toy, and read their first book in a mall. They may have smoked their first cigarette or first joint or turned them down, had their first kiss or lost their virginity in the mall parking lot. Teenagers in America now spend more time in the mall than anywhere else but home and school. Mostly it is their choice, but some of that mall time is put in as the result of two-paycheck and single-parent households, and the lack of other viable alternatives. But are these kids being harmed by the mall?

3   I wondered first of all what difference it makes for adolescents to experience so many important moments in the mall. They are, after all, at play in the fields of its little world and they learn its ways; they adapt to it and make it adapt to them. It's here that these kids get their street sense, only it's mall sense. They are learning the ways of a large-scale artificial environment: its subtleties and flexibilities, its particular pleasures and resonances, and the attitudes it fosters.

4   The presence of so many teenagers for so much time was not something mall developers planned on. In fact, it came as a big surprise. But kids became a fact of mall life very early, and the International Council of Shopping Centers found it necessary to commission a study, which they published along with a guide to mall managers on how to handle the teenage incursion.

5   The study found that "teenagers in suburban centers are bored and come to the shopping centers mainly as a place to go. Teenagers in suburban centers spent more time fighting, drinking, littering, and walking than did their urban counterparts, but presented fewer overall problems." The report observed that "adolescents congregated in groups of two to four and predominantly at locations selected by them rather than management." This probably had something to do with the decision to install game arcades, which allow management to channel these restless adolescents into naturally contained areas away from major traffic points of adult shoppers.

6   The guide concluded that mall management should tolerate and even encourage the teenage presence because, in the words of the report, "The vast majority support the same set of values as does shopping center management." *The same set of values* means simply that mall kids are already preprogrammed to be consumers and that the mall can put the finishing touches to them as hard-core, lifelong shoppers just like everybody else. That, after all, is what the mall is about. So it shouldn't be surprising that in spending a lot of time there, adolescents find little that challenges the assumption that the goal of life is to make money and buy products, or that just about everything else in life is to be used to serve those ends.

7   Growing up in a high-consumption society already adds inestimable pressure to kids' lives. Clothes consciousness has invaded the grade schools, and popularity is linked with having the best, newest clothes in the currently acceptable styles. Even what they read has been affected. "Miss [Nancy] Drew wasn't obsessed with her wardrobe," noted *The Wall Street Journal.* "But today the mystery in teen fiction for

girls is what outfit the heroine will wear next." Shopping has become a
survival skill and there is certainly no better place to learn it than the
mall, where its importance is powerfully reinforced and certainly never
questioned.

8   The mall as a university of suburban materialism, where Valley Girls
and Boys from coast to coast are educated in consumption, has its other
lessons in this era of change in family life and sexual mores and their
economic and social ramifications. The plethora of products in the mall,
plus the pressure on teens to buy them, may contribute to the phe-
nomenon that psychologist David Elkind calls "the hurried child": kids
who are exposed to too much of the adult world too quickly, and must
respond with a sophistication that belies their still-tender emotional development. Certainly the adult products marketed for children—form-
fitting designer jeans, sexy tops for preteen girls—add to the social
pressure to look like an adult, along with the homegrown need to understand adult finances (why mothers must work) and adult emotions (when
parents divorce).

9   Kids spend so much time at the mall partly because their parents
allow it and even encourage it. The mall is safe, it doesn't seem to harbor any unsavory activities, and there is adult supervision; it is, after
all, a controlled environment. So the temptation, especially for working parents, is to let the mall be their babysitter. At least the kids aren't
watching TV. But the mall's role as a surrogate mother may be more
extensive and more profound.

10   Karen Lansky, a writer living in Los Angeles, has looked into the subject and she told me some of her conclusions about the effects on its
teenaged denizens of the mall's controlled and controlling environment.
"Structure is the dominant idea, since true 'mall rats' lack just that in
their home lives," she said, "and adolescents about to make the big leap
into growing up crave more structure than our modern society cares to
acknowledge." Karen pointed out some of the elements malls supply that
kids used to get from their families, like warmth (Strawberry Shortcake
dolls and similar cute and cuddly merchandise), old-fashioned mothering
("We do it all for you," the fast-food slogan), and even home cooking
(the "homemade" treats at the food court).

11   The problem in all this, as Karen Lansky sees it, is that while
families nurture children by encouraging growth through the assumption of responsibility and then by letting them rest in the bosom of the
family from the rigors of growing up, the mall as a structural mother

encourages passivity and consumption, as long as the kid doesn't make trouble. Therefore all they learn about becoming adults is how to act and how to consume.

12   Kids are in the mall not only in the passive role of shoppers—they also work there, especially as fast-food outlets infiltrate the mall's enclosure. There they learn how to hold a job and take responsibility, but still within the same value context. When *CBS Reports* went to Oak Park Mall in suburban Kansas City, Kansas, to tape part of their hour-long consideration of malls, "After the Dream Comes True," they interviewed a teenaged girl who worked in a fast-food outlet there. In a sequence that didn't make the final program, she described the major goal of her present life, which was to perfect the curl on top of the ice-cream cones that were her store's specialty. If she could do that, she would be moved from the lowly soft-drink dispenser to the more prestigious ice-cream division, the curl on top of the status ladder at her restaurant. These are the achievements that are important at the mall.

13   Other benefits of such jobs may also be overrated, according to Laurence D. Steinberg of the University of California at Irvine's social ecology department, who did a study on teenage employment. Their jobs, he found, are generally simple, mindlessly repetitive, and boring. They don't really learn anything, and the jobs don't lead anywhere. Teenagers also work primarily with other teenagers; even their supervisors are often just a little older than they are. "Kids need to spend time with adults," Steinberg told me. "Although they get benefits from peer relationships, without parents and other adults it's one-sided socialization. They hang out with each other, have age-segregated jobs, and watch TV."

14   Perhaps much of this is not so terrible or even so terribly different. Now that they have so much more to contend with in their lives, adolescents probably need more time to spend with other adolescents without adult impositions, just to sort things out. Though it is more concentrated in the mall (and therefore perhaps a clearer target), the value system there is really the dominant one of the whole society. Attitudes about curiosity, initiative, self-expression, empathy, and disinterested learning aren't necessarily made in the mall; they are mirrored there, perhaps a bit more intensely—as through a glass brightly.

15   Besides, the mall is not without its educational opportunities. There are bookstores, where there is at least a short shelf of classics at great prices, and other books from which it is possible to learn more than

how to do sit-ups. There are tools, from hammers to VCRs, and products, from clothes to records, that can help the young find and express themselves. There are older people with stories, and places to be alone or to talk one-on-one with a kindred spirit. And there is always the passing show.

16   The mall itself may very well be an education about the future. I was struck with the realization, as early as my first forays into Greengate [Mall], that the mall is only one of a number of enclosed and controlled environments that are part of the lives of today's young. The mall is just an extension, say of those large suburban schools—only there's Karmelkorn instead of chem lab, the ice rink instead of the gym: It's high school without the impertinence of classes.

17   Growing up, moving from home to school to the mall—from enclosure to enclosure, transported in cars—is a curiously continuous process, without much in the way of contrast or contact with unenclosed reality. Places must tend to blur into one another. But whatever differences and dangers there are in this, the skills these adolescents are learning may turn out to be useful in their later lives. For we seem to be moving inexorably into an age of preplanned and regulated environments, and this is the world they will inherit.

18   Still, it might be better if they had more of a choice. One teenaged girl confessed to *CBS Reports* that she sometimes felt she was missing something by hanging out at the mall so much. "But I'm here," she said, "and this is what I have."

QUESTIONS ON CONTENT, STRUCTURE, AND STYLE

1. Why does Kowinski begin his essay with stories of teenagers he's heard about?

2. What question or problem is Kowinski addressing in this essay? Who might be his primary audience?

3. Why does Kowinski quote from the study by the International Council of Shopping Centers? What point is he trying to make about the values of teens in the malls?

4. Kowinski refers to the mall as the "university of suburban materialism." What lessons does this university teach?

5. According to Kowinski and writer Karen Lansky, the mall is also a "surrogate mother." Do you agree with this view? Why/why not?

6. What's wrong with jobs at the mall? Is Kowinski overlooking any advantages?

7. Why does Kowinski mention some of the benefits of spending time in the malls? Why do you think Kowinski mentions these benefits toward the end of his essay?

8. What analogy does Kowinski make between malls and the world of the future? Do you find this analogy convincing?

9. Are the words of the teenage girl an appropriate concluding note for this essay? Why/why not?

10. Summarize Kowinski's attitude toward his subject matter. Do you share his attitude? What effect, if any, did his essay have on your opinion of malls?

VOCABULARY

subtleties (3)	ramifications (8)	infiltrate (12)
resonances (3)	plethora (8)	empathy (14)
inestimable (7)	unsavory (9)	impertinence (16)
mores (8)	surrogate (9)	

SUGGESTIONS FOR WRITING

1. Did you and your friends spend time in high school at the local mall? At some other hangout? Write an essay describing the causes or effects of spending your hours in this particular place. Does your view of your hangout differ from Kowinski's view of the mall?

2. Kowinski believes the mall contributes to the assumption that "the goal of life is to make money and buy products." What other influences on a teenager's life contribute to this unfortunate assumption? Write an essay on one important influence, using enough concrete examples to make your point persuasive.

3. In his essay Kowinski refers to David Elkind, a psychologist whose popular book *The Hurried Child* argues that today's children are rushed into adulthood too quickly. Write an essay in which you agree or disagree with this theory. (Before you write, you might read "They Stole Our Childhood," on p. 52–54 of this text, which describes the effects of divorce on some children.)

Once More to the Lake
(August 1941)

E. B. WHITE

Elwyn Brooks White was an editor and writer for *The New Yorker* and a columnist for *Harper's Magazine*. He is well known for his essays, collected in volumes including *One Man's Meat* (1943), *The Second Tree from the Corner* (1954), and *The Points of My Compass* (1962), and for his children's books, *Charlotte's Web* (1952) and *Stuart Little* (1945). This essay, written in 1941, originally appeared in *Harper's*.

1   ONE SUMMER, along about 1904, my father rented a camp on a lake in Maine and took us all there for the month of August. We all got ringworm from some kittens and had to rub Pond's Extract on our arms and legs night and morning, and my father rolled over in a canoe with all his clothes on; but outside of that the vacation was a success and from then on none of us ever thought there was any place in the world like that lake in Maine. We returned summer after summer—always on August 1st for one month. I have since become a salt-water man, but sometimes in summer there are days when the restlessness of the tides and the fearful cold of the sea water and the incessant wind which blows across the afternoon and into the evening make me wish for the placidity of a lake in the woods. A few weeks ago this feeling got so strong I bought myself a couple of bass hooks and a spinner and returned to the lake where we used to go, for a week's fishing and to revisit old haunts.

2   I took along my son, who had never had any fresh water up his nose and who had seen lily pads only from train windows. On the journey over to the lake I began to wonder what it would be like. I wondered how time would have marred this unique, this holy spot—the coves and streams, the hills that the sun set behind, the camps and the paths behind the camps. I was sure the tarred road would have found it out and I wondered in what other ways it would be desolated. It is strange how much you can remember about places like that once you allow

your mind to return into the grooves which lead back. You remember one thing, and that suddenly reminds you of another thing. I guess I remembered clearest of all the early mornings, when the lake was cool and motionless, remembered how the bedroom smelled of the lumber it was made of and of the wet woods whose scent entered through the screen. The partitions in the camp were thin and did not extend clear to the top of the rooms, and as I was always the first up I would dress softly so as not to wake the others, and sneak out into the sweet outdoors and start out in the canoe, keeping close along the shore in the long shadows of the pines. I remembered being very careful never to rub my paddle against the gunwale for fear of disturbing the stillness of the cathedral.

3   The lake had never been what you would call a wild lake. There were cottages sprinkled around the shores, and it was in farming country although the shores of the lake were quite heavily wooded. Some of the cottages were owned by nearby farmers, and you would live at the shore and eat your meals at the farmhouse. That's what our family did. But although it wasn't wild, it was a fairly large and undisturbed lake and there were places in it which, to a child at least, seemed infinitely remote and primeval.

4   I was right about the tar: it led to within half a mile of the shore. But when I got back there, with my boy, and we settled into a camp near a farmhouse and into the kind of summertime I had known, I could tell that it was going to be pretty much the same as it had been before—I knew it, lying in bed the first morning, smelling the bedroom, and hearing the boy sneak quietly out and go off along the shore in a boat. I began to sustain the illusion that he was I, and therefore by simple transposition, that I was my father. This sensation persisted, kept cropping up all the time we were there. It was not an entirely new feeling, but in this setting it grew much stronger. I seemed to be living a dual existence. I would be in the middle of some simple act, I would be picking up a bait box or laying down a table fork, or I would be saying something, and suddenly it would be not I but my father who was saying the words or making the gesture. It gave me a creepy sensation.

5   We went fishing the first morning. I felt the same damp moss covering the worms in the bait can, and saw the dragonfly alight on the tip of my rod as it hovered a few inches from the surface of the water. It was the arrival of this fly that convinced me beyond any doubt that everything was as it always had been, that the years were a mirage and there

had been no years. The small waves were the same, chucking the row-boat under the chin as we fished at anchor, and the boat was the same boat, the same color green and the ribs broken in the same places, and under the floor-boards the same fresh-water leavings and debris—the dead helgramite,[1] the wisps of moss, the rusty discarded fishhook, the dried blood from yesterday's catch. We stared silently at the tips of our rods, at the dragonflies that came and went. I lowered the tip of mine into the water, tentatively, pensively dislodging the fly, which darted two feet away, poised, darted two feet back, and came to rest again a little farther up the rod. There had been no years between the ducking of this dragonfly and the other one—the one that was part of memory. I looked at the boy, who was silently watching his fly, and it was my hands that held his rod, my eyes watching. I felt dizzy and didn't know which rod I was at the end of.

6   We caught two bass, hauling them in briskly as though they were mackerel, pulling them over the side of the boat in a businesslike manner without any landing net, and stunning them with a blow on the back of the head. When we got back for a swim before lunch, the lake was exactly where we had left it, the same number of inches from the dock, and there was only the merest suggestion of a breeze. This seemed an utterly enchanted sea, this lake you could leave to its own devices for a few hours and come back to, and find that it had not stirred, this constant and trustworthy body of water. In the shallows, the dark, water-soaked sticks and twigs, smooth and old, were undulating in clusters on the bottom against the clean ribbed sand, and the track of the mussel was plain. A school of minnows swam by, each minnow with its small individual shadow, doubling the attendance, so clear and sharp in the sunlight. Some of the other campers were in swimming, along the shore, one of them with a cake of soap, and the water felt thin and clear and unsubstantial. Over the years there had been this person with the cake of soap, this cultist, and here he was. There had been no years.

7   Up to the farmhouse to dinner through the teeming, dusty field, the road under our sneakers was only a two-track road. The middle track was missing, the one with the marks of the hooves and the splotches of dried, flaky manure. There had always been three tracks to choose

---

[1] A helgramite is an insect sometimes used for bait.

from in choosing which track to walk in; now the choice was narrowed down to two. For a moment I missed terribly the middle alternative. But the way led past the tennis court, and something about the way it lay there in the sun reassured me; the tape had loosened along the backline, the alleys were green with plantains and other weeds, and the net (installed in June and removed in September) sagged in the dry noon, and the whole place steamed with mid-day heat and hunger and emptiness. There was a choice of pie for dessert, and one was blueberry and one was apple, and the waitresses were the same country girls, there having been no passage of time, only the illusion of it as in a dropped curtain—the waitresses were still fifteen; their hair had been washed, that was the only difference—they had been to the movies and seen the pretty girls with the clean hair.

8   Summertime, oh summertime, pattern of life indelible, the fade-proof lake, the woods unshatterable, the pasture with the sweet-fern and the juniper forever and ever, summer without end; this was the background, and the life along the shore was the design, the cottages with their innocent and tranquil design, their tiny docks with the flagpole and the American flag floating against the white clouds in the blue sky, the little paths over the roots of the trees leading from camp to camp and the paths leading back to the outhouses and the can of lime for sprinkling, and at the souvenir counters at the store the miniature birch-bark canoes and the post cards that showed things looking a little better than they looked. This was the American family at play, escaping the city heat, wondering whether the newcomers in the camp at the head of the cove were "common" or "nice," wondering whether it was true that the people who drove up for Sunday dinner at the farmhouse were turned away because there wasn't enough chicken.

9   It seemed to me, as I kept remembering all this, that those times and those summers had been infinitely precious and worth saving. There had been jollity and peace and goodness. The arriving (at the beginning of August) had been so big a business in itself, at the railway station the farm wagon drawn up, the first smell of the pine-laden air, the first glimpse of the smiling farmer, and the great importance of the trunks and your father's enormous authority in such matters, and the feel of the wagon under you for a long ten-mile haul, and at the top of the last long hill catching the first view of the lake after eleven months of not

seeing this cherished body of water. The shouts and cries of the other campers when they saw you, and the trunks to be unpacked, to give up their rich burden. (Arriving was less exciting nowadays, when you sneaked up in your car and parked it under a tree near the camp and took out the bags and in five minutes it was all over, no fuss, no loud wonderful fuss about trunks.)

10   Peace and goodness and jollity. The only thing that was wrong now, really, was the sound of the place, an unfamiliar nervous sound of the outboard motors. This was the note that jarred, the one thing that would sometimes break the illusion and set the years moving. In those other summertimes all motors were inboard; and when they were at a little distance, the noise they made was a sedative, an ingredient of summer sleep. They were one-cylinder and two-cylinder engines, and some were make-and-break and some were jump-spark, but they all made a sleepy sound across the lake. The one-lungers throbbed and fluttered, and the twin-cylinder ones purred and purred, and that was a quiet sound too. But now the campers all had outboards. In the daytime, in the hot mornings, these motors made a petulant, irritable sound; at night, in the still evening when the afterglow lit the water, they whined about one's ears like mosquitoes. My boy loved our rented outboard, and his great desire was to achieve singlehanded mastery over it, and authority, and he soon learned the trick of choking it a little (but not too much), and the adjustment of the needle valve. Watching him I would remember the things you could do with the old one-cylinder engine with the heavy flywheel, how you could have it eating out of your hand if you got really close to it spiritually. Motor boats in those days didn't have clutches, and you would make a landing by shutting off the motor at the proper time and coasting in with a dead rudder. But there was a way of reversing them, if you learned the trick, by cutting the switch and putting it on again exactly on the final dying revolution of the flywheel, so that it would kick back against compression and begin reversing. Approaching a dock in a strong following breeze, it was difficult to slow up sufficiently by the ordinary coasting method, and if a boy felt he had complete mastery over his motor, he was tempted to keep it running beyond its time and then reverse it a few feet from the dock. It took a cool nerve, because if you threw the switch a twentieth of a second too soon you would catch the flywheel when it still had speed enough to go up past center, and the boat would leap ahead, charging bull-fashion at the dock.

11   We had a good week at the camp. The bass were biting well and the
sun shone endlessly, day after day. We would be tired at night and lie
down in the accumulated heat of the little bedrooms after the long hot
day and the breeze would stir almost imperceptibly outside and the
smell of the swamp drift in through the rusty screens. Sleep would
come easily and in the morning the red squirrel would be on the roof,
tapping out his gay routine. I kept remembering everything, lying in
bed in the mornings—the small steamboat that had a long rounded
stern like the lip of a Ubangi, and how quietly she ran on the moonlight
sails, when the older boys played their mandolins and the girls sang and
we ate doughnuts dipped in sugar, and how sweet the music was on the
water in the shining night, and what it had felt like to think about girls
then. After breakfast we would go up to the store and the things were
in the same place—the minnows in a bottle, the plugs and spinners dis-
arranged and pawed over by the youngsters from the boys' camp, the
fig newtons and the Beeman's gum. Outside, the road was tarred and
cars stood in front of the store. Inside, all was just as it had always
been, except there was more Coca-Cola and not so much Moxie and
root beer and birch beer and sarsaparilla. We would walk out with a
bottle of pop apiece and sometimes the pop would backfire up our
noses and hurt. We explored the streams, quietly, where the turtles
slid off the sunny logs and dug their way into the soft bottom; and we
lay on the town wharf and fed worms to the tame bass. Everywhere
we went I had trouble making out which was I, the one walking at my
side, the one walking in my pants.

12   One afternoon while we were there at that lake a thunderstorm
came up. It was like the revival of an old melodrama that I had seen
long ago with childish awe. The second-act climax of the drama of the
electrical disturbance over a lake in America had not changed in any
important respect. This was the big scene, still the big scene. The
whole thing was so familiar, the first feeling of oppression and heat and
a general air around camp of not wanting to go very far away. In
midafternoon (it was all the same) a curious darkening of the sky, and
a lull in everything that had made life tick; and then the way the boats
suddenly swung the other way at their moorings with the coming of a
breeze out of the new quarter, and the premonitory rumble. Then the
kettle drum, then the snare, then the bass drum and cymbals, then
crackling light against the dark, and the gods grinning and licking their
chops in the hills. Afterward the calm, the rain steadily rustling in the

calm lake, the return of light and hope and spirits, and the campers running out in joy and relief to go swimming in the rain, their bright cries perpetuating the deathless joke about how they were getting simply drenched, and the children screaming with delight at the new sensation of bathing in the rain, and the joke about getting drenched linking the generations in a strong indestructible chain. And the comedian who waded in carrying an umbrella.

13   When the others went swimming my son said he was going in too. He pulled his dripping trunks from the line where they had hung all through the shower, and wrung them out. Languidly, and with no thought of going in, I watched him, his hard little body, skinny and bare, saw him wince slightly as he pulled up around his vitals the small, soggy, icy garment. As he buckled the swollen belt suddenly my groin felt the chill of death.

QUESTIONS ON CONTENT, STRUCTURE, AND STYLE

1. How does White introduce this essay? Why?

2. What gives White a "creepy sensation"?

3. What things about the lake have remained unchanged from White's boyhood?

4. What things around the lake have changed? What is the one jarring note that "set the years moving"?

5. What is the effect of the first sentence in paragraph 8? Sentence 3 in paragraph 9?

6. Evaluate White's use of specific sensory detail in his descriptions of the lake and the surrounding area. Support your answer with examples.

7. In what ways is this essay ordered and unified?

8. What images are used in paragraph 12 to depict the thunderstorm?

9. Why does White feel "the chill of death" as he watches his son put on his wet swimsuit? What is the relationship between this final comment and White's recurring feeling that he is his father?

10. This essay is primarily developed by what expository strategy? Is this an effective choice?

VOCABULARY

incessant (1)

placidity (1)

desolated (2)

primeval (3)

undulating (6)

unsubstantial (6)

indelible (8)

imperceptibly (11)

mandolins (11)

languidly (13)

SUGGESTIONS FOR WRITING

1. If you have returned to your hometown since you've been at college, write an essay comparing the way you see some familiar place (your room, high school, local hangout, etc.) now to the way you used to see it. Has it changed—or have *you*?

2. Write an essay describing a vacation of your childhood that was full of "jollity and peace and goodness." What made this particular vacation so special? Remember to use enough details to recreate the experience clearly for the reader.

3. Describe the worst vacation you ever had, again using vivid details to make your reader experience the trip with you. What is the most important piece of advice you would give someone about to make a similar trip?

Today's Terror: Kids Killing Kids

ROBERT C. MAYNARD

Robert C. Maynard was a journalist and editor, whose column on modern life and political issues appeared in newspapers throughout the country until his death in 1993. Maynard had been as associate editor for the *Washington Post*, senior editor for *Encore* magazine, and editor (and later owner) of the *Oakland Tribune*. He also founded the Institute for Journalism Education at the University of California, Berkeley, in 1977. This column was published in July 1990.

1   IT WAS not easy to listen to Monica Reed on television the other night. She was eyewitness to a terror in our times. Her brother, 13-year-old Kevin Reed, had been walking home on a quiet East Oakland, Calif., street with two of his friends. A car drove by and a young man inside opened fire on the three children.

2   "I laid him in my lap," said Monica, who reached Kevin's side within minutes of the shooting. "I tried CPR, but it wouldn't work, and then his hands and arms got real cold and his head got heavy. I think then I knew . . . he was going to die."

3   Thus did Kevin Reed, a likable, friendly child, become another national statistic. The FBI and medical community say there is a rising tide of urban homicide. They say the victims and the assailants are children.

4   America's police chiefs say the same thing: the weapons available to young people are more powerful, and those using them are younger than ever.

5   The Rev. J. Alfred Smith Sr. of East Oakland's Allen Temple Baptist Church, appalled at Kevin's death and the injury of his two companions, has called for a radical solution. He wants an amnesty to encourage youngsters to turn in their weapons.

6   As a method of reducing youth homicides, police are not impressed with Smith's idea. It has been tried before. At best a lot of iron gets turned in and the killing keeps on.

7   Smith's idea should not be so readily dismissed, because it has a value greater than merely capturing weapons. It could be the beginning of an

idea to capture the minds of young people with guns. All too often, their ideas about guns are formed from the sanitized versions of mayhem they see on television.

8   If an amnesty program were linked to an education program, the following might happen: once the amnesty period is closed, every youngster who is caught with a weapon would have to spend 10 hours on Friday and Saturday night in the emergency operating room of the county hospital. The following week, the same youngster would be required to spend a like amount of time in the county morgue witnessing autopsies of gun victims.

9   We are allowing children today to inhabit a world of fantasy about weapons. They need to face the reality that lies beneath the fantasy.

10   Physicians and criminologists tell an interesting story about today's urban violence. They say the homicide rate from guns dipped in the middle '70s and early '80s. The reason for this was the battlefield experience of Vietnam.

11   Today the story is different. "People used to use Saturday night specials, which were cheap and small and did not do as much damage as these big guns are doing," said John J. Townsend, chief of Chicago detectives. "More people are dying from their wounds because a semiautomatic or .357 magnum really tears up the body."

12   Gun education, like drug and sex education, must begin in the home. Unfortunately, too much home education consists of television. That is why it is good that clergy across the country are beginning to grapple with the problem of guns and children.

13   It is too late for Kevin Reed, but there are thousands like him at risk every day in America.

QUESTIONS ON CONTENT, STRUCTURE, AND STYLE

1. What problem is Maynard addressing in this essay?

2. Why does Maynard begin his essay with Monica Reed's story? How typical is this scene in cities today?

3. What solution does the Rev. J. Alfred Smith, Jr., suggest? Why are the police not impressed with this plan?

4. What value does Maynard see in Smith's idea?

5. According to Maynard, where do too many young people get their ideas about guns? What's wrong with this view of guns and violence?

6. Why does Maynard refer to Vietnam? Do you find this point convincing? Why/why not?

7. Describe Maynard's education program. What effect does Maynard want to have on children caught with guns?

8. Why does Maynard quote the chief of Chicago detectives?

9. Why does Maynard think the clergy should become more involved in the "problem of guns and children"?

10. Do you think Maynard's proposals would work in your community? In large urban areas? What strengths and weaknesses do you see in Maynard's ideas?

Vocabulary

appalled (5)	mayhem (7)
amnesty (5)	autopsies (8)
sanitized (7)	grapple (12)

Suggestions for Writing

1. Write an essay describing an incident of violence that you have witnessed. What caused this incident? What effects did this event have on you?

2. If you were to design an educational program to reduce the number of youth homicides or to slow the growth of gang activity, how would you try to "capture the minds" of young children? Would your program incorporate Maynard's suggestions? Write an essay describing what you consider a realistic plan for your community.

3. Write an essay in which you agree or disagree with Maynard's view that television is at fault for giving too many young people unrealistic ideas about guns and violence.

Homesick

BRENDA BELL

Brenda Bell is a journalist and freelance writer who has published many
articles in newspapers and magazines across the country, including
recent work for the *Los Angeles Times Magazine*. A versatile observer of
contemporary life, Bell has written articles that range from sage commentary on responsible parenting to indepth investigation of a teenage
murderer. This personal look at an "odd ailment" was published in the
Seattle Times Pacific Magazine in 1991.

1   MY FRIEND Norma says she can't keep reading the book I sent her because it makes her too homesick. "When that happens, I just go to bed
and cry—I did that last weekend—and my husband really *really* doesn't
like it, so I have to avoid certain things," she told me in her matter-of-
fact way.

2   Like me, Norma is from Texas, and she has spent a goodly portion
of the past two decades away from home, following the career path
of one husband or another. Her current abode is on top of a hill in
Hawaii, which most people would consider the most pleasant of her
various exiles, with an Army officer who is hands down the best of all
her husbands.

3   But she very nearly balked at accompanying him there, and the
combined stress of the move and family matters back home sent her
into a tailspin for months. Her Christmas card that first year, a photo
of the smiling couple beside a sylvan stream, carried the churlish yet
triumphant message: "Lest you think this is Hawaii, this picture was
taken on the Medina River in the Texas Hill Country, which is *my* idea
of paradise."

4   I love it when Norma acts this way, because it's even worse than the
way I act. Being homesick for a harsh place like Texas while living in
an environment of spectacular natural beauty and benign climate
tends to provoke bad behavior in the afflicted ones, causing them to be
viewed with puzzled annoyance rather than sympathy. Fortunately for
us all, there are few victims of homesickness anymore. In a society

that venerates moving up and moving on, this odd ailment is dying out altogether, like pleurisy and those archaic diseases that involve what our grandmothers called "sinking spells."

5   This was made clear during my sojourn some years ago in Washington, D.C., a city regarded by many of its inhabitants as the riveting pulse-point of the Western world. In my profession, which is journalism, the "other" Washington is a sort of heaven-on-earth where you go if you're really good, really pushy and work really, really hard. And if you're really lucky, you get to stay there forever, riding taxis to work and appearing on "MacNeil/Lehrer" from time to time with a White House press pass on a little chain around your neck.

6   Though I didn't fit any of those Type A categories, I wound up in D.C. nevertheless, plugging away on silly stories and taking pensive walks in the middle of the day. As far as I could tell, everyone else was deliriously happy with his or her good fortune to be at the nerve center of Where It's All Happening; *real* journalists no more get homesick than *real* jet pilots clutch barf bags. I was awed by them and their rootless equanimity. "Why me?" I mused during my daily hauls between Capitol Hill and the office. "Am I a wimp or what?"

7   Then one day on the subway I fell into conversation with a colleague from *The Washington Post,* who made a lot more money than I and by definition was infinitely more savvy and sophisticated. We talked of a trip I was planning back to Texas, to which I looked forward with unabashed eagerness. It prompted the strangest confession I have ever heard.

8   He told me he had grown up somewhere in the Midwest, in one or another of those vowel states—Ohio, Illinois, Indiana—but felt no particular attachment to it. Now that he was older, he said wistfully, he yearned for a sense of belonging to a certain place. On his vacations he usually went West—hence his many questions about Texas and what it was like—and felt particularly drawn to New Mexico. (You and a trillion others, I almost joshed, but he seemed so serious, I kept quiet.)

9   Maybe New Mexico would be *the place,* he went on, with a wan hopefulness that belied his urbane manner, his regulation rep tie and press-pass necklace. Maybe it would be the compass point his spirit craved. "I envy you," he said finally. "I'd give anything to know what that's like, to feel that way about someplace—any place at all."

10   Looking at it that way made me almost proud to be homesick. I wasn't a wimp after all! Just a sensitive person with a spiritual connection to my roots! *You* should be so lucky!

11   That attitude works fine in theory, but not so well in practice. People like other people to be, well, happy. Sometimes in a moment of good cheer punctuating our comfortable existence in a lovely house on a beautiful island,[1] a friend will turn on me suddenly and say, in so many words, "There! Aren't you happy *now?*"—as if by catching me unawares my joy will leap out from the cage where I have peevishly locked it away.

12   But the truth is, it is on those really spectacular days—the look of the clouds, maybe, or the feel of an unusually warm breeze—when my longing for home strikes me hardest, with a physical force that almost knocks the wind out of me. Of all my friends, only Norma understands the strength of this passion. She resolutely ignores the well-meaning advice of those who implore her to "make the best of it" and cheer up. "If I wanted to be happy, I'd be happy," she says with perfect logic.

13   I think of it as the ugly-man syndrome: imagine yourself in love with Karl Malden[2] while your friends keep fixing you up with Kevin Costner and Mel Gibson. "Kevin's got a great underbite," you say, "but I can't stand the way he walks." Or "Mel was fine to look at, but he's no fun to talk to." It's ugly old Karl you want, and only Karl, and you could listen to him talk forever.

14   When people ask me what I could possibly miss about Texas, I have a hard time explaining in terms they understand. There *is* the talking, of course, and the stories—"telling lies," we call it. In the Northwest, people talk to communicate. In many other parts of the world, mere communication is only one function of conversation. Texans consider talking a kind of art form, an important means of self-expression, as well as a stylized code of social exchange. You can't have a decent oral tradition without at least a century of porch-sitting to develop it. When's the last time you sat around on a porch trading stories?

15   I miss outrageousness, too—that peculiar extremism you find in many Texans, which is considered a character flaw in the subdued Northwest. Norma told me of an acquaintance in Hawaii who was

[1] Bell lives on an island near Seattle, Washington.
[2] Karl Malden is an actor also known for his credit card commercials on television.

fascinated with *Lonesome Dove*[3] but confessed he couldn't relate to Larry McMurtry's characters. "How does he make *those people* up?" he asked Norma. "Oh, honey," replied Norma, who was once married to the supremely macho patriarch of an old Hill Country ranching clan who often neglected his women, but never his guns or his whiskey. "He *doesn't* make them up."

16   These days Norma finds succor in a passable Mexican food joint in Honolulu and the barbecued ribs she has flown in from Austin for special occasions. For the next three years until her husband retires from the Army, I imagine her marking off the days on the wall like the prisoners in that horrendous Turkish prison in the movie *The Midnight Express*. Except in her prison, palm trees sway in the trade winds and frangipani blossoms scent the air.

17   Ah, nature's beauty. Riding the ferry across Elliott Bay, I marvel at the voluptuousness of the scenery: the close-hauled sailboats, the changing colors of the water, the pink-tinged mountain ranges at sunset. Like any tourist, I crest a hill in Seattle and am dumbfounded by a surprise vista. Thumbing through "Northwest Best Places," I dog-ear the gorgeous places to visit next: the ocean, the British Columbia whale migration, the glaciers, the hot springs, the Okanagon, the islands. I will hike, bike, row, sail and do my best to live the Northwest lifestyle, or as much of it as I can afford.

18   But this longing I have, and will always have, is not about scenery or lifestyle or anything I can rationally explain. It's about home, and it's lodged so deep in my bones it cannot be expunged. It's that old dog Karl I want, and I no longer apologize for it or ponder the reasons why. You needn't let it worry you, either.

19   Hey, if I wanted to be happy, I'd be happy.

QUESTIONS ON CONTENT, STRUCTURE, AND STYLE

1. Why does Bell tell about her friend Norma's Christmas card? Why does she like her friend's attitude?

2. What "odd ailment" do Bell and Norma share? Why does this "sickness" seem to be dying out?

---

[3] *Lonesome Dove,* a novel about Texas during the cattle drives, won a Pulitzer Prize in 1986 and was made into an award-winning television mini-series.

3. Why was Bell not completely happy in Washington, D.C.? What was preventing her from feeling like a "real" journalist?

4. How did her conversation with *The Washington Post* reporter temporarily improve her attitude?

5. What is the "ugly-man syndrome" and how does Bell use it to explain her feelings about Texas?

6. What two reasons does Bell give for missing her Texas home? Why does she refer to Norma's former husband?

7. Why does Bell compare Norma in Hawaii to the prisoner in the movie *The Midnight Express?* Why does she acknowledge the beauty of the Pacific Northwest but then claim "it's that old dog Karl I want"?

8. Cite some examples of Bell's humor. What do her personal stories add to the overall tone of this essay? The stories about Norma?

9. Evaluate the last sentences that conclude this essay. Who is she quoting in the last line and why? Are the sentiment and tone of this ending consistent with the rest of Bell's article?

10. Summarize what Bell is saying about the feeling of homesickness. Have you ever experienced this feeling? Or do you, like the reporter on the subway, still yearn for a sense of belonging to a certain place?

VOCABULARY

abode (2)	*pleurisy (4)*	*equanimity (6)*
balked (3)	*archaic (4)*	*unabashed (7)*
sylvan (3)	*sojourn (5)*	*succor (16)*
churlish (3)	*pensive (6)*	*expunged (18)*

SUGGESTIONS FOR WRITING

1. Write an essay describing a particular place for which you have a special feeling. Help your reader to understand your sense of this place. Do you have memories of people or events tied to this place? Or it is the scene itself that makes its claim on you?

2. Bell characterizes Texas as blessed with storytellers and outrageous characters. Write an essay in which you characterize a particular place by telling a favorite story or legend about it or its people. What does the story reveal about the unique features or "personality" of this place?

3. In her essay on homesickness Bell tries to define a feeling that she says is difficult to put into words. Select some other abstract feeling and offer your explanation of its meaning. Consider such possibilities as sibling rivalry, jealousy, friendship, self-respect, or even the sense of deja-vu. Try to use as many examples and details as you can to make your explanation as clear as possible.

The Road Not Taken

ROBERT FROST

Robert Frost was a twentieth-century poet whose poems frequently focus on the characters, events, and scenes of New England. Three of his many volumes of poetry won Pulitzer Prizes: *New Hampshire* (1923), *Collected Poems* (1930), and *A Further Range* (1936). Frost taught at Amherst College, Dartmouth, Yale, and Harvard and was one of the founders of the Bread Loaf School in Vermont. This poem was first published in 1916.

> Two roads diverged in a yellow wood,
> And sorry I could not travel both
> And be one traveler, long I stood
> And looked down one as far as I could
> 5 To where it bent in the undergrowth;
>
> Then took the other, as just as fair,
> And having perhaps the better claim,
> Because it was grassy and wanted wear;
> Though as for that the passing there
> 10 Had worn them really about the same,

And both that morning equally lay
In leaves no step had trodden black.
Oh, I kept the first for another day!
Yet knowing how way leads on to way,
15 I doubted if I should ever come back.

I shall be telling this with a sigh
Somewhere ages and ages hence:
Two roads diverged in a wood, and I—
I took the one less traveled by,
20 And that has made all the difference.

QUESTIONS ON CONTENT, STRUCTURE, AND STYLE

1. Who is speaking in this poem?

2. What decision was the speaker facing?

3. Why is this decision difficult? What lies ahead?

4. How do the roads differ? What is similar about them?

5. Which road did the traveler choose?

6. What does the speaker mean when he says, "Yet knowing how way leads on to way, / I doubted if I should ever come back" (lines 14–15)?

7. How does the speaker imagine he will be telling his story later in his life? Why might he be feeling that way?

8. Put into your own words the last three lines of the poem. What is the "difference" the speaker refers to?

9. Explain how Frost uses the story of the diverging roads as a metaphor or symbol of importance in human life. Who does the traveler represent? The two roads going in different directions?

10. Think of times in your life when you were faced with choices that would have moved you in opposite directions. Do you tend to take the paths "less traveled by"? What difference have your choices made?

VOCABULARY

diverged (line 1)
trodden (line 12)
hence (line 17)

SUGGESTIONS FOR WRITING

1. Reread your answer to question 10 above. Write an essay focusing on one time in your life when you chose an unpopular plan of action or took a path "less traveled." Explain how your decision "made all the difference."

2. Write an essay explaining a decision you once regretted but feel proud of today. What have you learned that you want to tell others?

3. Write an essay using some scene in nature as a metaphor for an important event or decision in your life.

Miss Brill

KATHERINE MANSFIELD

Kathleen Beauchamp was born in New Zealand but moved as a young adult to England, where she lived and wrote using the name of Katherine Mansfield. She is the author of several volumes of short stories, including *In A German Pension* (1911), *Bliss and Other Stories* (1920), and *The Garden Party* (1922), published to great critical acclaim shortly before her death from tuberculosis at age 35. This story may be found in *The Collected Short Stories of Katherine Mansfield* (1945).

1   ALTHOUGH IT was so brilliantly fine—the blue sky powdered with gold and great spots of light like white wine splashed over the Jardins Publiques[1]—Miss Brill was glad that she had decided on her fur. The air was motionless, but when you opened your mouth there was just a faint

[1] Public gardens or park.

chill, like a chill from a glass of iced water before you sip, and now and again a leaf came drifting—from nowhere, from the sky. Miss Brill put up her hand and touched her fur. Dear little thing! It was nice to feel it again. She had taken it out of its box that afternoon, shaken out the moth-powder, given it a good brush, and rubbed the life back into the dim little eyes. "What has been happening to me?" said the sad little eyes. Oh, how sweet it was to see them snap at her again from the red eiderdown! . . . But the nose, which was of some black composition, wasn't at all firm. It must have had a knock, somehow. Never mind—a little dab of black sealing-wax when the time came—when it was absolutely necessary. . . . Little rogue! Yes, she really felt like that about it. Little rogue biting its tail just by her left ear. She could have taken it off and laid in on her lap and stroked it. She felt a tingling in her hands and arms, but that came from walking, she supposed. And when she breathed, something light and sad—no, not sad, exactly—something gentle seemed to move in her bosom.

2   There were a number of people out this afternoon, far more than last Sunday. And the band sounded louder and gayer. That was because the Season had begun. For although the band played all the year round on Sundays, out of season it was never the same. It was like some one playing with only the family to listen; it didn't care how it played if there weren't any strangers present. Wasn't the conductor wearing a new coat, too? She was sure it was new. He scraped with his foot and flapped his arms like a rooster about to crow, and the bandsmen sitting in the green rotunda blew out their cheeks and glared at the music. Now there came a little "flutey" bit—very pretty!—a little chain of bright drops. She was sure it would be repeated. It was; she lifted her head and smiled.

3   Only two people shared her "special" seat: a fine old man in a velvet coat, his hands clasped over a huge carved walking-stick, and a big old woman, sitting upright, with a roll of knitting on her embroidered apron. They did not speak. This was disappointing, for Miss Brill always looked forward to the conversation. She had become really quite expert, she thought, at listening as though she didn't listen, at sitting in other people's lives just for a minute while they talked around her.

4   She glanced, sideways, at the old couple. Perhaps they would go soon. Last Sunday, too, hadn't been as interesting as usual. An Englishman and his wife, he wearing a dreadful Panama hat and she button boots. And she'd gone on the whole time about how she ought to wear

spectacles; she knew she needed them; but that it was no good getting any; they'd be sure to break and they'd never keep on. And he'd been so patient. He'd suggested everything—gold rims, the kind that curved round your ears, little pads inside the bridge. No, nothing would please her. "They'll always be sliding down my nose!" Miss Brill had wanted to shake her.

5   The old people sat on the bench, still as statues. Never mind, there was always the crowd to watch. To and fro, in front of the flower-beds and the band rotunda, the couples and groups paraded, stopped to talk, to greet, to buy a handful of flowers from the old beggar who had his tray fixed to the railings. Little children ran among them, swooping and laughing; little boys with big white silk bows under their chins, little girls, little French dolls, dressed up in velvet and lace. And sometimes a tiny staggerer came suddenly rocking into the open from under the trees, stopped, stared, as suddenly sat down "flop," until its small high-stepping mother, like a young hen, rushed scolding to its rescue. Other people sat on the benches and green chairs, but they were nearly always the same. Sunday after Sunday, and—Miss Brill had often noticed—there was something funny about nearly all of them. They were odd, silent, nearly all old, and from the way they stared they looked as though they'd just come from dark little rooms or even—even cupboards!

6   Behind the rotunda the slender trees with yellow leaves down drooping, and through them just a line of sea, and beyond the blue sky with gold-veined clouds.

7   Tum-tum-tum tiddle-um! tiddle-um! tum tiddley-um tum ta! blew the band.

8   Two young girls in red came by and two young soldiers in blue met them, and they laughed and paired and went off arm-in-arm. Two peasant women with funny straw hats passed, gravely, leading beautiful smoke-colored donkeys. A cold, pale nun hurried by. A beautiful woman came along and dropped her bunch of violets, and a little boy ran after to hand them to her, and she took them and threw them away as if they'd been poisoned. Dear me! Miss Brill didn't know whether to admire that or not! And now an ermine toque[2] and a gentleman in grey met just in front of her. He was tall, stiff, dignified, and she was wearing the

---

[2] A "toque" is a woman's hat; this one is made of ermine, a white fur, that has faded with age.

ermine toque she'd bought when her hair was yellow. Now everything, her hair, her face, even her eyes, was the same color as the shabby ermine, and her hand, in its cleaned glove, lifted to dab her lips, was a tiny yellowish paw. Oh, she was so pleased to see him—delighted! She rather thought they were going to meet that afternoon. She described where she'd been—everywhere, here, there, along by the sea. The day was so charming—didn't he agree? And wouldn't he, perhaps? . . . But he shook his head, lighted a cigarette, slowly breathed a great deep puff into her face, and, even while she was still talking and laughing, flicked the match away and walked on. The ermine toque was alone; she smiled more brightly than ever. But even the band seemed to know what she was feeling and played more softly, played tenderly, and the drum beat, "The Brute! The Brute!" over and over. What would she do? What was going to happen now? But as Miss Brill wondered, the ermine toque turned, raised her hand as though she'd seen some one else, much nicer, just over there, and pattered away. And the band changed again and played more quickly, more gaily than ever, and the old couple on Miss Brill's seat got up and marched away, and such a funny old man with long whiskers hobbled along in time to the music and was nearly knocked over by four girls walking abreast.

9   Oh, how fascinating it was! How she enjoyed it! How she loved sitting here, watching it all! It was like a play. It was exactly like a play. Who could believe the sky at the back wasn't painted? But it wasn't till a little brown dog trotted on solemn and then slowly trotted off, like a little "theatre" dog, a little dog that had been drugged, that Miss Brill discovered what it was that made it so exciting. They were all on the stage. They weren't only the audience, not only looking on; they were acting. Even she had a part and came every Sunday. No doubt somebody would have noticed if she hadn't been there; she was part of the performance after all. How strange she'd never thought of it like that before! And yet it explained why she made such a point of starting from home at just the same time each week—so as not to be late for the performance—and it also explained why she had quite a queer, shy feeling at telling her English pupils how she spent her Sunday afternoons. No wonder! Miss Brill nearly laughed out loud. She was on the stage. She thought of the old invalid gentleman to whom she read the newspaper four afternoons a week while he slept in the garden. She had got quite used to the frail head on the cotton pillow, the hollowed eyes, the open mouth, and the high pinched nose. If he'd been dead she

mightn't have noticed for weeks; she wouldn't have minded. But suddenly he knew he was having the paper read to him by an actress! "An actress!" The old head lifted; two points of light quivered in the old eyes. "An actress—are ye?" And Miss Brill smoothed the newspaper as though it were the manuscript of her part and said gently: "Yes, I have been an actress for a long time."

10   The band had been having a rest. Now they started again. And what they played was warm, sunny, yet there was just a faint chill—a something, what was it?—not sadness—no, not sadness—a something that made you want to sing. The tune lifted, lifted, the light shone; and it seemed to Miss Brill that in another moment all of them, all the whole company, would begin singing. The young ones, the laughing ones who were moving together, they would begin, and the men's voices, very resolute and brave, would join them. And then she too, she too, and the others on the benches—they would come in with a kind of accompaniment—something low, that scarcely rose or fell, something so beautiful—moving. . . . And Miss Brill's eyes filled with tears and she looked smiling at all the other members of the company. Yes, we understand, we understand, she thought—though what they understood she didn't know.

11   Just at that moment a boy and a girl came and sat down where the old couple had been. They were beautifully dressed; they were in love. The hero and heroine, of course, just arrived from his father's yacht. And still soundlessly singing, still with that trembling smile, Miss Brill prepared to listen.

12   "No, not now," said the girl. "Not here, I can't."

13   "But why? Because of that stupid old thing at the end there?" asked the boy. "Why does she come here at all—who wants her? Why doesn't she keep her silly old mug at home?"

14   "It's her fu-fur which is so funny," giggled the girl. "It's exactly like a fried whiting."

15   "Ah, be off with you!" said the boy in an angry whisper. Then: "Tell me, ma petite chère——"

16   "No, not here," said the girl. "Not yet."

17   On her way home she usually bought a slice of honey-cake at the baker's. It was her Sunday treat. Sometimes there was an almond in her slice, sometimes not. It made a great difference. If there was an almond it was like carrying home a tiny present—a surprise— something that might very well not have been there. She hurried on

the almond Sundays and struck the match for the kettle in quite a dashing way.

18   But today she passed the baker's by, climbed the stairs, went into the little dark room—her room like a cupboard—and sat down on the red eiderdown. She sat there for a long time. The box that the fur came out of was on the bed. She unclasped the necklet quickly; quickly, without looking, laid it inside. But when she put the lid on she thought she heard something crying.

QUESTIONS ON CONTENT, STRUCTURE, AND STYLE

1. How does Miss Brill regard her fur piece at the story's beginning? Have you ever seen fur pieces (or pictures of them) such as the one Mansfield describes, complete with face and paws?

2. Why do you think Mansfield called her main character Miss Brill? Why are readers never aware of her first name?

3. Cite some details about Miss Brill's life: what, for example does she do for a living? for pleasure? What do her observations about the conductor's new coat tell us about her routine on Sundays?

4. At what secret activity is she "really quite expert"? What does this activity say about Miss Brill's participation in the lives of other people?

5. As Miss Brill watches those people who frequent the park Sunday after Sunday, she notes "something funny about nearly all of them." How do they appear to her? Where, according to Miss Brill, might they have come from?

6. What do Miss Brill's reactions to the woman who threw away the violets and the man with the cigarette reveal about her character?

7. Miss Brill joyfully thinks of life in the park as what? What role does she play?

8. Miss Brill's positive feelings of community with the other people in the park are dispelled by what intrusion? Why is Miss Brill's first description of the couple ironic in light of their comments?

9. What change does Miss Brill undergo? Why is her home now described as a "little dark room . . . like a cupboard"?

10. How does Miss Brill's response to the fur at the end of the story reflect the way she now looks at herself? Why is "something crying"?

VOCABULARY

eiderdown (1)   invalid (9)
rogue (1)   resolute (10)
rotunda (2)

SUGGESTIONS FOR WRITING

1. Miss Brill sees herself (and her activities and environment as well) differently after her last Sunday in the park. Write an essay contrasting a view you once held of yourself to a later, vastly different opinion. Why did your view change? Was the change a positive one? Or a negative or sad one, like Miss Brill's?

2. Mansfield's story shows how one conversation can dramatically change a person's point of view. Write an essay in which you explain how powerful words have changed your life or the life of someone close to you, for better or worse.

3. Write an essay of analysis that explains the role of several minor characters in this short story. How do Miss Brill's observations about them contribute to our understanding of her character? Or, if you prefer, write an essay in which you analyze the function of the fur piece and the honey-cake in this story. How do these two items reflect Miss Brill's change of perspective?

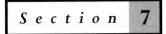

Section **7**

SOCIAL ISSUES:
FREEDOMS AND CHOICES

"Smoking Is Among Our Inalienable Vices"
BY ERNEST VAN DEN HAAG

*"Free Speech on Campus: An Argument for the Right
to Offend"*
BY CLARENCE PAGE

"A Scientist: 'I Am the Enemy'"
BY RON KARPATI

"How about Low-Cost Drugs for Addicts?"
BY LOUIS NIZER

"Screams from Somewhere Else"
BY ROGER ROSENBLATT

"The Unknown Citizen"
BY W. H. AUDEN

"A White Heron"
BY SARAH ORNE JEWETT

Smoking Is Among Our
Inalienable Vices

ERNEST VAN DEN HAAG

Ernest van den Haag is a professor of jurisprudence and public policy at Fordham University Law School. Formerly a psychoanalyst at New York University, he is also the author of *The Fabric of Society* (1957) and numerous articles for newspapers and magazines such as *Partisan Review* and *Harper's*. This newspaper editorial appeared in 1985.

1   ENOUGH IS enough, and we have seen enough of the harassment and intimidation of smokers.

2   True, smoking is bad for the smoker's health, and when he finally suffers his heart attack, or gets lung cancer, abstinent taxpayers have to pay for his hospitalization. As a result, many non-smokers favor laws prohibiting smoking, at least in public and semipublic places. This may seem logical, but it puts us, as a society, on a dangerous, slippery slope, raising the prospect that we will soon be preventing all kinds of other people from doing what they want because of hazards to their health and our pocketbooks.

3   After all, taxpayers are also compelled to help pay for the hospitalization of drinkers, obese overeaters and those too lazy to exercise. Should we, then, have legal regulation of eating, drinking and exercising? How much liberty—the liberty to enjoy one's own habits and even vices—are we willing to sacrifice?

4   People smoke, or drink, or eat the wrong things, despite bad physical effects, because of the psychological gratification they obtain. In his 60s, Sigmund Freud underwent the first of more than 30 painful operations for oral cancer. He was told that it was caused by cigar smoking, but he continued nevertheless. In his 72nd year he wrote "I owe to the cigar a great intensification of my capacity to work and . . . of my self-control." By then, he had an artificial jaw and palate. He smoked till he died, in his 80s.

5   Most non-smokers simply cannot understand this, and they scornfully label it "addiction." I prefer to call it a dependence, like reliance on a lover. Such a reliance may be enjoyable and productive; and it may have bad, even tragic, effects as well. But even when the bad effects

271

become clear, one may want to continue because of the gratifications: The habit, once formed, is usually hard to shake. If one is deprived of the lover, or of the cigars, one suffers withdrawal symptoms, be they physical or psychological. Love is seldom called an addiction. Why should smoking be?

6   The non-smoking taxpayer is right about one thing: He should not have to pay for hospitalizations caused by smoking. Instead, we should impose a federal tax on tobacco sufficient to pay all the extra costs that smoking causes. Insurance companies, too, might charge higher rates to smokers and drinkers.

7   But what about the health effects of "passive smoking" and the annoyance that smoking may cause?

8   Some people are indeed allergic to smoke, and any civilized person will avoid smoking when they are around. Allergic people should, in turn, avoid places and occasions known to be smokey—discotheques, bars or dinner with Winston Churchill. But allergies to smoking have increased amazingly in recent years—a sudden increase that suggests that many of them are hysterical, or faked, to justify the imposition of the nonsmoker's preference on smokers.

9   In fact, dubious statistics to the contrary and except in instances of rare genuine allergies, smoking does not ordinarily endanger the health of non-smokers unless they are exposed to smoke for a long time in an unventilated space.

10   As for annoyance, life is full of annoyances, some hazardous to health, that we must tolerate for the sake of other people, who want, or need, to do what annoys us. We all have to breathe polluted air, even if we never ride in a car or bus, simply because others want to.

11   Far more people refrain from smoking now than in the past—which is fine. But harassment will not increase their number. Nor will the prohibition of cigarette advertising. Marijuana does quite well without such promotion. People learn to smoke, or drink, from others, not from advertisements.

12   Is there nothing to be done? Certainly, wherever possible we should separate non-smokers from smokers and provide ventilation. We do so now on big airplanes. But in most other places, in offices and restaurants, for instance, smokers and non-smokers will have to rely on mutual tolerance. Courtesy cannot be replaced by onesided and unenforceable regulations that, even if temporarily effective, will in the long run simply discredit the law.

QUESTIONS ON CONTENT, STRUCTURE, AND STYLE

1. Van den Haag sets forth what sort of tone in the essay's introduction?

2. Where does the essay's thesis appear?

3. How does van den Haag discredit the argument that taxpayers suffer unjustly because they must pay for smokers' health care? Is his reasoning persuasive?

4. Why does the author mention Freud in this essay?

5. Van den Haag draws an analogy between the habit of smoking and the reliance on a lover. Do you find this comparison convincing? Why or why not?

6. What financial penalties does van den Haag suggest for smokers?

7. What are the two arguments against smoking that van den Haag raises in the last half of his essay?

8. How does van den Haag refute each of these arguments? Is his rebuttal effective?

9. Characterize the tone of the conclusion; is it the same tone as the introduction? Is the conclusion appropriate?

10. Evaluate the persuasiveness of this essay. Which arguments are the most and least convincing? Why?

VOCABULARY

inalienable (title)	abstinent (2)	imposition (8)
harassment (1)	gratification (4)	dubious (9)
intimidation (1)	reliance (5)	unventilated (9)

SUGGESTIONS FOR WRITING

1. If you disagree with Ernest van den Haag's position, write an editorial that refutes his arguments and defends yours. Consider submitting your editorial to your local newspaper.

2. Television has banned advertisements for cigarettes, but newspapers and magazines have not. Write an essay urging the total prohibition

of cigarette advertising or the reinstatement of such advertising on television.

3. Smoking in open-air stadiums is now illegal in some parts of the United States. Should smokers be allowed to light up in such places? Familiarize yourself with the latest research on the dangers of secondary smoke, and then write an essay that argues your position on this controversy.

Free Speech on Campus:
An Argument for the Right to Offend

CLARENCE PAGE

Clarence Page is a nationally syndicated columnist for the *Chicago Tribune* newspaper. His twice-weekly columns frequently focus on social and political topics of national interest; he has also written for the *Chicago Magazine* and has worked in television. In 1989 he won a Pulitzer Prize for distinguished commentary in journalism. This column appeared in newspapers across the country in April 1991.

1   "I ALWAYS read your column," a woman said recently, "although I don't always agree with you."

2   So what? Where do people get the notion that they're supposed to agree with everything they read? Don't they know the right to offend is a precious American right?

3   I try to exercise it often. Judging by some of my mail, I'm getting pretty good at it. Unfortunately, the fine art of offense has fallen on hard times, squeezed by the recklessness of too many amateurs on one side and a rising wave of sensitivity on the other.

4   Nowhere is this more true than on college campuses.

5   At the University of Michigan, for example, a student was charged with violating the school's language code when he suggested in class that homosexuality might be a disease.

6   At the University of Wisconsin-Eau Claire, a student was put on probation and had to do community service work at a shelter for battered women because he yelled vulgarities at a woman who criticized the athletic department.

7   At the University of California at Berkeley, a professor was drowned out by protesting students after he suggested that white and Asian students suffered under affirmative-action programs.

8   I don't agree with any of these speakers, but those who overreact risk slipping and sliding down to their level of ignorance.

9   It is informative to note that the Michigan student who ran afoul of a rule intended to protect minorities happened to be black. So was another Michigan student who was punished under the same rules for using the expletive "white trash." It's hardly the first time a censor's rule whipped back snakelike to bite those it was intended to protect.

10   Then there are those who argue that women and minorities should be exempt from such rules because they do not belong to an "oppressor class." As a member of a minority group, African-Americans, I take exception to that. To take away from me the ability ever to become an "oppressor" is to imply that I can never aspire to the obligations, along with the rights, that full humanity entails.

11   All this in the name of "sensitivity" to the feelings of women, minorities and the "differently abled," which in some circles is the "politically correct" way to refer to the disabled. Count me as one minority group member who says "thanks, but no thanks" to sensitivity that stifles the free discourse universities are supposed to encourage.

12   After all, one person's rational view is another person's claptrap. The American people are not perfect. We have produced 2 Live Crew and David Duke. But the nation has grown strong by letting the claptrap express itself, then fall of its own dead weight.

13   "Think for yourselves and let others enjoy the privilege to do so too," Voltaire advised. Unfortunately, to many of today's campus thinkers, Voltaire is just another DWEM (dead white European male), a product of a civilization that historically suppressed the rights of minorities and therefore should be replaced in curriculum with female and Third World authors.

14   No question that women and non-Europeans have been squeezed out of university studies for too long. Unfortunately, some proponents have gone to the other extreme.

15   Rep. Henry Hyde, R-Ill., in an unusual alliance with the American Civil Liberties Union, has taken a modest stab at stemming the tide. His proposed Collegiate Speech Protection Act would extend First Amendment rights now enjoyed by students at public colleges and universities to the students of private colleges and universities.

16   Unfortunately, Hyde proposes to remedy objectionable rules by urging Congress to pass what looks like yet another objectionable rule. Under the guise of expanding the rights of students, his bill would constrain the right of private universities to set their own rules, including rules that call for civilized behavior, free of congressional meddling.

17   Hyde, a conservative who usually advocates removing government from the people's backs, apparently recognized the hidden dangers of putting more government on college administrators' backs when he included in his bill an exemption for educational institutions "controlled by a religious organization" if application of the proposed law "would not be consistent with the religious tenets of such organization."

18   One wonders what will happen when, under Hyde's rule, a student heretic demands his or her rights too. Yes, whether it's a matter of "political correctness" or "theological correctness," Congress has no business telling colleges where to put their limits.

19   No offense.

QUESTIONS ON CONTENT, STRUCTURE, AND STYLE

1. What is Page's opinion of campus rules that punish students for offensive language?

2. What, according to Page, has happened to "the fine art of offense"?

3. Why does Page present examples from the Universities of Michigan, Wisconsin, and California?

4. Why do many colleges have regulations that govern the use of obscenity or "hate" speech?

5. What are Page's arguments against such regulations?

6. Why does Page identify himself as an African-American? How is such identification part of his argument?

7. Why does Page refer to 2 Live Crew and David Duke? to Voltaire?

8. What is Page's opinion of the proposed Collegiate Speech Protection Act? Of the exemption for schools controlled by religious organizations?

9. Evaluate Page's introduction and his two-word conclusion. Are they effective? Why/why not?

10. Does your campus have a speech code? Do you agree with Page that such rules should be struck down? Or do students on campus have a right to be protected from certain kinds of remarks by their classmates?

VOCABULARY

expletive (9)   *guise (16)*
"politically correct" (11)   *tenets (17)*
discourse (11)   *theological (18)*
proponents (14)

SUGGESTIONS FOR WRITING

1. Some of those who oppose Page's position argue that racial or sexist insults fall under the "fighting words" exception to First Amendment protection. Such language, they maintain, does not comprise ideas or invite dialogue but is only designed to injure or harass. Investigate this controversy thoroughly and write an essay that presents your opposition's view as clearly as your own.

2. Suppose your campus newspaper, which is supported by funds from students' fees, ran a political cartoon that some students and administrators felt promoted a racist stereotype. Your school administration now demands that the newspaper staff submit in advance of publication all such cartoons to a faculty editorial board for approval; the newspaper staff protests that its rights of free speech are being violated. Write a guest editorial arguing your opinion on this controversy.

3. Debate over free speech often rages over art and music. In recent years, critics have condemned much popular music, especially rap

and rock, for lyrics they believe encourage murder, rape, racism, homophobia, sexism, and even teen suicide. Do you find any of these charges true today? If so, what action, if any, do you advocate? Should children be protected from such lyrics? Write an essay arguing your point of view on violence or obscenity in music, music videos, or any art form today.

A Scientist: 'I Am the Enemy'

RON KARPATI

Ron Karpati is a pediatrician involved in immunological research, studies that often involve the use of animals in experiments. In 1989 Karpati published the following essay, which argues the necessity of animals in medical research, in the "My Turn" column of Newsweek magazine, a column of opinion that is written by readers of the magazine.

1   I AM the enemy! One of those vilified, inhumane physician-scientists involved in animal research. How strange, for I have never thought of myself as an evil person. I became a pediatrician because of my love for children and my desire to keep them healthy. During medical school and residency, however, I saw many children die of leukemia, prematurity and traumatic injury—circumstances against which medicine has made tremendous progress, but still has far to go. More important, I also saw children, alive and healthy, thanks to advances in medical science such as infant respirators, potent antibiotics, new surgical techniques and the entire field of organ transplantation. My desire to tip the scales in favor of the healthy, happy children drew me to medical research.

2   My accusers claim that I inflict torture on animals for the sole purpose of career advancement. My experiments supposedly have no relevance to medicine and are easily replaced by computer simulation. Meanwhile, an apathetic public barely watches, convinced that the issue

has no significance, and publicity-conscious politicians increasingly give way to the demands of the activists.

3   We in medical research have also been unconscionably apathetic. We have allowed the most extreme animal-rights protesters to seize the initiative and frame the issue as one of "animal fraud." We have been complacent in our belief that a knowledgeable public would sense the importance of animal research to the public health. Perhaps we have been mistaken in not responding to the emotional tone of the argument created by those sad posters of animals by waving equally sad posters of children dying of leukemia or cystic fibrosis.

4   Much is made of the pain inflicted on these animals in the name of medical science. The animal-rights activists contend that this is evidence of our malevolent and sadistic nature. A more reasonable argument, however, can be advanced in our defense. Life is often cruel, both to animals and human beings. Teenagers get thrown from the back of a pickup truck and suffer severe head injuries. Toddlers, barely able to walk, find themselves at the bottom of a swimming pool while a parent checks the mail. Physicians hoping to alleviate the pain and suffering these tragedies cause have but three choices: create an animal model of the injury or disease and use that model to understand the process and test new therapies; experiment on human beings—some experiments will succeed, most will fail—or finally, leave medical knowledge static, hoping that accidental discoveries will lead us to the advances.

5   Some animal-rights activists would suggest a fourth choice, claiming that computer models can simulate animal experiments, thus making the actual experiments unnecessary. Computers can simulate, reasonably well, the effects of well-understood principles on complex systems, as in the application of the laws of physics to airplane and automobile design. However, when the principles themselves are in question, as is the case with the complex biological systems under study, computer modeling alone is of little value.

6   One of the terrifying effects of the effort to restrict the use of animals in medical research is that the impact will not be felt for years and decades: drugs that might have been discovered will not be; surgical techniques that might have been developed will not be, and fundamental biological processes that might have been understood will remain mysteries. There is the danger that politically expedient solutions will be found to placate a vocal minority, while the consequences of those

decisions will not be apparent until long after the decisions are made and the decision makers forgotten.

7   Fortunately, most of us enjoy good health, and the trauma of watching one's child die has become a rare experience. Yet our good fortune should not make us unappreciative of the health we enjoy or the advances that make it possible. Vaccines, antibiotics, insulin and drugs to treat heart disease, hypertension and stroke are all based on animal research. Most complex surgical procedures, such as coronary-artery bypass and organ transplantation, are initially developed in animals. Presently undergoing animal studies are techniques to insert genes in humans in order to replace the defective ones found to be the cause of so much disease. These studies will effectively end if animal research is severely restricted.

8   In America today, death has become an event isolated from our daily existence—out of the sight and thoughts of most of us. As a doctor who has watched many children die, and their parents grieve, I am particularly angered by people capable of so much compassion for a dog or a cat, but with seemingly so little for a dying human being. These people seem so insulated from the reality of human life and death and what it means.

9   Make no mistake, however: I am not advocating the needlessly cruel treatment of animals. To the extent that the animal-rights movement has made us more aware of the needs of these animals, and made us search harder for suitable alternatives, they have made a significant contribution. But if the more radical members of this movement are successful in limiting further research, their efforts will bring about a tragedy that will cost many lives. The real question is whether an apathetic majority can be aroused to protect its future against a vocal, but misdirected, minority.

QUESTIONS ON CONTENT, STRUCTURE, AND STYLE

1. Why does Karpati start his essay "I am the enemy!"? Why does he tell about his medical school experiences? What tone does this first paragraph establish for the writer?

2. What is Karpati's position on using animals in medical research?

3. Where does Karpati summarize the opposition to his view? Why would he present these objections in this order?

4. What does Karpati gain by criticizing, in paragraph 3, the medical research professionals for their complacency?

5. In paragraphs 4 and 5, Karpati discusses computer simulations. Do you find his reasons for rejecting such simulations convincing? Why/why not?

6. Do Karpati's predictions in paragraph 6 seem reasonable? Persuasive? Why/why not?

7. Why does Karpati talk about how we view death in paragraph 8? What does it allow him to say about his opposition? About his readers?

8. If paragraph 8 were removed, would the impact of Karpati's argument be lessened or strengthened?

9. Evaluate this essay's conclusion. What role does highly connotative language play in Karpati's appeal for action?

10. Do you find Karpati's argument persuasive? What are his strongest and weakest points?

VOCABULARY

vilified (1)
inhumane (1)
simulation (2)
apathetic (2)

unconscionably (3)
malevolent (4)
placate (6)

SUGGESTIONS FOR WRITING

1. If you disagree with Karpati, write an essay that refutes his argument and defends your own reasons. Assume your essay will also appear in *Newsweek*'s "My Turn" column.

2. Is there experimentation on animals at your college or in your community? Are you aware of any local industries that use animals to test products such as cosmetics or household goods? Investigate and write a report on any such activities in your area. Consider using material gained from interviews to present a vivid picture of what you discover in your investigation.

3. Medical research brings up a number of ethical dilemmas. For example, should scientists be allowed to sell artificial body parts they may invent? Should poor people be allowed to sell certain body parts if science learns to perfect transplants of all kinds? Focus on an ethical question of this kind and write a paper arguing for your position.

How about Low-Cost Drugs for Addicts?

LOUIS NIZER

Louis Nizer is an attorney, perhaps best known for defending country humorist John Henry Faulk in a case that defeated the practice of "blacklisting" radio, television, and movie stars during the Communist witch-hunts of the McCarthy Era in the 1950s. He is the author of nine books about his life as a trial lawyer. This article was written as an editorial for the *New York Times* in 1986.

1   WE ARE losing the war against drug addiction. Our strategy is wrong. I propose a different approach.

2   The Government should create clinics, manned by psychiatrists, that would provide drugs for nominal charges or even free to addicts under controlled regulations. It would cost the Government only 20 cents for a heroin shot, for which the addicts must now pay the mob more than $100, and there are similar price discrepancies in cocaine, crack and other such substances.

3   Such a service, which would also include the staff support of psychiatrists and doctors, would cost a fraction of what the nation now spends to maintain the land, sea and air apparatus necessary to interdict illegal imports of drugs. There would also be a savings of hundreds of millions of dollars from the elimination of the prosecutorial procedures that stifle our courts and overcrowd our prisons.

4   We see in our newspapers the triumphant announcements by Government agents that they have intercepted huge caches of cocaine, the street prices of which are in the tens of millions of dollars. Should we be gratified? Will this achievement reduce the number of addicts by one? All it will do is increase the cost to the addict of his illegal supply.

5   Many addicts who are caught committing a crime admit that they have mugged or stolen as many as six or seven times a day to accumulate the $100 needed for a fix. Since many of them need two or three fixes a day, particularly for crack, one can understand the terror in our streets and homes. It is estimated that there are in New York City alone 200,000 addicts, and this is typical of cities across the nation. Even if we were to assume that only a modest percentage of a city's addicts engage in criminal conduct to obtain the money for the habit, requiring multiple muggings and thefts each day, we could nevertheless account for many of the tens of thousands of crimes each day in New York City alone.

6   Not long ago, a Justice Department division issued a report stating that more than half the perpetrators of murder and other serious crimes were under the influence of drugs. This symbolizes the new domestic terror in our nation. This is why our citizens are unsafe in broad daylight on the most traveled thoroughfares. This is why typewriters and television sets are stolen from offices and homes and sold for a pittance. This is why parks are closed to the public and why murders are committed. This is why homes need multiple locks, and burglary systems, and why store windows, even in the most fashionable areas, require iron gates.

7   The benefits of the new strategy to control this terrorism would be immediate and profound.

8   First, the mob would lose the main source of its income. It could not compete against a free supply for which previously it exacted tribute estimated to be hundreds of millions of dollars, perhaps billions, from hopeless victims.

9   Second, pushers would be put out of business. There would be no purpose in creating addicts who would be driven by desperate compulsion to steal and kill for the money necessary to maintain their habit. Children would not be enticed. The mob's macabre public-relations program is to tempt children with free drugs in order to create customers for the future. The wave of street crimes in broad daylight

would diminish to a trickle. Homes and stores would not have to be fortresses. Our recreational areas could again be used. Neighborhoods would not be scandalized by sordid street centers where addicts gather to obtain their supply from slimy merchants.

10   Third, police and other law-enforcement authorities, domestic or foreign, would be freed to deal with traditional nondrug crimes.

11   There are several objections that might be raised against such a salutary solution.

12   First, it could be argued that by providing free drugs to the addict we would consign him to permanent addiction. The answer is that medical and psychiatric help at the source would be more effective in controlling the addict's descent than the extremely limited remedies available to the victim today. I am not arguing that the new strategy will cure everything. But I do not see many addicts being freed from their bonds under the present system.

13   In addition, as between the addict's predicament and the safety of our innocent citizens, which deserves our primary concern? Drug-induced crime has become so common that almost every citizen knows someone in his immediate family or among his friends who has been mugged. It is these citizens who should be our chief concern.

14   Another possible objection is that addicts will cheat the system by obtaining more than the allowable free shot. Without discounting the resourcefulness of the bedeviled addict, it should be possible to have Government cards issued that would be punched so as to limit the free supply in accord with medical authorization.

15   Yet all objections become trivial when matched against the crisis itself. What we are witnessing is the demoralization of a great society: the ruination of its school children, athletes and executives, the corrosion of the workforce in general.

16   Many thoughtful sociologists consider the rapidly spreading drug use the greatest problem that our nation faces—greater and more real and urgent than nuclear bombs or economic reversal. In China, a similar crisis drove the authorities to apply capital punishment to those who trafficked in opium—an extreme solution that arose from the deepest reaches of frustration.

17   Free drugs will win the war against the domestic terrorism caused by illicit drugs. As a strategy, it is at once resourceful, sensible and simple. We are getting nowhere in our efforts to hold back the ocean of supply. The answer is to dry up demand.

QUESTIONS ON CONTENT, STRUCTURE, AND STYLE

1. What is Nizer's main purpose in this essay?
2. Describe the overall organization of this essay. What advantages does this organizational plan have for Nizer's purpose?
3. Note the manner in which Nizer begins his essay. Is this beginning an effective choice for this essay? Why/why not?
4. How does Nizer try to show a causal relationship between drug use and crime in our country? Is he convincing?
5. Why does Nizer choose to use only one sentence for paragraph 7 and for paragraph 11?
6. Summarize the benefits of Nizer's plan. Do you agree with these statements? Why/why not?
7. What objections does Nizer try to counter? Do you think his answers are persuasive? Why/why not?
8. Why, near the end of his essay, does Nizer mention China and its opium problem? Is this an effective technique?
9. Nizer concludes by using an ocean image. How does this image summarize his main point?
10. Evaluate Nizer's argument. How might he answer critics who claim that easier access to drugs will increase the number of drug users (addicts, "experimenters," and underage youth) in our country and increase the frequency of drug use, with both increases compounding already-existing problems of mental health, public safety, and poverty, especially in the inner-cities?

VOCABULARY

nominal (2)	stifle (3)	predicament (13)
discrepancies (2)	caches (4)	bedeviled (14)
interdict (3)	macabre (9)	demoralization (15)
prosecutorial (3)	salutary (11)	corrosion (15)

SUGGESTIONS FOR WRITING

1. Nizer wrote his opinions for an editorial in a large New York newspaper. Write a response editorial in which you argue for or against

Nizer's plan. If you support his argument, you might add additional benefits you see or you might elaborate on his plan (for example, how might he handle twelve-year-olds who lined up for free heroin?). If you oppose his plan, you need to refute his major arguments as well as presenting your own opinions. Would Nizer's plan increase the number of drug users—or the frequency of drug use— in our country?

2. One frequently hears people making a comparison between the prohibition of drugs, particularly marijuana, and the Prohibition laws of 1920–1933 that outlawed liquor. Read about the Prohibition Era in this country and the crime associated with bootlegging. Write an essay in which you argue for or against the similarities of the two problems—and their solutions.

3. Write an essay in which you explain the effects of someone's drug use on your life. How has this drug use shaped your attitude toward drugs? Toward those who sell or continue to abuse drugs?

Screams from Somewhere Else

ROGER ROSENBLATT

During the 1970s, Roger Rosenblatt served as director of expository writing at Harvard University. He later became editor of *The New Republic* and served on the editorial board of *The Washington Post,* where he was also a columnist. He has published *Black Fiction* (1974), *Children of War* (1983), and *Witness: The World Since Hiroshima* (1985). A senior writer for *Time* magazine until 1988, he then served as editor for *US News and World Report* from 1988 to 1989. This essay appeared in *Time* in 1987.

1   THE SCREAM is one of the indigenous sounds of city life, like an automobile alarm that whoops and heaves, then stops, leaving the question hanging like a hawk as to whether a car was broken into, or did its owner set off the alarm by accident, and then lay it to rest. With human

screams, the question is more complicated, since screams are not mechanical or automatic. Did you hear that, Harry? What could it be? A scream of delight, of fright? Hilarity, Harry? Do you think that someone is laughing too hard? Could it be hysteria, madness? Or is it a scream of blue murder? What should we do, Harry, if it is a scream of blue murder? And where is it coming from, anyway? Could you tell? *I* couldn't tell.

2   A Manhattan couple was charged last week with the murder by beating of their six-year-old adopted daughter. Neighbors never had any difficulty telling where the screams were coming from, though sometimes they may have had trouble discerning exactly who was doing the screaming, the six-year-old girl or the woman who lived with the father. The woman is accused of "acting in concert" in the murder, but clearly her own life buckled under regular punches. She wore dark glasses, and would attribute her recomposed face to a mugging or a fall in the kitchen. Over the years, colleagues and friends chose to believe the mugging and accident stories. Neighbors who heard the screams firsthand placed dozens of telephone calls to the police and to city authorities, who investigated but could prove no harm. The authorities did not hear the screams. After her beatings, the child lay brain dead, and the couple was in custody. Now no one in that building hears the screams.

3   But in other buildings in New York, in other cities, in all the cities, new screams will take up the slack. Sometimes the authorities will respond, sometimes not. The beating of women and children will continue in the hidden boxes of apartments: evil, secret noise. You will hear the scream, and someone else will tell you that it wasn't a scream, it was a kettle whistle; and no one will be sure if there ever was a scream, until a body lies in evidence. How is the citizen-listener to react? Rush wildly through the corridors until the sound is unmistakable? Push open some stranger's door to confront some stranger's scream? Much courage is required for that. Much recklessness as well. The helplessness you feel in such situations is dizzying; and even when you act, someone in power can let you down. You could be wrong. Foolish. You could be sued.

4   Civilization is tested by its screams. One has the choice to hear or not to hear; to detect location or not to detect location; to discover cause; to help or not to help. Along the many lines of choice, excuses and mistakes are possible, even reasonable. One is left with oneself and the screams, like two opponents. The Kitty Genovese case of 1964

keeps coming back, in which a young woman in Queens screamed for help, and everybody heard, and nobody helped. What were we to do? Edvard Munch's famous painting of *The Cry* keeps coming back, equally scary and bewildering. What *are* we to do?

5   You never know how you will react to a scream until you hear one. I can tell you how you will react at first. You will freeze. Your head will snap like an alarmed bird's and your eyes will swell, long before any practical choices begin to form between hiding under the bed and leaping to the rescue. You will freeze because you will recognize the sound. It comes from you; all the panic and the pain; all the screams of one's life, uttered and quashed, there in that dreadful eruption that has scattered the air. All yours.

6   The scream that comes from somewhere else comes from you. You have to go to it. You have to open the door to make it stop.

QUESTIONS ON CONTENT, STRUCTURE, AND STYLE

1. What is Rosenblatt's purpose in writing this essay? What does he want his readers to understand and to do?

2. The essay begins, in paragraph 1, with an unknown person questioning someone named Harry. Why is this conversation presented here?

3. Why does Rosenblatt go into detail about the six-year-old girl in Manhattan?

4. In paragraph 3 Rosenblatt poses, through a series of questions and possible answers, what complex problem for the reader? Why?

5. What does Rosenblatt mean when he argues that "civilization is tested by its screams"? Do you agree?

6. Who was Kitty Genovese and why does Rosenblatt refer to her? (*Hint:* For a thorough answer, you might wish to turn to p. 197 of this text.) Have you ever seen a picture of Munch's painting *The Cry*? If so, how did you react to it?

7. Why does Rosenblatt repeat his view that the screams from somewhere else "come from you"?

8. Characterize Rosenblatt's "voice" in this essay. What do his images (such as abused children in "hidden boxes of apartments"; oneself

and the screams as "two opponents"; your head snapping to attention like an "alarmed bird's"; and so on) contribute to this essay?

9. Why does Rosenblatt choose to aim many of his comments directly at "you"? Is this an effective choice for this essay? Why/why not?

10. Evaluate this essay's overall effectiveness. Do you find Rosenblatt persuasive? What is your personal response to his call for action in the conclusion?

VOCABULARY

indigenous (1)
discerning (2)
quashed (5)

SUGGESTIONS FOR WRITING

1. In his essay, Rosenblatt is clearly aware of the risks one takes becoming "involved" in unknown, potentially volatile situations; he nevertheless admonishes us to "open the door." Write an essay in which you describe a time when you did, in fact, become involved in a crisis and your help turned the situation around. What did you learn from this experience that might encourage others to offer help when needed?

2. Write your own powerful call for involvement in some problem in your community. Consider such contemporary issues as the homeless; abused children; safe houses for battered women and children; street crime; the neglected mentally ill, elderly, or infirm, and so on. What could college students do to help alleviate any one of these problems?

3. The six-year-old child Rosenblatt refers to in his essay was Lisa Steinberg, who died in 1987 from severe beatings at the hands of her adopted father, Joel Steinberg, a New York attorney. Her adoptive mother, Hedda Nussbaum, a former book editor and writer, was also arrested in connection with the crime. Research this well-known, tragic case and use it as evidence in an essay arguing a specific plan of action in the prevention or detection of child abuse or domestic violence.

The Unknown Citizen

W. H. AUDEN

Wystan Hugh Auden is regarded as one of the major poets of the twentieth century. Born in England, Auden became an American citizen after World War II and spent many years in New York City. Some of Auden's works include *Poems* (1930), *On This Island* (1936), *Another Time* (1940), *The Quest* (1951), *The Shield of Achilles* (1955), and *Homage to Clio* (1960).

To JS/07/M378

He was found by the Bureau of Statistics to be
One against whom there was no official complaint,
And all the reports on his conduct agree
That, in the modern sense of an old-fashioned word, he was a
    saint,
5 For in everything he did he served the Greater Community,
Except for the War till the day he retired
He worked in a factory and never got fired,
But satisfied his employers, Fudge Motors Inc.
Yet he wasn't a scab or odd in his views,
10 For his Union reports that he paid his dues,
(Our report on his Union shows it was sound)
And our Social Psychology workers found
That he was popular with his mates and liked a drink.
The Press are convinced that he bought a paper every day
15 And that his reactions to advertisements were normal in every
    way.
Policies taken out in his name prove that he was fully insured.
And his Health-card shows he was once in hospital but left it
    cured.
Both Producers Research and High-Grade Living declare
He was fully sensible to the advantages of the Installment Plan

20 And had everything necessary to the Modern Man,
    A phonograph, a radio, a car and a frigidaire.
    Our researchers into Public Opinion are content
    That he held the proper opinions for the time of year;
    When there was peace, he was for peace; when there was war,
      he went.
25 He was married and added five children to the population,
    Which our Eugenist says was the right number for a parent of
      his generation,
    And our teachers report that he never interfered with their
      education.
    Was he free? Was he happy? The question is absurd:
30 Had anything been wrong, we should certainly have heard.

QUESTIONS ON CONTENT, STRUCTURE, AND STYLE

1. Describe in a few sentences the character called "the unknown citizen." What are his distinguishing personality traits?

2. Why is he called a "saint" in today's world?

3. Why is the dedication "To JS/07/M378" especially appropriate for this person?

4. Are we supposed to admire the unknown citizen? What do lines such as "he held the proper opinions for the time of year" suggest about the man's ability to think or act for himself?

5. What other lines emphasize this man's sense of conformity?

6. Who are the "we" of the last line?

7. Why do "we" think the questions "Was he free? Was he happy?" are absurd ones?

8. Why is the title of this poem ironic?

9. What was Auden's purpose in writing this poem? What point was he trying to make about "the Modern Man"?

10. What is the overall tone of this poem? When did you first recognize this tone?

VOCABULARY

scab (line 9)
frigidaire (line 21)
Eugenist (line 26)

SUGGESTIONS FOR WRITING

1. Perhaps there was a time in your life when you chose to conform to some rule, regulation, or social custom, but later you regretted your decision. Write an essay describing the situation and what you learned from it.

2. On the other hand, perhaps you've broken an accepted rule or played the non-conformist. Write an essay describing the effects of your actions.

3. Describe a run-in you've had with a bureaucracy, using the incident to call for a change or improvement that would help others.

A White Heron

SARAH ORNE JEWETT

Sarah Orne Jewett was born in Maine in 1849, and much of her fiction focused on the simple life of rural New England and the independent but sometimes lonely people who lived there. Like other "regional" writers, Jewett tried to realistically recreate the settings, people, speech patterns, and daily life common to her section of the country while presenting universal themes and feelings. Some of her better-known works include *Deephaven* (1877), *A Country Doctor* (1884), *The Country of the Pointed Firs* (1896), and *A White Heron* (1886), the collection from which this story was taken.

I

1   THE WOODS were already filled with shadows one June evening, just before eight o'clock, though a bright sunset still glimmered faintly among

the trunks of the trees. A little girl was driving home her cow, a plodding, dilatory, provoking creature in her behavior, but a valued companion for all that. They were going away from the western light, and striking deep into the dark woods, but their feet were familiar with the path, and it was no matter whether their eyes could see it or not.

2   There was hardly a night the summer through when the old cow could be found waiting at the pasture bars; on the contrary, it was her greatest pleasure to hide herself away among the high huckleberry bushes, and though she wore a loud bell she had made the discovery that if one stood perfectly still it would not ring. So Sylvia had to hunt for her until she found her, and call Co'! Co'! with never an answering Moo, until her childish patience was quite spent. If the creature had not given good milk and plenty of it, the case would have seemed very different to her owners. Besides, Sylvia had all the time there was, and very little use to make of it. Sometimes in pleasant weather it was a consolation to look upon the cow's pranks as an intelligent attempt to play hide and seek, and as the child had no playmates she lent herself to this amusement with a good deal of zest. Though this chase had been so long that the wary animal herself had given an unusual signal of her whereabouts, Sylvia had only laughed when she came upon Mistress Moolly at the swamp-side, and urged her affectionately homeward with a twig of birch leaves. The old cow was not inclined to wander farther, she even turned in the right direction for once as they left the pasture, and stepped along the road at a good pace. She was quite ready to be milked now, and seldom stopped to browse.

3   Sylvia wondered what her grandmother would say because they were so late. It was a great while since she had left home at half-past five o'clock, but everybody knew the difficulty of making this errand a short one. Mrs. Tilley had chased the horned torment too many summer evenings herself to blame any one else for lingering, and was only thankful as she waited that she had Sylvia, nowadays, to give such valuable assistance. The good woman suspected that Sylvia loitered occasionally on her own account, there never was such a child for straying about out-of-doors since the world was made! Everybody said that it was a good change for a little maid who had tried to grow for eight years in a crowded manufacturing town, but, as for Sylvia herself, it seemed as if she never had been alive at all before she came to live at the farm. She thought often with wistful compassion of a wretched dry geranium that belonged to a town neighbor.

4   "'Afraid of folks,'" old Mrs. Tilley said to herself, with a smile, after
she had made the unlikely choice of Sylvia from her daughter's houseful
of children, and was returning to the farm. "'Afraid of folks,' they said!
I guess she won't be troubled no great with 'em up to the old place!"
When they reached the door of the lonely house and stopped to unlock
it, and the cat came to purr loudly, and rub against them, a deserted
pussy, indeed, but fat with young robins, Sylvia whispered that this was
a beautiful place to live in, and she never should wish to go home.

5   The companions followed the shady wood-road, the cow taking
slow steps, and the child very fast ones. The cow stopped long at the
brook to drink, as if the pasture were not half a swamp, and Sylvia
stood still and waited, letting her bare feet cool themselves in the shoal
water, while the great twilight moths struck softly against her. She
waded on through the brook as the cow moved away, and listened to
the thrushes with a heart that beat fast with pleasure. There was a stirring in the great boughs overhead. They were full of little birds and
beasts that seemed to be wide awake, and going about their world, or
else saying good-night to each other in sleepy twitters. Sylvia herself
felt sleepy as she walked along. However, it was not much farther to
the house, and the air was soft and sweet. She was not often in the
woods so late as this, and it made her feel as if she were a part of the
gray shadows and the moving leaves. She was just thinking how long it
seemed since she first came to the farm a year ago, and wondering if
everything went on in the noisy town just the same as when she was
there; the thought of the great red-faced boy who used to chase and
frighten her made her hurry along the path to escape from the shadow
of the trees.

6   Suddenly this little woods-girl is horror-stricken to hear a clear
whistle not very far away. Not a bird's-whistle, which would have a
sort of friendliness, but a boy's whistle, determined, and somewhat aggressive. Sylvia left the cow to whatever sad fate might await her, and
stepped discreetly aside into the bushes, but she was just too late. The
enemy had discovered her, and called out in a very cheerful and persuasive tone, "Halloa, little girl, how far is it to the road?" and trembling
Sylvia answered almost inaudible, "A good ways."

7   She did not dare to look boldly at the tall young man, who carried a
gun over his shoulder, but she came out of her bush and again followed
the cow, while he walked alongside.

8   "I have been hunting for some birds," the stranger said kindly, "and I have lost my way, and need a friend very much. Don't be afraid," he added gallantly. "Speak up and tell me what your name is, and whether you think I can spend the night at your house, and go out gunning early in the morning."

9   Sylvia was more alarmed than before. Would not her grandmother consider her much to blame? But who could have foreseen such an accident as this? It did not seem to be her fault, and she hung her head as if the stem of it were broken, but managed to answer "Sylvy," with much effort when her companion again asked her name.

10   Mrs. Tilley was standing in the doorway when the trio came into view. The cow gave a loud moo by way of explanation.

11   "Yes, you'd better speak up for yourself, you old trial! Where'd she tucked herself away this time, Sylvy?" But Sylvia kept an awed silence; she knew by instinct that her grandmother did not comprehend the gravity of the situation. She must be mistaking the stranger for one of the farmer lads of the region.

12   The young man stood his gun beside the door, and dropped a lumpy game-bag beside it; then he bade Mrs. Tilley good-evening, and repeated his wayfarer's story, and asked if he could have a night's lodging.

13   "Put me anywhere you like," he said. "I must be off early in the morning, before day; but I am very hungry, indeed. You can give me some milk at any rate, that's plain."

14   "Dear sakes, yes," responded the hostess, whose long slumbering hospitality seemed to be easily awakened. "You might fare better if you went out on the main road a mile or so, but you're welcome to what we've got. I'll milk right off, and you make yourself at home. You can sleep on husks or feathers," she proffered graciously. "I raised them all myself. There's good pasturing for geese just below here towards the ma'sh. Now step round and set a plate for the gentleman, Sylvy!" And Sylvia promptly stepped. She was glad to have something to do, and she was hungry herself.

15   It was a surprise to find so clean and comfortable a little dwelling in this New England wilderness. The young man had known the horrors of its most primitive housekeeping, and the dreary squalor of that level of society which does not rebel at the companionship of hens. This was the best thrift of an old-fashioned farmstead, though on such a small scale that it seemed like a hermitage. He listened eagerly to the old

woman's quaint talk, he watched Sylvia's pale face and shining gray eyes with ever growing enthusiasm, and insisted that this was the best supper he had eaten for a month; and afterward the new-made friends sat down in the door-way together while the moon came up.

16   Soon it would be berry-time, and Sylvia was a great help at picking. The cow was a good milker, though a plaguy thing to keep track of, the hostess gossiped frankly, adding presently that she had buried four children, so Sylvia's mother, and a son (who might be dead) in California were all the children she had left. "Dan, my boy, was a great hand to go gunning," she explained sadly. "I never wanted for pa'tridges or gray squer'ls while he was to home. He's been a great wand'rer, I expect, and he's no hand to write letters. There, I don't blame him, I'd ha' seen the world myself if it had been so I could."

17   "Sylvy takes after him," the grandmother continued affectionately, after a minute's pause. "There ain't a foot o' ground she don't know her way over, and the wild creaturs counts her one o' themselves. Squer'ls she'll tame to come an' feed right out o' her hands, and all sorts o' birds. Last winter she got the jay birds to bangeing here, and I believe she'd 'a' scanted herself of her own meals to have plenty to throw out amongst 'em, if I hadn't kep' watch. Anything but crows, I tell her, I'm willin' to help support—though Dan he had a tamed one o' them that did seem to have reason same as folks. It was round here a good spell after he went way. Dan an' his father they didn't hitch,—but he never held up his head ag'in after Dan had dared him an' gone off."

18   The guest did not notice this hint of family sorrows in his eager interest in something else.

19   "So Sylvy knows all about birds, does she?" he exclaimed, as he looked around at the little girl who sat, very demure but increasingly sleepy, in the moonlight. "I am making a collection of birds myself. I have been at it ever since I was a boy." (Mrs. Tilley smiled.) "There are two or three very rare ones I have been hunting for these five years. I mean to get them on my own ground if they can be found."

20   "Do you cage 'em up?" asked Mrs. Tilley doubtfully, in response to his enthusiastic announcement.

21   "Oh, no, they're stuffed and preserved, dozens and dozens of them," said the ornithologist, "and I have shot or snared every one myself. I caught a glimpse of a white heron three miles from here on Saturday, and have followed it in this direction. They have never been found in this district at all. The little white heron, it is," and he turned again to

arrow presently to his home in the green world beneath. Then Sylvia, well satisfied, makes her perilous way down again, not daring to look far below the branch she stands on, ready to cry sometimes because her fingers ache and her lamed feet slip. Wondering over and over again what the stranger would say to her, and what he would think when she told him how to find his way straight to the heron's nest.

38   "Sylvy, Sylvy!" called the busy old grandmother again and again, but nobody answered, and the small husk bed was empty, and Sylvia had disappeared.

39   The guest waked from a dream, and remembering his day's pleasure hurried to dress himself that it might sooner begin. He was sure from the way the shy little girl looked once or twice yesterday that she had at least seen the white heron, and now she must really be made to tell. Here she comes now, paler than ever, and her worn old frock is torn and tattered, and smeared with pine pitch. The grandmother and the sportsman stand in the door together and question her, and the splendid moment has come to speak of the dead hemlock-tree by the green marsh.

40   But Sylvia does not speak after all, though the old grandmother fretfully rebukes her, and the young man's kind appealing eyes are looking straight in her own. He can make them rich with money; he has promised it, and they are poor now. He is so well worth making happy, and he waits to hear the story she can tell.

41   No, she must keep silence! What is it that suddenly forbids her and makes her dumb? Has she been nine years growing, and now, when the great world for the first time puts out a hand to her, must she thrust it aside for a bird's sake? The murmur of the pine's green branches is in her ears, she remembers how the white heron came flying through the golden air and how they watched the sea and the morning together, and Sylvia cannot speak; she cannot tell the heron's secret and give its life away.

42   Dear loyalty, that suffered a sharp pang as the guest went away disappointed later in the day, that could have served and followed him and loved him as a dog loves! Many a night Sylvia heard the echo of his whistle haunting the pasture path as she came home with the loitering cow. She forgot even her sorrow at the sharp report of his gun and the piteous sight of thrushes and sparrows dropping silent to the ground, their songs hushed and their pretty feathers stained and wet with blood. Were the birds better friends than their hunter might have been,—who

can tell? Whatever treasures were lost to her, woodlands and summertime, remember! Bring your gifts and graces and tell your secrets to this lonely country child!

QUESTIONS ON CONTENT, STRUCTURE, AND STYLE

1. What sort of girl is Sylvia at the beginning of the story? Outgoing or shy? A lover of rural life or the busy city? In what ways does she remind her grandmother of her son Dan?

2. Characterize the young hunter. How are he and Sylvia different? How does his view of the farm and local wildlife contrast to Sylvia's?

3. Why does the young man want the white heron? Why is his offer of ten dollars so important to Sylvia and her family?

4. What sorts of mixed feelings does Sylvia have for the young man? Why? How do you think the young man sees her?

5. Why does Sylvia decide to climb the great pine tree? Does this action show a new development in her personality?

6. Look closely at the description of Sylvia's climb to the top of the tree. How is her new view of a "vast and awesome world" a symbolic part of the choice before her?

7. Why does Jewett devote so many paragraphs to the description of the wildlife Sylvia sees from her perch in the tree?

8. What does Jewett mean when she summarizes Sylvia's choice: "when the great world for the first time puts out a hand to her, must she thrust it aside for a bird's sake?" Why do you think Sylvia decides to remain silent about the location of the heron's nest? What does the heron mean to her?

9. Later, is Sylvia happy with her choice? Do you think she made the right decision? Why/why not? (Pose a similar choice for yourself: would you disclose the location of an American eagle or an endangered mountain gorilla to a hunter in exchange for a sum of money?)

10. Describe Jewett's style as a "regionalist" writer. How does she try to capture the flavor of rural New England? In what ways is her

style "realistic"? In what ways does it show the sentimental style of some popular late nineteenth-century fiction?

VOCABULARY

dilatory (1)	inaudible (6)	divining (26)
consolation (2)	wayfarer's (12)	premonition (27)
lingering (3)	proffered (14)	elusive (28)
loitered (3)	hermitage (15)	boughs (29)
shoal (5)	demure (19)	vexed (37)
discreetly (6)	ornithologist (21)	rebukes (40)

SUGGESTIONS FOR WRITING

1. Write an essay describing a time in your life when you, like Sylvia, had to choose between personal gain (financial or perhaps some other benefit) and your loyalty to someone or something. How did you decide? Are you still happy with your decision? Why/why not?

2. In this story, Sylvia makes a difficult decision regarding the life of a white bird. Today there are many difficult environmental decisions frequently demanding that we choose between preserving wildlife and public lands or destroying them to create products, jobs, or energy. Research one controversy—preferably a local environmental issue, but national and global ones abound (lumber in the Northwest, the destruction of the Rain Forests in South America, oil drilling in Alaska, the whaling industry, strip mining, and so on). After you've read about your subject, focus on one specific aspect of the controversy to write about. Show that you understand both sides of the controversy as you argue for your point of view.

3. Sylvia is attracted to the young man in this story, but she is, at the same time, repelled by the hunting and killing that are part of his hobby and his study of birds. Write an essay that supports or refutes one of the following claims: (1) the hunting of animals is never justified; (2) endangered animals should be protected at all costs; (3) zoos are more harmful to animals than helpful; (4) some environmental—protection laws (or groups) are too extreme; (5) more government funds should go into supporting wildlife programs/public lands. For a strong essay, use specific examples or cases as evidence to support your arguments when possible.

SCENES OF OUR PAST

"Ellis Island"

BY IRVING HOWE

"Impressions of an Indian Childhood"

BY GERTRUDE SIMMONS BONNIN (ZITKALA-SA)

"The Holocaust Remembered"

BY *THE NEW YORK TIMES* EDITORIAL STAFF

"Walking on the Moon"

BY DAVID R. SCOTT

"I Have a Dream"

BY MARTIN LUTHER KING, JR.

"Disgrace"

BY DAVID HALL

"The Blue Hotel"

BY STEPHEN CRANE

Ellis Island

IRVING HOWE

Irving Howe was a professor of English at City University of New York. He wrote many books and articles on literature, politics, and history and edited over a half-dozen volumes of short stories and poems. Some of his books include *Politics and the Novel* (1957), *William Faulkner: A Critical Study* (1975), and *Socialism and America* (1985). This selection is taken from *World of Our Fathers* (1983), which chronicles immigration into this country at the turn of the century.

Note: Ellis Island is a small island in New York Bay, near the south end of Manhattan Island. First used as an arsenal by the U.S. government, Ellis Island became in 1892 the official port of entry for thousands of immigrants from Europe. For these thousands of travel-weary men, women, and children, most of whom did not speak English, the scrutiny of papers and often demeaning physical and mental examinations on Ellis Island comprised their first American experience. The government abandoned Ellis Island as an immigration center in 1954, but because the Island played such an important part in so many families' histories, it was declared a national historic site and has been restored as a memorial to our American past.

1 "THE DAY of the emigrants' arrival in New York was the nearest earthly likeness to the final Day of Judgment, when we have to prove our fitness to enter Heaven." So remarked one of those admirable journalists who in the early 1900's exposed themselves to the experience of the immigrants and came to share many of their feelings. No previous difficulties roused such overflowing anxiety, sometimes self-destructive panic, as the anticipated test of Ellis Island. Nervous chatter, foolish rumors spread through each cluster of immigrants:

> "There is Ellis Island!" shouted an immigrant who had already been in the United States and knew of its alien laws. The name acted like magic. Faces grew taut, eyes narrowed. There, in those red buildings, fate awaited them. Were they ready to enter? Or were they to be sent back?

> "Only God knows," shouted an elderly man, his withered hand gripping the railing.

307

2   Numbered and lettered before debarking, in groups corresponding
to entries on the ship's manifest, the immigrants are herded onto the
Customs Wharf. "Quick! Run! Hurry!" shout officials in half a dozen
languages.

3   On Ellis Island they pile into the massive hall that occupies the entire width of the building. They break into dozens of lines, divided by
metal railings, where they file past the first doctor. Men whose breathing is heavy, women trying to hide a limp or deformity behind a large
bundle—these are marked with chalk, for later inspection. Children
over the age of two must walk by themselves, since it turns out that not
all can. (A veteran inspector recalls: "Whenever a case aroused suspicion, the alien was set aside in a cage apart from the rest indicating
why he had been isolated.") One out of five or six needs further medical checking—H chalked for heart, K for hernia, Sc for scalp, X for
mental defects.

4   An interpreter asks each immigrant a question or two: can he respond with reasonable alertness? Is he dull-witted? A question also to
each child: make sure he's not deaf or dumb. A check for TB, regarded
as "the Jewish disease."

5   Then a sharp turn to the right, where the second doctor waits, a
specialist in "contagious and loathsome diseases." Leprosy? Venereal
disease? Fauvus, "a contagious disease of the skin, especially of the
scalp, due to a parasitic fungus, marked by the formation of yellow flat-
tened scabs and baldness"?

6   Then to the third doctor, often feared the most. He

> stands directly in the path of the immigrant, holding a little stick
> in his hand. By a quick movement and the force of his own com-
> pelling gaze, he catches the eyes of his subject and holds them. You
> will see the immigrant stop short, lift his head with a quick jerk,
> and open his eyes very wide. The inspector reaches with a swift
> movement, catches the eyelash with his thumb and finger, turns it
> back, and peers under it. If all is well, the immigrant is passed on
> . . . Most of those detained by the physician are Jews.

7   The eye examination hurts a little. It terrifies the children. Nurses
wait with towels and basins filled with disinfectant. They watch for
trachoma, cause of more than half the medical detentions. It is a

torment hard to understand, this first taste of America, with its poking of flesh and prying into private parts and mysterious chalking of clothes.

8   Again into lines, this time according to nationality. They are led to stalls at which multilingual inspectors ask about character, anarchism, polygamy, insanity, crime, money, relatives, work. You have a job waiting? Who paid your passage? Anyone meeting you? Can you read and write? Ever in prison? Where's your money?

9   For Jewish immigrants, especially during the years before agencies like the Hebrew Immigrant Aid Society (HIAS) could give them advice, these questions pose a dilemma: to be honest or to lie? Is it good to have money or not? Can you bribe these fellows, as back home, or is it a mistake to try? Some are so accustomed to bend and evade and slip a ruble into a waiting hand that they get themselves into trouble with needless lies. "Our Jews," writes a Yiddish paper,

> love to get tangled up with dishonest answers, so that the officials have no choice but to send them to the detention area. A Jew who had money in his pocket decided to lie and said he didn't have a penny. . . . A woman with four children and pregnant with a fifth, said her husband had been in America fourteen years. . . . The HIAS man learned that her husband had recently arrived, but she thought fourteen years would make a better impression. The officials are sympathetic. They know the Jewish immigrants get "confused" and tell them to sit down and "remember." Then they let them in.

Especially bewildering is the idea that if you say you have a job waiting for you in the United States, you are liable to deportation—because an 1885 law prohibits the importation of contract labor. But doesn't it "look better" to say a job is waiting for you? No, the HIAS man patiently explains, it doesn't. Still, how can you be sure *he* knows what he's talking about? Just because he wears a little cap with those four letters embroidered on it?

10   Except when the flow of immigrants was simply beyond the staff's capacity to handle it, the average person passed through Ellis Island in about a day. Ferries ran twenty-four hours a day between the island and both the Battery and points in New Jersey. As for the unfortunates

detained for medical or other reasons, they usually had to stay at Ellis Island for one or two weeks. Boards of special inquiry, as many as four at a time, would sit in permanent session, taking up cases where questions had been raised as to the admissibility of an immigrant, and it was here, in the legal infighting and appeals to sentiment, that HIAS proved especially valuable.

11   The number of those detained at the island or sent back to Europe during a given period of time varied according to the immigration laws then in effect . . . and, more important, according to the strictness with which they were enforced. It is a sad irony, though familiar to students of democratic politics, that under relatively lax administrations at Ellis Island, which sometimes allowed rough handling of immigrants and even closed an eye to corruption, immigrants had a better chance of getting past the inspectors than when the commissioner was a public-spirited Yankee intent upon literal adherence to the law.

12   Two strands of opinion concerning Ellis Island have come down to us, among both historians and the immigrant masses themselves: first, that the newcomers were needlessly subjected to bad treatment, and second, that most of the men who worked there were scrupulous and fair, though often overwhelmed by the magnitude of their task.

13   The standard defense of Ellis Island is offered by an influential historian of immigration, Henry Pratt Fairchild:

> During the year 1907 five thousand was fixed as the maximum number of immigrants who could be examined at Ellis Island in one day; yet during the spring of that year more than fifteen thousand immigrants arrived at the port of New York in a single day.
>
> As to the physical handling of the immigrants, this is [caused] by the need for haste. . . . The conditions of the voyage are not calculated to land the immigrant in an alert and clear-headed state. The bustle, confusion, rush and size of Ellis Island complete the work, and leave the average alien in a state of stupor. . . . He is in no condition to understand a carefully-worded explanation of what he must do, or why he must do it, even if the inspector had the time to give it. The one suggestion which is immediately comprehensible to him is a pull or a push; if this is not administered with actual violence, there is no unkindness in it.

14   Reasonable as it may seem, this analysis meshed Yankee elitism with a defense of the bureaucratic mind. Immigrants *were* disoriented by the time they reached Ellis Island, but they remained human beings with all the sensibilities of human beings; the problem of numbers *was* a real one, yet it was always better when interpreters offered a word of explanation than when they resorted to "a pull or a push." Against the view expressed by Fairchild, we must weigh the massive testimony of the immigrants themselves, the equally large body of material gathered by congressional investigators, and such admissions, all the more telling because casual in intent, as that of Commissioner Corsi: "Our immigration officials have not always been as humane as they might have been." The Ellis Island staff was often badly overworked, and day after day it had to put up with an atmosphere of fearful anxiety which required a certain deadening of response, if only by way of self-defense. But it is also true that many of the people who worked there were rather simple fellows who lacked the imagination to respect cultural styles radically different from their own.

15   One interpreter who possessed that imagination richly was a young Italo-American named Fiorello La Guardia, later to become an insurgent mayor of New York. "I never managed during the years I worked there to become callous to the mental anguish, the disappointment and the despair I witnessed almost daily. . . . At best the work was an ordeal." For those who cared to see, and those able to feel, there could finally be no other verdict.

QUESTIONS ON CONTENT, STRUCTURE, AND STYLE

1. Why does Howe begin his essay with the quotation from the journalist? What comparison does the journalist draw and what does it tell you about the function of Ellis Island?

2. Throughout the essay Howe uses language such as "numbered," "herded," "marked with chalk," "set aside in a cage," "poked," and "led to stalls." What image does such language create? What is Howe suggesting about the way immigrants were viewed by the officials?

3. Why does Howe devote the first half of his essay to describing, step by step, the process through which the immigrants passed? Why not just summarize the process briefly for the readers?

4. Of all the health examinations, Howe chooses to elaborate on the role of the third doctor. Is this an effective choice? How might you have reacted?

5. Why does Howe recount some of the dilemmas immigrants faced while trying to make themselves appear model citizens? Who eventually helped the Jewish immigrants?

6. Note that in paragraphs 4, 8, and 9 Howe uses questions to detail the scene. In each paragraph, who is asking the questions? What do these questions contribute to our understanding of the scene at the Island and why does Howe vary the speakers of these questions?

7. What are the two strands of opinion concerning Ellis Island and why does Howe present both of them?

8. Why does he quote Henry Pratt Fairchild and how does he counter this historian's opinion?

9. Why does Howe conclude his essay by quoting the well-known former New York mayor, Fiorello La Guardia?

10. Summarize in one or two sentences Howe's primary purpose in writing about Ellis Island. What dominant impression do you think he was trying to present? Did he succeed?

VOCABULARY

taut (1)
alien (1)
debarking (2)
multilingual (8)

anarchism (8)
polygamy (8)
detention (9)
deportation (9)

scrupulous (12)
disoriented (14)
sensibilities (14)
insurgent (15)

SUGGESTIONS FOR WRITING

1. Many families have handed down stories of their ancestors' immigration to this country. If possible, interview several relatives to help you reconstruct the story of your family's coming to America. Consider such questions as these: What reasons did your relative(s) have for coming? What hardships or obstacles did they encounter and overcome? What personal sacrifices did they make to become part of

a new country? Turn your discoveries into an essay that illustrates the values that make your family heritage unique and admirable.

2. Arguments rage today about immigration to this country. Former Governor Richard Lamb of Colorado, for example, has repeatedly called for a halt to immigration, arguing that America can no longer afford to share its resources as it once did. Others counter by insisting that our country profits by immigration and that, moreover, we have a moral obligation to accept refugees from countries suffering from war, tyranny, or poverty. Research this on-going debate, and write an essay that argues your position persuasively while acknowledging the positions of those opposed to your view.

3. In his discussion of the Ellis Island officials, Howe states that the men may have been "rather simple fellows who lacked the imagination to respect cultural styles radically different from their own." Do you think that Americans have changed much in their treatment of immigrants? Write an essay that illustrates your community's (your classmates'? your own?) response to people who are culturally or ethnically "different" from the majority. (At some universities students are now being required to take a course in "multiculturalism" that acquaints them with the values and views of other cultures or ethnic groups. You might wish to investigate such courses and evaluate their effectiveness. Should your college adopt such a course?)

Impressions of an Indian Childhood

GERTRUDE SIMMONS BONNIN (ZITKALA-SA)

Gertrude Simmons Bonnin, also known as Zitkala-Sa (Red Bird), was a Yankton Sioux born in 1876 and raised on a South Dakota reservation. When she was eight, she left home to attend a missionary school, where, according to common practice, she was taught to renounce her Native American customs and language. Trained as a teacher, Bonnin later became a well-known violinist and a political activist; she organized and was the president of the National Council of American Indians. In addition to the autobiographical selections here, she wrote stories for *Harper's Monthly* and published two books, *Old Indian Legends* (1901) and *American Indian Stories* (1921).

VII. The Big Red Apples

1   THE FIRST turning away from the easy, natural flow of my life occurred in an early spring. It was in my eighth year; in the month of March, I afterward learned. At this age I knew but one language, and that was my mother's native tongue.

2   From some of my playmates I heard that two paleface missionaries were in our village. They were from that class of white men who wore big hats and carried large hearts, they said. Running direct to my mother, I began to question her why these two strangers were among us. She told me, after I had teased much, that they had come to take away Indian boys and girls to the East. My mother did not seem to want me to talk about them. But in a day or two, I gleaned many wonderful stories from my playfellows concerning the strangers.

3   "Mother, my friend Judéwin is going home with the missionaries. She is going to a more beautiful country than ours; the palefaces told her so!" I said wistfully, wishing in my heart that I too might go.

4   Mother sat in a chair, and I was hanging on her knee. Within the last two seasons my big brother Dawée had returned from a three years' education in the East, and his coming back influenced my mother to take a farther step from her native way of living. First it was a change from the buffalo skin to the white man's canvas that covered

our wigwam. Now she had given up her wigwam of slender poles, to live, a foreigner, in a home of clumsy logs.

5   "Yes, my child, several others besides Judéwin are going away with the palefaces. Your brother said the missionaries had inquired about his little sister," she said, watching my face very closely.

6   My heart thumped so hard against my breast, I wondered if she could hear it.

7   "Did he tell them to take me, mother?" I asked, fearing lest Dawée had forbidden the palefaces to see me, and that my hope of going to the Wonderland would be entirely blighted.

8   With a sad, slow smile, she answered: "There! I knew you were wishing to go, because Judéwin has filled your ears with the white men's lies. Don't believe a word they say! Their words are sweet, but, my child, their deeds are bitter. You will cry for me, but they will not even soothe you. Stay with me, my little one! Your brother Dawée says that going East, away from your mother, is too hard an experience for his baby sister."

9   Thus my mother discouraged my curiosity about the lands beyond our eastern horizon; for it was not yet an ambition for Letters that was stirring me. But on the following day the missionaries did come to our very house. I spied them coming up the footpath leading to our cottage. A third man was with them, but he was not my brother Dawée. It was another, a young interpreter, a paleface who had a smattering of the Indian language. I was ready to run out to meet them, but I did not dare to displease my mother. With great glee, I jumped up and down on our ground floor. I begged my mother to open the door, that they would be sure to come to us. Alas! They came, they saw, and they conquered!

10   Judéwin had told me of the great tree where grew red, red apples; and how we could reach out our hands and pick all the red apples we could eat. I had never seen apple trees. I had never tasted more than a dozen red apples in my life; and when I heard of the orchards of the East, I was eager to roam among them. The missionaries smiled into my eyes, and patted my head. I wondered how mother could say such hard words against them.

11   "Mother, ask them if little girls may have all the red apples they want, when they go East," I whispered aloud, in my excitement.

12   The interpreter heard me, and answered: "Yes, little girl, the nice red apples are for those who pick them; and you will have a ride on the iron horse if you go with these good people."

13   I had never seen a train, and he knew it.

14   "Mother, I'm going East! I like big red apples, and I want to ride on the iron horse! Mother, say yes!" I pleaded.

15   My mother said nothing. The missionaries waited in silence; and my eyes began to blur with tears, though I struggled to choke them back. The corners of my mouth twitched, and my mother saw me.

16   "I am not ready to give you any word," she said to them. "To-morrow I shall send you my answer by my son."

17   With this they left us. Alone with my mother, I yielded to my tears, and cried aloud, shaking my head so as not to hear what she was saying to me. This was the first time I had ever been so unwilling to give up my own desire that I refused to hearken to my mother's voice.

18   There was a solemn silence in our home that night. Before I went to bed I begged the Great Spirit to make my mother willing I should go with the missionaries.

19   The next morning came, and my mother called me to her side. "My daughter, do you still persist in wishing to leave your mother?" she asked.

20   "Oh, mother, it is not that I wish to leave you, but I want to see the wonderful Eastern land," I answered.

21   My dear old aunt came to our house that morning, and I heard her say, "Let her try it."

22   I hoped that, as usual, my aunt was pleading on my side. My brother Dawée came for mother's decision. I dropped my play, and crept close to my aunt.

23   "Yes, Dawée, my daughter, though she does not understand what it all means, is anxious to go. She will need an education when she is grown, for then there will be fewer real Dakotas, and many more pale-faces. This tearing her away, so young, from her mother is necessary, if I would have her an educated woman. The palefaces, who owe us a large debt for stolen lands, have begun to pay a tardy justice in offering some education to our children. But I know my daughter must suffer keenly in this experiment. For her sake, I dread to tell you my reply to the missionaries. Go, tell them that they may take my little daughter, and that the Great Spirit shall not fail to reward them according to their hearts."

24   Wrapped in my heavy blanket, I walked with my mother to the carriage that was soon to take us to the iron horse. I was happy. I met my playmates, who were also wearing their best thick blankets. We showed

one another our new beaded moccasins, and the width of the belts that girdled our new dresses. Soon we were being drawn rapidly away by the white man's horses. When I saw the lonely figure of my mother vanish in the distance, a sense of regret settled heavily upon me. I felt suddenly weak, as if I might fall limp to the ground. I was in the hands of strangers whom my mother did not fully trust. I no longer felt free to be myself, or to voice my own feelings. The tears trickled down my cheeks, and I buried my face in the folds of my blanket. Now the first step, parting me from my mother, was taken, and all my belated tears availed nothing. . . .

25 Having driven thirty miles to the ferryboat, we crossed the Missouri in the evening. Then riding again a few miles eastward, we stopped before a massive brick building. I looked at it in amazement, and with a vague misgiving, for in our village I had never seen so large a house. Trembling with fear and distrust of the palefaces, my teeth chattering from the chilly ride, I crept noiselessly in my soft moccasins along the narrow hall, keeping very close to the bare wall. I was as frightened and bewildered as the captured young of a wild creature.

The School Days of an Indian Girl

I. The Land of Red Apples

26 There were eight in our party of bronzed children who were going East with the missionaries. Among us were three young braves, two tall girls, and we three little ones, Judéwin, Thowin, and I.

27 We had been very impatient to start on our journey to the Red Apple Country, which, we were told, lay a little beyond the great circular horizon of the Western prairie. Under a sky of rosy apples we dreamt of roaming as freely and happily as we had chased the cloud shadows on the Dakota plains. We had anticipated much pleasure from a ride on the iron horse, but the throngs of staring palefaces disturbed and troubled us.

28 On the train, fair women, with tottering babies on each arm, stopped their haste and scrutinized the children of absent mothers. Large men, with heavy bundles in their hands, halted near by, and riveted their glassy blue eyes upon us.

29 I sank deep into the corner of my seat, for I resented being watched. Directly in front of me, children who were no larger than I hung themselves upon the backs of their seats, with their bold white faces

toward me. Sometimes they took their forefingers out of their mouths and pointed at my moccasined feet. Their mothers, instead of reproving such rude curiosity, looked closely at me, and attracted their children's further notice to my blanket. This embarrassed me, and kept me constantly on the verge of tears.

30   I sat perfectly still, with my eyes downcast, daring only now and then to shoot long glances around me. Chancing to turn to the window at my side, I was quite breathless upon seeing one familiar object. It was the telegraph pole which strode by at short paces. Very near my mother's dwelling, along the edge of a road thickly bordered with wild sunflowers, some poles like these had been planted by white men. Often I had stopped, on my way down the road, to hold my ear against the pole, and, hearing its low moaning, I used to wonder what the paleface had done to hurt it. Now I sat watching for each pole that glided by to be the last one. . . .

31   It was night when we reached the school grounds. The lights from the windows of the large buildings fell upon some of the icicled trees that stood beneath them. We were led toward an open door, where the brightness of the lights within flooded out over the heads of the excited palefaces who blocked the way. My body trembled more from fear than from the snow I trod upon. . . . We were taken along an upward incline of wooden boxes, which I learned afterward to call a stairway. At the top was a quiet hall, dimly lighted. Many narrow beds were in one straight line down the entire length of the wall. In them lay sleeping brown faces, which peeped just out of the coverings. I was tucked into bed with one of the tall girls, because she talked to me in my mother tongue and seemed to soothe me.

32   I had arrived in the wonderful land of rosy skies, but I was not happy, as I had thought I should be. My long travel and the bewildering sights had exhausted me. I fell asleep, heaving deep, tired sobs. My tears were left to dry themselves in streaks, because neither my aunt nor my mother was near to wipe them away.

II. The Cutting of My Long Hair

33   The first day in the land of apples was a bitter-cold one; for the snow still covered the ground, and the trees were bare. A large bell rang for breakfast, its loud metallic voice crashing through the belfry overhead and into our sensitive ears. The annoying clatter of shoes on bare floors

gave us no peace. The constant clash of harsh noises, with an undercurrent of many voices murmuring an unknown tongue, made a bedlam within which I was securely tied. And though my spirit tore itself in struggling for its lost freedom, all was useless.

34   A paleface woman, with white hair, came up after us. We were placed in a line of girls who were marching into the dining room. These were Indian girls, in stiff shoes and closely clinging dresses. The small girls wore sleeved aprons and shingled[1] hair. As I walked noiselessly in my soft moccasins, I felt like sinking to the floor, for my blanket had been stripped from my shoulders. I looked hard at the Indian girls, who seemed not to care that they were even more immodestly dressed than I, in their tightly fitting clothes. While we marched in, the boys entered at an opposite door. I watched for the three young braves who came in our party. I spied them in the rear ranks, looking as uncomfortable as I felt.

35   A small bell was tapped, and each of the pupils drew a chair from under the table. Supposing this act meant they were to be seated, I pulled out mine and at once slipped into it from one side. But when I turned my head, I saw that I was the only one seated, and all the rest at our table remained standing. Just as I began to rise, looking shyly around to see how chairs were to be used, a second bell was sounded. All were seated at last, and I had to crawl back into my chair again. I heard a man's voice at one end of the hall, and I looked around to see him. But all the others hung their heads over their plates. As I glanced at the long chain of tables, I caught the eyes of a paleface woman upon me. Immediately I dropped my eyes, wondering why I was so keenly watched by the strange woman. The man ceased his mutterings, and then a third bell was tapped. Every one picked up his knife and fork and began eating. I began crying instead, for by this time I was afraid to venture anything more.

36   But this eating by formula was not the hardest trial in that first day. Late in the morning, my friend Judéwin gave me a terrible warning. Judéwin knew a few words of English; and she had overheard the paleface woman talk about cutting our long, heavy hair. Our mothers had taught us that only unskilled warriors who were captured had their hair shingled by the enemy. Among our people, short hair was worn by mourners, and shingled hair by cowards!

---

[1] Cut short and tapered at the back of the neck.

37   We discussed our fate some moments, and when Judéwin said, "We have to submit, because they are strong," I rebelled.

38   "No, I will not submit! I will struggle first!" I answered.

39   I watched my chance, and when no one noticed I disappeared. I crept up the stairs as quietly as I could in my squeaking shoes,—my moccasins had been exchanged for shoes. Along the hall I passed, without knowing whither I was going. Turning aside to an open door, I found a large room with three white beds in it. The windows were covered with dark green curtains, which made the room very dim. Thankful that no one was there, I directed my steps toward the corner farthest from the door. On my hands and knees I crawled under the bed, and cuddled myself in the dark corner.

40   From my hiding place I peered out, shuddering with fear whenever I heard footsteps near by. Though in the hall loud voices were calling my name, and I knew that even Judéwin was searching for me, I did not open my mouth to answer. Then the steps were quickened and the voices became excited. The sounds came nearer and nearer. Women and girls entered the room. I held my breath, and watched them open closet doors and peep behind large trunks. Some one threw up the curtains, and the room was filled with sudden light. What caused them to stoop and look under the bed I do not know. I remember being dragged out, though I resisted by kicking and scratching wildly. In spite of myself, I was carried downstairs and tied fast in a chair.

41   I cried aloud, shaking my head all the while until I felt the cold blades of the scissors against my neck, and heard them gnaw off one of my thick braids. Then I lost my spirit. Since the day I was taken from my mother I had suffered extreme indignities. People had stared at me. I had been tossed about in the air like a wooden puppet. And now my long hair was shingled like a coward's! In my anguish I moaned for my mother, but no one came to comfort me. Not a soul reasoned quietly with me, as my own mother used to do; for now I was only one of many little animals driven by a herder.

QUESTIONS ON CONTENT, STRUCTURE, AND STYLE

1. What changes have taken place in Native American life and in the life of Bonnin's family by the time she leaves for school?

2. How do the white missionaries encourage her to leave her family to attend school? What is represented by the red apples?

3. Bonnin's mother is reluctant to let her daughter go to the school. Why does she first hesitate then decide to let her go?

4. How is Bonnin treated by white passengers on the train? How does this treatment make her feel?

5. In this essay, Bonnin describes many sights she sees for the first time. How does her choice of descriptive language reveal her youth and inexperience? Choose some examples from the essay to illustrate your answer.

6. Bonnin presents a number of vivid scenes in the essay. Which one, in your view, is most fully developed and effective? Why?

7. What is the central idea of this essay? Where is this best stated?

8. Why is the cutting of Bonnin's hair so upsetting? What does her hair symbolize?

9. Which of the following sensory appeals does Bonnin use in her description—sight, sound, taste, touch, smell? Cite one vivid example for each type of sensory appeal that you can find in the essay. How do these descriptions affect the reader?

10. What is the contrast between the Bonnin's vision of "the land of the red apples" and its reality?

VOCABULARY

wistfully (3)	*smattering (9)*	*scrutinized (28)*
blighted (7)	*hearken (17)*	*reproving (29)*
soothe (8)	*persist (19)*	*whither (39)*
Letters (9)	*keenly (23)*	

SUGGESTIONS FOR WRITING

1. Have you, like Bonnin, had an experience that robbed you of personal or cultural dignity? In a narrative essay using dialogue and vivid description, recreate this experience for a specific audience of your choosing.

2. Compare this essay to Dick Gregory's "Shame" (pp. 165–168). What similarities and/or differences do you see in these two memories of a child in conflict with authority?

3. For how long was Bonnin's treatment typical of Native American education in this country? Why were Native Americans encouraged to reject their language, customs, and religion? How have such educational practices changed? Research some aspect of this topic that intrigues you, and write an informative essay that would interest a general audience of college-age readers.

The Holocaust Remembered

This editorial appeared in *The New York Times* on April 23, 1993, the day after the dedication of the United States Holocaust Memorial Museum. The editorial not only praises the opening of the museum but also responds to several of the project's critics and reminds us why such memorials are both appropriate and important.

Note: Acclaimed for its unique design, the U.S. Holocaust Memorial Museum in Washington, D.C., is located next door to the Smithsonian Institution. Its architect James Freed has said that he "wanted to convey the feeling of constantly being watched, of things closing in." To achieve this feeling, the museum contains a number of off-kilter panels, winding hallways, barred passages, and even a walk into one of the windowless boxcars that transported victims to the death camps. Upon entering the museum, each visitor may pick up a computer-generated ID card of a Holocaust victim and follow this person's fate as a myriad of exhibits describe the progression of Nazi terrorism.

1 THE NEW Holocaust Memorial Museum was dedicated in Washington yesterday [April 22, 1993]; so America, being America, is all tangled up in debate. Should there be a Holocaust museum in the United States? Couldn't it cheapen or distort this horrific chapter in history? Should it focus on the extermination of Jews? Should it even *be?*

2 Let the debate continue. But let it not obscure and confuse. Too much hair-splitting could obliterate the point of what this and all other memorials to inhumanity are about—absolute evil. A Holocaust Museum teaches about evil; it tells those who don't know, or who do not want to

know, how people—weak, ignorant, remarkably unremarkable people led by amoral, twisted demagogues—tortured, starved, gassed, burned and otherwise murdered millions of people. Because of their religion and ethnic identity.

3   That reality helps answer the questions critics have raised. First, why should it be in the United States, when the Holocaust took place in Europe? Why *not* the United States, haven for millions of Holocaust survivors and a democracy that, in its flawed, uneven way, is indisputably dedicated to justice and human rights?

4   What about the charge that the museum risks cheapening, or even glorifying, the Holocaust? It could have. But it doesn't. The design by James Freed, who suffered through childhood in Nazi Germany, communicates sensitively through its starkness and simplicity.

5   Should it focus on the death of Jews? Others were murdered in Hitler's Germany—homosexuals, Gypsies, Catholics, Russian prisoners, the handicapped. Their deaths are remembered and mourned. But *six million* Jews died in the Holocaust. Two-thirds of European Jewry were rounded up and killed in Auschwitz, Treblinka, Bergen-Belsen, Dachau and other abominations designed for killing. "While not all victims were Jews," said Elie Wiesel,[1] "all Jews were victims."

6   As for its being created in the first place, the answer is straightforward. The world does need reminding. Neo-Nazis say the Holocaust never happened. In a recent Roper poll sponsored by the American Jewish Committee, 34 percent of the adults surveyed, and 37 percent of the high school youths, said it was possible the Holocaust never happened, or didn't know if it happened.

7   Maybe some people cannot conceive of such evil so they dismiss it. Maybe they are, some of them, infected with anti-Semitism. But more likely it's ignorance that civilized society has the most to worry about, as it always has.

8   And that, ultimately, is what validates the museum's existence. It teaches what must be taught. How can anyone doubt the need for such instruction in a world that has produced "ethnic cleansing"?

[1] Elie Wiesel is a winner of the Nobel Peace Prize and a concentration camp survivor who has dedicated his life to keeping alive the memory of the Holocaust. The author of many books, including the novel *Night,* Wiesel delivered a moving speech at the Museum's dedication ceremony.

9   If anything, build more Holocaust museums. Build a memorial museum about slavery, about every brutal event and benighted spot on the planet. They serve, as do the struggles of Sarajevo, Belfast, Bombay, Soweto to remind the world again and again, as President Clinton said yesterday, "how fragile are the safeguards of civilization."

QUESTIONS ON CONTENT, STRUCTURE, AND STYLE

1. What, according to this editorial, is the point of the Holocaust Memorial?

2. Why is there debate over this memorial? What is the danger of such debate?

3. How does the editorial answer those critics who feel the memorial should not have been erected in the United States? Do you agree with this answer?

4. Other critics charge that the museum might cheapen or even glorify the Holocaust. Explain what you think those critics might be afraid of. How could a museum "cheapen" its subject?

5. Why is author Elie Wiesel directly quoted in this editorial? What criticism do his words try to answer?

6. Why are the results from the Roper poll so important to the debate over the building of the museum? Do you find the results surprising? How would you have answered such a poll?

7. What, according to this editorial, is the biggest problem civilized society has to confront when dealing with such evil as the Holocaust? What ultimately validates the museum's existence?

8. What does the phrase "ethnic cleansing" refer to? Why is this reference relevant to this discussion?

9. Other critics have argued that a museum-memorial to those victimized by slavery should have been built in America before a memorial to the Holocaust victims. How well does this editorial confront this argument? On which side of this argument do you stand?

10. Why does this editorial refer to places such as Sarajevo and Soweto and then conclude with the words of President Clinton? Is this an effective ending for this editorial? Explain.

Vocabulary

dedicated (1)	*obscure (2)*	*haven (3)*
distort (1)	*hair-splitting (2)*	*indisputably (3)*
horrific (1)	*obliterate (2)*	*anti-Semitism (7)*
extermination (1)	*demagogues (2)*	*benighted (9)*

Suggestions for Writing

1. Research some aspect of the Holocaust that interests or puzzles you. Write an essay on your topic that informs your readers while reminding them "how fragile are the safeguards of civilization." Don't overlook the many acts of heroism, such as Raoul Wallenberg's work, the admirable conduct of the Danes and their King, the resistance fighters in the Warsaw Ghetto and other areas, or the many stories of people who hid those persecuted by the Nazis. (Or, if you prefer, research one of the many controversies of World War II. For example, what were the arguments for and against the Japanese internment camps in America? For dropping the bomb? For maintaining neutrality until after Pearl Harbor? For turning away European refugees fleeing Hitler as late as 1939?)

2. Design a questionnaire that asks a specific group of readers to reveal their knowledge of the Holocaust or of some other important struggle such as apartheid in South Africa, slavery in America, the treatment of the Native Americans, women's rights, etc. (You may need to do some reading about your topic beforehand.) Write an essay that reveals and analyzes your results. What do your results say about people's awareness of your topic? Compare your results to the Roper poll. Are your subjects more or less informed?

3. Read an excellent article on the Holocaust Museum in the April 1993 issue of *Smithsonian* in which the author, Robert C. Lautman, describes his walk through the memorial in vivid detail. After reading the article and studying the accompanying photographs of the museum, write an essay that supports or refutes *The New York Times'* claim that the museum does not cheapen or misrepresent the Holocaust. Or, if you have been to a memorial site that particularly moved you, write about this experience. Describe your visit and explain why you feel the memorial captures just the right feeling. How does the memorial's design contribute to this feeling?

Walking on the Moon

DAVID R. SCOTT

As an Apollo astronaut, David R. Scott is one of a select group of people to have walked on the moon, an experience he recreates in the following essay first published in *National Geographic*. Born in 1932, the
son of an Air Force Brigadier General, Scott began training as an
astronaut in 1963 after serving as an Air Force jet pilot. With James B.
Irvin and Alfred Worden, he piloted the Endeavour in the 1971 Apollo
15 mission, a journey he describes as "steps into a frontier that will
never end."

1   SIXTY FEET above the moon, the blast of our single rocket churns up a
gray tumult of lunar dust that seems to engulf us. Blinded, I feel the
rest of the way down "on the gauges." With an abrupt jar, our lunar
module, or LM, strikes the surface and shudders to rest. We have hit
our target squarely—a large amphitheater girded by mountains and a
deep canyon, at the eastern edge of a vast plain.

2   As Jim Irvin and I wait for the dust to settle, I recall the twelve rev-
olutions we have just spent in lunar orbit aboard our Apollo 15 spaceship *Endeavour*. Each two hours found us completing a full circuit of
earth's ancient satellite—one hour knifing through lunar night, then
sunrise and an hour of daylight. As we orbited, I found a particular fascination in that sector of the darkened moon bathed in earthshine. The
light reflected by our planet illuminates the sleeping moon much more
brightly than moonlight silvers our own night. The mountains and
crater rims are clearly seen.

3   I will always remember *Endeavour* hurtling through that strange night
of space. Before us and above us stars spangled the sky with their distant icy fire; below lay the moon's far side, an arc of impenetrable
blackness that blotted the firmament. Then, as our moment of sunrise
approached, barely discernible streamers of light—actually the glowing gases of the solar corona millions of miles away—played above the
moon's horizon. Finally the sun exploded into our view like a visual
thunderclap. Abruptly, completely, in less than a second, its harsh light
flooded into the spaceship and dazzled our eyes.

4   As we looked into the early lunar morning from *Endeavour,* the moonscape stretched into the distance, everything the color of milk chocolate. Long angular shadows accentuated every hill, every crater. As the sun arched higher, the plains and canyons and mountains brightened to a gunmetal gray, while the shadows shrank. At full lunar noontide, the sun glared down upon a bleached and almost featureless world.

5   Now we have come to rest on the moon, and the last of the dust settles outside the LM. We throw the switches that convert this hybrid vehicle from spacecraft to dwelling. Thus begin our 67 hours of lunar residence. We are on a still and arid world where each blazing day and each subfreezing night stretch through 355 earth hours. We have landed in the bright morning of a moon day. When we depart, the sun will not have reached zenith.

6   It is sobering to realize that we are the only living souls on this silent sphere, perhaps the only sentient beings in our solar system not confined to earth. Though we have slipped the bonds of our home planet, we remain earthmen. So we keep our clocks set to Houston time and gear our lives to the 24-hour cycle we have always known.

7   Opening the top hatch for a preliminary reconnaissance, I peer out at a world seemingly embalmed in the epoch of its creation. Each line, each form blends into the harmonious whole of a single fluid sculpture. Craters left by "recent" meteorites—merely millions of years ago—stand out, startlingly white, like fresh scar tissue against the soft beige of the undulating terrain.

8   I steal a moment and glance straight up into the black sky where the crystalline sphere of earth—all blue and white, sea and clouds—gleams in the abyss of space. In that cold and boundless emptiness, our planet provides the only glow of color. For 30 minutes my helmeted head pivots above the open hatch as I survey and photograph the wonderland of the lunar surface. The incredible variety of landforms in this restricted area (on the moon, the horizon lies a scant mile and a half from a viewer) fills me with pleasant surprise. To the south an 11,000-foot ridge rises above the bleak plain. To the east stretch the hulking heights of an even higher summit. On the west a winding gorge plunges to depths of more than 1,000 feet. Dominating the northeastern horizon, a great mountain stands in noble splendor almost three miles above us. Ours is the first expedition to land amid lunar mountains. Never quickened by life, never assailed by wind and rain, they loom still and serene, a tableau of forever. Their majesty overwhelms me.

9   Eight years' training in lunar geology makes me instantly aware of intriguing details. A dark line like a bathtub ring smudges the bases of the mountains. Was it left by the subsiding lake of lava that filled the immense cavity of Palus Putredinis, on the fringes of Mare Imbrium, billions of years ago? Mare Imbrium, on whose edge we have landed, stretches across the face of the moon for some 650 miles. The celestial projectile that excavated it must have been huge—perhaps as much as 50 miles across—and it slammed into the moon with a velocity many times greater than that of a rifle bullet.

10   When we descend the ladder of the LM and step onto the moon's surface, Jim and I feel a gratifying sense of freedom. For five days we have been crammed into the tight confines of the spacecraft that brought us here. Now, all at once, we regain the luxury of movement. But, we quickly discover, locomotion on the moon has its own peculiar restrictions. At one-sixth of earth's gravity, we weigh only a sixth our normal poundage. Our gait quickly evolves into a rhythmic, bounding motion that possesses all the lightness and ease of strolling on a trampoline.

11   At the same time, since the mass of our bodies and personal gear—and hence, our inertia—remains unchanged, starting and stopping require unusual exertion. I learn to get under way by thrusting my body forward, as though I were stepping into a wind. To stop, I dig in my heels and lean backward.

12   To fall on the moon—and I did several times—is to rediscover childhood. You go down in slow motion, the impact is slight, the risk of injury virtually nil. Forsaking the adult attitude that regards a fall not only as a loss of dignity but also a source of broken bones, the moon walker—like a child—accepts it as yet another diversion. Only the clinging moon dust, the untoward demand on the oxygen supply occasioned by the exertion of getting up, pall the pleasure of a tumble. Personally I find the one-sixth gravity of the moon more enjoyable than the soothing weightlessness of space. I have the same sense of buoyancy, but the moon provides a reassuringly fixed sense of up and down.

13   As we unload and begin to assemble our equipment—including the battery-powered four-wheeled Rover that will carry us across the moonscape at a jaunty six or so miles an hour—I gaze around at the plains and mountains that have become our world. My eyes trace a curiously contoured, totally alien wasteland. I scale the lofty mountains and feel a strange, indescribable emotion: No naked eye has ever seen them; no foot has ever trod them. I am an intruder in an eternal wilderness.

14   The flowing moonscape, unmarred by a single jagged peak, reminds me of earth's uplands covered by a heavy blanket of fresh snow. Indeed, the dark-gray moon dust—its consistency seems to be somewhat between coal dust and talcum powder—mantles virtually every physical feature of the lunar surface. Our boots sink gently into it as we walk; we leave sharply chiseled footprints.

15   Color undergoes an odd transformation here. Everything underfoot or nearby is gray, yet this hue blends gradually into the uniform golden tan that characterizes distant objects. And this small spectrum moves with the walker. Most of the scattered rocks share the same gray tint as the dust, but we find two that are jet black, two of pastel green, several with sparkling crystals, some coated with glass, and one that is white. As we advance, we are surrounded by stillness. No wind blows. No sound echoes. Only shadows move. Within the space suit, I hear the reassuring purr of the miniaturized machines that supply vital oxygen and shield me from the blistering 150°F. surface heat of lunar morning.

16   Any of a thousand malfunctions in a space suit or the LM could condemn an astronaut to swift death. Yet we have a quiet confidence in our own abilities, and boundless faith in the engineers and technicians who have fashioned the ingenious devices that transport and sustain us in space. Often, in the course of my stay on the moon, I recall the words of American poet Edwin Markham: "There is a destiny which makes us brothers; none goes his way alone."

17   At first we experience a troubling deception with perspective. Without the familiar measuring sticks of our native planet—trees, telephone poles, clouds, and haze—we cannot determine whether an object stands close at hand or at a considerable distance, or whether it is large or small. Gradually our eyes learn to cope with the craters—mammoth, medium, and minuscule—that dot virtually every inch of the surface. And gradually the moon becomes a friendlier place. A thought occurs to me: Would human beings born on the moon be able to find their way among the trees and clouds of earth?

18   Each excursion on the lunar surface is planned to last seven hours, almost to the limit of a space suit's life-sustaining capabilities. We dig and drill into the surface, gather rocks and soil, take endless photographs. The photographs, it seems to me, provide us with a testament that transcends time, for we may be photographing the distant past of our own planet. The Rover functions impeccably as we ride from site to site, accumulating fragments of history. We bounce and pitch across

omnipresent chuckholelike craters. The motion exactly resembles that of a small boat in a rough sea; so does the physical effect. Incredible as it seems, in the arid environment of the moon, seasickness could become an occupational hazard.

19   After each of our expeditions, we climb—sapped of energy—back into the LM. With its oxygen and food and water, it is a tiny artificial earth that comforts us in the void. Removing our space suits and attending to our housekeeping chores consumes two hours. For the first twenty minutes we are conscious of a pervasive odor, similar to that of gunpowder, from the moon dust we have tracked in. Our air-purifying system soon dispels the acrid scent, but the fine, adhesive dust clings to everything. Back on earth, no amount of cleaning will convert our space suits from the gray hue acquired on the moon to their once pristine and sparkling white.

20   The better to sleep, we create the illusion of night. We place opaque shades over the windows of the LM to exclude the harsh sunlight reflected from the moon's surface. Then we go through all the homey activities of sunset on earth, even to snapping on overhead lights. When finally we switch them off, we settle into hammocks. On earth, I have always found hammocks uncomfortable. But here my 30-pound body adapts marvelously to the canvas crescent, and I easily fall into dreamless sleep.

21   Bounding along in the Rover on our third and final expedition, we begin to feel fully at home in our new habitat. The craters now seem familiar and help us gauge distances. And we venture across the horizon—the first astronauts ever to do so—without anxiety. Should the sophisticated Rover navigation system fail, we have a small cardboard sun compass fashioned by a technician in Houston—a frail instrument much shriveled by the savage lunar sunlight and coated with moon dust—that will give us our bearings. But our newfound confidence stems less from instruments than from the fact that we have come to know and understand our surroundings.

22   On our return we even dare a shortcut. The Rover bounces between undulations and crater walls that mask our view of the LM for long minutes, but we emerge on target. Arriving at the LM, I experience a sense of impending loss. Soon I will leave the moon, probably forever. And, in a peculiar way, I have come to feel a strange affection for this peaceful, changeless companion of the earth.

23   As I mount the ladder for the last time, I halt and glance back at the Rover. It seems poised and ready for its next task. And poised in that same eager attitude it could remain for thousands, perhaps millions of years—a driverless vehicle lost in the loneliness of this lifeless realm. Beside it, like staunch sentinels through the long millenniums, will hulk the LM descent stage and the assorted equipment of our mission. The vacuum of space, which knows only negligible decay, will confer upon all of it—even to the footprints we have left in the undrifting dust—a permanence akin to immortality.

24   The thought haunts us that the end of the Apollo flights may mark man's last visit to the moon for a long time. American manned exploration of deep space is scheduled for an indefinite hiatus. Most scientists have already suggested that, when it resumes, all effort should concentrate upon reaching Mars and beyond. So our lunar artifacts—bypassed in the race to the planets—could remain undisturbed for eternity.

25   Clutching the ladder, I raise my eyes from the now-familiar moonscape to earth, glowing in the black heavens—that incredibly vivid sphere, so blue, so beautiful, so beloved. And so bedeviled: by ecological balances gone awry, by scattered starvation, by a shortage of energy that may motivate us to seek sources beyond our earth. Our Apollo crew believes that a technology capable of exploring space can and will help resolve such problems. We feel a sense of pride in the accomplishments of our program, yet we cannot escape a sense of deep concern for the fate of our planet and our species. This concern has led us to add certain items to the equipment we are leaving on the moon. The sum of these articles, we hope, will form a résumé of our era in the continuing story of the human race.

26   In eons to come, should astronauts from the deeps of space—from other solar systems in other galaxies—pass this way, they may find our spoor, our abandoned gear. A plaque of aluminum affixed to the deserted LM descent stage portrays the two hemispheres of our planet; upon it are engraved the name of our spacecraft, the date of our mission and a roster of the crew. From these data, the equipment, and even the dimensions of our footprints, intelligent beings will readily deduce what kind of creatures we were and whence we came. We leave a piece of fauna—a falcon feather—and of flora—a four-leaf clover.

27   In a little hollow in the moon dust we place a stylized figurine of a man in a space suit and beside it another metal plaque bearing the names

of the 14 spacemen—Russians and Americans—who have given their lives so that man may range the cosmos. Finally we deposit a single book: the Bible.

28   Our mission ends in fatigue and elation. Amazing success has rewarded the first extended scientific expedition to the moon. After debriefing and helping in the analyses of our findings, our crew disbands.

29   Now, two years later, I continue to work in the Lyndon B. Johnson Space Center near Houston. Frequently I reflect upon those three most memorable days of my life. Although I can reconstruct them virtually moment by moment, sometimes I can scarcely believe that I have actually walked on the moon.

30   Occasionally, while strolling on a crisp autumn night or driving a straight Texas road, I look up at the moon riding bright and proud over the clouds. My eye picks out the largest circular splotch on the silvery surface: Mare Imbrium. There, at the eastern edge of that splotch, I once descended in a spaceship. Again I feel that I will probably never return, and the thought stirs a pang of nostalgia. For when I look at the moon I do not see a hostile, empty world. I see the radiant body where man has taken his first steps into a frontier that will never end.

QUESTIONS ON CONTENT, STRUCTURE, AND STYLE

1. What is Scott's purpose in writing this essay? Why is this subject so well suited for a descriptive essay for a general audience?

2. Note Scott's use of figurative language. Which similes are particularly effective in showing the reader what it is like on the moon's surface? Why is figurative language especially useful, given Scott's subject?

3. Is this essay written primarily in present or past tense? How does this affect the reader?

4. As readers who have never been on the moon's surface, we depend on Scott's description to let us "see" through his eyes. Choose a descriptive passage from the essay that is particularly effective to you, explaining why you chose it from among the many possibilities.

5. How does Scott's attitude toward his visit to the moon come through in his writing tone? Describe this attitude/tone.

6. Why does Scott allude to Edwin Markham's words, "There is a destiny which makes us brothers; none goes his way alone"?

7. Review paragraph 25. How does Scott's trip to the moon affect his views of earth?

8. In paragraphs 26 and 27, Scott describes the artifacts intentionally left behind on the moon's surface in case other "astronauts from the deeps of space" should "pass this way." Explain why, in your opinion, they might have chosen to leave each of these items. What does each item say about our culture?

9. What is the dominant idea of Scott's essay? How do the last few paragraphs of the essay affect the overall impact of the essay on the reader?

10. Have you ever seen the famous black-and-white pictures of the moon walks? Did Scott's descriptions change your views of what it is like on the moon's surface? What part of his essay was most surprising or interesting to you?

VOCABULARY

tumult (1)	zenith (5)	inertia (11)
lunar (1)	sentient (6)	diversion (12)
girded (1)	reconnaissance (7)	buoyancy (12)
impenetrable (3)	epoch (7)	transcends (18)
discernible (3)	quickened (8)	pervasive (19)
accentuated (4)	tableau (8)	nostalgia (30)
hybrid (5)	locomotion (10)	

SUGGESTIONS FOR WRITING

1. Since the termination of the Apollo program, our country has debated whether NASA should resume its exploration of the moon and—as Scott notes—other planets like Mars. Should the U.S. allocate resources for resuming these programs? What are the benefits of such exploration? What are the costs? In a persuasive essay, present your views on this subject.

2. If you, like the Apollo astronauts, could choose a few items to represent earth's culture for other, unknown civilizations, what would

you choose and why? Write an essay that presents these artifacts and your explanation of their value.

3. If you had the chance, would you travel into space in a space shuttle, rocket, or space station? What personal qualities do you believe are necessary to be an astronaut? As author Tom Wolfe described it, do you have "the right stuff"? In an essay examining your own temperament and character, show why you either would or would not be a good candidate for space travel.

I Have a Dream

MARTIN LUTHER KING, JR.

The Rev. Martin Luther King, Jr., president of the Southern Christian Leadership Conference, was the most well-known leader of the civil rights movement of the 1960s and the recipient of the 1964 Nobel Peace Prize. He was assassinated in 1968. King delivered this speech in 1963 at a celebration of the Emancipation Proclamation, before a crowd of thousands who had marched to the Lincoln Memorial in Washington, D.C., to protest racial discrimination.

1   FIVE SCORE years ago, a great American, in whose symbolic shadow we stand, signed the Emancipation Proclamation. This momentous decree came as a great beacon light of hope to millions of Negro slaves who had been seared in the flames of withering injustice. It came as a joyous daybreak to end the long night of captivity.

2   But one hundred years later, we must face the tragic fact that the Negro is still not free. One hundred years later, the life of the Negro is still sadly crippled by the manacles of segregation and the chains of discrimination. One hundred years later, the Negro lives on a lonely island of poverty in the midst of a vast ocean of material prosperity. One hundred years later, the Negro is still languished in the corners of American society and finds himself an exile in his own land. So we have come here today to dramatize an appalling condition.

3   In a sense we have come to our nation's Capital to cash a check. When the architects of our republic wrote the magnificent words of the Constitution and the Declaration of Independence, they were signing a promissory note to which every American was to fall heir. This note was a promise that all men would be guaranteed the unalienable rights of life, liberty, and the pursuit of happiness.

4   It is obvious today that America has defaulted on this promissory note insofar as her citizens of color are concerned. Instead of honoring this sacred obligation, America has given the Negro people a bad check; a check which has come back marked "insufficient funds." But we refuse to believe that the bank of justice is bankrupt. We refuse to believe that there are insufficient funds in the great vaults of opportunity of this nation. So we have come to cash this check—a check that will give us upon demand the riches of freedom and the security of justice. We have also come to this hallowed spot to remind America of the fierce urgency of *now*. This is no time to engage in the luxury of cooling off or to take the tranquilizing drug of gradualism. *Now* is the time to make real the promises of Democracy. *Now* is the time to rise from the dark and deso-late valley of segregation to the sunlit path of racial justice. *Now* is the time to open the doors of opportunity to all of God's children. *Now* is the time to lift our nation from the quicksands of racial injustice to the solid rock of brotherhood.

5   It would be fatal for the nation to overlook the urgency of the mo-ment and to underestimate the determination of the Negro. This swel-tering summer of the Negro's legitimate discontent will not pass until there is an invigorating autumn of freedom and equality. 1963 is not an end, but a beginning. Those who hope that the Negro needed to blow off steam and will now be content will have a rude awakening if the nation returns to business as usual. There will be neither rest nor tranquillity in America until the Negro is granted his citizenship rights. The whirl-winds of revolt will continue to shake the foundations of our nation until the bright day of justice emerges.

6   But there is something that I must say to my people who stand on the warm threshold which leads into the palace of justice. In the pro-cess of gaining our rightful place we must not be guilty of wrongful deeds. Let us not seek to satisfy our thirst for freedom by drinking from the cup of bitterness and hatred. We must forever conduct our struggle on the high plane of dignity and discipline. We must not

allow our creative protest to degenerate into physical violence. Again and again we must rise to the majestic heights of meeting physical force with soul force. The marvelous new militancy which has engulfed the Negro community must not lead us to a distrust of all white people, for many of our white brothers, as evidenced by their presence here today, have come to realize that their destiny is tied up with our destiny and their freedom is inextricably bound to our freedom. We cannot walk alone.

7   And as we walk, we must make the pledge that we shall march ahead. We cannot turn back. There are those who are asking the devotees of civil rights, "When will you be satisfied?" We can never be satisfied as long as the Negro is the victim of the unspeakable horrors of police brutality. We can never be satisfied as long as our bodies, heavy with fatigue of travel, cannot gain lodging in the motels of the highways and the hotels of the cities. We cannot be satisfied as long as the Negro's basic mobility is from a smaller ghetto to a larger one. We can never be satisfied as long as a Negro in Mississippi cannot vote and a Negro in New York believes he has nothing for which to vote. No, no, we are not satisfied, and we will not be satisfied until justice rolls down like waters and righteousness like a mighty stream.

8   I am not unmindful that some of you have come here out of great trials and tribulations. Some of you have come fresh from narrow jail cells. Some of you have come from areas where your quest for freedom left you battered by the storms of persecution and staggered by the winds of police brutality. You have been the veterans of creative suffering. Continue to work with the faith that unearned suffering is redemptive.

9   Go back to Mississippi, go back to Alabama, go back to South Carolina, go back to Georgia, go back to Louisiana, go back to the slums and ghettos of our northern cities, knowing that somehow this situation can and will be changed. Let us not wallow in the valley of despair.

10   I say to you today, my friends, that in spite of the difficulties and frustrations of the moment I still have a dream. It is a dream deeply rooted in the American dream.

11   I have a dream that one day this nation will rise up and live out the true meaning of its creed: "We hold these truths to be self-evident; that all men are created equal."

12   I have a dream that one day on the red hills of Georgia the sons of former slaves and the sons of former slaveowners will be able to sit down together at the table of brotherhood.

13   I have a dream that one day even the state of Mississippi, a desert state sweltering with the heat of injustice and oppression, will be transformed into an oasis of freedom and justice.

14   I have a dream that my four little children will one day live in a nation where they will not be judged by the color of their skin but by the content of their character.

15   I have a dream today.

16   I have a dream that one day the state of Alabama, whose governor's lips are presently dripping with the words of interposition and nullification, will be transformed into a situation where little black boys and black girls will be able to join hands with little white boys and white girls and walk together as sisters and brothers.

17   I have a dream today.

18   I have a dream that one day every valley shall be exalted, every hill and mountain shall be made low, the rough places will be made plain, and the crooked places will be made straight, and the glory of the Lord shall be revealed, and all flesh shall see it together.

19   This is our hope. This is the faith with which I return to the South. With this faith we will be able to hew out of the mountain of despair a stone of hope. With this faith we will be able to transform the jangling discords of our nation into a beautiful symphony of brotherhood. With this faith we will be able to work together, to pray together, to struggle together, to go to jail together, to stand up for freedom together, knowing that we will be free one day.

20   This will be the day when all of God's children will be able to sing with new meaning

> My country, 'tis of thee,
> Sweet land of liberty,
>   Of thee I sing:
> Land where my fathers died,
> Land of the pilgrims' pride
> From every mountainside
>   Let freedom ring.

21   And if America is to be a great nation this must become true. So let freedom ring from the prodigious hilltops of New Hampshire. Let freedom ring from the mighty mountains of New York. Let freedom ring from the heightening Alleghenies of Pennsylvania!

22   Let freedom ring from the snowcapped Rockies of Colorado!

23   Let freedom ring from the curvacious peaks of California!

24   But not only that; let freedom ring from Stone Mountain of Georgia.

25   Let freedom ring from Lookout Mountain of Tennessee!

26   Let freedom ring from every hill and molehill of Mississippi. From every mountainside, let freedom ring.

27   When we let freedom ring, when we let it ring from every village and every hamlet, from every state and every city, we will be able to speed up that day when all of God's children, black men and white men, Jews and Gentiles, Protestants and Catholics, will be able to join hands and sing in the words of the old Negro spiritual, "Free at last! free at last! thank God almighty, we are free at last!"

QUESTIONS ON CONTENT, STRUCTURE, AND STYLE

1. King begins his speech with reference to what nineteenth-century event?

2. What contrast does King draw in paragraph 2? Why?

3. What is the effect of repeating "one hundred years later" in paragraph 2? Cite at least two other examples of effective repetition.

4. Identify the dominant imagery presented in paragraphs 3 and 4.

5. What warning does King give if the nation "returns to business as usual"?

6. Why does King make a plea for nonviolence?

7. What is the oratorical effect of mixing short sentences ("I have a dream today") with the longer ones in paragraphs 10–18?

8. Throughout the essay King uses abundant imagery to help his audience visualize his message. Frequently these images are presented in the same sentence as paired opposites:

   "joyous daybreak . . . long night of captivity" (paragraph 1)

   "summer of . . . discontent . . . autumn of freedom" (paragraph 5)

   "whirlwinds of revolt . . . until the bright day of justice" (paragraph 5) "heat of injustice . . . oasis of freedom" (paragraph 13)

"jangling discords . . . symphony of brotherhood" (paragraph 19).

What do these antithetical images add to the tone and effectiveness of King's speech?

9. Identify King's use of patriotic and spiritual songs, the Bible, and the Declaration of Independence. Why did he borrow from these sources? Why did he end his speech by quoting the old spiritual?

10. What were King's main purposes in delivering such a speech? Had you been in the audience that day, what reaction would you have had?

VOCABULARY

manacles (2)	*invigorating (5)*	*interposition (16)*
promissory (3)	*inextricably (6)*	*nullification (16)*
unalienable (3)	*redemptive (8)*	

SUGGESTIONS FOR WRITING

1. Write an essay analyzing the power of King's speech, explaining his effective uses of repetition, imagery, and sentence variation. Or write an essay that incorporates many of King's techniques; use repetition and imagery to emphasize a point you would like to make about a current controversial issue.

2. Write an essay in which you show the purely oratory qualities of this selection. What choices did King make to ensure that his listening audience could easily follow his speech?

3. Do you think that King's dream has come to pass? Are we still a nation divided by racism? Write an essay that presents your view on racism in our country today. (You might focus this large topic by limiting the scope of your paper to your community or to your campus.)

Disgrace

DAVID HALL

David Hall received his Ph.D. in English from the University of Texas, Austin, in 1978. He has published numerous poems and stories, including one that won the Texas Institute of Letters award for best short fiction. He has also had plays produced across the country. This poem was first published in *Encore* in 1975, five years after Hall served as an artillery First Lieutenant in Vietnam.

    If Juan Rodriguez is alive today
    I'd like to tell him that
    to step on a mine
    your first step into war
5 is no disgrace.

    What will my mother say?
    he asked the medics
    bending over him
    knowing he shouldn't see
10 what all he'd lost.

    What will she think of her clumsy son?

    I'd like to say
    I've seen good men
    take longer,
15 long enough to think their country
    putrefied.

    I knew one boy
    who ate gunpowder
    and died

20 I'd like to say
    I've seen men cry
    and try to swat the bullets
    away like bees

and watched one black man
25 scared of dying
shoot off both his knees.

I huddled half my year in mud
and couldn't remember my mother's face.

Believe me Juan
30 your friends who stayed
went far beyond disgrace.

QUESTIONS ON CONTENT, STRUCTURE, AND STYLE

1. From whose point of view is this poem written?

2. Who is Juan Rodriguez and why does he feel disgraced?

3. What is the poet's attitude toward Juan? Why?

4. What does the poet try to tell Juan about some of the other soldiers?

5. Why does the poet mention that he couldn't remember his mother's face? How does this comment relate to Juan's reference to his mother in line 6?

6. What kind of "disgrace" might the poet be talking about in the last stanza?

7. Identify the only simile in the poem; what is its purpose?

8. Analyze the poem's use of rhyme. What pattern is present? Why does the poet maintain this pattern?

9. If you had not been told that the setting of this poem was Vietnam, might you have guessed it? Why/why not?

10. Contrast the views of "disgrace" in war that are presented here to your own view. Are they different or similar?

VOCABULARY

medics (line 7)
putrefied (line 16)

SUGGESTIONS FOR WRITING

1. During the Vietnam War, many young men declared themselves "conscientious objectors" and refused to fight in a war they felt unjust. Should people of draft age have the right to object to fighting in a particular war? Or should only those with traditional religious opposition to fighting in general be exempt? Write an essay defending your position.

2. In his poem, Hall tries to define "disgrace" within the context of an unpopular war. In an essay, explain your own definition of "disgrace" in a particular context, making your meaning clear either by presenting multiple examples as Hall does or by describing a longer incident or two that illustrate your point about "disgraceful" behavior. (Some examples: What constitutes "disgrace" in sports? In one's family? In one's close circle of friends?)

3. Interview a Vietnam veteran and write an essay based on that person's most vivid memory or most valuable insight during or after the war. (If you can't find a veteran, you might use another poem or piece of short fiction or prose written by a Vietnam vet.)

The Blue Hotel

STEPHEN CRANE

Stephen Crane was a nineteenth-century novelist, short-story writer, and journalist. His two most famous novels are *Maggie, A Girl of the Streets* (1893), originally rejected by publishers because of its sympathetic treatment of a young girl turned prostitute, and *The Red Badge of Courage* (1895), still admired as one of the best war stories ever written. This story was published in *The OpenBoat and Other Tales of Adventure* in 1898.

I

1   THE PALACE Hotel at Fort Romper was painted a light blue, a shade that is on the legs of a kind of heron, causing the bird to declare its position against any background. The Palace Hotel, then, was always screaming and howling in a way that made the dazzling winter landscape of Nebraska seem only a gray swampish hush. It stood alone on the prairie, and when the snow was falling the town two hundred yards away was not visible. But when the traveler alighted at the railway station he was obliged to pass the Palace Hotel before he could come upon the company of low clap-board houses which composed Fort Romper, and it was not to be thought that any traveler could pass the Palace Hotel without looking at it. Pat Scully, the proprietor, had proved himself a master of strategy when he chose his paints. It is true that on clear days, when the great trans-continental expresses, long lines of swaying Pullmans, swept through Fort Romper, passengers were overcome at the sight, and the cult that knows the brown-reds and the subdivisions of the dark greens of the East expressed shame, pity, horror, in a laugh. But to the citizens of this prairie town, and to the people who would naturally stop there, Pat Scully had performed a feat. With this opulence and splendor, these creeds, classes, egotisms, that steamed through Romper on the rails day after day, they had no color in common.

2   As if the displayed delights of such a blue hotel were not sufficiently enticing, it was Scully's habit to go every morning and evening to meet

the leisurely trains that stopped at Romper and work his seductions upon any man that he might see wavering, gripsack in hand.

3   One morning, when a snow-crusted engine dragged its long string of freight cars and its one passenger coach to the station, Scully performed the marvel of catching three men. One was a shaky and quick-eyed Swede, with a great shining cheap valise; one was a tall bronzed cowboy, who was on his way to a ranch near the Dakota line; one was a little silent man from the East, who didn't look it, and didn't announce it. Scully practically made them prisoners. He was so nimble and merry and kindly that each probably felt it would be the height of brutality to try to escape. They trudged off over the creaking board sidewalks in the wake of the eager little Irishman. He wore a heavy fur cap squeezed tightly down on his head. It caused his two red ears to stick out stiffly, as if they were made of tin.

4   At last, Scully, elaborately, with boisterous hospitality, conducted them through the portals of the blue hotel. The room which they entered was small. It seemed to be merely a proper temple for an enormous stove, which, in the center, was humming with god-like violence. At various points on its surface the iron had become luminous and glowed yellow from the heat. Beside the stove Scully's son Johnnie was playing High-Five with an old farmer who had whiskers both gray and sandy. They were quarreling. Frequently the old farmer turned his face toward a box of sawdust—colored brown from tobacco juice—that was behind the stove, and spat with an air of great impatience and irritation. With a loud flourish of words Scully destroyed the game of cards, and bustled his son upstairs with part of the baggage of the new guests. He himself conducted them to three basins of the coldest water in the world. The cowboy and the Easterner burnished themselves fiery red with this water, until it seemed to be some kind of a metal polish. The Swede, however, merely dipped his fingers gingerly and with trepidation. It was notable that throughout this series of small ceremonies the three travelers were made to feel that Scully was very benevolent. He was conferring great favors upon them. He handed the towel from one to the other with an air of philanthropic impulse.

5   Afterward they went to the first room, and, sitting about the stove, listened to Scully's officious clamor at his daughters, who were preparing the midday meal. They reflected in the silence of experienced men who tread carefully amid new people. Nevertheless, the old farmer, stationary, invincible in his chair near the warmest part of

the stove, turned his face from the sawdust box frequently and addressed a glowing commonplace to the strangers. Usually he was answered in short but adequate sentences by either the cowboy or the Easterner. The Swede said nothing. He seemed to be occupied in making furtive estimates of each man in the room. One might have thought that he had the sense of silly suspicion which comes to guilt. He resembled a badly frightened man.

6   Later, at dinner, he spoke a little, addressing his conversation entirely to Scully. He volunteered that he had come from New York, where for ten years he had worked as a tailor. These facts seemed to strike Scully as fascinating, and afterward he volunteered that he had lived at Romper for fourteen years. The Swede asked about the crops and the price of labor. He seemed barely to listen to Scully's extended replies. His eyes continued to rove from man to man.

7   Finally, with a laugh and a wink, he said that some of these Western communities were very dangerous; and after his statement he straightened his legs under the table, tiled his head, and laughed again, loudly. It was plain that the demonstration had no meaning to the others. They looked at him wondering and in silence.

II

8   As the men trooped heavily back into the front room, the two little windows presented views of a turmoiling sea of snow. The huge arms of the wind were making attempts—mighty, circular, futile—to embrace the flakes as they sped. A gate-post like a still man with a blanched face stood aghast amid this profligate fury. In a hearty voice Scully announced the presence of a blizzard. The guests of the blue hotel, lighting their pipes, assented with grunts of lazy masculine contentment. No island of the sea could be exempt in the degree of this little room with its humming stove. Johnnie, son of Scully, in a tone which defined his opinion of his ability as a card-player, challenged the old farmer of both gray and sandy whiskers to a game of High-Five. The farmer agreed with a contemptuous and bitter scoff. They sat close to the stove, and squared their knees under a wide board. The cowboy and the Easterner watched the game with interest. The Swede remained near the window, aloof, but with a countenance that showed signs of an inexplicable excitement.

9   The play of Johnnie and the gray-beard was suddenly ended by another quarrel. The old man arose while casting a look of heated scorn
at his adversary. He slowly buttoned his coat, and then stalked with
fabulous dignity from the room. In the discreet silence of all other men
the Swede laughed. His laughter rang somehow childish. Men by this
time had begun to look at him askance, as if they wished to inquire
what ailed him.

10   A new game was formed jocosely. The cowboy volunteered to become the partner of Johnnie, and they all then turned to ask the Swede
to throw in his lot with the little Easterner. He asked some questions
about the game, and learning that it wore many names, and that he had
played it when it was under an alias, he accepted the invitation. He
strode toward the men nervously, as if he expected to be assaulted. Finally, seated, he gazed from face to face and laughed shrilly. This laugh
was so strange that the Easterner looked up quickly, the cowboy sat intent and with his mouth open, and Johnnie paused, holding the cards
with still fingers.

Afterward there was a short silence. Then Johnnie said: "Well,
let's get at it. Come on now!" They pulled their chairs forward until
their knees were bunched under the board. They began to play, and
their interest in the game caused the others to forget the manner of
the Swede.

The cowboy was a board-whacker. Each time that he held superior
cards he whanged them, one by one, with exceeding force, down upon
the improvised table, and took the tricks with a glowing air of prowess
and pride that sent thrills of indignation into the hearts of his opponents. A game with a board-whacker in it is sure to become intense.
The countenances of the Easterner and the Swede were miserable
whenever the cowboy thundered down his aces and kings, while Johnnie, his eyes gleaming with joy, chuckled and chuckled.

Because of the absorbing play none considered the strange ways of the
Swede. They paid strict heed to the game. Finally, during a lull caused
by a new deal, the Swede suddenly addressed Johnnie: "I suppose there
have been a good many men killed in this room." The jaws of the others
dropped and they looked at him.

"What in hell are you talking about?" said Johnnie.

15   The Swede laughed again his blatant laugh, full of a kind of false
courage and defiance. "Oh, you know what I mean all right," he
answered.

"I'm a liar if I do!" Johnnie protested. The card was halted, and the men stared at the Swede. Johnnie evidently felt that as the son of the proprietor he should make a direct inquiry. "Now, what might you be drivin' at, mister?" he asked. The Swede winked at him. It was a wink full of cunning. His fingers shook on the edge of the board. "Oh, maybe you think I have been to nowheres. Maybe you think I'm a tenderfoot?"

"I don't know nothin' about you," answered Johnnie, "and I don't give a damn where you've been. All I got to say is that I don't know what you're driving at. There hain't never been nobody killed in this room."

The cowboy, who had been steadily gazing at the Swede, then spoke. "What's wrong with you, mister?"

Apparently it seemed to the Swede that he was formidably menaced. He shivered and turned white near the corners of his mouth. He sent an appealing glance in the direction of the little Easterner. During these moments he did not forget to wear his air of advanced pot-valor. "They say they don't know what I mean," he remarked mockingly to the Easterner.

20   The latter answered after prolonged and cautious reflection. "I don't understand you," he said, impassively.

The Swede made a movement then which announced that he thought he had encountered treachery from the only quarter where he had expected sympathy if not help. "Oh, I see you are all against me. I see——"

The cowboy was in a state of deep stupefaction. "Say," he cried, as he tumbled in the deck violently down upon the board. "Say, what are you gittin' at, hey?"

The Swede sprang up with the celerity of a man escaping from a snake on the floor. "I don't want to fight!" he shouted. "I don't want to fight!"

The cowboy stretched his long legs indolently and deliberately. His hands were in his pockets. He spat into the sawdust box. "Well, who the hell thought you did?" he inquired.

25   The Swede backed rapidly toward a corner of the room. His hands were out protectingly in front of his chest, but he was making an obvious struggle to control his fright. "Gentlemen," he quavered, "I suppose I am going to be killed before I can leave this house! I suppose I am going to be killed before I can leave this house!" In his eyes was the dying swan look. Through the windows could be seen the snow turning blue in the shadow of dusk. The wind tore at the house and some loose thing beat regularly against the clap-boards like a spirit tapping.

A door opened, and Scully himself entered. He paused in surprise as he noted the tragic attitude of the Swede. Then he said: "What's the matter here?"

The Swede answered him swiftly and eagerly: "These men are going to kill me."

"Kill you!" ejaculated Scully. "Kill you! What are you talkin'?"

The Swede made the gesture of a martyr.

30   Scully wheeled sternly upon his son. "What is this, Johnnie?"

The lad had grown sullen. "Damned if I know," he answered. "I can't make no sense to it." He began to shuffle the cards, fluttering them together with an angry snap. "He says a good many men have been killed in this room, or something like that. And he says he's goin' to be killed here too. I don't know what ails him. He's crazy, I shouldn't wonder."

Scully then looked for explanation to the cowboy, but the cowboy simply shrugged his shoulders.

"Kill you?" said Scully again to the Swede. "Kill you? Man, you're off your nut."

"Oh, I know," burst out the Swede. "I know what will happen. Yes, I'm crazy—yes. Yes, of course, I'm crazy—yes. But I know one thing—" There was a sort of sweat of misery and terror upon his face. "I know I won't get out of here alive."

35   The cowboy drew a deep breath, as if his mind was passing into the last stages of dissolution. "Well, I'm dog-goned," he whispered to himself.

Scully wheeled suddenly and faced his son. "You've been troublin' this man!"

Johnnie's voice was loud with its burden of grievance. "Why, good Gawd, I ain't done nothin' to 'im."

The Swede broke in. "Gentlemen, do not disturb yourselves. I will leave this house. I will go 'way because—" He accused them dramatically with his glance. "Because I do not want to be killed."

Scully was furious with his son. "Will you tell me what is the matter, you young divil? What's the matter, anyhow? Speak out!"

40   "Blame it," cried Johnnie in despair, "don't I tell you I don't know. He—he says we want to kill him, and that's all I know. I can't tell what ails him."

The Swede continued to repeat: "Never mind, Mr. Scully, never mind. I will leave this house. I will go away, because I do not wish to be killed. Yes, of course, I am crazy—yes. But I know one thing! I will go away. I will leave this house. Never mind, Mr. Scully, never mind. I will go away."

"You will not go 'way," said Scully. "You will not go 'way until I hear the reason of this business. If anybody has troubled you I will take care of him. This is my house. You are under my roof, and I will not allow any peaceable man to be troubled here." He cast a terrible eye upon Johnnie, the cowboy, and the Easterner.

"Never mind, Mr. Scully, never mind. I will go 'way. I do not wish to be killed." The Swede moved toward the door, which opened upon the stairs. It was evidently his intention to go at once for his baggage.

"No, no," shouted Scully peremptorily; but the white-faced man slid by him and disappeared. "Now," said Scully severely, "what does this mane?"

45   Johnnie and the cowboy cried together: "Why, we didn't do nothin' to 'im!"

Scully's eyes were cold. "No," he said, "you didn't?"

Johnnie swore a deep oath. "Why, this is the wildest loon I ever see. We didn't do nothin' at all. We were jest sittin' here playin' cards and he—"

The father suddenly spoke to the Easterner. "Mr. Blanc," he asked, "what has these boys been doin'?"

The Easterner reflected again. "I didn't see anything wrong at all," he said at last slowly.

50   Scully began to howl. "But what does it mane?" He stared ferociously at his son. "I have a mind to lather you for this, me boy."

Johnnie was frantic. "Well, what have I done?" he bawled at his father.

III

"I think you are tongue-tied," said Scully finally to his son, the cowboy and the Easterner, and at the end of this scornful sentence he left the room.

Upstairs the Swede was swiftly fastening the straps of his great valise. Once his back happened to be half-turned toward the door, and hearing a noise there, he wheeled and sprang up, uttering a loud cry. Scully's wrinkled visage showed grimly in the light of the small lamp he carried. This yellow effulgence, streaming upward, colored only his prominent features, and left his eyes, for instance, in mysterious shadow. He resembled a murderer.

"Man, man!" he exclaimed, "have you gone daffy?"

"Oh, no! Oh, no!" rejoined the other. "There are people in this world who know pretty nearly as much as you do—understand?"

For a moment they stood gazing at each other. Upon the Swede's deathly pale cheeks were two spots brightly crimson and sharply edged, as if they had been carefully painted. Scully placed the light on the table and sat himself on the edge of the bed. He spoke ruminatively. "By cracky, I never heard of such a thing in my life. It's a complete muddle. I can't for the soul of me think how you ever got this idea into your head." Presently he lifted his eyes and asked: "And did you sure think they were going to kill you?"

The Swede scanned the old man as if he wished to see into his mind. "I did," he said at last. He obviously suspected that this answer might precipitate an outbreak. As he pulled on a strap his whole arm shook, the elbow wavering like a bit of paper.

Scully banged his hand impressively on the foot-board of the bed. "Why, man, we're goin' to have a line of ilictric street-cars in this town next spring."

"A line of electric street-cars," repeated the Swede stupidly.

"And," said Scully, "there's a new railroad goin' to be built down from Broken Arm to here. Not to mintion the four churches and the smashin' big brick school-house. Then there's the big factory, too. Why, in two years Romper'll be a met-tro-*pol*-is."

Having finished the preparation of his baggage, the Swede straightened himself. "Mr. Scully," he said with sudden hardihood, "how much do I owe you?"

"You don't owe me anythin'," said the old man angrily.

"Yes, I do," retorted the Swede. He took seventy-five cents from his pocket and tendered it to Scully; but the latter snapped his fingers in disdainful refusal. However, it happened that they both stood gazing in a strange fashion at three silver pieces on the Swede's open palm.

"I'll not take your money," said Scully at last. "Not after what's been goin' on here." Then a plan seemed to strike him. "Here," he cried, picking up his lamp and moving toward the door. "Here! Come with me a minute."

"No," said the Swede in overwhelming alarm.

"Yes," urged the old man. "Come on! I want you to come and see a picter—just across the hall—in my room."

The Swede must have concluded that his hour was come. His jaw dropped and his teeth showed like a dead man's. He ultimately followed Scully across the corridor, but he had the step of one hung in chains.

Scully flashed the light high on the wall of his own chamber. There was revealed a ridiculous photograph of a little girl. She was leaning against a balustrade of gorgeous decoration, and the formidable band to her hair was prominent. The figure was as graceful as an upright sled-stake, and, withal, it was of the hue of lead. "There," said Scully tenderly. "That's the picter of my little girl that died. Her name was Carrie. She had the purtiest hair you ever saw! I was that fond of her, she—"

Turning then he saw that the Swede was not contemplating the picture at all, but, instead, was keeping keen watch on the gloom in the rear.

70   "Look, man!" shouted Scully heartily. "That's the picter of my little gal that died. Her name was Carrie. And then here's the picter of my oldest boy, Michael. He's a lawyer in Lincoln an' doin' well. I gave that boy a grand eddycation, and I'm glad for it now. He's a fine boy. Look at 'im now. Ain't he bold as blazes, him there in Lincoln, an honored an' respicted gintleman. An honored an' respicted gintleman," concluded Scully with a flourish. And so saying, he smote the Swede jovially on the back.

The Swede faintly smiled.

"Now," said the old man, "there's only one more thing." He dropped suddenly to the floor and thrust his head beneath the bed. The Swede could hear his muffled voice. "I'd keep it under me piller if it wasn't for that boy Johnnie. Then there's the old woman—Where is it now? I never put it twice in the same place. Ah, now come out with you!"

Presently he backed clumsily from under the bed, dragging with him an old coat rolled into a bundle. "I've fetched him," he muttered. Kneeling on the floor he unrolled the coat and extracted from its heart a large yellow-brown whisky bottle.

His first maneuver was to hold the bottle up to the light. Reassured, apparently, that nobody had been tampering with it, he thrust it with a generous movement toward the Swede.

75   The weak-kneed Swede was about to eagerly clutch this element of strength, but he suddenly jerked his hand away and cast a look of horror upon Scully.

"Drink," said the old man affectionately. He had arisen to his feet, and now stood facing the Swede.

There was a silence. Then again Scully said: "Drink!"

The Swede laughed wildly. He grabbed the bottle, put it to his mouth, and as his lips curled absurdly around the opening and his throat worked, he kept his glance burning with hatred upon the old man's face.

IV

After the departure of Scully the three men, with the cardboard still upon their knees, preserved for a long time an astounded silence. Then Johnnie said: "That's the dod-dangest Swede I ever see."

80   "He ain't no Swede," said the cowboy scornfully.

"Well, what is he then?" cried Johnnie. "What is he then?"

"It's my opinion," replied the cowboy deliberately, "he's some kind of a Dutchman." It was a venerable custom of the country to entitle as Swedes all light-haired men who spoke with a heavy tongue. In consequence the idea of the cowboy was not without its daring. "Yes, sir," he repeated. "It's my opinion this feller is some kind of a Dutchman."

"Well, he says he's a Swede, anyhow," muttered Johnnie sulkily. He turned to the Easterner: "What do you think, Mr. Blanc?"

"Oh, I don't know," replied the Easterner.

85   "Well, what do you think makes him act that way?" asked the cowboy.

"Why, he's frightened!" The Easterner knocked his pipe against a rim of the stove. "He's clear frightened out of his boots."

"What at?" cried Johnnie and cowboy together.

The Easterner reflected over his answer.

"What at?" cried the others again.

90   "Oh, I don't know, but it seems to me this man has been reading dime-novels, and he thinks he's right out in the middle of it—the shootin' and stabbin' and all."

"But," said the cowboy, deeply scandalized, "this ain't Wyoming, ner none of them places. This is Nebrasker."

"Yes," added Johnnie, "an' why don't he wait till he gits *out West?*"

The traveled Easterner laughed. "It isn't different there even—not in these days. But he thinks he's right in the middle of hell."

Johnnie and the cowboy mused long.

95   "It's awful funny," remarked Johnnie at last.

"Yes," said the cowboy. "This is a queer game. I hope we don't git snowed in, because then we'd have to stand this here man bein' around with us all the time. That wouldn't be no good."

"I wish pop would throw him out," said Johnnie.

Presently they heard a loud stamping on the stairs, accompanied by ringing jokes in the voice of old Scully, and laughter, evidently from the Swede. The men around the stove stared vacantly at each other. "Gosh," said the cowboy. The door flew open, and old Scully, flushed and anecdotal, came into the room. He was jabbering at the Swede, who followed him, laughing bravely. It was the entry of two roysterers from a banquet hall.

"Come now," said Scully sharply to the three seated men, "move up and give us a chance at the stove." The cowboy and the Easterner obediently sidled their chairs to make room for the newcomers. Johnnie, however, simply arranged himself in a more indolent attitude, and then remained motionless.

100   "Come! Git over, there," said Scully.

"Plenty of room on the other side of the stove," said Johnnie.

"Do you think we want to sit in the draught?" roared the father.

But the Swede here interposed with a grandeur of confidence. "No, no. Let the boy sit where he likes," he cried in a bullying voice to the father.

"All right! All right!" said Scully deferentially. The cowboy and the Easterner exchanged glances of wonder.

105   The five chairs were formed in a crescent about one side of the stove. The Swede began to talk; he talked arrogantly, profanely, angrily. Johnnie, the cowboy and the Easterner maintained a morose silence, while old Scully appeared to be receptive and eager, breaking in constantly with sympathetic ejaculations.

Finally the Swede announced that he was thirsty. He moved in his chair, and said that he would go for a drink of water.

"I'll git it for you," cried Scully at once.

"No," said the Swede contemptuously. "I'll get it for myself." He arose and stalked with the air of an owner off into the executive parts of the hotel.

As soon as the Swede was out of hearing Scully sprang to his feet and whispered intensely to the others. "Upstairs he thought I was tryin' to poison 'im."

110   "Say," said Johnnie, "this makes me sick. Why don't you throw 'im out in the snow?"

"Why, he's all right now," declared Scully. "It was only that he was from the East and he thought this was a tough place. That's all. He's all right now."

The cowboy looked with admiration upon the Easterner. "You were straight," he said. "You were on to that there Dutchman."

"Well," said Johnnie to his father, "he may be all right now, but I don't see it. Other time he was scared, and now he's too fresh."

Scully's speech was always a combination of Irish brogue and idiom, Western twang and idiom, and scraps of curiously formal diction taken from the story-books and newspapers. He now hurled a strange mass of language at the head of his son. "What do I keep? What do I keep? What do I keep?" he demanded in a voice of thunder. He slapped his knee impressively, to indicate that he himself was going to make reply, and that all should heed. "I keep a hotel," he shouted. "A hotel, do you mind? A guest under my roof has sacred privileges. He is to be intimidated by none. Not one word shall he hear that would prijudice him in favor of goin' away. I'll not have it. There's no place in this here town where they can say they iver took in a guest of mine because he was afraid to stay here." He wheeled suddenly upon the cowboy and the Easterner. "Am I right?"

115   "Yes, Mr. Scully," said the cowboy, "I think you're right."

"Yes, Mr. Scully," said the Easterner, "I think you're right."

V

At six-o'clock supper, the Swede fizzed like a fire-wheel. He sometimes seemed on the point of bursting into riotous song, and in all his madness he was encouraged by old Scully. The Easterner was incased in reserve; the cowboy sat in wide-mouthed amazement, forgetting to eat, while Johnnie wrathily demolished great plates of food. The daughters of the house when they were obliged to replenish the biscuits approached as warily as Indians, and, having succeeded in their purposes, fled with ill-concealed trepidation. The Swede domineered the whole feast, and he gave it the appearance of a cruel bacchanal. He seemed to have grown suddenly taller; he gazed, brutally disdainful, into every face. His voice rang through the room. Once when he jabbed out harpoon-fashion with his fork to pinion a biscuit the weapon nearly impaled the hand of the Easterner which had been stretched quietly out for the same biscuit.

After supper, as the men filed toward the other room, the Swede smote Scully ruthlessly on the shoulder. "Well, old boy, that was a good square meal." Johnnie looked hopefully at his father; he knew that shoulder was tender from an old fall; and indeed it appeared for a moment as if Scully was going to flame out over the matter, but in the end he smiled a sickly smile and remained silent. The others understood from his manner that he was admitting his responsibility for the Swede's new viewpoint.

Johnnie, however, addressed his parent in an aside. "Why don't you license somebody to kick you downstairs?" Scully scowled darkly by a way of reply.

120   When they were gathered about the stove, the Swede insisted on another game of High-Five. Scully gently deprecated the plan at first, but the Swede turned a wolfish glare upon him. The old man subsided, and the Swede canvassed the others. In his tone there was always a great threat. The cowboy and the Easterner both remarked indifferently that they would play. Scully said that he would presently have to go to meet the 6:58 train, and so the Swede turned menacingly upon Johnnie. For a moment their glances crossed like blades, and then Johnnie smiled and said: "Yes, I'll play."

They formed a square with the little board on their knees. The Easterner and the Swede were again partners. As the play went on, it was noticeable that the cowboy was not board-whacking as usual. Meanwhile, Scully, near the lamp, had put on his spectacles and, with an appearance curiously like an old priest, was reading a newspaper. In time he went out to meet the 6:58 train, and, despite his precautions, a gust of polar wind whirled into the room as he opened the door. Besides scattering the cards, it chilled the players to the marrow. The Swede cursed frightfully. When Scully returned, his entrance disturbed a cozy and friendly scene. The Swede again cursed. But presently they were once more intent, their heads bent forward and their hands moving swiftly. The Swede had adopted the fashion of board-whacking.

Scully took up his paper and for a long time remained immersed in matters which were extraordinarily remote from him. The lamp burned badly, and once he stopped to adjust the wick. The newspaper as he turned from page to page rustled with a slow and comfortable sound. Then suddenly he heard three terrible words: "You are cheatin'!"

Such scenes often prove that there can be little of dramatic import in environment. Any room can present a tragic front; any room can be comic. This little den was now hideous as a torture-chamber. The new faces of the men themselves had changed it upon the instant. The Swede held a huge fist in front of Johnnie's face, while the latter looked steadily over it into the blazing orbs of his accuser. The Easterner had grown pallid; the cowboy's jaw had dropped in that expression of bovine amazement which was one of his important mannerisms. After the three words, the first sound in the room was made by Scully's paper as it floated forgotten to his feet. His spectacles had also fallen from his nose, but by a clutch he has saved them in air. His hand, grasping the spectacles, now remained poised awkwardly and near his shoulder. He stared at the card-players.

Probably the silence was while a second elapsed. Then, if the floor had been suddenly twitched out from under the men they could not have moved quicker. The five had projected themselves headlong toward a common point. It happened that Johnnie in rising to hurl himself upon the Swede had stumbled slightly because of his curiously instinctive care for the cards and the board. The loss of the moment allowed time for the arrival of Scully, and also allowed the cowboy time to give the Swede a great push which sent him staggering back. The men found tongue together, and hoarse shouts of rage, appeal or fear burst from every throat. The cowboy pushed and jostled feverishly at the Swede, and the Easterner and Scully clung wildly to Johnnie; but, through the smoky air, above the swaying bodies of the peace-compellers, the eyes of the two warriors ever sought each other in glances of challenge that were at once hot and steely.

125   Of course the board had been overturned, and now the whole company of cards was scattered over the floor, where the boots of the men trampled the fat and painted kings and queens as they gazed with their silly eyes at the war that was waging above them.

Scully's voice was dominating the yells. "Stop now! Stop, I say! Stop, now—"

Johnnie, as he struggled to burst through the rank formed by Scully and the Easterner, was crying: "Well, he says I cheated! He says I cheated! I won't allow no man to say I cheated! If he says I cheated, he's a —————— —————!"

The cowboy was telling the Swede: "Quit, now! Quit, d'ye hear—"

The screams of the Swede never ceased. "He did cheat! I saw him! I saw him—"

130   As for the Easterner, he was importuning in a voice that was not heeded. "Wait a moment, can't you? Oh, wait a moment. What's the good of a fight over a game of cards? Wait a moment—"

In this tumult no complete sentences were clear. "Cheat"—"Quit"— "He says"—These fragments pierced the uproar and rang out sharply. It was remarkable that whereas Scully undoubtedly made the most noise, he was the least heard of any of the riotous band.

Then suddenly there was a great cessation. It was as if each man had paused for breath, and although the room was still lighted with the anger of men, it could be seen that there was no danger of immediate conflict, and at once Johnnie, shouldering his way forward, almost succeeded in confronting the Swede. "What did you say I cheated for? What did you say I cheated for? I don't cheat and I won't let no man say I do!"

The Swede said: "I saw you! I saw you!"

"Well," cried Johnnie, "I'll fight any man what says I cheat!"

135   "No, you won't," said the cowboy. "Not here."

"Ah, be still, can't you?" said Scully, coming between them.

The quiet was sufficient to allow the Easterner's voice to be heard. He was repeating: "Oh, wait a moment, can't you? What's the good of a fight over a game of cards? Wait a moment."

Johnnie, his red face appearing above his father's shoulder, hailed the Swede again. "Did you say I cheated?"

The Swede showed his teeth. "Yes."

140   "Then," said Johnnie, "we must fight."

"Yes, fight," roared the Swede. He was like a demoniac. "Yes, fight! I'll show you what kind of a man I am! I'll show you who you want to fight! Maybe you think I can't fight! Maybe you think I can't! I'll show you, you skin,[1] you card-sharp! Yes, you cheated! You cheated! You cheated!"

"Well, let's git at it, then, mister," said Johnnie coolly.

The cowboy's brow was beaded with sweat from his efforts in intercepting all sorts of raids. He turned in despair to Scully. "What are you goin' to do now?"

---

[1] Cheater.

A change had come over the Celtic visage of the old man. He now seemed all eagerness; his eyes glowed.

145   "We'll let them fight," he answered stalwartly. "I can't put up with it any longer. I've stood this damned Swede till I'm sick. We'll let them fight."

VI

The men prepared to go out of doors. The Easterner was so nervous that he had great difficulty in getting his arms into the sleeves of his new leather-coat. As the cowboy drew his fur-cap down over his ears his hands trembled. In fact, Johnnie and old Scully were the only ones who displayed no agitation. These preliminaries were conducted without words.

Scully threw open the door. "Well, come on," he said. Instantly a terrific wind caused the flame of the lamp to struggle at its wick, while a puff of black smoke sprang from the chimney-top. The stove was in mid-current of the blast, and its voice swelled to equal the roar of the storm. Some of the scarred and bedabbled cards were caught up from the floor and dashed helplessly against the further wall. The men lowered their heads and plunged into the tempest as into a sea.

No snow was falling, but great whirls and clouds of flakes, swept up from the ground by the frantic winds, were streaming southward with the speed of bullets. The covered land was blue with the sheen of an unearthly satin, and there was no other hue save where at the low black railway station—which seemed incredibly distant—one light gleamed like a tiny jewel. As the men floundered into a thigh-deep drift, it was known that the Swede was bawling out something. Scully went to him, put a hand on his shoulder and projected an ear. "What's that you say?" he shouted.

"I say," bawled the Swede again, "I won't stand much show against this gang. I know you'll all pitch on me."

150   Scully smote him reproachfully on the arm. "Tut, man," he yelled. The wind tore the words from Scully's lips and scattered them far a-lee.

"You are all a gang of—" boomed the Swede, but the storm also seized the remainder of this sentence.

Immediately turning their backs upon the wind, the men had swung around a corner to the sheltered side of the hotel. It was the function of the little house to preserve here, amid this great devastation of snow, an irregular V-shape of heavily-incrusted grass, which crackled beneath the feet. One could imagine the great drifts piled against the windward side. When the party reached the comparative peace of this spot it was found that the Swede was still bellowing.

"Oh, I know what kind of a thing this is! I know you'll all pitch on me. I can't lick you all!"

Scully turned upon him panther-fashion. "You'll not have to whip all of us. You'll have to whip my son Johnnie. An' the man what troubles you durin' that time will have me to dale with."

155   The arrangements were swiftly made. The two men faced each other, obedient to the harsh commands of Scully, whose face, in the subtly luminous gloom, could be seen set in the austere impersonal lines that are pictured on the countenances of the Roman veterans. The Easterner's teeth were chattering, and he was hopping up and down like a mechanical toy. The cowboy stood rock-like.

The contestants had not stripped off any clothing. Each was in his ordinary attire. Their fists were up, and they eyed each other in a calm that had the elements of leonine cruelty in it.

During this pause, the Easterner's mind, like a film, took lasting impressions of three men—the iron-nerved master of the ceremony; the Swede, pale, motionless, terrible; and Johnnie, serene yet ferocious, brutish yet heroic. The entire prelude had in it a tragedy greater than the tragedy of action, and this aspect was accentuated by the long mellow cry of the blizzard, as it sped the tumbling and wailing flakes into the black abyss of the south.

"Now!" said Scully.

The two combatants leaped forward and crashed together like bullocks. There was heard the cushioned sound of blows, and of a curse squeezing out from between the tight teeth of one.

160   As for the spectators, the Easterner's pent-up breath exploded from him with a pop of relief, absolute relief from the tension of the preliminaries. The cowboy bounded into the air with a yowl. Scully was immovable as from supreme amazement and fear at the fury of the fight which he himself had permitted and arranged.

For a time the encounter in the darkness was such a perplexity of flying arms that it presented no more detail than would a swiftly-revolving wheel. Occasionally a face, as if illumined by a flash of light, would shine out, ghastly and marked with pink spots. A moment later, the men might have been known as shadows, if it were not for the involuntary utterance of oaths that came from them in whispers.

Suddenly a holocaust of warlike desire caught the cowboy, and he bolted forward with the speed of a broncho. "Go it, Johnnie; go it! Kill him! Kill him!"

Scully confronted him. "Kape back," he said; and by his glance the cowboy could tell that this man was Johnnie's father.

To the Easterner there was a monotony of unchangeable fighting that was an abomination. This confused mingling was eternal to his sense, which was concentrated in a longing for the end, the priceless end. Once the fighters lurched near him, and as he scrambled hastily backward, he heard them breathe like men on the rack.

165   "Kill him, Johnnie! Kill him! Kill him!" The cowboy's face was contorted like one of those agony-masks in museums.

"Keep still," said Scully icily.

Then there was a sudden loud grunt, incomplete, cut-short, and Johnnie's body swung away from the Swede and fell with sickening heaviness to the grass. The cowboy was barely in time to prevent the mad Swede from flinging himself upon his prone adversary. "No, you don't," said the cowboy, interposing an arm. "Wait a second."

Scully was at his son's side. "Johnnie! Johnnie, me boy?" His voice had a quality of melancholy tenderness. "Johnnie? Can you go on with it?" He looked anxiously down into the bloody pulpy face of his son.

There was a moment of silence, and then Johnnie answered in his ordinary voice: "Yes, I—it—yes."

170   Assisted by his father he struggled to his feet. "Wait a bit now till you git your wind," said the old man.

A few paces away the cowboy was lecturing the Swede. "No, you don't! Wait a second!"

The Easterner was plucking at Scully's sleeve. "Oh, this is enough," he pleaded. "This is enough! Let it go as it stands. This is enough!"

"Bill," said Scully, "git out of the road." The cowboy stepped aside. "Now." The combatants were actuated by a new caution as they advanced toward collision. They glared at each other, and then the Swede aimed a lightning blow that carried with it his entire weight. Johnnie was evidently half-stupid from weakness, but he miraculously dodged, and his fist sent the over-balanced Swede sprawling.

The cowboy, Scully and the Easterner burst into a cheer that was like a chorus of triumphant soldiery, but before its conclusion the Swede had scuffled agilely to his feet and come in berserk abandon at his foe. There was another perplexity of flying arms, and Johnnie's body again swung away and fell, even as a bundle might fall from a roof. The Swede instantly staggered to a little wind-waved tree and leaned upon it, breathing like an engine, while his savage and flame-lit eyes roamed from face to face as the men bent over Johnnie. There was a splendor of isolation in his situation at this time which the Easterner felt once when, lifting his eyes from the man on the ground, he beheld that mysterious and lonely figure, waiting.

175   "Are you any good yet, Johnnie?" asked Scully in a broken voice.

The son gasped and opened his eyes languidly. After a moment he answered: "No—I ain't—any good—any—more." Then, from shame and bodily ill, he began to weep, the tears furrowing down through the blood-stains on his face. "He was too—too—too heavy for me."

Scully straightened and addressed the waiting figure. "Stranger," he said, evenly, "it's all up with our side." Then his voice changed into that vibrant huskiness which is commonly the tone of the most simple and deadly announcements. "Johnnie is whipped."

Without replying, the victor moved off on the route to the front door of the hotel.

The cowboy was formulating new and unspellable blasphemies. The Easterner was startled to find that they were out in a wind that seemed to come direct from the shadowed arctic floes. He heard again the wail of the snow as it was flung to its grave in the south. He knew now that all this time the cold had been sinking into him deeper and deeper, and he wondered that he had not perished. He felt indifferent to the condition of the vanquished man.

180   "Johnnie, can you walk?" asked Scully.

"Did I hurt—hurt him any?" asked the son.

"Can you walk, boy? Can you walk?"

Johnnie's voice was suddenly strong. There was a robust impatience in it. "I asked you whether I hurt him any!"

"Yes, yes, Johnnie," answered the cowboy consolingly; "he's hurt a good deal."

185   They raised him from the ground, and as soon as he was on his feet he went tottering off, rebuffing all attempts at assistance. When the party rounded the corner they were fairly blinded by the pelting of the snow. It burned their faces like fire. The cowboy carried Johnnie through the drift to the door. As they entered some cards again rose from the floor and beat against the wall.

The Easterner rushed to the stove. He was so profoundly chilled that he almost dared to embrace the glowing iron. The Swede was not in the room. Johnnie sank into a chair, and folding his arms on his knees, buried his face in them. Scully, warming one foot and then the other at a rim of the stove, muttered to himself with Celtic mournfulness. The cowboy had removed his fur-cap, and with a dazed and rueful air he was now running one hand through his tousled locks. From overhead they could hear the creaking of boards, as the Swede trampled here and there in his room.

The sad quiet was broken by the sudden flinging open of a door that led toward the kitchen. It was instantly followed by an inrush of women. They precipitated themselves upon Johnnie amid a chorus of lamentation. Before they carried their prey off to the kitchen, there to be bathed and harangued with that mixture of sympathy and abuse which is a feat of their sex, the mother straightened herself and fixed old Scully with an eye of stern reproach. "Shame be upon you, Patrick Scully!" she cried. "Your own son, too. Shame be upon you!"

"There, now! Be quiet, now!" said the old man weakly.

"Shame be upon you, Patrick Scully!" The girls, rallying to this slogan, sniffed disdainfully in the direction of those trembling accomplices, the cowboy and the Easterner. Presently they bore Johnnie away, and left the three men to dismal reflection.

VII

190 "I'd like to fight this here Dutchman myself," said the cowboy, breaking a long silence.

Scully wagged his head sadly. "No, that wouldn't do. It wouldn't be right. It wouldn't be right."

"Well, why wouldn't it?" argued the cowboy. "I don't see no harm in it."

"No," answered Scully with mournful heroism. "It wouldn't be right. It was Johnnie's fight, and now we mustn't whip the man just because he whipped Johnnie."

"Yes, that's true enough," said the cowboy; "but—he better not get fresh with me, because I couldn't stand no more of it."

195 "You'll not say a word to him," commanded Scully, and even then they heard the tread of the Swede on the stairs. His entrance was made

theatric. He swept the door back with a bang and swaggered to the middle of the room. No one looked at him. "Well," he cried, insolently, at Scully, "I s'pose you'll tell me now how much I owe you?"

The old man remained stolid. "You don't owe me nothin'."

"Huh!" said the Swede, "huh! Don't owe 'im nothin'."

The cowboy addressed the Swede. "Stranger, I don't see how you come to be so gay around here."

Old Scully was instantly alert. "Stop!" he shouted, holding his hand forth, fingers upward. "Bill, you shut up!"

200   The cowboy spat carelessly into the sawdust box. "I didn't say a word, did I?" he asked.

"Mr. Scully," called the Swede, "how much do I owe you?" It was seen that he was attired for departure, and that he had his valise in his hand.

"You don't owe me nothin'," repeated Scully in his same imperturbable way.

"Huh!" said the Swede. "I guess you're right. I guess if it was any way at all, you'd owe me somethin'. That's what I guess." He turned to the cowboy. "'Kill him! Kill him! Kill him!'" he mimicked, and then guffawed victoriously. "'Kill him!'" he was convulsed with ironical humor.

But he might have been jeering the dead. The three men were immovable and silent, staring with glassy eyes at the stove.

205   The Swede opened the door and passed into the storm, giving one derisive glance backward at the still group.

As soon as the door was closed, Scully and the cowboy leaped to their feet and began to curse. They trampled to and fro, waving their arms and smashing into the air with their fists. "Oh, but that was a hard minute!" wailed Scully. "That was a hard minute! Him there leerin' and scoffin'! One bang at his nose was worth forty dollars to me that minute! How did you stand it, Bill?"

"How did I stand it?" cried the cowboy in a quivering voice. "How did I stand it? Oh!"

The old man burst into sudden brogue. "I'd loike to take that Swade," he wailed, "and hould 'im down on a shtone flure and bate 'im to a jelly wid a shtick!"

The cowboy groaned in sympathy. "I'd like to git him by the neck and ha-ammer him"—he brought his hand down on a chair with a noise like a pistol-shot—"hammer that there Dutchman until he couldn't tell himself from a dead coyote!"

210   "I'd bate 'im until he—"

"I'd show *him* some things—"

And then together they raised a yearning fanatic cry. "Oh-o-oh! if we only could—"

"Yes!"

"Yes!"

215   "And then I'd—"

"O-o-oh!"

VIII

The Swede, tightly gripping his valise, tacked across the face of the storm as if he carried sails. He was following a line of little naked gasping trees, which he knew must mark the way of the road. His face, fresh from the pounding of Johnnie's fists, felt more pleasure than pain in the wind and the driving snow. A number of square shapes loomed upon him finally, and he knew them as the houses of the main body of the town. He found a street and made travel along it, leaning heavily upon the wind whenever, at a corner, a terrific blast caught him.

He might have been in a deserted village. We picture the world as thick with conquering and elate humanity, but here, with the bugles of the tempest pealing, it was hard to imagine a peopled earth. One viewed the existence of man then as a marvel, and conceded a glamour of wonder to these lice which were caused to cling to a whirling, fire-smote, ice-locked, disease-stricken, space-lost bulb. The conceit of man was explained by this storm to be the very engine of life. One was a coxcomb not to die in it. However, the Swede found a saloon.

In front of it an indomitable red light was burning, and the snow-flakes were made blood-color as they flew through the circumscribed territory of the lamp's shining. The Swede pushed open the door of the saloon and entered. A sanded expanse was before him, and at the end of it four men sat about a table drinking. Down one side of the room extended a radiant bar, and its guardian was leaning upon his elbows listening to the talk of the men at the table. The Swede dropped his valise upon the floor, and, smiling fraternally upon the barkeeper, said: "Gimme some whisky, will you?" The man placed a bottle, a whisky-glass, and a glass of ice-thick water upon the bar. The Swede poured himself an abnormal portion of whisky and drank it in three gulps. "Pretty bad night," remarked the bartender indifferently. He was making the pretension of blindness, which is usually a distinction of his class; but it could have been seen that he was furtively studying the half-erased blood-stains on the face of the Swede. "Bad night," he said again.

220   "Oh, it's good enough for me," replied the Swede, hardily, as he poured himself some more whisky. The barkeeper took his coin and maneuvered it through its reception by the highly-nickeled cash-machine. A bell rang; a card labeled "20 cts." had appeared.

"No," continued the Swede, "this isn't too bad weather. It's good enough for me."

"So?" murmured the barkeeper languidly.

The copious drams made the Swede's eyes swim, and he breathed a trifle heavier. "Yes, I like this weather. I like it. It suits me." It was apparently his design to impart a deep significance to these words.

"So?" murmured the bartender again. He turned to gaze dreamily at the scroll-like birds and bird-like scrolls which had been drawn with soap upon the mirrors back of the bar.

225   "Well, I guess I'll take another drink," said the Swede presently. "Have something?"

"No, thanks; I'm not drinkin'," answered the bartender. Afterward he asked: "How did you hurt your face?"

The Swede immediately began to boast loudly. "Why, in a fight. I thumped the soul out of a man down here at Scully's hotel."

The interest of the four men at the table was at last aroused.

"Who was it?" said one.

230   "Johnnie Scully," blustered the Swede. "Son of the man what runs it. He will be pretty near dead for some weeks, I can tell you. I made a nice thing of him, I did. He couldn't get up. They carried him in the house. Have a drink?"

Instantly the men in some way incased themselves in reserve. "No, thanks," said one. The group was of curious formation. Two were prominent local business men; one was the district-attorney; and one was a professional gambler of the kind known as "square." But a scrutiny of the group would not have enabled an observer to pick the gambler from the men of more reputable pursuits. He was, in fact, a man so delicate in manner, when among people of fair class, and so judicious in his choice of victims, that in the strictly masculine part of the town's life he had come to be explicitly trusted and admired. People called him a thoroughbred. The fear and contempt with which his craft was regarded was undoubtedly the reason that his quiet dignity shone conspicuous above the quiet dignity of men who might be merely hatters, billiard-markers or grocery clerks. Beyond an occasional unwary traveler, who came by rail, this gambler was supposed to prey solely upon reckless and senile farmers, who, when flush with good crops, drove into town in all the pride and confidence of an absolutely invulnerable stupidity. Hearing at times in circuitous fashion of the despoilment of such a farmer, the important men of Romper invariably laughed in contempt of the victim, and if they thought of the wolf at all, it was with a kind of pride at the knowledge that he would never dare think of attacking their wisdom and courage. Besides, it was popular that this gambler had a real wife and two real children in a neat cottage in a suburb, where he led an exemplary home life, and when any one even suggested a discrepancy in his character, the crowd immediately vociferated descriptions of this virtuous family circle. Then men who led exemplary home lives, and men who did not lead exemplary home lives, all subsided in a bunch, remarking that there was nothing more to be said.

However, when a restriction was placed upon him—as, for instance, when a strong clique of members of the new Pollywog Club refused to permit him, even as a spectator, to appear in the rooms of the organization—the candor and gentleness with which he accepted the judgment disarmed many of his foes and made his friends more desperately partisan. He invariably distinguished between himself and a respectable Romper man so quickly and frankly that his manner actually appeared to be a continual broadcast compliment.

And one must not forget to declare the fundamental fact of his entire position in Romper. It is irrefutable that in all affairs outside of his business, in all matters that occur eternally and commonly between man and man, this thieving card-player was so generous, so just, so moral, that, in a contest, he could have put to flight the consciences of nine-tenths of the citizens of Romper.

And so it happened that he was seated in this saloon with the two prominent local merchants and the district-attorney.

235   The Swede continued to drink raw whisky, meanwhile babbling at the barkeeper and trying to induce him to indulge in potations. "Come on. Have a drink. Come on. What—no? Well, have a little one then. By gawd, I've whipped a man to-night, and I want to celebrate. I whipped him good, too. Gentlemen," the Swede cried to the men at the table, "have a drink?"

"Ssh!" said the barkeeper.

The group at the table, although furtively attentive, had been pretending to be deep in talk, but now a man lifted his eyes toward the Swede and said shortly: "Thanks. We don't want any more."

At this reply the Swede ruffled out his chest like a rooster. "Well," he exploded, "it seems I can't get anybody to drink with me in this town. Seem so, don't it? Well!"

"Ssh!" said the barkeeper.

240 "Say," snarled the Swede, "don't you try to shut me up. I won't have it. I'm a gentleman, and I want people to drink with me. And I want 'em to drink with me now. *Now*—do you understand?" He rapped the bar with his knuckles.

Years of experience had calloused the bartender. He merely grew sulky. "I hear you," he answered.

"Well," cried the Swede, "listen hard then. See those men over there? Well, they're going to drink with me, and don't you forget it. Now you watch."

"Hi!" yelled the barkeeper, "this won't do!"

"Why won't it?" demanded the Swede. He stalked over to the table, and by chance laid his hand upon the shoulder of the gambler. "How about this?" he asked, wrathfully. "I asked you to drink with me."

245 The gambler simply twisted his head and spoke over his shoulder. "My friend, I don't know you."

"Oh, hell!" answered the Swede, "come and have a drink."

"Now, my boy," advised the gambler kindly, "take your hand off my shoulder and go 'way and mind your own business." He was a little slim man, and it seemed strange to hear him use this tone of heroic patronage to the burly Swede. The other man at the table said nothing.

"What? You won't drink with me, you little dude! I'll make you then! I'll make you!" The Swede had grasped the gambler frenziedly at the throat, and was dragging him from his chair. The other men sprang up. The barkeeper dashed around the corner of his bar. There was a great tumult, and then was seen a long blade in the hand of the gambler. It shot forward, and a human body, this citadel of virtue, wisdom, power, was pierced as easily as if it had been a melon. The Swede fell with a cry of supreme astonishment.

The prominent merchants and the district-attorney must have at once tumbled out of the place backward. The bartender found himself hanging limply to the arm of a chair and gazing into the eyes of a murderer.

250   "Henry," said the latter, as he wiped his knife on one of the towels that hung beneath the bar-rail, "you tell 'em where to find me. I'll be home, waiting for 'em." Then he vanished. A moment afterward the barkeeper was in the street dinning through the storm for help, and, moreover, companionship.

The corpse of the Swede, alone in the saloon, had its eyes fixed upon a dreadful legend that dwelt a-top of the cash-machine. "This registers the amount of your purchase."

IX

Months later, the cowboy was frying pork over the stove of a little ranch near the Dakota line, when there was a quick thud of hoofs outside, and, presently, the Easterner entered with the letters and the papers.

"Well," said the Easterner at once, "the chap that killed the Swede has got three years. Wasn't much, was it?"

"He has? Three years?" The cowboy poised his pan of pork, while he ruminated upon the news. "Three years. That ain't much."

255   "No. It was a light sentence," replied the Easterner as he unbuckled his spurs. "Seems there was a good deal of sympathy for him in Romper."

"If the bartender had been any good," observed the cowboy thoughtfully, "he would have gone in and cracked that there Dutchman on the head with a bottle in the beginnin' of it and stopped all this here murderin'."

"Yes, a thousand things might have happened," said the Easterner tartly.

The cowboy returned his pan of pork to the fire, but his philosophy continued. "It's funny, ain't it? If he hadn't said Johnnie was cheatin' he'd be alive this minute. He was an awful fool. Game played for fun, too. Not for money. I believe he was crazy."

"I feel sorry for that gambler," said the Easterner.

260   "Oh, so do I," said the cowboy. "He don't deserve none of it for killin' who he did."

"The Swede might not have been killed if everything had been square."

"Might not have been killed?" exclaimed the cowboy. "Everythin' square? Why, when he said that Johnnie was cheatin' and acted like such a jackass? And then in the saloon he fairly walked up to git hurt?"

With these arguments the cowboy browbeat the Easterner and reduced him to rage.

"You're a fool!" cried the Easterner viciously. "You're a bigger jackass than the Swede by a million majority. Now let me tell you one thing. Let me tell you something. Listen! Johnnie *was* cheating!"

"'Johnnie,'" said the cowboy blankly. There was a minute of silence, and then he said robustly: "Why, no. The game was only for fun."

265 "Fun or not," said the Easterner, "Johnnie was cheating. I saw him. I know it. I saw him. And I refused to stand up and be a man. I let the Swede fight it out alone. And you—you were simply puffing around the place and wanting to fight. And then old Scully himself! We are all in it! This poor gambler isn't even a noun. He is kind of an adverb. Every sin is the result of a collaboration. We, five of us, have collaborated in the murder of this Swede. Usually there are from a dozen to forty women really involved in every murder, but in this case it seems to be only five men—you, I, Johnnie, old Scully, and that fool of an unfortunate gambler came merely as a culmination, the apex of a human movement, and gets all the punishment."

The cowboy, injured and rebellious, cried out blindly into this fog of mysterious theory. "Well, I didn't do anythin', did I?"

Questions on Content, Structure, and Style

1. Where is the Blue Hotel? This story is set in what approximate time period? What time of year?

2. What hints are there in the first sections of the story that Johnnie cheats at cards?

3. Why does the Swede act like "a badly frightened man"? What is his vision of the West? Where might he have picked up these ideas about the West?

4. Why does Scully try to tell the Swede about Fort Romper's churches, school-house, forthcoming electric street-cars, and his children? What mistake in judgment does Scully then make? How is the Swede transformed?

5. Describe the character of the Easterner. How does he differ in manner from the cowboy and Johnnie? What is his original attitude toward the fight?

6. How does Crane picture man's role in world, according to his description in section VIII? Why does Crane describe the snowflakes in the saloon's red light as "blood-color"?

7. Look closely at Crane's description of the gambler and his relationship to the people of Fort Romper. What does the line "this thieving card-player was so generous, so just, so moral, that, in a contest, he could have put to flight the consciences of nine-tenths of the citizens" say about the townspeople?

8. Analyze the use of the cash-register as an ironic symbol of the Swede's fate. Does the Swede "buy" his own death? How would you feel if Crane had stopped his story at the end of section VIII?

9. What is the purpose of section IX? What does the Easterner mean when he says, "This poor gambler isn't even a noun. He is kind of an adverb. Every sin is the result of a collaboration"? Do you agree with the Easterner's view of the murder? Why/why not?

10. Why does Crane end his story with the cowboy's statement "Well, I didn't do anythin', did I?", a refrain that appears in various forms throughout the story. What, if anything, do you think Crane was trying to say in this story about personal honesty and responsibility to others?

VOCABULARY

valise (3)	effulgence (53)	judicious (231)
profligate (8)	disdainful (63)	exemplary (231)
jocosely (10)	trepidation (117)	citadel (248)
indolently (24)	bacchanal (117)	culmination (265)
visage (53)	coxcomb (218)	

SUGGESTIONS FOR WRITING

1. Write an essay that analyzes the character of the Swede. How do his misconceptions contribute to his death? Is the hotel dangerous? In your reading of the story, who is most responsible for the tragedy that takes place? Do you think Crane would agree with you?

2. Write an essay analyzing Crane's use of irony throughout this story. You might consider, for example, the Swede's perceptions,

the Easterner's name, the gambler's character, or the cowboy's refrain. Or write an essay that analyzes one of the story's major symbols, such as the snowstorm, the cards, the cash register, or the Blue Hotel itself. How does this symbol work to help the reader understand the story's theme or characters?

3. People the world over are fascinated with characters and stories of the Old West. Investigate a Western "hero" (or anti-hero) and write an essay in which you try to account for his or her popularity. What role, if any, did dime-novels and newspaper stories (such as the ones the Swede may have read) play in creating legends? What were people such as Doc Holliday, Wyatt Earp, Belle Starr, Chief Seattle, Annie Oakley, Wild Bill Hickok, or Buffalo Bill really like? (Your essay might contrast the reality to the legend, if you find a disparity between the two.)

LANGUAGE:
READING, WRITING, CREATING

Twenty-Six Ways to Start Writing

Donald Murray

Donald Murray is a writer of poetry, fiction, and nonfiction, whose editorial writing won him a Pulitzer Prize in 1954. He has served as the director of writing programs at the University of New Hampshire and is a frequent speaker on the writing process. His helpful advice for writers and teachers of writing has appeared in numerous journals and texts, including *Write to Learn* (1984), which contains the useful suggestions listed below, *Read to Write* (1986), and *The Craft of Revision* (1991).

1   A PROMISE: If you write until your hair's white, your eyes make the print blur, and your hands tremble on the typewriter keys, it will still be hard to start writing.

2   Writing reveals us to ourselves and eventually to others, and we do not want to be exposed on the page. The writing is never as good as we hoped, so it is natural that we resist this exposure. We have to find ways to get over this understandable psychological hurdle, this normal stage fright before the blank page.

3   Writing is also a commitment. Once we have put down one line, sometimes just one word, we have made a choice, and the direction of our writing, its limits, its pace, its dimensions, its voice, its meaning are all constrained. Everything is not possible, and we face the realities of making meaning with language.

4   The process approach described in this book is itself an attempt to get us writing in a normal way. We collect material, focus it, and order it. At least 60 percent of our time and effort is spent in planning and preparation for writing so that we will be ready, often eager, to make a run at the blank page. If we aren't ready to write it may mean that we need to go back to collect, focus, or order.

5   Experienced writers, however, still find it hard to get started writing. Here are some of the tricks they use:

6   ***1.   Make Believe You Are Writing a Letter to a Friend.*** Put "Dear_____" at the top of the page and start writing. Tom Wolfe did this on one of his first New Journalism pieces. He wrote the editor a letter saying why he couldn't write the piece he'd been assigned. The letter flowed along in such a wonderful, easy fashion that the editor

took the salutation off and ran it. It established a new style for contemporary journalism.

7   *2. Switch Your Writing Tools.*   If you normally type, write by hand. If you write by hand, type. Switch from pen to pencil or pencil to pen. Switch from unlined paper to lined paper, or vice versa. Try larger paper or smaller, colored paper or white paper. Use a bound notebook or a spiral notebook, a legal pad or a clipboard. Tools are a writer's toys, and effective, easy writing is the product of play.

8   *3. Talk about the Piece of Writing with Another Writer, and Pay Close Attention to What You Say.*   You may be telling yourself how to write the piece. You may even want to make notes as you talk on the telephone or in person. Pay attention to words or combinations of words that may become a voice and spark a piece of writing.

9   *4. Write Down the Reasons You Are Not Writing.* Often when you see the problem you will be able to avoid it. You may realize that your standards are too high, or that you're thinking excessively of how one person will respond to your piece, or that you're trying to include too much. Once you have defined the problem you may be able to dispose of it.

10   *5. Describe the Process You Went Through When a Piece of Writing Went Well.*   You may be able to read such an account in your journal. We need to reinforce the writing procedures that produce good writing. A description of what worked before may tell us that we need to delay at this moment, or it may reveal a trick that got us going another time. We should keep a careful record of our work habits and the tricks of our trade, so that we have a positive resource to fall back on.

11   *6. Interview Other Writers to Find Out How They Get Started.*   Try your classmates' tricks and see if they work for you.

12   *7. Make Writing a Habit.*   For years I started every day by putting a pocket timer on for fifteen minutes and writing before I had a cup of coffee. Now the timer's not necessary. When writing, any kind of writing, is a normal activity it's much easier to start on a particular writing project. You are used to spoiling clean paper the same way joggers are used to wearing out running shoes.

13   *8. Switch the Time of Day.*   I tried to write this chapter just before noontime. Nothing. Well, not nothing, just the first

paragraph and a feeling of total hopelessness. Now it is early morning the next day and the writing is perking. Sometimes writing at night when you are tired lowers your critical sense in a positive way, and other times you can jump out of bed in the morning and get a start on the writing before your internal critic catches up with you.

14   *9. Call the Draft an Experiment or an Exercise.*   All my courses are experimental, so I don't have to worry too much about failing as a teacher—failure is normal during experiments—and I'm ready to try new ways to teach. Good writing is always an experiment. Make a run at it. See if it will work. The poet Mekeel McBride is always writing "exercises" in her journals. Since they are just exercises and not poems she doesn't have to get uptight about them, but of course if an exercise turns into a poem she'll accept it.

15   *10. Dictate a Draft.*   Use a tape recorder, and then transcribe it from that. You may want to transcribe it carefully, or just catch the gist of what you had to say. No matter how experienced we are as writers we are a million times more experienced as speakers, and it's often easier to get started writing by talking than by simply writing.

16   *11. Quit.*   Come back later and try again. You can't force writing. You have to keep making runs at it. Come back ten minutes later, or later that day, or the next day. Keep trying until the writing flows so fast you have to run along behind it trying to keep up.

17   *12. Read.*   Some writers read over what they've written, and they may even edit it or recopy it as a way of sliding into the day's writing. I can't do that; I despair too much, and when I read my own writing I feel I have to start over again; it's worthless, hopeless. If you don't feel that way, however, it may be a good device to go over the previous day's work and then push on to the new writing, the way an experienced house painter will paint back into the last brush stroke and then draw the new paint forward.

18   *13. Write Directly to a Reader.*   The too-critical reader can keep us from writing, but we can also get writing by imagining an especially appreciative reader, or a reader who needs the information we have to convey. If we can feel that reader's hunger for what we have to say it will draw us into the text. Sometimes as I have been writing this book, I must confess, I've imagined the enjoyment I expect Don

Graves, Chip Scanlan, or Nedah Abbott[1] to feel at an unexpected turn of phrase, a new insight, or a different approach. I read their faces as I write the way I read and speak to friendly faces in an audience.

19   **14. Take a Walk, Lift Weights, Jog, Run, Dance, Swim.** Many writers have found that the best way to get started writing is by getting the blood coursing through the body and the brain. As they get their physical body tuned up their brain starts to get into high gear. Exercise is also the kind of dumb, private activity that allows the mind to free itself of stress and interruption and rehearse what may be written when the exercise is done.

20   **15. Change the Place Where You Write.**   I write in my office at home, but I also write on a lap desk in the living room or on the porch. I like to take the car and drive down by Great Bay, where I can look up from my lap desk and watch a heron stalk fish or a seagull soar— the way I would like to write, without effort. Some writers cover their windows and write to a wall. I like to write to a different scene. Right now, for example, I'm looking at the green ocean of Indiana farmland and a marvelously angry gray sky as I drive west and write by dictation. In the 1920s writers thought the cafes of Paris were the best places to write. I don't think I could work on those silly little tables, but my ideal writing place would be in a booth in a busy lunchroom where nobody knows me. Yesterday morning I started writing in a Denny's in a city in Michigan; it was a fine place to write. When my writing doesn't go well I move around. I imagine that the muse is looking for me, and if it can't find me at home I'll go out somewhere where I may be more visible.

21   **16. Draw a Picture, in Your Mind or on Paper.**   Take a photograph. Cut a picture from a magazine and put it on your bulletin board. When small children start writing they usually first draw a picture. They do on paper what experienced writers usually do in their mind—they visualize the subject. Last summer I started my writing sessions by making a sketch of a rubber tree that stands on our porch. I wasn't writing about the rubber tree, but the activity of drawing seemed to help me get started and stimulated the flow of writing.

22   **17. Free Write.**   Write as hard and as fast and free as you can. See if language will lead you towards a meaning. As I have said

[1] Donald Graves teaches writing at the University of New Hampshire; Christopher Scanlan is a writer for the Providence *Journal-Bulletin;* Nedah Abbott was Murray's editor.

before, free writing isn't very free, for the text starts to develop its own form and direction. But the act of writing freely is one of the techniques that can unleash your mind.

23   *18.   Stop in the Middle of a Sentence.*   This is a good trick when the writing is going well and you are interrupted or come to the end of the day's writing during a long project. Many well-known writers have done this, and I've found that it really helps me at times. If I can pick up the draft and finish an ordinary sentence, then I am immediately back into the writing. If I've stopped at the end of a sentence or a paragraph it's much harder to get going. And if I've stopped at the end of a chapter it may take days or weeks to get the next chapter started.

24   *19.   Write the Easy Parts First.*   If you're stuck on a section or a beginning, skip over it and write the parts of the draft that you are ready to write. Once you've got those easy, strong pieces of writing done then you'll be able to build a complete draft by connecting those parts. A variation on this is to write the end first, as I've suggested in other parts of the text, or to plunge in and grab the beast wherever you can get hold of it. Once you have a working text you can extend it backwards or forwards as it requires.

25   *20.   Be Silly.*   You're not writing anyway, so you might as well make a fool of yourself. I've numbered the day's quota of pages and then filled them in. One of my writer neighbors loves cigars, but he won't let himself have a cigar until he finishes his daily quota. Reward yourself with a cup of coffee or a dish of ice cream, or a handful of nuts. It is no accident that some writers are fat; they keep rewarding themselves with food. Do whatever you have to do to keep yourself writing. Jessamyn West writes in bed the first thing in the morning. If the doorbell rings she can't answer it; she isn't up and dressed. Use timers, count pages, count words (you may not be able to say the writing went well, but you'll be able to say "I did 512 words," or "I completed two pages"), play music, write standing up (Thomas Wolfe wrote on the top of an icebox, Ernest Hemingway put his typewriter on a bureau), start the day writing in the bathtub as Nabokov did. Nothing is silly if it gets you started writing.

26   *21.   Start the Writing Day by Reading Writing that Inspires You.*   This is dangerous for me, because I may get so interested in the reading I'll never write, or I'll pick up the voice of another writer. I can't, for example, read William Faulkner when I'm writing

fiction: a poor New Hampshire imitation of that famous Mississippian is not a good way to go. The other day, however, when I couldn't get started writing I read a short story by Mary Gordon, one of my favorite authors. Reading a really good writer should make you pack up your pen and quit the field, but most of us find reading other writers inspiring. I put down Mary Gordon's short story and was inspired to write.

27 **22. Read What Other Writers Have Written about Writing.** I may not write as well as they do, but we work at the same trade, and it helps me to sit around and chat with them. You may want to start a "commonplace book," an eighteenth-century form of self-education in which people made their personal collections of wise or witty sayings. I've collected what writers have said about writing in my own commonplace book, which has now grown to twenty-four three-inch-thick notebooks. Some of my favorite quotes from that collection appear before each chapter in this book as well as in the text. I find it comforting to hear that the best writers have many of the same problems I do and browse through these quotes as a way of starting writing.

28 **23. Break Down the Writing Task into Reasonable Goals.** A few years ago I watched on TV as the first woman to climb a spectacular rock face in California made it to the top. It had taken her days, and as soon as she got over the edge a TV reporter stuck a microphone in her face and asked her what she'd thought of as she kept working her way up the cliff. She said she kept reminding herself that you eat an elephant one bite at a time. You also write a long piece of writing one page, or one paragraph, at a time. John Steinbeck said, "When I face the desolate impossibility of writing 500 pages a sick sense of failure falls on me and I know I can never do it. Then I gradually write one page and then another. One day's work is all I can permit myself to contemplate." If you contemplate a book you'll never write it, but if you write just a page a day you'll have a 365-page draft at the end of a year. If you're stuck, you may be trying to eat an elephant at one gulp. It may be wiser to tell yourself that you'll just get the first page, or perhaps just the lead, done that day. That may seem possible, and you'll start writing.

29 **24. Put Someone Else's Name on It.** I've been hired as a ghostwriter to create a text for politicians or industrialists. I've had little trouble writing when someone else's name is on the work. Most of the time when I can't write I'm excessively self-conscious.

Sometimes I've put a pseudonym on a piece of work and the writing has taken off.

30   **25. *Delegate the Writing to Your Subconscious.***   Often I will tell my subconscious what I'm working on, and then I'll do something that doesn't take intense concentration and allows my subconscious mind to work. I walk around bookstores or a library, watch a dull baseball game or movie on TV, take a nap, go for a walk or a drive. Some people putter around the house or work in the garden. Whatever you do, you're allowing your mind to work on the problem. Every once in a while a thought, an approach, a lead, a phrase, a line, or a structure will float up to the conscious mind. If it looks workable then go to your writing desk; if it doesn't shove it back down underwater and continue whatever you're doing until something new surfaces.

31   **26. Listen.**   Alice Walker says, "If you're silent for a long time, people just arrive in your mind." As Americans we are afraid of silence, and I'm guilty too. I tend to turn on the car radio if I'm moving the car twenty feet from the end of the driveway into the garage. One of the best ways to get started writing is to do nothing. Waste time. Stare out the window. Try to let your mind go blank. This isn't easy, as those who have tried meditation know. But many times our minds, distracted by trivia, are too busy to write. Good writing comes out of silence, as Charles Simic says. "In the end, I'm always at the beginning. Silence—an endless mythical condition. I think of explorers setting out over an unknown ocean. . . ." We have to cultivate a quietness, resist the panic that the writing won't come, and allow ourselves to sink back into the emptiness. If we don't fight the silence, but accept it, then usually, without being aware of it, the writing will start to come.

32   These are some ways to get writing. You will come up with others if you make a list of techniques from other parts of your life that may apply here. A theater major may have all sorts of exercises and theater games that can spark writing. A scientist will be able to apply techniques of setting up experiments to setting up the experiment of writing. Art majors know how to attack a white canvas, and ski team members know how to shove off at the top of a steep slope. Keep a record of methods of starting writing that work for you. The more experienced you become, the harder it may be to start writing, but you will also have developed more ways of starting words down a page.

QUESTIONS ON CONTENT, STRUCTURE, AND STYLE

1. Why, according to Murray, do we resist starting to write?

2. How much of our time might be spent in the prewriting stage, before we put pen to paper?

3. What was Murray's purpose in writing this part of his book?

4. Why does Murray use the first person "I" (and "we") and address the reader as "you"?

5. Why does Murray include stories of his own writing difficulties and successes?

6. Why does Murray quote or paraphrase numerous professional writers?

7. What is the purpose of including the story about the mountain climber?

8. Evaluate the effectiveness of Murray's "voice" in this selection. What are some of the ways he achieves this tone?

9. Murray presented his material through a lengthy list of suggestions. Was this the most effective method of organization? Why or why not?

10. In the last paragraph of this excerpt Murray notes that other parts of one's life might offer additional techniques for getting started. Can you add one or two hints suggested by your academic major or by some other interest in your life?

VOCABULARY

constrained (3)   desolate (28)
gist (15)   contemplate (28)

SUGGESTIONS FOR WRITING

1. When you tackle your next writing assignment, make notes about your own prewriting and composing processes. How do *you* get started? Do your techniques work successfully? If so, write a brief description that you could share with a classmate who's having trouble facing the blank page. If you're unhappy with your own

composing methods, write a thoughtful analysis of your problem and suggest a possible solution for yourself.

2. Write an essay entitled "Beating Writer's Block." Your essay can be serious or lighthearted.

3. Imitate Murray's helpful tone in an essay that discusses at least four ways to accomplish something successfully.

The Qualities of Good Writing

JACQUELINE BERKE

A professor at Drew University for more than thirty years, Jacqueline Berke was awarded the university's Scholar/Teacher of the Year Award in 1986. The author of the highly regarded writing text *Twenty Questions for the Writer,* Berke has also contributed to a number of anthologies. In the following excerpt from *Twenty Questions,* Berke discusses the necessary components of effective writing.

1   EVEN BEFORE you set out, you come prepared by instinct and intuition to make certain judgments about what is "good." Take the following familiar sentence, for example: "I know not what course others may take, but as for me, give me liberty or give me death." Do you suppose this thought of Patrick Henry's would have come ringing down through the centuries if he had expressed this sentiment not in one tight, rhythmical sentence but as follows?

> It would be difficult, if not impossible, to predict on the basis of my limited information as to the predilections of the public, what the citizenry at large will regard as action commensurate with the present provocation, but after arduous consideration I personally feel so intensely and irrevocably committed to the position of social, political, and economic independence, that rather than submit to foreign and despotic control which is anathema to me, I will make the ultimate sacrifice of which humanity is capable—under the aegis of personal honor, ideological conviction, and existential commitment, I will sacrifice my own mortal existence.

2   How does this rambling, high-flown paraphrase measure up to the
bold "Give me liberty or give me death"? Who will deny that something
is "happening" in Patrick Henry's rousing challenge that not only fails
to happen in the paraphrase but is actually negated there? Would you
bear with this long-winded, pompous speaker to the end? If you were to
judge this statement strictly on its rhetoric (its choice and arrangement
of words), you might aptly call it more boring than brave. Perhaps a
plainer version will work better:

> Liberty is a very important thing for a person to have. Most peo-
> ple—at least the people I've talked to or that other people have
> told me about—know this and therefore are very anxious to pre-
> serve their liberty. Of course I can't be absolutely sure about what
> other folks are going to do in this present crisis, what with all
> these threats and everything, but I've made up my mind that I'm
> going to fight because liberty is really a very important thing to
> me; at least that's the way I feel about it.

3   This flat, "homely" prose, weighted down with what the French author Gustave Flaubert called "fatty deposits," is grammatical enough.
As in the pompous paraphrase, every verb agrees with its subject, every
comma is in its proper place; nonetheless it lacks the qualities that
make a statement—of one sentence or one hundred pages—pungent,
vital, moving, and memorable.

4   Let us isolate these qualities and describe them briefly.

Economy

5   The first quality of good writing is *economy.* In an appropriately slender volume entitled *The Elements of Style,* authors William Strunk Jr.
and E. B. White state the case for economy concisely:

> A sentence should contain no unnecessary words, for the same rea-
> son that a drawing should have no unnecessary lines and a machine
> no unnecessary parts. This requires not that the writer make all his
> sentences short or that he avoid all detail . . . but that every
> word tell.

6   In other words, economical writing is *efficient* and *aesthetically satis-fying*. While it makes a minimum demand on the energy and patience of readers, it returns to them a maximum of sharply compressed meaning. This is one of your basic responsibilities as a writer: to inflict no unnecessary words on your reader—just as a dentist inflicts no unnecessary pain, a lawyer no unnecessary risk. Economical writing avoids strain and at the same time promotes pleasure by producing a sense of form and right proportion, a sense of words that fit the ideas they embody. Economical writing contains no "deadwood" to dull the reader's attention, not an extra, useless phrase to clog the free flow of ideas, one following swiftly and clearly upon another.

Simplicity

7   Another basic quality of good writing is *simplicity*. Here again this does not require that you make all your sentences primer-like or that you reduce complexities to the bare bone, but rather that you avoid embellishment and embroidery. A natural, unpretentious style is best. It signifies sincerity, for one thing: when people say what they *really mean,* they tend to say it with disarming simplicity. But paradoxically, simplicity or naturalness does not come naturally. By the time we are old enough to write, most of us have grown so self-conscious that we stiffen, sometimes to the point of rigidity, when we are called upon to make a statement in speech or in writing. It is easy to offer the kindly advice "Be yourself" but many people do not feel like themselves when they take a pencil in hand or sit down at a typewriter. During the early days of the Second World War, when air raids were feared in New York City and blackouts were instituted, an anonymous writer—probably a young civil service worker at City Hall—produced and distributed the following poster:

> Illumination
> Is Required
> to be
> Extinguished
> on These Premises
> After Nightfall

8   What this meant, of course, was simply "Lights Out After Dark."
But apparently that direct imperative—clear and to the point—did not
sound "official" enough, so the writer resorted to long Latinate words
and involved syntax (note the awkward passives "*Is* Required" and "*to be*
Extinguished") to establish a tone of dignity and authority. In contrast,
how beautifully simple are the words of the translators of the King
James Version of the Bible, who felt no need for flourish, flamboyance,
or grandiloquence. The Lord did not loftily or bombastically proclaim
that universal illumination was required to be instantaneously installed. Simply but majestically "God said, Let there be light: and there
was light. . . . And God called the light Day, and the darkness He
called Night."

9   Most memorable declarations have been spare and direct. The
French author Andre Maurois noted that Abraham Lincoln and John F.
Kennedy seemed to "speak to each other across the span of a century,"
for both men embodied noble themes in eloquently simple terms. Said
Lincoln in his second Inaugural Address "With malice toward none,
with charity for all, with firmness in the right as God gives us to see
the right, let us strive on to finish the work we are in. . . ." One hundred years later President Kennedy made his Inaugural dedication:
"With a good conscience our only sure reward, with history the final
judge of our deeds, let us go forth to lead the land we love. . . ."

Clarity

10   A third fundamental element of good writing is *clarity*. Some people
question whether it is always possible to be clear. After all, certain ideas
are inherently complicated and inescapably difficult. True enough. But
the responsible writer recognizes that writing should not add to the
complications nor increase the difficulty: it should not set up an additional roadblock to understanding. If writers understand their own ideas
and want to convey them to others, they are obliged to render those
ideas in clear, orderly, readable, understandable prose—else why bother
writing in the first place? Actually, obscure writers are usually confused themselves, uncertain of what they want to say or what they
mean; they have not yet completed that process of thinking through and
reasoning into the heart of the subject.

11   Whatever the topic, whatever the occasion, expository writing should be readable, informative, and, wherever possible, engaging. At its best it may even be poetic.

12   Even in technical writing, where the range of styles is necessarily limited, you must always be aware of "the reader over your shoulder." Take topics such as how to follow postal regulations for overseas mail, how to change oil in an engine, or how to produce aspirin from salicylic acid. Here are technical descriptions that defy a memorable turn of phrase. Such writing is of necessity cut and dried, dispassionate, and bloodless. But it need not be tedious or confusing to readers who want to find out about mailing letters, changing oil, or making aspirin. Readers who are looking for such information should have reasonably easy access to it. Written instructions should be clear, spare, direct, and, most of all, *human:* No matter how technical the subject, all writing is done *for* human beings *by* human beings. Writing, like language itself, is a strictly human enterprise. Machines may stamp letters, measure oil, and convert acids, but only human beings talk and write about these procedures so that other human beings may better understand them. It is always appropriate, therefore, to be human in the way you write.

Rhetorical Stance

13   Part of this humanity must stem from your sense of who your readers are. You must assume a "rhetorical stance." Indeed this is a fundamental principle of rhetoric: *nothing should ever be written in a vacuum.* You should identify your audience, hypothetical or real, so that you may speak to them in an appropriate voice. A student, for example, should never "just write," without visualizing a definite group of readers—fellow students, perhaps, or the educated community at large (intelligent nonspecialists). Without such definite readers in mind, you cannot assume a suitable and appropriate relationship to your material, your purpose, and your audience. A proper rhetorical stance, in other words, requires that you have an active sense of the following:

1. Who you are as a writer

2. Who your readers are

3. Why you are addressing them and on what occasion

4. Your relationship to your subject matter

5. How you want your readers to relate to the subject matter

"Courtship" Devices

14   In addition to a rhetorical stance, a writer should draw upon those personal and aesthetic effects that enhance a statement without distorting it and that delight—or at least sustain—a reader's attention. "One's case," said Aristotle, "should, in justice, be fought on the strength of the facts alone." This would be ideal: mind speaking to mind. The truth is, however, that people do not react solely on rational grounds, or, to quote Aristotle in a more cynical mood, "External matters do count much, because of the sorry nature of the audience." Facing reality then, you should try to "woo" the reader through a kind of "courtship." You should try, as Carl Rogers reminds us, to break down the natural barriers and fears that separate people, whether their encounters are face to face or on the printed page.

15   You must personalize your relationship with the reader by using those rhetorical devices that enable you to emerge from the page as a human being, with a distinctive voice and, in a broad sense, a personality. When the writer and reader come together, the occasion should be special, marked by a common purpose and an element of pleasure.

16   Rhetoric provides a rich storehouse of courting devices, and we shall consider these in Part Three. For example, the pleasant rhythm of a balanced antithesis is evident in President Kennedy's immortal statement, ". . . ask not what your country can do for you; ask what you can do for your country." The lilting suspense of a periodic sentence (one that suspends its subject or predication until the end) appears in Edward Gibbon's delightful account of how he came to write the famous *Decline and Fall of the Roman Empire*:

> It was at Rome, on the 15th of October 1764, as I sat musing amidst the ruins of the Capitol, while the barefooted friars were singing vespers in the temple of Jupiter, that the idea of writing the decline and fall of the city first started to my mind.

17   Simeon Potter, a modern scholar, has observed that the word picture Gibbon draws, although brief, is "artistically perfect":

The rhythm is stately and entirely satisfying. The reader is held in suspense to the end. Had he wished, and had he been less of an artist, Gibbon might have said exactly the same things in a different way, arranging them in their logical and grammatical order: "The idea of writing the decline and fall of the city first started to my mind as I sat musing amidst the ruins of the Capitol at Rome on the 15th of October 1764, while the barefooted friars were singing vespers in the temple of Jupiter." What has happened? It is not merely that a periodic sentence has been re-expressed as a loose one. The emphasis is now all wrong and the magnificent cadence of the original is quite marred. All is still grammatically correct, but "proper words" are no longer in "proper places." The passage has quite lost its harmonious rhythm.

18   In addition, then, to economy, simplicity, and clarity—the foundation of sound, dependable rhetoric—include this marvelous dimension of "harmonious rhythm," of proper words in proper places. If you are sensitive to these strategies, you will delight as well as inform your reader, and in delighting, reinforce your statement.

QUESTIONS ON CONTENT, STRUCTURE, AND STYLE

1. What does Berke accomplish with her two revisions of Patrick Henry's famous words?

2. Who might benefit most from reading this essay?

3. Paraphrase Berke's definition of economy.

4. Why, according to Berke, is simplicity often lost in writing?

5. In your view, how are the qualities of simplicity and clarity related in writing? Can you have one without the other?

6. Why, according to Berke, must writers have a clear rhetorical stance?

7. What are "courtship devices"?

8. Throughout the essay, Berke refers to other writers' views of good writing. How does this affect her reading audience?

9. Is Berke's essay written in a style that illustrates the qualities she discusses? In short, does she practice what she preaches? Support your response with specific references to the essay.

10. Which of these qualities of good prose come naturally for you in your own writing? With which qualities do you struggle?

VOCABULARY

intuition *(1)*	paradoxically *(7)*	bombastically *(8)*
pompous *(3)*	imperative *(8)*	render *(10)*
aesthetically *(6)*	Latinate *(8)*	dispassionate *(12)*
embellishment *(7)*	syntax *(8)*	antithesis *(16)*
disarming *(7)*	grandiloquence *(8)*	

SUGGESTIONS FOR WRITING

1. In your writing for your major or your profession, which of Berke's qualities of good writing do you believe is most important? Write a persuasive essay using examples, as Berke does, to illustrate your opinion.

2. Review a work by one of your favorite authors and describe—using specific examples from the piece of writing—how he or she uses these qualities of good writing. You may find that a writer ignores some of these principles. If so, is he or she successful in bending the rules? Explain.

3. Review the letters to the editor of a daily newspaper and choose one that does not have the necessary qualities of good writing. In a well-detailed essay supported by specific references to both the letter of your choice and Berke's essay, show how the letter fails.

The Great Person-Hole Cover Debate:
A Modest Proposal

LINDSY VAN GELDER

Lindsy Van Gelder has been a reporter for United Press International and the *New York Post* and is a writer for *MS.* magazine. Van Gelder has contributed to a number of other publications, including *Redbook, Esquire,* and *Rolling Stone.* This essay was published in 1980 in *MS.* magazine.

1   I WASN'T looking for trouble. What I was looking for, actually, was a little tourist information to help me plan a camping trip to New England.

2   But there it was, on the first page of the 1979 edition of the State of Vermont *Digest of Fish and Game Laws and Regulations:* a special message of welcome from one Edward F. Kehoe, commissioner of the Vermont Fish and Game Department, to the reader and would-be camper, *i.e.,* me.

3   This person (*i.e.,* me) is called "the sportsman."

4   "We have no 'sportswomen, sportspersons, sportsboys, or sportsgirls,'" Commissioner Kehoe hastened to explain, obviously anticipating that some of us sportsfeminists might feel a bit overlooked. "But," he added, "we are pleased to report that we do have many great sportsmen who are women, as well as young people of both sexes."

5   It's just that the Fish and Game Department is trying to keep things "simple and forthright" and to respect "longstanding tradition." And anyway, we really ought to be flattered, "sportsman" being "a meaningful title being earned by a special kind of dedicated man, woman, or young person, as opposed to just any hunter, fisherman, or trapper."

6   I have heard this particular line of reasoning before. In fact, I've heard it so often that I've come to think of it as The Great Person-Hole Cover Debate, since gender-neutral manholes are invariably brought into the argument as evidence of the lengths to which humorless, Newspeak-spouting feminists will go to destroy their mother tongue.

7   Consternation about woman-handling the language comes from all sides. Sexual conservatives who see the feminist movement as a unisex plot and who long for the good olde days of *vive la différence,* when men were men and women were women, nonetheless do not rally behind the notion that the term "mankind" excludes women.

8   But most of the people who choke on expressions like "spokesperson" aren't right-wing misogynists, and this is what troubles me. Like the undoubtedly well-meaning folks at the Vermont Fish and Game Department, they tend to reassure you right up front that they're only trying to keep things "simple" and to follow "tradition," and that some of their best men are women, anyway.

9   Usually they wind up warning you, with great sincerity, that you're jeopardizing the worthy cause of women's rights by focusing on "trivial" side issues. I would like to know how anything that gets people so defensive and resistant can possibly be called "trivial," whatever else it might be.

10   The English language is alive and constantly changing. Progress—both scientific and social—is reflected in our language, or should be.

11   Not too long ago, there was a product called "flesh-colored" Band-Aids. The flesh in question was colored Caucasian. Once the civil rights movement pointed out the racism inherent in the name, it was dropped. I cannot imagine reading a thoughtful, well-intentioned company policy statement explaining that while the Band-Aids would continue to be called "flesh-colored" for old time's sake, black and brown people would now be considered honorary whites and were perfectly welcome to use them.

12   Most sensitive people manage to describe our national religious traditions as "Judeo-Christian," even though it takes a few seconds longer to say than "Christian." So why is it such a hardship to say "he or she" instead of "he"?

13   I have a modest proposal for anyone who maintains that "he" is just plain easier: since "he" has been the style for several centuries now—and since it really includes everybody anyway, right?—it seems only fair to give "she" a turn. Instead of having to ponder over the intricacies of, say, "Congressman" versus "Congress person" versus "Representative," we can simplify things by calling them all "Congresswoman."

14   Other clarifications will follow: "a woman's home is her castle . . ." "a giant step for all womankind" . . . "all women are created equal" . . . "Fisherwoman's Wharf." . . .

15   And don't be upset by the business letter that begins "Dear Madam,"
fellas. It means you, too.

QUESTIONS ON CONTENT, STRUCTURE, AND STYLE

1. What is "The Great Person-Hole Cover Debate"?

2. Why does Van Gelder include the reference to the "message of welcome" from Kehoe?

3. Explain Van Gelder's play on words when she writes "Consternation about woman-handling the language comes from all sides."

4. Who is opposed to the language changes Van Gelder believes are needed and what are their reasons for wanting to keep a "man"-based language?

5. Describe Van Gelder's style. How is her tone important in reaching her audience? To what well-known essay does "A Modest Proposal" refer?

6. Why does the author offer the "Band-Aids" and "Judeo-Christian" examples? How does this strengthen her argument?

7. What is the proposal that Van Gelder offers? How serious is she about this?

8. In the final paragraph, Van Gelder directly addresses the "fellas" in her reading audience. Why does she do this, and how do you suppose she believes that they will react to her proposal?

9. How did you respond to Van Gelder's "modest proposal"? How does audience reaction to this proposal help Van Gelder make her case? What is her unstated, more serious proposal?

10. Note that this essay was originally published in 1980. Have there been changes in the use of gender-specific language in America since then? Offer examples to support your view.

VOCABULARY

forthright (5)	*consternation (7)*	*misogynists (8)*
invariably (6)	*unisex (7)*	*jeopardizing (9)*
Newspeak (6)	vive la différence *(7)*	*intricacies (13)*

SUGGESTIONS FOR WRITING

1. Do you agree with Van Gelder's view that terms referring only to men should be made gender neutral or more inclusive of women? If so, write an essay stating your position, offering points other than those presented by Van Gelder in support of your claim. If not, write an essay presenting your view; be sure to refute those points raised by Van Gelder.

2. Van Gelder's essay touches on an on-going question: do cultural values affect and change language or does language affect and change cultural values? In a persuasive essay based on personal experience and current as well as past events, argue for one of these views or some combination of the two.

3. Van Gelder uses humor to raise a serious point about an issue she believes is very important. What current issues are of great importance to you? Present your own "modest proposal" for a subject you care deeply about, using Van Gelder's humorous tone and style as a guide.

The Best Refuge for Insomniacs

LANCE MORROW

Shortly after graduating from Harvard, Lance Morrow began a career as a writer for *Time* that has spanned nearly thirty years. In addition to his award-winning essays and cover stories for the magazine, he has written several books, including *The Chief: A Memoir of Fathers and Sons* (1984), a chronicle of his relationship with his father, former *Saturday Evening Post* writer Hugh Morrow. "The Best Refuge for Insomniacs" was first published in *Time* in 1991.

1   I KNOW a woman whose son died by drowning on the night of his high school graduation. She told me she got through the weeks and months afterward by reading and rereading the works of Willa Cather. The calm and clarity of Cather's prose stabilized the woman and helped her through the time.

2   We have rafts that we cling to in bad weather—consolations, little solidarities, numbers we dial, people we wake up in the middle of the night.

3   Somehow it is not much fun to wake up the television set. The medium is a microwave: it makes reality taste wrong. Television transforms the world into a bright dust of electrons, noisy and occasionally toxic. Turn on the set and lingering dreams float out to mingle with CNN. Dreams are not an electronic medium.

4   During the war in the gulf, the escapist magician made urgent reality inescapable. Television became spookier than usual in its metaphysical way: the instant global connection that is informative and hypnotic and jumpy all at once—immediate and unreal. The sacramental anchormen dispensed their unctions and alarms. During the war, I found shelter in books in the middle of the night. They are cozier. The global electronic collective, the knife of the news, could wait until the sun came up. The mind prefers to be private in its sleepless stretches.

5   Read what? I am not talking exactly about reading to escape. Nor about reading to edify and impress oneself. *Paradise Lost* is not much help at 3 in the morning, except of course as a heavy sleeping potion. I mean the kind of reading one does to keep sane, to touch other intelligences, to absorb a little grace. In Vietnam the soldiers said, "He is a man you can walk down the road with." They meant, a man you can trust when the road is very dangerous. Every reader knows there are certain books you can go down the road with.

6   Everyone has his or her own list—each list no doubt is peculiar, idiosyncratic. The books you keep for the middle of the night serve a deeply personal purpose, one of companionship. Your connection with them is a mystery of affinities. Each mind has its night weather, its topographies. I like certain books about fly fishing, for example, especially Norman Maclean's brilliant *A River Runs Through It*, which, like fishing itself, sometimes makes sudden, taut connections to divinity.

7   One man rereads the adventures of Sherlock Holmes. He cherishes their world, the fogs and bobbies, the rational wrapped in an ambient madness, the inexplicable each time yielding its secret in a concluding sunburst, a sharp clarity.

8   Television news, when it flies in raw and ragged, can be lacerating. The medium destroys sequence. Reading restores to the mind a stabilization of linear prose, a bit of the architecture of thought. First one sentence, then another, building paragraphs, whole pages, chapters, books,

until eventually something like an attention span returns and perhaps a steadier regard for cause and effect. War (and television) shatters. Reading, thoughts reconstruct. The mind in reading is active, not passive-depressive.

9   There is no point in being too reverent about books. *Mein Kampf* was—is—a book. Still, some books have the virtue of being processed through an intelligence. Writers make universes. To enter that creation gives the reader some intellectual dignity and a higher sense of his possibilities. The dignity encourages relief and acceptance. The universe may be the splendid, twittish neverland of P. G. Wodehouse (escape maybe, but a steadying one) or Anthony Trollope's order, or Tolkien's. I know a married couple who got through a tragic time by reading Dickens to each other every night. Years ago, recovering from a heart operation, I read Shelby Foote's three-volume history of the American Civil War—a universe indeed, the fullest, most instructive tragedy of American history, all of the New World's Homer and Shakespeare enacted in four years. People find the books they need.

10   I like writers who have struggled with a dark side and persevered: Samuel Johnson, for example; his distinction and his majestic sanity both achieved the hard way. He emerged very human and funny and with astonishing resources of kindness. I have been reading Henry James' letters in the middle of the night. If James' novels are sometimes tiresome, his letters, which he produced in amazing quantity, are endlessly intelligent and alive. To a friend named Grace Norton, who was much afflicted, he wrote, "Remember that every life is a special problem which is not yours but another's and content yourself with the terrible algebra of your own . . . We all live together, and those of us who love and know, live so most." He told her, "Even if we don't reach the sun, we shall at least have been up in a balloon."

11   Odd that 19th century writers should write a prose that seems so stabilizing in the late 20th. Ralph Waldo Emerson is good to have beside the bed between 3 and 6 in the morning. So is the book of *Job*. Poetry: Wallace Stevens for his strange visual clarities, Robert Frost for his sly moral clarities, Walt Whitman for his spaciousness and energy. Some early Hemingway. I read the memoirs of Nadezhda Mandelstam (*Hope Against Hope; Hope Abandoned*), the widow of Osip Mandelstam, a Soviet poet destroyed by Stalin. I look at *The Wind in the Willows* out of admiration for Mr. Toad and for what he has to teach about folly and resilience.

12   The contemplation of anything intelligent—it need not be writing—helps the mind through the black hours. Mozart, for example; music like bright ice water, or, say, the memory of the serene Palladian lines of Jefferson at Monticello. These things realign the mind and teach it not to be petty. All honest thought is a form of prayer. I read Samuel Johnson ("Despair is criminal") and go back to sleep.

Questions on Content, Structure, and Style

1. Re-read the opening line of Morrow's essay. Is it effective in capturing a reader's attention? Why? How does it prepare the reader for the content of the essay?

2. In what way, according to Morrow, can books become "rafts we cling to in bad weather"?

3. Why does Morrow reject television as a source of solace in times of trouble?

4. What is the effect of the religious imagery in paragraph 4 as Morrow discusses television ("sacramental," "unctions")?

5. What difference between reading and television does Morrow emphasize in paragraph 8?

6. In paragraphs 9, 10, and 11, Morrow discusses specific authors and books. How does this enhance his essay? Is it necessary for a reader to know these writers and works to understand this section? Explain.

7. Morrow writes, "Every reader knows there are certain books you can go down the road with." What are those books for you? Why?

8. In his closing paragraph, Morrow expands his focus to include music and architecture. How does this broader focus affect you as a reader? Explain your response.

9. Why does Morrow conclude his essay with the line from Johnson, "Despair is criminal"? How does this reflect the body of his essay?

10. As Morrow notes, all of us have "rafts" that we turn to in times of need. What are your rafts? Books? Music? Friends? Exercise? Discuss the activities that bring you comfort, escape, or perhaps even a solution to problems.

VOCABULARY

clarity (1)   *unctions (4)*   *taut (6)*
stabilized (1)   *collective (4)*   *ambient (7)*
solidarities (2)   *edify (5)*   Mein Kampf *(9)*
toxic (3)   *idiosyncratic (6)*   *resilience (11)*
metaphysical (4)   *affinities (6)*   *petty (12)*
sacramental (4)   *topographies (6)*

SUGGESTIONS FOR WRITING

1. In a well-developed essay, describe a time in your life when you found solace in reading. Explain to your audience why a particular book or author helped you in that situation, using specific references to the book(s) in question.

2. Morrow writes that books give readers "intellectual dignity and a higher sense of [their] possibilities." Has a particular piece of writing affected you in this way? Describe the effects of one such book on your views or goals.

3. Compare Morrow's essay to Dave Barry's "Horrors!" (pp. 139–140). Both essays address the impact of books on readers, yet they differ completely in tone, style, and message. In a contrast essay using specific references to the essays, show how these two authors present very different views of the same topic.

Printed Noise

GEORGE F. WILL

George Will is a journalist and television commentator best known for his conservative, and sometimes controversial, opinions. After earning a Ph.D. in political science at Princeton, Will taught briefly, served as a congressional aide and speech writer, and wrote for the *National Review*. Although his widely syndicated newspaper columns most frequently focus on current political issues, this 1977 column presents an irreverent look at modern abuse of language.

1 THE FLAVOR list at the local Baskin-Robbins ice cream shop is an anarchy of names like "Peanut Butter 'N' Chocolate" and "Strawberry Rhubarb Sherbert." These are not the names of things that reasonable people consider consuming, but the names are admirably businesslike, briskly descriptive.

2 Unfortunately, my favorite delight (chocolate-coated vanilla flecked with nuts) bears the unutterable name "Hot Fudge Nutty Buddy," an example of the plague of cuteness in commerce. There are some things a gentleman simply will not do, and one is announce in public a desire for a "Nutty Buddy." So I usually settle, sullenly, for plain vanilla.

3 But I am not the only person suffering for immutable standards of propriety. The May issue of *Atlantic* contains an absorbing tale of lonely heroism at a Burger King.

4 A gentleman requested a ham and cheese sandwich that the Burger King calls a Yumbo. The girl taking orders was bewildered.

5 "Oh," she eventually exclaimed, "you mean a Yumbo."

6 Gentleman: "The ham and cheese. Yes."

7 Girl, nettled: "It's called a Yumbo. Now, do you want a Yumbo or not?"

8 Gentleman, teeth clenched: "Yes, thank you, the ham and cheese."

9 Girl: "Look, I've got to have an order here. You're holding up the line. You want a Yumbo, don't you? You want a Yumbo!"

10 Whereupon the gentleman chose the straight and narrow path of virtue. He walked out rather than call a ham and cheese a Yumbo. His

principles are anachronisms but his prejudices are impeccable, and he is on my short list of civilization's friends.

11   That list includes the Cambridge don who would not appear outdoors without a top hat, not even when routed by fire at 3 a.m., and who refused to read another line of Tennyson after he saw the poet put water in fine port. The list includes another don who, although devoutly Tory, voted Liberal during Gladstone's day because the duties of Prime Minister kept Gladstone too busy to declaim on Holy Scripture. And high on the list is the grammarian whose last words were: "I am about to—or I am going to—die: either expression is correct."

12   Gentle reader, can you imagine any of these magnificent persons asking a teen-age girl for a "Yumbo"? Or uttering "Fishamagig" or "Egg McMuffin" or "Fribble" (that's a milk shake, sort of).

13   At one point in the evolution of American taste, restaurants that were relentlessly fun, fun, fun were built to look like lemons or bananas. I am told that in Los Angeles there was the Toed Inn, a strange spelling for a strange place shaped like a giant toad. Customers entered through the mouth, like flies being swallowed.

14   But the mature nation has put away such childish things in favor of menus that are fun, fun, fun. Seafood is "From Neptune's Pantry" or "Denizens of the Briny Deep." And "Surf 'N Turf," which you might think is fish and horsemeat, actually is lobster and beef.

15   To be fair, there are practical considerations behind the asphyxiatingly cute names given hamburgers. Many hamburgers are made from portions of the cow that the cow had no reason to boast about. So sellers invent distracting names to give hamburgers cachet. Hence "Whoppers" and "Heroburgers."

16   But there is no excuse for Howard Johnson's menu. In a just society it would be a flogging offense to speak of "steerburgers," clams "fried to order" (which probably means they don't fry clams for you unless you order fried clams), a "natural cut" (what is an "unnatural" cut?) of sirloin, "oven-baked" meat loaf, chicken pot pie with "flaky crust," "golden croquettes," "grilled-in-butter Frankforts (sic)," "liver with smothered onions" (smothered by onions?), and a "hearty" Reuben sandwich.

17   America is marred by scores of Dew Drop Inns serving "crispy green" salads, "garden fresh" vegetables, "succulent" lamb, "savory" pork, "sizzling" steaks, and "creamy" or "tangy" coleslaw. I've nothing against

Homeric adjective ("wine-dark sea," "winged-footed Achilles") but isn't coleslaw just coleslaw?

18   Americans hear the incessant roar of commerce without listening to it, and read the written roar without really noticing it. Who would notice if a menu proclaimed "creamy" steaks and "sizzling" coleslaw?

19   Such verbal litter is to language as Musak is to music. As advertising blather becomes the nation's normal idiom, language becomes printed noise.

QUESTIONS ON CONTENT, STRUCTURE, AND STYLE

1. Explain the title's paradox. How does the title try to capture the reader's attention?

2. According to Will, what effect has "printed noise" had on the American consumer?

3. Why does Will include the example of the gentleman and the "Yumbo"?

4. Describe the writer's tone (examine paragraphs 10–13, for example). What effect does this tone have on the reader?

5. Why does Will use phrases like "immutable standards of propriety" (paragraph 3)?

6. What point is Will making about language use in paragraph 18?

7. Who is Will's audience? What is the effect of paragraph 12 where he asks a question of the "gentle reader"?

8. In his closing paragraph, Will offers the analogy, "Such verbal litter is to language as Musak is to music." What does he mean?

9. Will gives specific examples of offensive language use at a number of restaurants. List a few examples of similarly tortured language from your own dining experiences.

10. Do you agree with Will that "advertising blather" is becoming the language of our country? Explain, using specific examples.

Vocabulary

anarchy *(1)*   anachronisms *(10)*   cachet *(15)*
sullenly *(2)*   impeccable *(10)*   incessant *(18)*
immutable *(3)*   don *(11)*   blather *(19)*
propriety *(3)*   routed *(11)*   idiom *(19)*
nettled *(7)*   declaim *(11)*

Suggestions for Writing

1. Columnist Ellen Goodman once wrote about an experience she'd had in a restaurant. She ordered a "fresh-fruit salad" from the menu, but she received a salad obviously composed of canned fruit. When she pointed out that the menu clearly read "fresh-fruit salad," the waitress replied, "Oh, honey, that's just what they CALL it." Write an essay in which you present other examples that illustrate the ways language is being used today to deceive or mislead consumers. You might want to focus your essay on advertising for a particular product, such as cars, liquor, cigarettes, or a household item.

2. Watch a television program or read a newspaper or magazine, keeping a close eye on all advertisements. Jot down examples of "verbal litter" that you notice. In an essay based on these observations, explain why you think this type of language is/is not justified in reaching its intended audience.

3. Take a drive in a commercial area, making note of the incorrect, "gimmicky" spellings you see on signs and stores ("Koffee Kavern," "drive thru," "Tuff Body Shoppe," "open all nite," etc.). Write an essay explaining the influence of such spellings. Are such gimmicks part of the "verbal litter" devaluing our language or do you find them playfully harmless? Compare/contrast your view to what George Will might think about such use of the English language.

since feeling is first

E. E. CUMMINGS

e. e. cummings was educated at Harvard University and served in the ambulance corps in World War I, an experience he describes in his novel *The Enormous Room* (1922). He studied art in Paris and developed an innovative style of writing poetry that uses words and punctuation in unusual, creative ways. His books of poetry include *Tulips and Chimneys* (1923), *XLI Poems* (1925), *Is 5* (1926), *Collected Poems* (1938), *Poems 1923–54* (1954), and *Poems* (1958).

since feeling is first
who pays any attention
to the syntax of things
will never wholly kiss you;
5   wholly to be a fool
while Spring is in the world

my blood approves,
and kisses are a better fate
than wisdom
10   lady i swear by all flowers. Don't cry
—the best gesture of my brain is less than
your eyelids' flutter which says

we are for each other: then
laugh, leaning back in my arms
15   for life's not a paragraph

And death i think is no parenthesis

QUESTIONS ON CONTENT, STRUCTURE, AND STYLE

1. Who is speaking in this poem? Characterize this person's state of mind as it is revealed here.

2. To whom are the comments in the poem addressed? What is the relationship between these two people?

3. Which season of the year is the most probable setting for this poem? Why do you think so?

4. What sort of person is being described in lines 2–6?

5. How does the speaker feel about someone who "pays attention to the syntax of things?"

6. What does the speaker mean when he says "kisses are a better fate than wisdom"? What effect is the speaker trying to have on his listener?

7. Identify and explain the grammatical metaphors in lines 15 and 16. What is the speaker saying about life and death?

8. Does cummings pay attention to the "syntax of things" in his poem? Is his choice effective?

9. How does the lack of conventional punctuation and capitalization in this poem reinforce its message?

10. Throughout the years, and especially in the sixteenth century, many poems have been written on the theme of "seize the day— tomorrow we'll be gone." Would you describe this poem as a modern treatment of that theme? Do you agree with the view of life expressed here?

VOCABULARY
syntax (line 3)
parenthesis (line 16)

SUGGESTIONS FOR WRITING

1. Think about a time in your life when you cast logic, good sense, or rules to the wind and allowed your feelings to be "first." Did such a choice bring positive or negative consequences? What did you learn from this incident? Write an essay that explains your view of the situation now.

2. Cummings uses the metaphors "life's not a paragraph/And death . . . no parenthesis." Write an essay explaining what you think the poet meant and then argue for or against this view of life by

giving examples from your own experience or from the lives of
others.

3. Write an essay based on a metaphor that reveals your own philosophy of life or an important belief. Don't rely on a cliché or worn-
   out homily. Create a fresh image and explain your metaphor clearly
   and persuasively.

The Open Window

H. H. MUNRO (SAKI)

Hector Hugh Munro was a journalist and short story writer who wrote
under the pseudonym Saki. His collections of stories include *Reginald*
(1904), *Reginald in Russia* (1910), *The Chronicles of Clovis* (1911), and
Beasts and Superbeasts (1914). This story is collected in *The Short Stories
of Saki,* published in 1930.

1   "MY AUNT will be down presently, Mr. Nuttel," said a very self-
possessed young lady of fifteen; "in the meantime you must try and put
up with me."

2   Framton Nuttel endeavoured to say the correct something which
should duly flatter the niece of the moment without unduly discounting
the aunt that was to come. Privately he doubted more than ever whether
these formal visits on a succession of total strangers would do much towards helping the nerve cure which he was supposed to be undergoing.

3   "I know how it will be," his sister had said when he was preparing to
migrate to this rural retreat; "you will bury yourself down there and
not speak to a living soul, and your nerves will be worse than ever from
moping. I shall just give you letters of introduction to all the people I
know there. Some of them, as far as I can remember, were quite nice."

4   Framton wondered whether Mrs. Sappleton, the lady to whom he
was presenting one of the letters of introduction, came into the nice
division.

5   "Do you know many of the people round here?" asked the niece,
when she judged that they had had sufficient silent communion.

6   "Hardly a soul," said Framton, "My sister was staying here, at the rectory, you know, some four years ago, and she gave me letters of introduction to some of the people here."

7   He made the last statement in a tone of distinct regret.

8   "Then you know practically nothing about my aunt?" pursued the self-possessed young lady.

9   "Only her name and address," admitted the caller. He was wondering whether Mrs. Sappleton was in the married or widowed state. An undefinable something about the room seemed to suggest masculine habitation.

10   "Her great tragedy happened just three years ago," said the child; "that would be since your sister's time."

11   "Her tragedy?" asked Framton; somehow in this restful country spot tragedies seemed out of place.

12   "You may wonder why we keep that window wide open on an October afternoon," said the niece, indicating a large French window[1] that opened on to a lawn.

13   "It is quite warm for the time of the year," said Framton; "but has that window got anything to do with the tragedy?"

14   "Out through that window, three years ago to a day, her husband and her two young brothers went off for their day's shooting. They never came back. In crossing the moor to their favourite snipe-shooting ground they were all engulfed in a treacherous piece of bog. It had been that dreadful wet summer, you know, and places that were safe in other years gave way suddenly without warning. Their bodies were never recovered. That was the dreadful part of it." Here the child's voice lost its self-possessed note and became falteringly human. "Poor aunt always thinks that they will come back some day, they and the little brown spaniel that was lost with them, and walk in at that window just as they used to do. That is why the window is kept open every evening till it is quite dusk. Poor dear aunt, she has often told me how they went out, her husband with his white waterproof coat over his arm, and Ronnie, her youngest brother, singing, 'Bertie, why do you bound?' as he always did to tease her, because she said it got on her nerves. Do you know, sometimes on still, quiet evenings like this, I almost get a creepy feeling that they will all walk in through that window——"

---

[1] Commonly referred to as "French doors" in this country—that is, double doors that often open to a patio.

15   She broke off with a little shudder. It was a relief to Framton when the aunt bustled into the room with a whirl of apologies for being late in making her appearance.

16   "I hope Vera has been amusing you?" she said.

17   "She has been very interesting," said Framton.

18   "I hope you don't mind the open window," said Mrs. Sappleton briskly; "my husband and brothers will be home directly from shooting, and they always come in this way. They've been out for snipe in the marshes today, so they'll make a fine mess over my poor carpets. So like you menfolk, isn't it?"

19   She rattled on cheerfully about the shooting and the scarcity of birds, and the prospects for duck in the winter. To Framton it was all purely horrible. He made a desperate but only partially successful effort to turn the talk on to a less ghastly topic; he was conscious that his hostess was giving him only a fragment of her attention, and her eyes were constantly straying past him to the open window and the lawn beyond. It was certainly an unfortunate coincidence that he should have paid his visit on this tragic anniversary.

20   "The doctors agree in ordering me complete rest, an absence of mental excitement, and avoidance of anything in the nature of violent physical exercise," announced Framton, who laboured under the tolerably widespread delusion that total strangers and chance acquaintances are hungry for the least detail of one's ailments and infirmities, their cause and cure. "On the matter of diet they are not so much in agreement," he continued.

21   "No?" said Mrs. Sappleton, in a voice which only replaced a yawn at the last moment. Then she suddenly brightened into alert attention—but not to what Framton was saying.

22   "Here they are at last!" she cried. "Just in time for tea, and don't they look as if they were muddy up to the eyes!"

23   Framton shivered slightly and turned towards the niece with a look intended to convey sympathetic comprehension. The child was staring out through the open window with dazed horror in her eyes. In a chill shock of nameless fear Framton swung round in his seat and looked in the same direction.

24   In the deepening twilight three figures were walking across the lawn towards the window; they all carried guns under their arms, and one of them was additionally burdened with a white coat hung over his shoulders. A tired brown spaniel kept close at their heels. Noiselessly they

neared the house, and then a hoarse young voice chanted out of the dusk: "I said, Bertie, why do you bound?"

25   Framton grabbed wildly at his stick and hat; the hall-door, the gravel-drive, and the front gate were dimly noted stages in his headlong retreat. A cyclist coming along the road had to run into the hedge to avoid imminent collision.

26   "Here we are, my dear," said the bearer of the white mackintosh, coming in through the window; "fairly muddy, but most of it's dry. Who was that who bolted out as we came up?"

27   "A most extraordinary man, a Mr. Nuttel," said Mrs. Sappleton; "could only talk about his illnesses, and dashed off without a word of good-bye or apology when you arrived. One would think he had seen a ghost."

28   "I expect it was the spaniel," said the niece calmly; "he told me he had a horror of dogs. He was once hunted into a cemetery somewhere on the banks of the Ganges[2] by a pack of pariah dogs, and had to spend the night in a newly dug grave with the creatures snarling and grinning and foaming just above him. Enough to make any one lose their nerve."

29   Romance[3] at short notice was her specialty.

QUESTIONS ON CONTENT, STRUCTURE, AND STYLE

1. Why does Nuttel bolt so suddenly from the house?

2. What is Vera's special talent?

3. What hints are we given early in the story that Vera is an exceptional girl?

4. Why is Nuttel a perfect victim for Vera's "speciality"?

5. Describe Vera's performance when she tells Nuttel of the hunting trip and when she sees the men return. Why is she convincing?

6. What does the setting (time and place) add to Vera's story?

7. How does Munro make this story humorous rather than tragic?

8. How does Munro build up to the twist in the last sentence? Why didn't he tell the reader about Vera's speciality earlier in the story?

[2] A river in India.
[3] "Romance" here refers to fictitious tales of extraordinary or mysterious adventures.

9. What does Vera's story about Nuttel's fear of dogs add to your understanding of her character? Of her relationship to her family?

10. Evaluate Vera's character. Do you think she is an inherently malicious deviant or merely a bright child with a talent for story-telling?

VOCABULARY

duly (2)	*ghastly (19)*
moping (3)	*mackintosh (26)*
falteringly (14)	*pariah (28)*

SUGGESTIONS FOR WRITING

1. Think of a time when you fabricated a story that pushed you into trouble—or one that allowed you to save face (or even saved your neck?). Describe the causes and consequences of this fiction, making clear to the reader the lesson you learned from this experience.

2. Have you ever been the victim of someone's lie or false story? Or have you ever been accused falsely of telling a lie? Write an essay that explains the situation and your attitude toward it.

3. Write an essay analyzing Saki's power with words that enables him to create lively characters and symbolic settings. Or, if you prefer, try your hand at writing your own story or narrative that concludes with an ironic twist or surprise.

INDEX

ACKNOWLEDGMENTS

Gage, Nicholas. "The Teacher Who Changed My Life" by Nicholas Gage. Reprinted with permission from Parade, Copyright © 1989. Nicholas Gage is the author of "Eleui" and "A Place For Us," from which this article was adapted.

Gansberg, Martin. "38 Who Saw Murder Didn't Call the Police," by Martin Gansberg, March 4, 1964. Copyright © 1964 by The New York Times Company. Reprinted by permission.

Gibbon, Peter H. "In Search of Heroes" by Peter H. Gibbon. From *Newsweek,* 1993, © 1993, Newsweek, Inc. All rights reserved. Reprinted by permission.

Goldberg, Lee. "They Stole Our Childhood" by Lee Goldberg. From *Newsweek,* copyright © by and reprinted by permission of Lee Goldberg.

Goodman, Ellen. "I Have Just Moved Into A New Car" by Ellen Goodman. Copyright © by The Washington Post Writers Group. Reprinted by permission.

Gregory, Dick. "Shame" by Dick Gregory. "Shame," from NIGGER: AN AUTOBIOGRAPHY by Dick Gregory. Copyright © 1964 by Dick Gregory Enterprises, Inc. Used by permission of Dutton Signet, a division of Penguin Books USA, Inc.

Howe, Irving. "Ellis Island" by Irving Howe, from *World of Our Fathers.* Copyright © 1976 by and reprinted by permission of Harcourt Brace and Company, Inc.

Karpati, Ron. "A Scientist: I Am the Enemy" by Ron Karpati. From Newsweek, Inc. Copyright © 1989 by and reprinted by permission of Ron Karpati.

Keillor, Garrison. "Attitude" by Garrison Keillor. Reprinted with the permission of Atheneum Publishers, an imprint of Macmillan Publishing Company from HAPPY TO BE HERE by Garrison Keillor. Copyright © 1982 by Garrison Keillor.

King, Jr. Martin Luther. "I Have a Dream" by Martin Luther King, Jr. Reprinted by arrangement with The Heirs to the Estate of Martin Luther King, Jr., c/o Joan Daves Agency as agent for the proprietor. Copyright 1963 by Martin Luther King, Jr., copyright renewed 1991 by Coretta Scott King.

Kowinski, William Severini. "Kids in the Mall" by William Severini Kowinski. "Kids in the Mall" from THE MALLING OF AMERICA by William Severini Kowinski. Copyright © 1985 by William Severini Kowinski. By permission of William Morrow & Company, Inc.

Mitford, Jessica. "To Bid the World Farewell" from THE AMERICAN WAY OF DEATH by Jessica Mitford. Reprinted by permission of Jessica Mitford. All rights reserved. Copyright © 1963, 1978 by Jessica Mitford.

Maynard, Robert. "Today's Terror: Kids Killing Kids" by Robert Maynard. Copyright 1990 by Universal Press Syndicate. Reprinted by permission.

Morrow, Lance. "The Best Refuge for Insomniacs" by Lance Morrow. Copyright 1991 Time Inc. Reprinted by permission.

Morrow, Lance. "A Dying Art: The Classy Exit Line" by Lance Morrow. Copyright 1984 Time Inc. Reprinted by permission.

Muller, Steven. "Our Youth Should Serve" by Steven Muller. From Newsweek, Inc., copyright © 1978.

Murray, Donald. "Twenty-Six Ways to Start Writing," by Donald Murray from *Write to Learn.* Copyright © 1984 by and reprinted by permission of Donald Murray.

Nizer, Louis. "How About Low-Cost Drugs for Addicts?" by Louis Nizer. Copyright © 1986 by The New York Times Company. Reprinted by permission.